C000157886

CIMA

Paper P2

Advanced Management Accounting

Study Text

CIMA

PUBLISHING

KAPLAN

PUBLISHING

Published by: Kaplan Publishing UK

Unit 2 The Business Centre, Molly Millars Lane, Wokingham, Berkshire RG41 2QZ

Copyright © 2014 Kaplan Financial Limited. All rights reserved.

No part of this publication may be reproduced, stored in a retrieval system or transmitted in any form or by any means electronic, mechanical, photocopying, recording or otherwise without the prior written permission of the publisher.

Acknowledgements

We are grateful to the CIMA for permission to reproduce past examination questions. The answers to CIMA Exams have been prepared by Kaplan Publishing, except in the case of the CIMA November 2010 and subsequent CIMA Exam answers where the official CIMA answers have been reproduced.

Notice

The text in this material and any others made available by any Kaplan Group company does not amount to advice on a particular matter and should not be taken as such. No reliance should be placed on the content as the basis for any investment or other decision or in connection with any advice given to third parties. Please consult your appropriate professional adviser as necessary. Kaplan Publishing Limited and all other Kaplan group companies expressly disclaim all liability to any person in respect of any losses or other claims, whether direct, indirect, incidental, consequential or otherwise arising in relation to the use of such materials.

Kaplan is not responsible for the content of external websites. The inclusion of a link to a third party website in this text should not be taken as an endorsement.

British Library Cataloguing in Publication Data

A catalogue record for this book is available from the British Library.

ISBN: 978-1-78415-127-0

Printed and bound in Great Britain.

Contents

Introduction

How to use the materials

These official CIMA learning materials have been carefully designed to make your learning experience as easy as possible and to give you the best chances of success in your Objective Test Examination.

The product range contains a number of features to help you in the study process. They include:

- a detailed explanation of all syllabus areas;
- extensive 'practical' materials;
- generous question practice, together with full solutions.

This Study Text has been designed with the needs of home study and distance learning candidates in mind. Such students require very full coverage of the syllabus topics, and also the facility to undertake extensive question practice. However, the Study Text is also ideal for fully taught courses.

The main body of the text is divided into a number of chapters, each of which is organised on the following pattern:

- **Detailed learning outcomes.** These describe the knowledge expected after your studies of the chapter are complete. You should assimilate these before beginning detailed work on the chapter, so that you can appreciate where your studies are leading.

- **Step-by-step topic coverage.** This is the heart of each chapter, containing detailed explanatory text supported where appropriate by worked examples and exercises. You should work carefully through this section, ensuring that you understand the material being explained and can tackle the examples and exercises successfully. Remember that in many cases knowledge is cumulative: if you fail to digest earlier material thoroughly, you may struggle to understand later chapters.

- **Activities.** Some chapters are illustrated by more practical elements, such as comments and questions designed to stimulate discussion.

- **Question practice.** The test of how well you have learned the material is your ability to tackle exam standard questions. Make a serious attempt at each question, but at this stage do not be too concerned about attempting the questions in Objective Test Examination conditions. It is more important to absorb the material thoroughly than to observe the time limits that would apply in the actual Objective Test Examination.

- **Solutions.** Avoid the temptation merely to 'audit' the solutions provided. It is an illusion to think that this provides the same benefits as you would gain from a serious attempt of your own. However, if you are struggling to get started on a question you should read the introductory guidance provided at the beginning of the solution, where provided, and then make your own attempt before referring back to the full solution.

If you work conscientiously through this Official CIMA Study Text according to the guidelines above you will be giving yourself an excellent chance of success in your Objective Test Examination. Good luck with your studies!

Quality and accuracy are of the utmost importance to us so if you spot an error in any of our products, please send an email to mykaplanreporting@kaplan.com with full details, or follow the link to the feedback form in MyKaplan.

Our Quality Co-ordinator will work with our technical team to verify the error and take action to ensure it is corrected in future editions.

Icon Explanations

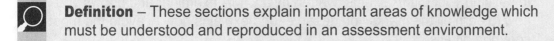 **Definition** – These sections explain important areas of knowledge which must be understood and reproduced in an assessment environment.

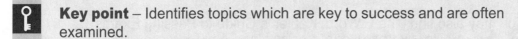 **Key point** – Identifies topics which are key to success and are often examined.

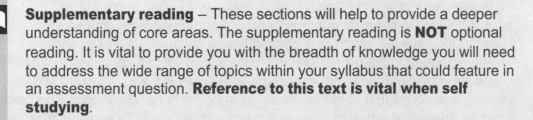 **Supplementary reading** – These sections will help to provide a deeper understanding of core areas. The supplementary reading is **NOT** optional reading. It is vital to provide you with the breadth of knowledge you will need to address the wide range of topics within your syllabus that could feature in an assessment question. **Reference to this text is vital when self studying**.

Test your understanding – Following key points and definitions are exercises which give the opportunity to assess the understanding of these core areas.

e.g Illustration – To help develop an understanding of particular topics. The illustrative examples are useful in preparing for the Test your understanding exercises.

Exclamation mark – This symbol signifies a topic which can be more difficult to understand. When reviewing these areas, care should be taken.

Study technique

Passing exams is partly a matter of intellectual ability, but however accomplished you are in that respect you can improve your chances significantly by the use of appropriate study and revision techniques. In this section we briefly outline some tips for effective study during the earlier stages of your approach to the Objective Test Examination. We also mention some techniques that you will find useful at the revision stage.

Planning

To begin with, formal planning is essential to get the best return from the time you spend studying. Estimate how much time in total you are going to need for each subject you are studying. Remember that you need to allow time for revision as well as for initial study of the material. You may find it helpful to read 'Pass First Time!' second edition by David R. Harris ISBN: 978-1-85617-798-6. This book will help you develop proven study and examination techniques. Chapter by chapter it covers the building blocks of successful learning and examination techniques. This is the ultimate guide to passing your CIMA exams, written by a CIMA examiner and shows you how to earn all the marks you deserve, and explains how to avoid the most common pitfalls.

You may also find 'The E Word: Kaplan's Guide to Passing Exams' by Stuart Pedley-Smith ISBN: 978-0-85732-205-0 helpful. Stuart Pedley-Smith is a senior lecturer at Kaplan Financial and a qualified accountant specialising in financial management. His natural curiosity and wider interests have led him to look beyond the technical content of financial management to the processes and journey that we call education. He has become fascinated by the whole process of learning and the exam skills and techniques that contribute towards success in the classroom. This book is for anyone who has to sit an exam and wants to give themselves a better chance of passing. It is easy to read, written in a common sense style and full of anecdotes, facts, and practical tips. It also contains synopses of interviews with people involved in the learning and examining process.

With your study material before you, decide which chapters you are going to study in each week, and which weeks you will devote to revision and final question practice.

Prepare a written schedule summarising the above and stick to it!

It is essential to know your syllabus. As your studies progress you will become more familiar with how long it takes to cover topics in sufficient depth. Your timetable may need to be adapted to allocate enough time for the whole syllabus.

Students are advised to refer to the notice of examinable legislation published regularly in CIMA's magazine (Financial Management), the students e-newsletter (Velocity) and on the CIMA website, to ensure they are up-to-date.

The amount of space allocated to a topic in the Study Text is not a very good guide as to how long it will take you. The syllabus weighting is the better guide as to how long you should spend on a syllabus topic.

Tips for effective studying

(1) Aim to find a quiet and undisturbed location for your study, and plan as far as possible to use the same period of time each day. Getting into a routine helps to avoid wasting time. Make sure that you have all the materials you need before you begin so as to minimise interruptions.

(2) Store all your materials in one place, so that you do not waste time searching for items every time you want to begin studying. If you have to pack everything away after each study period, keep your study materials in a box, or even a suitcase, which will not be disturbed until the next time.

(3) Limit distractions. To make the most effective use of your study periods you should be able to apply total concentration, so turn off all entertainment equipment, set your phones to message mode, and put up your 'do not disturb' sign.

(4) Your timetable will tell you which topic to study. However, before diving in and becoming engrossed in the finer points, make sure you have an overall picture of all the areas that need to be covered by the end of that session. After an hour, allow yourself a short break and move away from your Study Text. With experience, you will learn to assess the pace you need to work at. Each study session should focus on component learning outcomes – the basis for all questions.

(5) Work carefully through a chapter, making notes as you go. When you have covered a suitable amount of material, vary the pattern by attempting a practice question. When you have finished your attempt, make notes of any mistakes you made, or any areas that you failed to cover or covered more briefly. Be aware that all component learning outcomes will be tested in each examination.

(6) Make notes as you study, and discover the techniques that work best for you. Your notes may be in the form of lists, bullet points, diagrams, summaries, 'mind maps', or the written word, but remember that you will need to refer back to them at a later date, so they must be intelligible. If you are on a taught course, make sure you highlight any issues you would like to follow up with your lecturer.

(7) Organise your notes. Make sure that all your notes, calculations etc. can be effectively filed and easily retrieved later.

Objective Test

Objective Test questions require you to choose or provide a response to a question whose correct answer is predetermined.

The most common types of Objective Test question you will see are:

- Multiple choice, where you have to choose the correct answer from a list of four possible answers. This could either be numbers or text.

- Multiple choice with more choices and answers, for example, choosing two correct answers from a list of eight possible answers. This could either be numbers or text.

- Single numeric entry, where you give your numeric answer, for example, profit is $10,000.

- Multiple entry, where you give several numeric answers.

- True/false questions, where you state whether a statement is true or false.

- Matching pairs of text, for example, matching a technical term with the correct definition.

- Other types could be matching text with graphs and labelling graphs/diagrams.

In every chapter of this Study Text we have introduced these types of questions, but obviously we have had to label answers A, B, C etc rather than using click boxes. For convenience we have retained quite a few questions where an initial scenario leads to a number of sub-questions. There will be questions of this type in the Objective Test Examination but they will rarely have more than three sub-questions.

Guidance re CIMA on-screen calculator

As part of the CIMA Objective Test software, candidates are now provided with a calculator. This calculator is on-screen and is available for the duration of the assessment. The calculator is available in each of the Objective Test Examinations and is accessed by clicking the calculator button in the top left hand corner of the screen at any time during the assessment.

All candidates must complete a 15-minute tutorial before the assessment begins and will have the opportunity to familiarise themselves with the calculator and practise using it, although they can also use a physical calculator.

Candidates may practise using the calculator by downloading and installing the practice exam at http://www.vue.com/athena/. The calculator can be accessed from the fourth sample question (of 12).

Please note that the practice exam and tutorial provided by Pearson VUE at http://www.vue.com/athena/ is not specific to CIMA and includes the full range of question types the Pearson VUE software supports, some of which CIMA does not currently use.

Fundamentals of Objective Tests

The Objective Tests are 90-minute assessments comprising 60 compulsory questions, with one or more parts. There will be no choice and all questions should be attempted.

Structure of subjects and learning outcomes

Each subject within the syllabus is divided into a number of broad syllabus topics. The topics contain one or more lead learning outcomes, related component learning outcomes and indicative knowledge content.

A learning outcome has two main purposes:

(a) To define the skill or ability that a well prepared candidate should be able to exhibit in the examination.

(b) To demonstrate the approach likely to be taken in examination questions.

The learning outcomes are part of a hierarchy of learning objectives. The verbs used at the beginning of each learning outcome relate to a specific learning objective, e.g.

Calculate the break-even point, profit target, margin of safety and profit/volume ratio for a single product or service.

The verb '**calculate**' indicates a level three learning objective. The following tables list the verbs that appear in the syllabus learning outcomes and examination questions.

CIMA VERB HIERARCHY

CIMA place great importance on the definition of verbs in structuring Objective Test Examinations. It is therefore crucial that you understand the verbs in order to appreciate the depth and breadth of a topic and the level of skill required. The Objective Tests will focus on levels one, two and three of the CIMA hierarchy of verbs. However they will also test levels four and five, especially at the management and strategic levels. You can therefore expect to be tested on knowledge, comprehension, application, analysis and evaluation in these examinations.

Level 1: KNOWLEDGE

What you are expected to know.

VERBS USED	DEFINITION
List	Make a list of.
State	Express, fully or clearly, the details of/facts of.
Define	Give the exact meaning of.

For example you could be asked to make a list of the advantages of a particular information system by selecting all options that apply from a given set of possibilities. Or you could be required to define relationship marketing by selecting the most appropriate option from a list.

Level 2: COMPREHENSION

What you are expected to understand.

VERBS USED	DEFINITION
Describe	Communicate the key features of.
Distinguish	Highlight the differences between.
Explain	Make clear or intelligible/state the meaning or purpose of.
Identify	Recognise, establish or select after consideration.
Illustrate	Use an example to describe or explain something.

For example you may be asked to distinguish between different aspects of the global business environment by dragging external factors and dropping into a PEST analysis.

Level 3: APPLICATION

How you are expected to apply your knowledge.

VERBS USED	DEFINITION
Apply	Put to practical use.
Calculate	Ascertain or reckon mathematically.
Demonstrate	Prove with certainty or exhibit by practical means.
Prepare	Make or get ready for use.
Reconcile	Make or prove consistent/compatible.
Solve	Find an answer to.
Tabulate	Arrange in a table.

For example you may need to calculate the projected revenue or costs for a given set of circumstances.

Level 4: ANALYSIS

How you are expected to analyse the detail of what you have learned.

VERBS USED	DEFINITION
Analyse	Examine in detail the structure of.
Categorise	Place into a defined class or division.
Compare/contrast	Show the similarities and/or differences between.
Construct	Build up or compile.
Discuss	Examine in detail by argument.
Interpret	Translate into intelligible or familiar terms.
Prioritise	Place in order of priority or sequence for action.
Produce	Create or bring into existence.

For example you may be required to interpret an inventory ratio by selecting the most appropriate statement for a given set of circumstances and data.

Level 5: EVALUATION

How you are expected to use your learning to evaluate, make decisions or recommendations.

VERBS USED	DEFINITION
Advise	Counsel, inform or notify.
Evaluate	Appraise or assess the value of.
Recommend	Propose a course of action.

For example you may be asked to recommend and select an appropriate course of action based on a short scenario.

P2
ADVANCED MANAGEMENT ACCOUNTING

Syllabus overview

Focusing primarily on the long term, P2 builds on the insights about costs and their drivers (from P1) to provide the competencies needed to analyse, plan and manage costs to support the implementation of the organisation's strategy. It shows how to manage and control the performance of various units of the organisation in line with both short-term budgets and long-term strategy. Finally, P2 covers investment decision making and the risks associated with such decisions. It provides the basis for developing deeper understanding of various types of risk affecting the strategy and operations of organisations (covered in P3).

Summary of syllabus

Weight	Syllabus topic
25%	**A.** Cost planning and analysis for competitive advantage
30%	**B.** Control and performance management of responsibility centres
30%	**C.** Long-term decision making
15%	**D.** Management control and risk

P2 – A. COST PLANNING AND ANALYSIS FOR COMPETITIVE ADVANTAGE (25%)

Learning outcomes
On completion of their studies, students should be able to:

Lead	Component	Indicative syllabus content
1 evaluate techniques for analysing and managing costs for competitive advantage.	(a) evaluate activity-based management	• Activity-based costing to derive 'long-run' costs appropriate for use in decision making. • Activity-based management and its use in improving the efficiency of repetitive overhead activities. • Direct and activity-based cost methods in tracing costs to 'cost objects', such as customers or distribution channels, and the comparison of such costs with appropriate revenues to establish 'tiered' contribution levels, as in the activity-based cost hierarchy. • Direct customer profitability and distribution channel profitability.
	(b) evaluate total quality management (TQM) techniques	• The impacts of just-in-time (JIT) production, the theory of constraints and total quality management on efficiency, inventory and cost. • The benefits of JIT production, total quality management and theory of constraints and the implications of these methods for decision making in the contemporary manufacturing environment. • Kaizen costing, continuous improvement and cost of quality reporting. • Process re-engineering and the elimination of non-value adding activities and reduction of activity costs.
	(c) discuss techniques for enhancing long-term profits	• Target costing and the determination of target costs from target prices. • Value analysis and quality function deployment. • The Value Chain and the management of contribution/profit generated throughout the chain. • Life cycle costing and its implications for marketing strategies.

Learning outcomes

On completion of their studies, students should be able to:

Lead	Component	Indicative syllabus content
	(d) apply learning curves to estimate time and cost for activities, products and services.	• Learning curves and their use in predicting product/service costs, including derivation of the learning rate and the learning index.

P2 – B. CONTROL AND PERFORMANCE MANAGEMENT OF RESPONSIBILITY CENTRES (30%)

Learning outcomes
On completion of their studies, students should be able to:

Lead	Component	Indicative syllabus content
1 discuss decision making in responsibility centres.	(a) discuss the information needed for decision making in different organisational structures	• Relevant cost information for cost centre managers: controllable and uncontrollable costs and budget flexing. • Relevant revenue and cost information for profit and investment centre managers: cost variability, attributable costs, controllable costs and identification of appropriate measures of profit centre 'contribution'. • Alternative measures of performance for responsibility centres.
	(b) prepare reports to inform decisions.	• Performance reports: recognising issues of controllable/uncontrollable costs, variable/fixed costs and tracing revenues and costs to particular cost objects.
2 discuss issues arising from the use of performance measures and budgets for control.	(a) prepare performance reports for the evaluation of projected and actual performance	• Key metrics for the assessment of financial consequences including profitability, liquidity and asset turnover ratios, return on investment, residual income and economic value. • Benchmarking. • Analysis of reporting by dimension (e.g. segment, product, channel).
	(b) discuss traditional and non-traditional approaches to performance measurement	• Non-financial performance indicators. • Balanced Scorecards (BSC).
	(c) discuss the criticisms and behavioural aspects of budgeting in responsibility centres.	• Behavioural issues in budgeting: participation in budgeting and its possible beneficial consequences for ownership and motivation; participation in budgeting and its possible adverse consequences for 'budget padding' and manipulation; setting budget targets for motivation; implications of setting standard costs etc. • Criticisms of budgeting and the arguments for and against 'beyond budgeting'.

Learning outcomes
On completion of their studies, students should be able to:

Lead	Component	Indicative syllabus content
3 evaluate issues arising from the division of the organisation into responsibility centres.	(a) discuss the likely behavioural consequences of performance measurement within an organisation	• The behavioural consequences of performance management and control in responsibility centres. • The behavioural consequences arising from divisional structures: internal competition and internal trading.
	(b) discuss transfer pricing systems	• The theory of transfer pricing, including perfect, imperfect and no market for the intermediate good. • Negotiated, market, cost-plus and variable cost-based transfer prices. Dual transfer prices and lump sum payments as means of addressing some of the issues that arise.
	(c) evaluate the effects of transfer prices.	• The motivation of divisional management. • Divisional and group profitability. • The autonomy of individual divisions.

P2 – C. LONG-TERM DECISION MAKING (30%)

Learning outcomes
On completion of their studies, students should be able to:

Lead	Component	Indicative syllabus content
1 evaluate information to support project appraisal.	(a) analyse information for use in long-term decision making (including consideration of tax, inflation and other factors)	• Relevant cash flows taking account of tax, inflation and other factors, and the use of perpetuities to derive 'final' project value where appropriate. • The identification and integration of non-financial factors in long-term decisions.
	(b) discuss the financial consequences of dealing with long-run projects, in particular the importance of accounting for the 'time value of money'	• The process of investment decision making, including origination of proposals, creation of capital budgets, go/no go decisions on individual projects (where judgements on qualitative issues interact with financial analysis). • Discounting, including the use of annuities in comparing projects with unequal lives and the profitability index in capital rationing situations. • Capital investment real options (i.e. to make follow-on investment, abandon or wait).
	(c) evaluate investment appraisal techniques and explain their results.	• The strengths and weaknesses of: payback, discounted payback, accounting rate of return (ARR), net present value (NPV), internal rate of return (IRR) and modified internal rate of return (based on a project's terminal value). • Prioritisation of projects that are mutually exclusive, and/or are subject to single-period capital rationing, and/or have unequal lives.
2 discuss pricing strategies and their consequences.	(a) discuss pricing strategies and their consequences.	• Pricing decisions for profit maximising in imperfect markets. **Note:** Tabular methods of solution are acceptable. • Pricing strategies and the financial consequences of market skimming, premium pricing, penetration pricing, loss leaders, product bundling/optional extras and product differentiation to appeal to different market segments.

P2 – D. MANAGEMENT CONTROL AND RISK (15%)

Learning outcomes
On completion of their studies, students should be able to:

Lead	Component	Indicative syllabus content
1 analyse information to assess its impact on long-term decisions.	(a) apply sensitivity analysis	• Sensitivity analysis to identify the input variables that most affect the chosen measure of project worth (payback, ARR, NPV or IRR).
	(b) analyse risk and uncertainty.	• Quantification of risk. • Probabilistic models and interpretation of distribution of project outcomes. • Decision trees. • Bayes Theorem. • Decision making in conditions of uncertainty.
2 discuss management's responsibilities with regard to risk.	(a) discuss risk management	• Upside and downside risk. • The TARA framework – transfer, avoid, reduce, accept. • Business risks. • Ethical implications and the public interest.
	(b) discuss the risks associated with the collection and use of information.	• Costs and benefits associated with investing in information systems. • Big Data.

PRESENT VALUE TABLE

Present value of 1.00 unit of currency, that is $(1+r)^{-n}$ where r = interest rate; n = number of periods until payment or receipt.

Periods (n)	Interest rates (r)									
	1%	2%	3%	4%	5%	6%	7%	8%	9%	10%
1	0.990	0.980	0.971	0.962	0.952	0.943	0.935	0.926	0.917	0.909
2	0.980	0.961	0.943	0.925	0.907	0.890	0.873	0.857	0.842	0.826
3	0.971	0.942	0.915	0.889	0.864	0.840	0.816	0.794	0.772	0.751
4	0.961	0.924	0.888	0.855	0.823	0.792	0.763	0.735	0.708	0.683
5	0.951	0.906	0.863	0.822	0.784	0.747	0.713	0.681	0.650	0.621
6	0.942	0.888	0.837	0.790	0.746	0.705	0.666	0.630	0.596	0.564
7	0.933	0.871	0.813	0.760	0.711	0.665	0.623	0.583	0.547	0.513
8	0.923	0.853	0.789	0.731	0.677	0.627	0.582	0.540	0.502	0.467
9	0.914	0.837	0.766	0.703	0.645	0.592	0.544	0.500	0.460	0.424
10	0.905	0.820	0.744	0.676	0.614	0.558	0.508	0.463	0.422	0.386
11	0.896	0.804	0.722	0.650	0.585	0.527	0.475	0.429	0.388	0.350
12	0.887	0.788	0.701	0.625	0.557	0.497	0.444	0.397	0.356	0.319
13	0.879	0.773	0.681	0.601	0.530	0.469	0.415	0.368	0.326	0.290
14	0.870	0.758	0.661	0.577	0.505	0.442	0.388	0.340	0.299	0.263
15	0.861	0.743	0.642	0.555	0.481	0.417	0.362	0.315	0.275	0.239
16	0.853	0.728	0.623	0.534	0.458	0.394	0.339	0.292	0.252	0.218
17	0.844	0.714	0.605	0.513	0.436	0.371	0.317	0.270	0.231	0.198
18	0.836	0.700	0.587	0.494	0.416	0.350	0.296	0.250	0.212	0.180
19	0.828	0.686	0.570	0.475	0.396	0.331	0.277	0.232	0.194	0.164
20	0.820	0.673	0.554	0.456	0.377	0.312	0.258	0.215	0.178	0.149

Periods (n)	Interest rates (r)									
	11%	12%	13%	14%	15%	16%	17%	18%	19%	20%
1	0.901	0.893	0.885	0.877	0.870	0.862	0.855	0.847	0.840	0.833
2	0.812	0.797	0.783	0.769	0.756	0.743	0.731	0.718	0.706	0.694
3	0.731	0.712	0.693	0.675	0.658	0.641	0.624	0.609	0.593	0.579
4	0.659	0.636	0.613	0.592	0.572	0.552	0.534	0.516	0.499	0.482
5	0.593	0.567	0.543	0.519	0.497	0.476	0.456	0.437	0.419	0.402
6	0.535	0.507	0.480	0.456	0.432	0.410	0.390	0.370	0.352	0.335
7	0.482	0.452	0.425	0.400	0.376	0.354	0.333	0.314	0.296	0.279
8	0.434	0.404	0.376	0.351	0.327	0.305	0.285	0.266	0.249	0.233
9	0.391	0.361	0.333	0.308	0.284	0.263	0.243	0.225	0.209	0.194
10	0.352	0.322	0.295	0.270	0.247	0.227	0.208	0.191	0.176	0.162
11	0.317	0.287	0.261	0.237	0.215	0.195	0.178	0.162	0.148	0.135
12	0.286	0.257	0.231	0.208	0.187	0.168	0.152	0.137	0.124	0.112
13	0.258	0.229	0.204	0.182	0.163	0.145	0.130	0.116	0.104	0.093
14	0.232	0.205	0.181	0.160	0.141	0.125	0.111	0.099	0.088	0.078
15	0.209	0.183	0.160	0.140	0.123	0.108	0.095	0.084	0.079	0.065
16	0.188	0.163	0.141	0.123	0.107	0.093	0.081	0.071	0.062	0.054
17	0.170	0.146	0.125	0.108	0.093	0.080	0.069	0.060	0.052	0.045
18	0.153	0.130	0.111	0.095	0.081	0.069	0.059	0.051	0.044	0.038
19	0.138	0.116	0.098	0.083	0.070	0.060	0.051	0.043	0.037	0.031
20	0.124	0.104	0.087	0.073	0.061	0.051	0.043	0.037	0.031	0.026

Please check the CIMA website for the latest version of the maths
tables and formulae sheets in advance of sitting your live assessment.

Cumulative present value of 1.00 unit of currency per annum, Receivable or Payable at the end of each year for n years $\frac{1-(1+r)^{-n}}{r}$

Periods (n)	Interest rates (r)									
	1%	2%	3%	4%	5%	6%	7%	8%	9%	10%
1	0.990	0.980	0.971	0.962	0.952	0.943	0.935	0.926	0.917	0.909
2	1.970	1.942	1.913	1.886	1.859	1.833	1.808	1.783	1.759	1.736
3	2.941	2.884	2.829	2.775	2.723	2.673	2.624	2.577	2.531	2.487
4	3.902	3.808	3.717	3.630	3.546	3.465	3.387	3.312	3.240	3.170
5	4.853	4.713	4.580	4.452	4.329	4.212	4.100	3.993	3.890	3.791
6	5.795	5.601	5.417	5.242	5.076	4.917	4.767	4.623	4.486	4.355
7	6.728	6.472	6.230	6.002	5.786	5.582	5.389	5.206	5.033	4.868
8	7.652	7.325	7.020	6.733	6.463	6.210	5.971	5.747	5.535	5.335
9	8.566	8.162	7.786	7.435	7.108	6.802	6.515	6.247	5.995	5.759
10	9.471	8.983	8.530	8.111	7.722	7.360	7.024	6.710	6.418	6.145
11	10.368	9.787	9.253	8.760	8.306	7.887	7.499	7.139	6.805	6.495
12	11.255	10.575	9.954	9.385	8.863	8.384	7.943	7.536	7.161	6.814
13	12.134	11.348	10.635	9.986	9.394	8.853	8.358	7.904	7.487	7.103
14	13.004	12.106	11.296	10.563	9.899	9.295	8.745	8.244	7.786	7.367
15	13.865	12.849	11.938	11.118	10.380	9.712	9.108	8.559	8.061	7.606
16	14.718	13.578	12.561	11.652	10.838	10.106	9.447	8.851	8.313	7.824
17	15.562	14.292	13.166	12.166	11.274	10.477	9.763	9.122	8.544	8.022
18	16.398	14.992	13.754	12.659	11.690	10.828	10.059	9.372	8.756	8.201
19	17.226	15.679	14.324	13.134	12.085	11.158	10.336	9.604	8.950	8.365
20	18.046	16.351	14.878	13.590	12.462	11.470	10.594	9.818	9.129	8.514

Periods (n)	Interest rates (r)									
	11%	12%	13%	14%	15%	16%	17%	18%	19%	20%
1	0.901	0.893	0.885	0.877	0.870	0.862	0.855	0.847	0.840	0.833
2	1.713	1.690	1.668	1.647	1.626	1.605	1.585	1.566	1.547	1.528
3	2.444	2.402	2.361	2.322	2.283	2.246	2.210	2.174	2.140	2.106
4	3.102	3.037	2.974	2.914	2.855	2.798	2.743	2.690	2.639	2.589
5	3.696	3.605	3.517	3.433	3.352	3.274	3.199	3.127	3.058	2.991
6	4.231	4.111	3.998	3.889	3.784	3.685	3.589	3.498	3.410	3.326
7	4.712	4.564	4.423	4.288	4.160	4.039	3.922	3.812	3.706	3.605
8	5.146	4.968	4.799	4.639	4.487	4.344	4.207	4.078	3.954	3.837
9	5.537	5.328	5.132	4.946	4.772	4.607	4.451	4.303	4.163	4.031
10	5.889	5.650	5.426	5.216	5.019	4.833	4.659	4.494	4.339	4.192
11	6.207	5.938	5.687	5.453	5.234	5.029	4.836	4.656	4.486	4.327
12	6.492	6.194	5.918	5.660	5.421	5.197	4.988	4.793	4.611	4.439
13	6.750	6.424	6.122	5.842	5.583	5.342	5.118	4.910	4.715	4.533
14	6.982	6.628	6.302	6.002	5.724	5.468	5.229	5.008	4.802	4.611
15	7.191	6.811	6.462	6.142	5.847	5.575	5.324	5.092	4.876	4.675
16	7.379	6.974	6.604	6.265	5.954	5.668	5.405	5.162	4.938	4.730
17	7.549	7.120	6.729	6.373	6.047	5.749	5.475	5.222	4.990	4.775
18	7.702	7.250	6.840	6.467	6.128	5.818	5.534	5.273	5.033	4.812
19	7.839	7.366	6.938	6.550	6.198	5.877	5.584	5.316	5.070	4.843
20	7.963	7.469	7.025	6.623	6.259	5.929	5.628	5.353	5.101	4.870

Activity-Based Costing and Activity-Based Management

Chapter learning objectives

Syllabus Link

Lead A: Evaluate techniques for analysing and managing costs for competitive advantage

Component A1a): Evaluate activity-based management

- Activity-based costing to derive 'long-run' costs appropriate for use in decision-making.

- Activity-based management and its uses in improving the efficiency of repetitive overhead activities.

- Direct and activity-based cost methods in tracing costs to 'cost objects' such as customers or distribution channels, and the comparison of such costs with appropriate revenues to establish 'tiered' contribution levels, as in the activity-based cost hierarchy.

- Direct customer profitability and distribution channel profitability.

1 Chapter summary

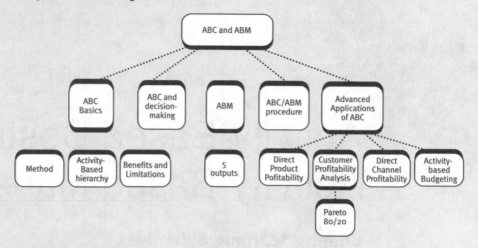

2 Knowledge brought forward

You will already have covered Activity-Based-Costing in previous CIMA papers. It is an important technique. In this chapter, we will explore ABC approaches such as Activity-Based Management, Direct Product Profitability, Direct Customer Profitability and Distribution Channel Profitability.

3 Activity-Based Costing: Basics revisited

In traditional absorption costing, overheads are charged to products using a predetermined overhead recovery rate. This overhead absorption rate (OAR) is based upon the volume of activity. A full unit cost is computed in order to satisfy financial accounting requirements.

However, it is always stressed that full product costs, using financial accounting principles, are not suitable for decision-making purposes. Instead, decisions should be based on a decision-relevant approach incorporating relevant/incremental cash flows.

With this approach, decisions such as introducing new products and special pricing decisions should be based on a study of only those incremental revenues and expenses that will vary with respect to the particular decision.

This approach requires that special studies be undertaken when the need arises. However, studies have shown that the majority of companies base their decision making upon full product cost.

In the late 1980s Cooper and Kaplan developed a more refined approach for assigning overheads to products and computing product cost. This new approach is called activity based costing (ABC). It is claimed that ABC provides product-cost information that is useful for decision-making purposes.

Activity-Based Costing is **'an approach to the costing and monitoring of activities which involves tracing resource consumption and costing final outputs. Resources are assigned to activities, and activities to cost objects based on consumption estimates. The latter utilise cost drivers to attach activity costs to outputs'.**

CIMA Official Terminology

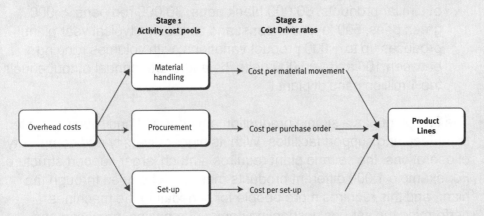

Traditional systems accurately measure volume-related resources that are consumed in proportion to the number of units produced of the individual products. Such resources include direct labour, materials, energy and machine-related costs.

However, many organisational resources exist for activities that are unrelated to physical volume. Non-volume related activities consist of support activities such as:

- materials handling
- material procurement
- set-ups
- production scheduling
- first-item inspection activities.

Traditional product-cost systems, which assume that products consume all activities in proportion to their production volumes, thus report distorted product costs.

Cooper and Kaplan – The Pen Factory

The distortions arising from the use of traditional product-costing systems are most pronounced in organisations that produce a diverse range of products which differ in volume and complexity. Cooper and Kaplan (1991) use the following example to illustrate the inability of traditional systems to report accurate product costs:

> 'Consider two hypothetical plants turning out a simple product: ball-point pens. The factories are the same size and have the same capital equipment. Every year plant I makes 1 million units of only one product: blue pens. Plant II, a full-line producer, also produces blue pens, but only 100,000 a year. Plant II also produces a variety of similar products: 80,000 black pens, 30,000 red pens, 5,000 green pens, 500 lavender pens, and so on. In a typical year plant II produces up to 1,000 product variations, with volumes ranging between 100 and 100,000 units. Its aggregate annual output equals the 1 million pens of plant I'.

The first plant has a simple production environment and requires limited manufacturing support facilities. With its higher diversity and complexity of operations, the second plant requires a much larger support structure. For example 1,000 different products must be scheduled through the plant, and this requires more people for scheduling the machines, performing the set-ups, inspecting items, purchasing, receiving and handling materials, and handling a large number of individual requests. Expenditure on support overheads will therefore be much higher in the second plant, even though the number of units produced and sold by both plants is identical. Furthermore, since the number of units produced is identical, both plants will have approximately the same number of direct labour hours, machine hours and material purchases. The much higher expenditure on support overheads in the second plant cannot therefore be explained in terms of direct labour, machine hours operated or the amount of materials purchased.

Traditional costing systems, however, use volume bases to allocate support overheads to products. In fact, if each pen requires approximately the same number of machine hours, direct labour hours or material cost, the reported cost per pen will be identical in plant II. Thus blue and lavender pens will have identical product costs, even though the lavender pens are ordered, manufactured, packaged and despatched in much lower volumes.

The small-volume products place a much higher relative demand on the support departments than a low share of volume might suggest. Intuitively, it must cost more to produce the low-volume lavender pen than the high-volume blue pen. Traditional volume-based costing systems therefore tend to overcost high-volume products and undercost low-volume products. To remedy this discrepancy **ABC** expands the second stage assignment bases for assigning overheads to products.

4 The ABC procedure

Cooper and Kaplan stated that it was the support activities that were the cause of many overheads, for example, material handling, quality inspection, setting up machinery, material acquisition, etc. Thus a simple three-step philosophy was developed:

- support activities cause cost
- the products consume these activities
- cost should, therefore, be charged on the basis of consumption of the activities.

```
                    ┌─────────────────────┐
                    │     ABC – Method     │
                    └─────────────────────┘
                              │
                              ▼
```

Identify the organisation's major activities. Ideally about 30 to 50 activities should be identified. However, over time, some large firms have been known to develop hundreds of activities. A suitable rule of thumb is to apply the 80/20 rule: identify the 20% of activities that generate 80% of the overheads, and analyse these in detail.

Estimate the costs associated with performing each activity – these costs are collected into **cost pools.**

Identify the factors that influence the cost pools. These are known as the **cost drivers**. For example, the number of set-ups will influence the cost of setting up machinery.

Calculate a cost driver rate, for example a rate per set-up, or a rate per material requisition, or a rate per inspection.

$$\text{Cost driver rate} = \frac{\text{Cost pool}}{\text{Level of cost drivers}}$$

Charge the overheads to the products by applying the cost driver rates to the activity usage of the products.

Favourable conditions for ABC

The purpose of moving from a traditional costing system to an activity-based system should be based on the premise that the new information provided will lead to action that will increase the overall profitability of the business.

This is most likely to occur when the analysis provided under the ABC system differs significantly from that which was provided under the traditional system, which is most likely to occur under the following conditions:

- when production overheads are high relative to direct costs, particularly direct labour
- where there is great diversity in the product range
- where there is considerable diversity of overhead resource input to products
- when consumption of overhead resources is not driven primarily by volume.

Information from an ABC analysis may indicate opportunities to increase profitability in a variety of ways, many of which are long-term. For example, an activity-based analysis may reveal that small-batch items are relatively expensive to produce, and are therefore unprofitable at current prices.

A number of responses to this information could be adopted. The first response might be to consider stopping production of such items, and concentrate on the apparently more profitable high-volume lines. Another approach would be to investigate how the production process could be organised in such a way as to bring the cost of producing small-batch items closer to that of producing high-volume goods.

By identifying the cost of carrying out particular activities, the new approach provides opportunities for directing attention to matters of cost control. It can therefore be viewed as a much longer-term technique than the word 'costing' in the title suggests. The establishment of an ABC product cost may thus be considered to be the beginning of the process, rather than an end in itself. The recent use of the term activity-based management suggests this forward-looking orientation, which is assuming increasing importance.

5 The activity-based cost hierarchy

Cooper and Kaplan (1991) propose a cost hierarchy framework that maintains that costs are driven by, and are variable with respect to, activities that occur at four levels:

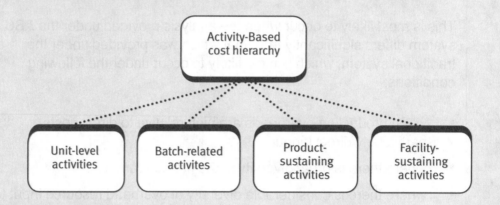

Unit-level activities are performed each time a unit of product is produced. They are consumed in direct proportion to the number of units produced. Expenses in this category include:

- direct labour
- direct materials
- energy costs
- machine maintenance.

Batch-related activities are performed each time a batch is produced. The cost of batch-related activities varies with the number of batches made, but is common (or fixed) for all the units within the batch.

For example, set-up resources are consumed when a machine is changed from one product to another. As more batches are produced, more set-up resources are consumed. It costs the same to set-up a machine for a run of 10 or 5,000 units.

Similarly, purchasing resources are consumed each time a purchasing order is processed, but the resources consumed are independent of the number of units included in the purchase order.

Product-sustaining activities are performed to support different products in the product line. They are performed to enable different products to be produced and sold, but the resources consumed are independent of how many units or batches are being produced.

Cooper and Kaplan (1991) identify engineering resources devoted to maintaining accurate bills of materials and routing each product as an example of product-sustaining activities. Product design costs and advertising costs of the specific product would also be counted as product-sustaining costs. The expenses of product-sustaining activities will tend to increase as the number of products manufactured increases.

Facility-sustaining activities. Some costs cannot be related to a particular product line, instead they are related to maintaining buildings and the facilities. Examples include:

- maintenance of the building
- plant security
- business rates.

6 ABC: Benefits and limitations

Benefits

(1) Provides more accurate product-line costings particularly where non-volume-related overheads are significant and a diverse product line is manufactured.

(2) Is flexible enough to analyse costs by cost objects other than products such as processes, areas of managerial responsibility and customers.

(3) Provides a reliable indication of long-run variable product cost which is particularly relevant to managerial decision making at a strategic level.

(4) Provides meaningful financial (periodic cost driver rates) and non-financial (periodic cost driver volumes) measures which are relevant for cost management and performance assessment at an operational level.

(5) Aids identification and understanding of cost behaviour and thus has the potential to improve cost estimation.

(6) Provides a more logical, acceptable and comprehensible basis for costing work.

Limitations

(1) Little evidence to date that ABC improves corporate profitability.

(2) ABC information is historic and internally orientated and therefore lacks direct relevance for future strategic decisions.

(3) Practical problems such as cost driver selection.

(4) Its novelty is questionable. It may be viewed as simply a rigorous application of conventional costing procedures.

[In the March 2013 PEG, the Examiner notes that candidates make a mistake when they believe that the introduction of Activity Based Costing will allow the company to reduce the selling price of every product.]

AT&T – Illustration

AT&T, the US telephone and telecommunications company, first used ABC in the early 1990s as a pilot project in its sales invoicing department according to Hobdy et al. (1994). It used the following types of activities to collect costs:

- Monitoring billing records

- Editing checks

- Validating data

- Correcting errors

- Printing, sorting and dispatching invoices.

It then spread the activity cost pools on cost drivers that included the following:

- No. of customers tested

- Change requests

- Service orders

- Customer locations

- Printer hours

- Pages printed.

AT&T found that ABC not only helped managers to manage the costs, but it also helped them improve operating processes and supplier relationships and to raise customer satisfaction.

This shows another role for ABC, namely its use as a one-off attention-directing technique to assess an activity and its impact on the business. Whether it continues to be used as a one-off technique or becomes an integral part of the costing systems is up to management.

ABC is also used in a wide range of service industries, from hospitals to credit card companies. Research into hospital costs and activities by Huang and Kirby (1994) has identified two main cost drivers for a hospital:

- The number of days spent in hospital. Costs included in this category were routine nursing care, meals and laundry.

- The number of admissions. Costs included in this category were obtaining and using the patient's medical history, preparation for surgery, after-surgery care and invoicing insurers and collecting funds.

This particular piece of research found that Medicare (i.e. the government reimbursement scheme) had been considerably over-charged because it dealt with older patients who stayed longer in hospital than others on private insurance. As a consequence the absorption rate used prior to ABC, which was a single day rate, gave a charge which was too high for long-stay patients.

7 ABC and decision making

Activity-Based Costing has a role in longer-term decision-making.

ABC systems are primarily designed to furnish management with cost information relating to an organisation's products.

However, the production of this information is not an end in itself. Indeed it is the use to which such activity-based information is put that represents its real purpose, and its value should be assessed against this end-result.

An ABC system produces historic information relating to its products or service provision, which is of much assistance to management in analysing and explaining an organisation's profitability. However, many commentators including Robin Kaplan and Robin Cooper have viewed ABC as supporting major areas of strategic decision making with organisations, these being:

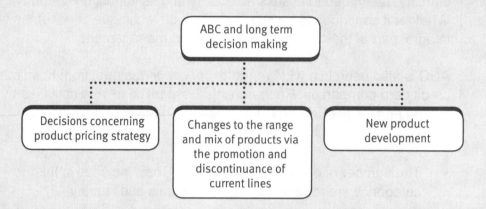

When ABC information is used in the above ways, then it will underpin policy decisions of senior management, and will therefore have a significant influence upon the longer term prosperity of an organisation.

Advocates of the use of ABC for strategic decision making maintain that its values lies in **greater accuracy attaching to product costing,** which in turn **increases the degree of reliability of cost information** used for the above purposes.

They further maintain that the use of ABC may give an indication for the **long-term variable cost of products**, which arguably is the most relevant cost information for use in decisions of the above type. Given the inherent uncertainty involved in strategic decision making, management may use ABC information in decision-modelling and sensitivity analysis to assist in the making of such decisions.

The end product of an ABC system is an estimate of the historic cost of each of an organisation's products. However, strategic decision making involves future time periods and thus it is future outlay costs that need to be taken into consideration, as opposed to historic costs.

Therefore, it is arguable that the results obtained from an ABC system should be aimed at assisting in the making of longer-term decisions. This is especially the case if ABC based product costs are viewed as estimates of longer term product costs as 'nothing is forever' and historic costs are susceptible to substantial change, since all factors of production become variable in the longer term.

Any cost information which has been produced based on past activities must be used with caution with regard to longer term decisions. Even so, ABC information may provide a sound starting point for the preparation of cost information to be used in strategic decision making. It has been argued that a significant advantage of ABC over conventional costing systems lies in its suitability for strategic decision making. Kaplan has argued that for decisions of a strategic nature, a long-term perspective is usual and maintains that an ABC system gives product cost information which matches this requirement particularly well.

This is evidenced by his assertion that **'conventional notions of fixed and variable costs are ignored because, for the purpose of product cost analysis, the time period is long enough to warrant treatment of virtually all costs as variable.'**

8 Activity Based Management

Activity-Based Management is a **'System of management which uses activity-based cost information for a variety of purposes including cost reduction, cost modelling and customer profitability analysis.'**

CIMA Official Terminology

ABM is simply using the information derived from an ABC analysis for cost management. ABM seeks to classify each activity within a process as a value-added or non-value-added activity:

Non-value-added activities are unnecessary and represent waste. The aim should be to eliminate them. For example, time spent dealing with customer complaints is wasted time, but cannot be reduced until the customers have nothing to complain about!

ABM focuses on activities within a process, decision making and planning relative to those activities and the need for continuous improvement of all organisational activity. Management and staff must determine which activities are critical to success and decide how these are to be clearly defined across all functions.

Everyone must co-operate in defining:

- cost pools
- cost drivers
- key performance indicators.

They must be trained and empowered to act; all must be fairly treated and success recognised.

9 Outputs from the ABM Information System

Organisations that are designing and implementing ABM will find there are five basic information outputs:

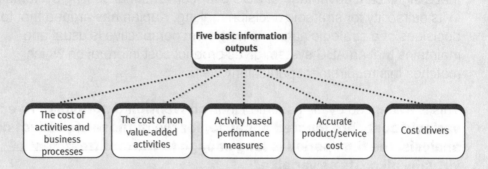

(1) **The cost of activities and business processes**. Since activities form the very core of what a business does, the basic output of the ABM system must be to provide relevant cost information about what a business does. Instead of reporting what money is spent for and by whom, costs are assigned to activities.

(2) **The cost of non value-added activities**. Identification of these wasteful activities is invaluable to management as it provides a crucial focal point for management.

(3) **Activity based performance measures**. Knowing the total cost of an activity is insufficient to measure activity performance. Activity measures of quality, cycle time, productivity and customer service may also be required to judge performance. Measuring the performance of activities provides a scorecard to report how well improvement efforts are working and is an integral part of continuous improvement.

(4) **Accurate product/service cost**. Products and services are provided to markets and customers through various distribution channels or contractual relationships. Because products and services consume resources at different rates and require different levels of support, costs must be accurately determined.

(5) **Cost drivers**. The final output from the ABM system is cost driver information. With this information it is possible to understand and manage these activity levels.

ABM can be used in assessing strategic decisions such as:

- whether to continue with a particular activity

- how cost structures measure up to those of competitors

- how changes in activities and components affect the suppliers and value chain.

Clearly ABM and employee empowerment takes a critical step forward beyond ABC by recognising the contribution that people make as the key resource in any organisation's success.

- It nurtures good communication and team work.
- It develops quality decision making.
- It leads to quality control and continuous improvement.

ABM will not reduce costs, it will only help the manager understand costs better.

Strategic activity management recognises that individual activities are part of a wider process. Activities are grouped to form a total process or service.

For example, serving a particular customer involves a number of discrete activities that form the total service. Strategic activity management attempts to classify each activity within the whole as a value-added or non-value-added activity. Non-value-added activities are unnecessary and should be eliminated.

Bellis-Jones (1992) noted that typically prior to the introduction of ABM, 35% of staff time was spent on diversionary (non-value-added) activities. After the introduction of ABM, total staff time declined and the percentage of time spent on diversionary activities fell to 20% of the reduced time.

Non-value-added activities are often caused by inadequacies within the existing processes and cannot be eliminated unless the inadequacy is addressed.

For example, dealing with customer complaints is a diversionary activity, but it cannot be eliminated unless the source of the complaints is eliminated. Another example is machine set-up time. Better product design so that fewer components or more standard components are used will reduce the set-up time between component runs. So management must concentrate on eliminating non-value-added activities.

But strategic activity management is more than just eliminating non-value-added activities, important though this is.

By identifying the cost and value drivers for each activity, the firm can develop both the activities and the linkages between them, and so better differentiate the firm from its competitors. In addition, by understanding the factors which influence the costs of each activity, the firm can take action to minimize those costs in the medium term.

ABC information can be used in an ABM system to assist strategic decisions, such as:

(1) Whether to continue with a particular activity.

(2) The effect on cost structure of a change in strategy, e.g. from mass production to smaller production runs.

(3) How changes in activities and components affect the suppliers and the value chain.

The value chain is simply a large activity map for the organisation and its position in the industry chain. It is covered in a later chapter of this Text.

10 Problems with implementing ABC/ABM

Much has been written in academic journals of the benefits of using ABC and ABM. The majority of organisations still do not use either. Why, if the majority of academics consider it to be so useful, do practitioners not employ ABC?

The obvious reason is that they do not agree on its usefulness or cost effectiveness in terms of costs and benefits. For ABC to be effective an accurate system is required with as many as 50 different activities identified and costs attributed to them. This requires considerable time and effort.

A certain amount of research has focused on the problems of implementing the system. Friedman and Lyne (1999) provide some clues as to why ABC has not been taken up with more enthusiasm from case study research they carried out. Some reasons they draw attention to are:

(1) Where it was devised for a single project that was not taken up the system got dropped as well. As communication between business units in a large organisation is often not very good, the work was not developed further by other units.

(2) Finance department opposed its implementation. Often finance staff appear less than dynamic and unable to perceive the needs of the production staff.

(3) General ledger information too poor to provide reliable ABC information. The resulting figures would have been no better than traditional absorption methods.

Of course, if organisations do not have reliable ABC information then they also forgo the cost management advantages of an ABM system. Since ABC provides the basic building blocks of activities, without ABC there can be no ABM.

Illustration – ABC and ABM

Tool of the trade

Financial Management; London; Nov 2001; Stephanie Gourdie;

A company in New Zealand is one of the few to have implemented activity-based management successfully but it needed careful planning and a radical rethink of company culture.

Since professors Robin Cooper and Robert Kaplan codified and developed activity-based costing, many organisations have implemented it, but few are using it for cost management. The original emphasis of ABC was on developing more accurate product costs. It was based on the principle that resource-consuming activities caused costs, not volume of products, as assumed by traditional cost-allocation methods. Overhead costs were allocated and traced back to activities that consumed resources, such as purchasing, set-ups and material handling.

A cost driver was then selected for each activity centre. The choice of driver was based on two things: it had to measure the resources a product used for a particular set of activities; and it had to be linked to the changes of costs in the activity centre (cause-effect relationship).

Cost drivers can include the number of purchase orders, material movements or setup hours. The overhead rate for each activity was worked out by dividing the activity cost by the capacity of the cost driver. The costs of products were determined by multiplying the number of the cost driver of the activity used by the product, by the overhead rate for that activity, for all activities used by that product.

ABC systems could then be applied to cost management. This was labelled activity based management (ABM), defined by Don Hansen and Maryanne Mowen as "a system-wide, integrated approach that focuses management's attention on activities with the objective of improving customer value and the profit achieved by providing this value".

The progression to ABM involved a shift in focus from the original ABC system – producing information on activity-based product costs to producing information to improve management of processes. The idea is to analyse the activities that make up a company's processes and the cost drivers of those activities, then question why the activities are being carried out and how well they are being performed. ABM provides the activity information and the costs of inefficient activities, and quantifies the benefits of continuous improvements.

Companies can then improve operations by re-engineering (complete redesign of processes), redesigning plant layouts, using common parts, outsourcing or strengthening supplier and customer relationships and developing alternative product designs.

Research on the implementation of ABC in Europe, shows that adoption of ABM remains low. One organisation in New Zealand has used ABM to improve the way it manages some of its processes, to get rid of non-value added activities and to reduce costs substantially through efficiencies. It has achieved this by following certain "dos and don'ts" in implementing accounting systems.

The organisation provides information services, record-keeping, testing, research and advisory services for New Zealand's agriculture sector. Its mission is to lead the world with its research and create wealth for its stakeholders, and its profit objective is to have enough resources to fund research and development. It has been through the same changes, including restructuring, that many New Zealand public sector organisations went through in the 1980s.

The drive to implement ABM began with calls for more efficiency and accountability and a need to be seen to have efficient business practices and be more customer-orientated. The emphasis was on efficiency, total quality and effectiveness – all of which were in the firm's mission statements and business plans.

The board constantly requested more information and ABM offered the management accounting team a way of providing better quality service. But ABM was a major undertaking and the team had to proceed carefully.

ABM required a major investment in time and resources. Apart from the cost of the software, staff had to be taken away from their existing jobs and trained to set up and use the system. The activity analysis stage, for example, was long and sometimes arduous: it took three people nine months to implement.

Since ABM's introduction, the models have been reviewed annually for budgets and actuals and updated for budgets, forecasts and actuals. This process takes three people between five and 10 weeks depending on the number and complexity of process changes.

Managers had to be clear about the potential benefits of ABM and what information the organisation wanted. Members of the management accounting team attended seminars and investigated several packages. They knew they wanted more than just an ABC package. They needed to establish product profitability, improve distribution of overheads, activities and costs of processes and find out how to improve these.

The organisation's clients, who were also its shareholders, believed they had the right to query prices. So the system had to provide information about the relationship between prices and costs. It also needed an integrated decision support system that could carry out business process efficiency simulations.

There are plans to extend the system to include calculations of customer profitability, activity-based budgeting, and the balanced scorecard. The balanced scorecard "translates an organisation's mission and strategy into operational objectives and performance measures for four different perspectives: the financial perspective; the customer perspective; the internal business process perspective; and the learning and growth perspective'. In other words, activities carried out in an organisation should be linked to its strategic objectives.

The next step was to decide which model to use. Some organisations operate standalone ABM systems using either spreadsheets or third-party packaged software. Others integrate the system in their wider information systems. The maximum business advantage cannot be achieved until ABM is an integral part of an organisation's reporting system.

The New Zealand organisation chose a software package that could map the process. This approach would suit any organisation with inputs, demands, processes and constrained resources. It already had a mainframe database of activity data and a separate accounting system. The use of dataware-housing allowed summary information from its two systems to be stored and accessed for multidimensional modelling, including accounting models for budgeting ABC costs, ABM information, simulations and forecasting.

It is important to pick a model that emphasises the operational understanding of all activities in the business. Instead of going down the financial decomposition analysis route – which analyses the accounting records of the organisation – the organisation chose the process model approach. This analyses the operations, identifying the key activities and resources consumed, by asking what people do, what resources are consumed and how. From the answers, appropriate activity drivers can be established, as can the inputs and outputs to each activity and the relationship between activities.

Managers gathered data from both operational and financial sources and carried out interviews to find out about processes. Some costs were allocated on traditional cost drivers, such as area, others on transactional cost drivers, such as number of visits by truck or technician. For each cost driver, costs were divided into fixed and variable. Some were more obvious than others and work was done to find an approximate division.

A pilot project was recommended in order to achieve results in six to eight weeks, develop a team of experts and convince managers of the benefits. The pilot chosen had defined inputs and outputs and was contained with simple and clear process flows. There was also clear output from each activity.

First, the project mapped the process showing different activities outside the ABM software. This procedure was useful as it helped the "mapper" to understand the components of the process and how they interacted. The pilot study initially involved high-level mapping but, with hindsight, it would have been easier if it had been less detailed.

A key point is to involve people other than just the management accounting team. The model approach enables this because much of the original information must be obtained from people in the field. So the organisation used the management accounting team to implement the system, but seconded members from the field to use local expertise.

As part of the new system, ownership of cost management had to be transferred from the accounting department to the departments and processes where costs were incurred. Some units were not happy about this, but since there was a shift in performance criteria meaning divisional managers' salaries depended on results, they were motivated to make it work. Perceptions of how different departments in the company worked had not changed, so staff did not feel threatened. People were keen to contribute, perhaps because of the good relationship between management accounts and other staff.

Agreement was obtained on criteria for measuring overheads and it turned out to be pretty straightforward to put numbers to activities and capacity levels. Tests showed that figures were generally reasonable and it is unlikely that investing far more time and resources would have made them significantly more accurate. Reports and graphs were prepared for each division so they could monitor their progress.

Implementing ABM meant a change in the culture of the whole organisation. It had to change from a public-sector-style company into a commercial enterprise (there is still ambivalence about how much profit it should make). The firm also had to worry about budgets and costs for the first time – it had never before had management accounting systems for cost management and budgeting.

Transition to the ABM system had to be gradual. First, the firm developed a cash objective budget system. From this, it built a simple ABC system model. Few products were dropped and the firm still expected to make a profit or break even. Economic conditions and other external factors were taken into account since there was a high proportion of fixed costs, but the new ABM philosophy made it clear to managers that the size of the "cake" was fixed.

The information from the ABM system was used to show managers where divisions were unprofitable. It was left to them to cut costs and become more efficient. At the moment, part of the general divisional managers' salaries is performance-related, but the aim is to extend this to more layers of management. Managers and staff are more aware of their portfolios.

Reports are made to the board twice a year, so the accounting system is particularly important. The first report is for the budget, detailed forecast and product profitability, and the second for actual compared with previous. The forecasting and budgeting processes both take two months. In January, managers are asked for their capital budgeting requirements and forecasts for the year until the end of May. Departments meet the following February to finalise their budgets. Budgets are completed by mid-April and the dollars are fed into the ABM model.

Senior managers have also had to change focus. The new system gives them more information about what is going on in divisions and they have had to adjust their management practices accordingly. The systems did create some concern about how big a slice of cake people would have, and operational divisions now question expenditure on overheads.

The organisation needed to link ABM to corporate objectives in the form of increased product profitability and improved value for customers. Performance measures for divisional managers included ABM improvements. Introducing ABM was not seen as a cost-cutting exercise and the processes were seen to be important and effective at meeting the needs of customers.

Overall, ABM was used to ensure the organisation was doing the thing right. The introduction of the balanced scorecard will ensure it is also doing the right thing.

TIPS FOR ABM

- Get the support of senior management
- Recognise that ABM requires a major investment in time and resources
- Know what ABM can achieve and what information you want from the system

- Decide which model to use

- Choose the model approach that emphasises the operational understanding of all activities in the business

- Involve people in the field

- Transfer ownership of cost management from the accounts department to the departments and processes where costs are incurred

- Don't underestimate the need to manage the change process

- Link ABM to corporate objectives in the form of increased product profitability and added value for customers.

11 Direct Product Profitability (DPP)

As traditional absorption costing, which normally uses labour hours as a basis for absorption, is rarely suitable for service and retail organisations other methods had to be devised. One relatively new way of spreading overheads in retail organisations, which is used in the grocery trade in particular, is direct product profitability (DPP).

Direct Product Profitability is **'used primarily within the retail sector...DPP involves the attribution of both the purchase price and other indirect costs (for example distribution, warehousing and retailing) to each product line. Thus a net profit, as opposed to a gross profit, can be identified for each product. The cost attribution process utilises a variety of measures (for example warehousing space and transport time) to reflect the resource consumption of individual products'.**

CIMA Official Terminology

DPP started in the USA in the 1960s at General Electric, and was then taken up and used by Proctor and Gamble in the 1980s. In 1985 the Food Marketing Institute in the USA laid down a standard approach to the system and two years later DPP was taken up by the Institute of Grocery Distribution in the UK. The system described below was introduced in the late 1980s and has since undergone transformation as activity-based costing has developed.

Retail organisations traditionally deducted the bought-in cost of the good from the selling price to give a gross margin. The gross margin is a useless measure for controlling the costs of the organisation itself or making decisions about the profitability of the different products. This is because none of the costs generated by the retail organisation itself are included in its calculation. For example, it does not include the storage costs of the different goods and these costs vary considerably from one good to another. A method was needed which related the indirect costs to the goods according to the way the goods used or created these costs.

The table below shows the DPP for Product A. Directly-attributable costs have been grouped into three categories and are deducted from the gross margin to determine the product's DPP.

Direct product profit for Product A

	$	$
Selling price		1.50
Less: bought-in price		(0.80)
Gross margin		**0.70**
Less: Direct product costs:		
Warehouse costs	0.16	
Transport costs	0.18	
Store costs	0.22	
		(0.56)
Direct product profit		**0.14**

Warehouse and store costs will include items such as labour, space and insurance costs, while transport costs will include labour, fuel and vehicle maintenance costs. The usual way to spread these costs across the different goods sold is in relation to volume or area occupied, as most costs increase in direct proportion to the volume of the product or the space it occupies.

However, there are some exceptions to this; for example, insurance costs may be better spread on value or on a risk index. Risk is greater with refrigerated or perishable goods. Refrigeration costs must only be related to those products that need to be stored in the refrigerator. Handling costs can also be treated in a different manner as they tend to vary with the number of pallets handled rather than the volume of the good itself. The labour involved in shelf-stacking may also need to be spread on a different basis.

The benefits of DPP may be summarised as:

- Better cost analysis
- Better pricing decisions
- Better management of store and warehouse space
- The rationalisation of product ranges
- Better merchandising decisions.

More On DPP

In recent years DPP has developed considerably in parallel with activity-based costing. DPP has become much more sophisticated and is now very similar to activity-based costing. One of the reasons for its development during the 1990s has been the development of EPOS and EFTPOS (electronic point of sale and electronic funds transfer point of sale) systems that have enabled access to the detailed data needed for direct product cost and profitability calculations.

Indirect costs may be analysed into basic cost categories as follows. These are very similar to those discussed later for activity-based costing.

- Overhead cost. This is incurred through an activity that is not directly linked to a particular product.
- Volume-related cost. Products incur this cost in relation to the space they occupy. This is the cost described previously and includes storage and transport costs.
- Product batch cost. This is often a time-based cost. If product items (i.e. a number of identical products which are handled together as a batch) are stacked on shelves, a labour time cost is incurred. If shipping documents have to be prepared for an order or batch, this again is a labour time cost.
- Inventory financing costs. This is the cost of tying up money in inventory and is the cost of the product multiplied by the company's cost of capital per day or per week.
- Each of the categories above will contain a number of individual activities, such as:
  (1) Checking incoming goods
  (2) Repacking or packing out for storing
  (3) Inspecting products
  (4) Refilling store shelf.

DPP software systems can be purchased to model costs. They require a number of key variables to analyse different situations. The variables are:

(a) **Buying and selling prices**. The retailer has the option to adjust the selling price. A price increase from a supplier can always be used to increase the gross margin, but the higher the selling price relative to other retailers the slower inventory movement is likely to be.

(b) **Rate of sale**. This is critical and needs to be as fast as possible in order to minimise space costs at the warehouse and the store, and to avoid loss of interest on money tied up in inventory.

(c) **Inventory-holding size**. The aim is to hold as little inventory as possible in keeping with JIT principles without running out of inventory.

(d) **Product size**. This is the cubic area that the product occupies and is important because space costs per item will be incurred according to size.

(e) **Pallet configuration**. The larger the number of cases on the pallet the cheaper handling costs per unit will be.

(f) **Ordering costs**. Obviously fewer orders will be cheaper but fewer orders will mean holding more inventory.

(g) **Distribution routes**. Are the goods transported direct to the store or is a central warehouse used? Transporting goods direct to the store is a high cost activity for the supplier and it is usually better to use a central warehouse, even for goods with a short shelf life.

[In the March 2013 PEG, the Examiner notes that when asked to describe Direct Product Profitability, the candidates provided 'answers that did not relate to this technique but simply described general selling price issues'.]

12 Customer Profitability Analysis

In many organisations, it is just as important to cost customers as it is to cost products. Different customers or groups of customers differ in their profitability. This is a relatively new technique that ABC makes possible because it creates cost pools for activities. Customers use some activities but not all, and different groups of customers have different 'activity profiles'.

Customer Profitability Analysis is **'the analysis of revenue streams and service costs associated with specific customers or customer groups'.**

CIMA Official Terminology

Service organisations such as a bank or a hotel in particular need to cost customers. A bank's activities for a customer will include the following types of activities:

- Withdrawal of cash
- Unauthorised overdraft
- Request for a statement
- Stopping a cheque
- Returning a cheque because of insufficient funds.

Different customers or categories of customers will each use different amounts of these activities and so customer profitability profiles can be built up, and customers can be charged according to the cost to serve them.

Example of CPA in a hotel

A hotel may have activities that are provided for specific types of customers, such as:

- well-laid-out gardens
- a swimming pool
- a bar.

Older guests may appreciate and use the garden, families the swimming pool and business guests the bar.

If the activities are charged to the relevant guests a correct cost per bed occupied can be calculated for this type of category. This will show the relative profitability and lead to strategies for encouraging the more profitable guests.

13 Customer profitability curve

Even a manufacturing organisation can benefit from costing its customers. Not all customers cost the same to serve even if they require the same products. Some customers may be located a long way from the factory and transport may cost more. Other customers may be disruptive and place rush orders that interrupt production scheduling and require immediate, special transport. Some customers need after sales service and help with technical matters, etc.

When an organisation analyses the profitability of its customers it is not unusual to find that a Pareto curve exists. That is 20 per cent of customers provide 80 per cent of the profit. This may be illustrated by a **customer profitability curve**. For example:

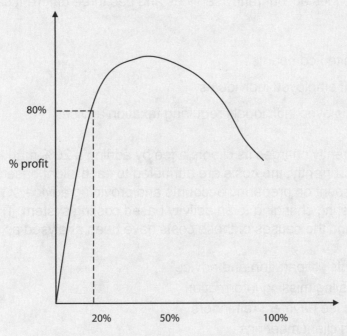

The diagram above shows that the last 80% of customers do not all generate profit. The last 50% actually reduce the total profit. There is no point in serving these customers as the situation stands but it may be foolish just to refuse to serve them. Instead it may be better to turn them into profitable customers if this is possible. A multifunctional team should be set up to find ways of making these customers profitable.

Usually it is the small volume/order customers who are unprofitable because of high production batch costs and order processing, etc. One organisation introduced a third party wholesaler into the supply chain and significantly reduced the cost of serving the small order customers. At the same time the organisation found that the product range and service to the small customers improved, and so the company saved costs and the customer received an improved service.

Illustration – CPA

From November 2010 exam

XY provides accountancy services and has three different categories of client:

- limited companies
- self employed individuals
- employed individuals requiring taxation advice.

XY currently charges its clients a fee by adding a 20% mark-up to total costs. Currently, the costs are attributed to each client based on the hours spent on preparing accounts and providing advice. XY is considering changing to an activity based costing system. The annual costs and the causes of these costs have been analysed as follows:

Accounts preparation and advice	$580,000
Requesting missing information	$30,000
Issuing fee payment reminders	$15,000
Holding client meetings	$60,000
Travelling to clients	$40,000

The following details relate to three of XY's clients and to XY as a whole:

	Client			XY
	A	B	C	
Hours spent on preparing accounts and providing advice	1,000	250	340	**18,000**
Requests for missing information	4	10	6	**250**
Payment reminders sent	2	8	10	**400**
Client meetings held	4	1	2	**250**
Miles travelled to clients	150	600	0	**10,000**

Required:

Prepare calculations to show the effect on fees charged to each of these three clients of changing to the new costing system.

[From the PEG November 2010 : Many candidates did not gain the marks available simply because they did not correctly answer the question. Candidates were asked to prepare calculations to show the effect on fees, as a result of changing to an ABC system. Therefore a **comparison** was needed of the fees generated from both systems. A significant number of candidates simply produced a chart showing the costs using an ABC approach. The layout of figures put forward by many candidates was extremely poor. A typical spreadsheet approach was required; simply three columns and a number of rows were required.]

Solution

Cost driver rates:

Accounts preparation and advice	$580,000/18,000 hours = $32.222 per hour
Requesting missing information	$30,000/250 times = $120 per request
Issuing fee payment reminders	$15,000/400 times = $37.50 per reminder
Holding client meetings	$60,000/250 meetings = $240 per meeting
Travelling to clients	$40,000/10,000 miles = $4 per mile

Client costs:

	Client		
	A	B	C
Accounts preparation and advice	$32,222	$8,055	$10,955
Requesting missing information	$480	$1,200	$720
Issuing fee payment reminders	$75	$300	$375
Holding client meetings	$960	$240	$480
Travelling to clients	$600	$2,400	$0
Total costs	$34,337	$12,195	$12,530
Total costs on original basis (*)	$40,280	$10,070	$13,695
Client fees – new basis (W1)	$41,204	$14,634	$15,036
Client fees – original basis	$48,336	$12,084	$16,434
Increase/(Decrease)	$(7,132)	$2,550	$(1,398)

(*) $725,000/18,000 hours = $40.28 per hour

> (W1) **Client fees calculations, new basis**
>
> Client A: Total costs $34,337 × (1 + 20% mark-up on costs) = $41,204
>
> Client B: Total costs $12,195 × (1 + 20% mark-up on costs) = $14,634
>
> Client C: Total costs $12,530 × (1 + 20% mark-up on costs) = $15,036

[In the March 2013 PEG, the Examiner notes that when asked to describe Customer Profitability Analysis, the candidates provided 'answers that did not relate to this technique but simply described general selling price issues'.]

14 Pareto analysis

Pareto analysis is based on the 80:20 rule that was a phenomenon first observed by Vilfredo Pareto, a nineteenth century Italian economist. He noticed that 80 per cent of the wealth of Milan was owned by 20 per cent of its citizens:

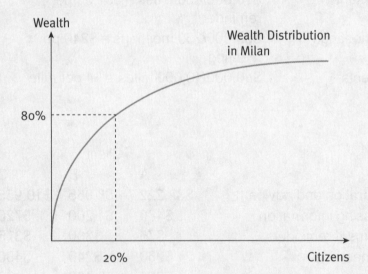

This phenomenon, or some kind of approximation of it (70:30, etc.), can be observed in many different business situations. The management accountant can use it in a number of different circumstances to help direct management's attention to the key control mechanisms or planning aspects.

The Pareto phenomenon often shows itself in relation to profitability. Often around 80 per cent of an organisation's contribution is generated by 20 per cent of the revenue. A situation similar to this can be seen in the figure below, where the contributions of five products are plotted on a cumulative basis. Twenty per cent of the sales revenue generates 80 per cent of the contribution:

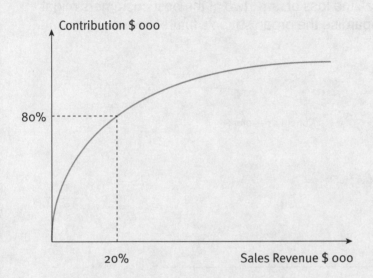

It is not always advisable to delete products from the range if they are not very profitable or their price cannot be increased, without carrying out careful analysis. The poor performers may be new products establishing themselves in the market and they may have a profitable future. However, the products that generate the largest proportion of the contribution need to be looked after. One reason for their profitability may be a high degree of branding which increases the contribution margin per unit. The company must continue to spend money promoting the brand so as to keep it in front of the public.

Pareto analysis has a number of different uses in business:

- Instead of analysing products, customers can be analysed for their relative profitability to the organisation. Again, it is often found that approximately 20 per cent of customers generate 80 per cent of the profit. There will always be some customers who are less profitable than others, just as some products are less profitable than others.

- The key with customers is to make sure that the overall profile does not degenerate and the aim should be to **improve the profile**. This can be seen in the figure below, where the solid line represents the present position and the two dotted lines represent a change in performance for the better and worse. The 'better profile' dotted line shows improved performance in the sense that customers are contributing more evenly to the profit, thus stabilising the position of the organisation. With the 'worse profile', the loss of, say, two of the best customers might seriously jeopardise the organisation's future:

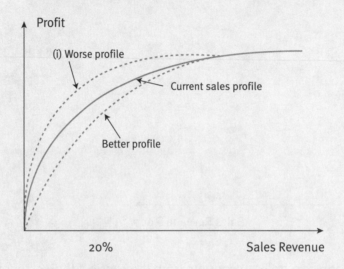

Another use for Pareto analysis is in inventory control where it may be found that only a few of the goods in inventory make up most of the value. A typical analysis of inventory may reveal the situation shown as follows:

Product	Value	% of value	% of volume	Action
A	High value	70%	10	Control carefully
B	Medium value	20%	20	Medium control
C	Little value	10%	70	No control

The outcome of this type of analysis may be to increase control and safeguards on the 10 per cent of the inventory that is of a particularly high value and to remove or reduce the controls on the inventory that is of little value. Alternatively it may be found that a few items take up most of the storage space and therefore storage costs are unduly high for these items. It may be possible to move towards a just-in-time system for these items only, thus saving money and space.

Another study might relate to activity-based costing and overheads. **It may show that 20 per cent of an organisation's cost drivers are responsible for 80 per cent of the total cost**. By analysing, monitoring and controlling those cost drivers that cause most cost, a better control and understanding of overheads will be obtained.

Procedure

(1) Rank the data in descending order.

(2) Find each figure as a percentage of the total.

(3) Turn this into a cumulative percentage.

(4) It is possible to draw a diagram to illustrate the principle, e.g. a component bar chart or a cumulative frequency graph.

Pareto analysis and charts

ABC Limited manufactures and sells seven products. The following data relates to the latest period:

Product	Contribution in $000
P	96
Q	36
R	720
S	240
T	12
U	60
V	24
	_____
	1,188
	_____

To prepare a Pareto chart of product contribution and comment on the results, the first step is to rearrange the products in descending order of contribution and calculate the cumulative contribution:

Product	Contribution in $	Cumulative Contribution in $000	Cumulative %
R	720	720	61
S	240	960	81
P	96	1,056	89
U	60	1,116	94
Q	36	1,152	97
V	24	1,176	99
T	12	1,188	100
	_____		
	1,188		
	_____		

The cumulative data can now be used to produce the required Pareto chart showing product contribution:

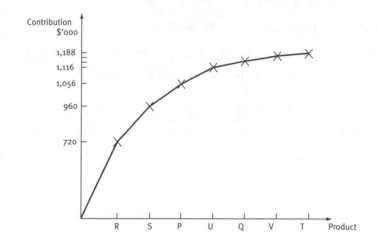

The analysis shows that more than 80 per cent of the total contribution is earned by two products: R and S. The position of these products needs protecting, perhaps through careful attention to branding and promotion. The other products require investigation to see whether their contribution can be improved through increased prices, reduced costs or increased volumes.

The term 'Pareto diagram' usually refers to a histogram or frequency chart on product quality – see figure below. In the 1950s Juran observed that a few causes of poor quality usually accounted for most of the quality problems – hence the name Pareto. The figure below shows a frequency chart for poor quality in boxed cakes, and it can easily be imagined how it could be turned into a Pareto chart.

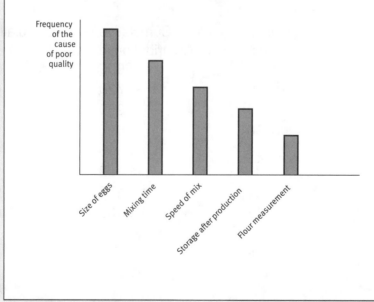

The purpose of the analysis, in this case, is to direct attention to the area where the best returns can be achieved by solving most of the quality problems, perhaps just with a single action. In this case more accurate grading of eggs by volume by the supplier may solve about 40 per cent of the total quality problem and if the mixing time is made more accurate at least 75 per cent of the problems will be removed.

15 Distribution channel profitability

Distribution channels are in simple terms the means of transacting with customers. The channel is the point of purchase which need not necessarily be the point of communication, payment, delivery and after sales support. Companies may transact with their customers through direct channels e.g. sales teams, telephone, shops, Internet or through indirect channels e.g. retailers, wholesalers, resellers, agents.

Regardless of whether a company's channels are direct or indirect they should always consider the ultimate needs of the customer and therefore use the channels to ensure that those needs are satisfied. Customers will look for ease of access to the supplier, reciprocal communication, products and services which satisfy their needs, prompt delivery, after sales support to name but a few.

The channel a company selects is therefore a critical driver to business profitability. A company should not only aim to satisfy the needs of the customer but must also ensure that the products and services that they are providing are profitable. The method of channel distribution chosen can account for a significant proportion of total cost and choosing the wrong channel can result in significant losses for that particular product or service. Key aspects that the company needs to consider in relation to their distribution channels include; access to the customer base, brand awareness, competitiveness, achieving sales and market targets, speed of payment, customer retention rates and most importantly of all profitability.

In companies it is just as important to cost channels as it is to cost products and customers. Different channels will differ in profitability. Activity based costing information makes this possible because it creates cost pools for activities. Channels will use some activities but not all, and different channels will have different 'activity profiles'. This makes channel profitability analysis possible and allows companies to build up distribution channel profitability profiles. It can be possible therefore for a company to identify costly distribution channels for low margin products or services which they are supplying through direct channels, and which may best be offered through indirect channels. This would result in reduced channel distribution costs, and a better profitability profile for the product or service.

16 Activity – Based Budgeting

As its name should suggest, activity-based budgeting (ABB) takes a similar approach to activity-based costing.

ABB is **'a method of budgeting based on an activity framework and utilising cost driver data in the budget-setting and variance feedback processes'**.

CIMA Official Terminology

Whereas ZBB is based on budgets (decision packages) prepared by responsibility centre managers, ABB is based on budgeting for activities.

The basic approach of ABB is to budget the costs for each cost pool or activity.

There will also be some general overhead costs that are not activity-related, such as factory rental costs and the salary cost of the factory manager. General overhead costs are budgeted separately.

(1) The cost driver for each activity is identified. A forecast is made of the number of units of the cost driver that will occur in the budget period.

(2) Given the estimate of the activity level for the cost driver, the activity cost is estimated. Where appropriate, a **cost per unit of activity** is calculated.

The advantages and disadvantages of ABB are similar to those provided by activity-based costing.

Advantages	Disadvantages
It draws attention to the costs of 'overhead activities'. This can be important where overhead costs are a large proportion of total operating costs.	A considerable amount of time and effort might be needed to establish an ABB system, for example to identify the key activities and their cost drivers.
It provides information for the control of activity costs, by assuming that they are variable, at least in the longer term.	Activity-based budgeting might not be appropriate for the organisation and its activities and cost structures.
It provides a useful basis for monitoring and controlling overhead costs, by drawing management attention to the actual costs of activities and comparing actual costs with what the activities were expected to cost.	A budget should be prepared on the basis of responsibility centres, with identifiable budget holders made responsible for the performance of their budget centre. A problem with ABB could be to identify clear individual responsibilities for activities.
It also provides useful control information by emphasising that activity costs might be controllable if the activity volume can be controlled.	It could be argued that in the short term many overhead costs are not controllable and do not vary directly with changes in the volume of activity for the cost driver. The only cost variances to report would be fixed overhead expenditure variances for each activity.
ABB can provide useful information for a total quality management (TQM) programme, by relating the cost of an activity to the level of service provided (for example, stores requisitions processed) – Do the user departments feel they are getting a cost-effective service?	

17 Practice Questions

Objective Test Question 1: ABC vs. traditional costing

Company A manufactures three smartphones. Company A currently operates a traditional absorption costing system, but has decided to use an activity based costing (ABC) system on a trial basis for its procurement operation. A time-based cost driver is used to charge the procurement costs to the smartphones under the ABC system. The following unit manufacturing costs have been determined using both traditional absorption costing and activity based costing:

	Traditional absorption costing	Activity Based Costing
Smartphone Type 1	$90	$108
Smartphone Type 2	$102	$104
Smartphone Type 3	$95	$85

Place each of the following statements in a grey cell, against the product to which it is most likely to relate:

Smartphone Type 1	
Smartphone Type 2	
Smartphone Type 3	

This smartphone uses a lot of parts and materials that are readily available.	This smartphone has relatively few components that are generally purchased in bulk.	This smartphone uses a lot of parts and materials that are difficult to obtain, and so puts the buying department under pressure.

Objective Test Question 2: Activity Based Management

An engineering company is thinking about implementing activity-based management principles. Which of the following is a correct definition of activity-based management? Select the ONE definition that applies.

(i)   ABM is an approach to the costing and monitoring of activities which involves tracing resources consumption and costing final outputs. Resources are assigned to activities and activities to cost objects based on consumption estimates. The latter utilise cost drivers to attach activities costs to outputs.

(ii) ABM involves the identification and evaluation of the activity drivers used to trace the cost of activities to cost objects. It may also involve selecting activity drivers with potential to contribute to the cost management function, with particular reference to cost reduction.

(iii) ABM is a method of budgeting based on an activity framework and utilising cost driver data in the budget setting and variance feedback processes.

(iv) ABM is a system of management which uses activity-based cost information for a variety of purposes including cost reduction, cost modelling and customer profitability analysis.

(v)   ABM is a grouping of all cost elements associated with an activity.

Objective Test Question 3: Direct Product Profitability

AB plc is a supermarket group which incurs the following costs:

(i)   The bought-in price of the good

(ii) Inventory financing costs

(iii) Shelf refilling costs

(iv) Costs of repacking or 'pack out' prior to storage before sale.

AB plc's calculation of Direct Product Profitability would include:

A   All of the above costs

B   All of the above costs, except (ii)

C   All of the above costs, except (iv)

D   Costs (i) and (ii) only

E   Cost (i) only

Data Set Question: Walken Supermarkets

Walken Supermarkets sells over 30,000 product lines. It wishes to introduce Direct Product Profitability analysis and a team of management accountants have ascertained the following information relating to the following year:

Budgeted weekly overhead	$
Warehouse costs	75,000
Supermarket costs	40,000 per supermarket
Transportation costs	400 per delivery

The warehouse is expected to handle 10,000 cubic metres (m^3) of goods.

Each supermarket will handle 5,000 m^3 of goods each week.

Each transportation vehicle holds 40 m^3 of goods.

Three products sold by Walken are Kitchen Roll (KR), Tinned Spaghetti (TS) and Toothpaste (T):

	KR	TS	T
Retail price per item	$1.00	$0.60	$1.75
Bought-in price per item	$0.60	$0.30	$1.00
Number of items per case	10	25	40
Number of cases per m^3	20	30	20
Time in warehouse	1 week	2 weeks	3 weeks
Time in supermarket	2 weeks	4 weeks	2 weeks

Required:

Calculate the following figures, in $, to four decimal places:

The net profit per kitchen roll $ [   ]

The net profit per tin of spaghetti $ [   ]

The net profit per tube of toothpaste $ [   ]

Integration Style Question: Casamia

PRE-SEEN MATERIAL

Casamia plc purchases a range of good quality gift and household products from around the world; it then sells these products through 'mail order' or retail outlets. The company receives 'mail orders' by post, telephone and Internet. Retail outlets are either department stores or Casamia plc's own small shops. The company started to set up its own shops after a recession in the early 1990s and regards them as the flagship of its business; sales revenue has gradually built up over the last 10 years. There are now 50 department stores and 10 shops.

The company has made good profits over the last few years but recently trading has been difficult. As a consequence, the management team has decided that a fundamental reappraisal of the business is now necessary if the company is to continue trading.

Meanwhile, the budgeting process for the coming year is proceeding. Casamia uses an activity-based costing (ABC) system and the following estimated cost information for the coming year is available:

Retail outlet costs:

Activity	Cost driver	Rate per cost driver	Per Year Department store	Own shop
Telephone queries and request to Casamia	Calls	$15	40 calls	350 calls
Sales visits to shops and stores by Casamia sales staff	Visits	$250	2 visits	4 visits
Shop orders	Orders	$20	25 orders	150 orders
Packaging	Deliveries	$100	28 deliveries	150 deliveries
Delivery to shops	Deliveries	$150	28 deliveries	150 deliveries

Staffing, rental and service costs for each of Casamia plc's own shops cost on average $300,000 a year.

Mail order costs:

Activity	Cost driver	Rate per cost driver		
		Post	Telephone	Internet
Processing 'mail orders'	Orders	$5	$6	$3
Dealing with 'mail order' queries	Orders	$4	$4	$1
		Number of packages per order		
Packaging and deliveries for 'mail orders' – cost per package $10	Packages	2	2	1

Task: Report

You receive the following email from the Financial Controller:

> **From:** Clara Fuchs (Financial Controller)
> **Sent:** 03 June, 10.23 a.m.
> **To:** Senior Management Accountant
> **Subject:** Activity-Based Costing
>
> Please prepare calculations on the expected profitability of the different types of sales outlets for the coming year.
>
> I intend to submit your report to the Board. I would welcome some comments on the results of the figures you have prepared, particularly in the context of the re-appraisal of the business.
>
> Please also advise on how the information you have submitted may be revised or expanded to be of more assistance, and suggest what other information is needed to make a more informed judgement.

Test your understanding answers

Objective Test Question 1: ABC vs. traditional costing

Smartphone Type 1	This smartphone uses a lot of parts and materials that are difficult to obtain, and so puts the buying department under pressure.
Smartphone Type 2	This smartphone has relatively few components that are generally purchased in bulk
Smartphone Type 3	This smartphone uses a lot of parts and materials that are readily available.

Smartphone 1 has a higher cost under ABC, which suggests a more complex item using specific parts and materials.

Smartphone 2 has a marginally higher cost under ABC, which suggests the use of mostly readily available components.

Smartphone 3 has a lower cost under ABC, which suggests a standard product using few, if any, specific or complex components.

Objective Test Question 2: Activity Based Management

The answer is (iv): ABM uses the information provided by an ABC analysis to improve organisational profitability.

Option (i) defines ABC.

Option (ii) defines activity driver analysis.

Option (iii) defines activity based budgeting.

Option (v) defines an activity cost pool.

Objective Test Question 3: Direct Product Profitability

The answer is A: All of the costs described can be identified with specific goods and would be deducted from the selling price to determine the direct product profit.

Data Set Question: Walken Supermarkets

Warehouse cost $75,000 ÷ 10,000 = $7.50 per m³

Supermarket cost $40,000 ÷ 5,000 = $8.00 per m³

Transportation cost $400 ÷ 40 = $10 per m³

	KR $	TS $	T $
Retail price	1.00	0.60	1.75
Less bought-in price	(0.60)	(0.30)	(1.00)
Gross margin	0.40	0.30	0.75
Less overheads:			
Warehouse costs (see workings)	0.0375	0.02	0.0281
Supermarket costs (see workings)	0.08	0.0427	0.02
Transportation costs (see workings)	0.05	0.0133	0.0125
Net profit	**0.2325**	**0.2240**	**0.6894**

Workings

Number of items per m³	10 × 20 = 200	25 × 30 = 750	40 × 20 = 800

Warehouse charge:

Kitchen roll ($7.50 ÷ 200) × 1 week = 0.0375

Tinned spaghetti ($7.50 ÷ 750) × 2 weeks = 0.02

Supermarket cost:

Kitchen roll ($8.00 ÷ 200) × 2 weeks = 0.08

Tinned spaghetti ($8.00 ÷ 750) × 4 weeks = 0.0427

Transportation costs:

Kitchen roll $10 per m³ (÷ 20 cases per m³) (÷ 10 items per case) = 0.05 per item

Tinned spaghetti $10 per m³ (÷ 30 cases per m³) (÷ 25 items per case) = 0.0133 per item

Integration Style Question: Casamia

REPORT

To: Financial Controller

From: Management Accountant

Date: 03 June 2014

Subject: Profitability of different types of sales outlets

The aim of this report is to determine the expected profitability of the different types of sales outlets for the coming year.

In summary, the calculations in the attached appendices (Appendix 'A' to 'E') show the following:

- Casamia's own shops will make a considerable 'loss'.

- The department store sales will not generate as good a profit as the 'mail order' side.

- The telephone mail order, that is 46% of the business, will generate 104% of the current total profit.

- The Internet business is not particularly profitable in the coming year, but it will presumably grow quite quickly. If this happens, the charge for maintaining the Internet, which is expressed by each order, will presumably decline as it is likely to be a semi-fixed cost.

(1) **Usefulness of information**

The calculations show the profitability of the different types of outlet for the coming year only, which is of some use. For example, it shows that Casamia's own shops make a considerable loss and it would appear, on the surface, that the company would be better off without them, perhaps transferring the business to franchises within department stores. It also indicates that the emphasis of the business should be switched to the mail order side, as it is more profitable and, in particular, to the telephone section.

(2) **The need for further information**

However, the latter shows how dangerous this kind of assumption can be because the telephone section may have peaked and, in future, growth in the Internet section may be at the expense of the telephone section. Therefore, decisions about future strategies cannot be made on predicted short-term costs and revenues. Any attempt to do so could prove disastrous. Growth in the market, competitors' moves, customers' needs and requirements must be the basis for any decisions.

The ABC costs could, however, be used to highlight areas for cost reduction and procedural changes which could assist longer-term profitability. ABC is a method for apportioning costs and it suffers from the same defects as every absorption method. In Casamia's case, the analysis does not look very detailed/accurate and so may be little better than a traditional absorption system.

The head office and warehousing costs need to be examined in detail to determine which type of outlet incurs what part of the cost, as these costs may be caused and used more by some types of outlets than others. If this is so, what would happen to cost if one type of outlet was abandoned and others increased in size?

(3) **Other information needed to make a more informed judgement is likely to be:**

Customers' changing purchasing habits

Same customer purchases across outlet types, that is, do customers buy from shops and order by telephone

Competitors' moves

New entrants into the market – especially in the Internet business

Future economic conditions

Exchange rate movements – as some goods are imported

Increase in disposable income

The image created by the different types of outlet, that is do their own shops create the brand or company name

Past data to establish trends.

Then, specific information will need to be collected for the fundamental reappraisal of the business. For example, if the decision to close Casamia's own shops was being considered, a detailed study of the interrelationship between outlets should be carried out, as having the products on display in shops might be necessary in order to maintain the high level of telephone orders. For instance, potential customers may visit to see colours, quality, and so on.

Products on display are also a form of advertising for the company and this would be lost if the shops were closed.

Appendix A : Calculation of net margin per type of outlet

	Department Store	Own shop	Mail order Post	Mail order Telephone	Mail order Internet
Sales revenue	50,000	1,000,000	150.00	300.00	100.00
Gross margin[1] (50,000 + 1.30, etc)	11,538	285,714	42.86	85.71	28.57
Less: Staffing etc.		300,000			
Telephone queries ($15 × 40, etc)	600	5,250			
Sales visits ($250 × 2, etc)	500	1,000			
Orders ($20 × 25, etc)	500	3,000			
Packaging ($100 × 28, etc)	2,800	15,000			
Delivery ($150 × 28, etc)	4,200	22,500			
Order cost			5.00	6.00	3.00
Queries			4.00	4.00	1.00
Packing & delivery ($10 × 2, etc)			20.00	20.00	10.00
Internet cost[2]					10.00
	8,600	**346,750**	**29.00**	**30.00**	**24.00**
Net margin	2,938	(61,036)	13.86	55.71	4.57
Net margin/sales	5.9%		9.2%	18.6%	4.6%
	4th	5th	2nd	1st	3rd

Appendix B : Calculation of total margin for each type of outlet

	Department Stores $000	Own shops $000	Mail order Post $000	Mail order Telephone $000	Mail order Internet $000	Total $000
Total revenue	2,500	10,000	3,600	14,400	800	31,300
Total net margin	146.90	(610.36)	332.64	2,674.08	36.56	2,579.82

Appendix C: Gross margin calculation for 30% of purchase cost

$$100 = 0.3X + X$$
$$X = 76.92\%$$
$$0.3\,X = 23.076\%$$
$$\$50,000 \times 23.076\% = \$11.538$$

Appendix D: Mail order

Total number of mail orders = 80,000. So number of Internet orders = 80,000 × 10% = 8,000

Internet link cost per order = $80,000/8,000 orders = $10

Appendix E: Calculation of total revenues and net margins ($000)

		Total revenue		Total net margin
Department Stores 50 outlets	(× $50,000)	$2,500	(× 2,938)	146.9
Own shops 10 outlets	(× $1,000,000)	10,000	(× $61,036)	(610.36)
Mail order – post				
80,000 × 30% = 24,000 orders	(× $150)	3,600	(× $13.86)	332.64
Mail order – telephone				
80,000 × 60% = 48,000 orders	(× $300)	14,400	(× $55.71)	2,674.08
Mail order – Internet				
80,000 × 10% = 8,000 orders	(× $100)	800	(× $4.57)	$36.56

2

The Modern Business Environment

Chapter learning objectives

Lead A1: Evaluate techniques for analysing and managing costs for competitive advantage

Component A1b): Evaluate Total Quality Management techniques

- The impacts of just-in-time (JIT) production, the theory of constraints and total quality management on efficiency, inventory and cost.

- The benefits of JIT production, total quality management and theory of constraints and the implications of these methods for decision in the contemporary manufacturing environment.

- Kaizen costing, continuous improvement and cost of quality reporting.

- Process re-engineering and the elimination of non-value adding activities and reduction of activity costs.

1 Chapter summary

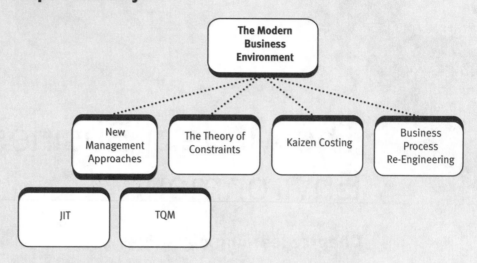

2 Introduction to the modern business environment

'To compete successfully in today's highly competitive global environment companies are making customer satisfaction an overriding priority, adopting new management approaches, changing their manufacturing systems and investing in new technologies. These changes are having a significant influence on management accounting systems.'

Colin Drury in ' Management and Cost Accounting'

The modern manufacturing environment is very different from the traditional production environment. It means that traditional costing methods are becoming less relevant.

In this chapter we explore how the modern production system has changed, and in the following chapters we examine how costing has adapted to this and created new ways to calculate a product's production cost.

3 Knowledge brought forward

You will already have covered some key concepts in Paper P1. We will build on this knowledge in P2 with more aspects of the modern business environment, but make sure you are comfortable with the assumed knowledge, that should have been brought forward as a base, in the following sections.

Characteristics of the modern business environment

Global environment

- Companies operate in a world economy.

- Customers and competitors come from all over the world.

- Products are made from components from around the world.

- Firms have to be world class to compete.

- International regulations.

Flexibility

- In a global environment, customers have far greater choice than ever before.

- There has been a huge increase in demand for new, cutting-edge innovative products.

- Customers are demanding ever-improving levels of service in cost, quality, reliability and delivery.

- Customers demand flexibility. Companies need to respond to this in order to survive.

As a consequence of this:

(1) many companies now have very diverse product ranges, with a high level of tailor-made products and services

(2) product life cycles have dramatically reduced, often from several years to just a few months.

The move away from standardised units of production towards individual customised units means that mass production techniques are redundant. Instead, it is of greatest importance to take an order from placement to completion in the shortest time possible. This means that production processes will be designed differently to accommodate flexibility of production rather than just throughput.

Employee empowerment

To ensure this flexibility, managers need to empower their employees to make decisions quickly, without reference to more senior managers. By empowering employees and giving them relevant information they will be able to respond faster to customers, increase process flexibility, reduce cycle times and improve morale.

Management accounting systems are moving from providing information to managers to monitor employees to providing information to employees to empower them to focus on continuous improvement.

World Class Manufacturing

The World Class Manufacturing approach to quality is quite different from the traditional approach because the primary emphasis is placed on the resolution of the problems that cause poor quality, rather than merely detecting it. These systems are more proactive and try to prevent problems from occurring in the first place rather than waiting for them to occur and then fixing them.

The system might be developed formally under Total Quality Management.

Just-In-Time

CIMA's *Official Terminology defines* 'Just-in-Time' as *a system whose objective is to produce or procure products or components as they are required by a customer or for use, rather than for inventory. A just-in-time system is a 'pull' system, which responds to demand, in contrast to a 'push' system, in which inventory acts as a buffer between the different elements of the system, such as purchasing, production and sales.'*

JIT **production** is defined as:

A production system which is driven by demand for finished products whereby each component on a production line is produced only when needed for the next stage.

JIT **purchasing** as:

A purchasing system in which material purchases are contracted so that the receipt and usage of material, to the maximum extent possible, coincide.

[In the PEG November 2010 Exam, the Examiner notes that some candidates failed to recognise that the system in the question was a form of JIT for production and inventory (but not for purchasing). Candidates also tend to write far too much for the marks available and often don't relate the answer to the scenario.

In the PEG March 2011 Exam, the Examiner regrets that some candidates do not include or mention that a JIT production system is based around the principle of zero inventories at all stages of production including finished goods. This is an important issue that specifically needs mentioning.]

These Official Terminology definitions give JIT the appearance of being merely an alternative production management system, with similar characteristics and objectives to techniques such as MRP. However, JIT is better described as a philosophy, or approach to management, as it encompasses a commitment to continuous improvement and the pursuit of excellence in the design and operation of the production management system.

Toyota

Organisations in the West have traditionally used a 'push' production flow system. This system has the following stages:

(1) Buy raw materials and put them into inventory.

(2) Produce a production schedule based on sales forecasts.

(3) Withdraw goods from inventory and make products according to the production schedule.

(4) Put completed units into finished goods store.

(5) Sell from finished goods store when customers request products.

Work in progress (WIP) is an unavoidable feature of such a system.

Toyota developed a different system known as JIT. This system is not a 'push' system but a 'pull' system. A product is not 'made' until the customer requests it, and components are not made until they are required by the next production stage. In a full JIT system virtually no inventory is held, that is no raw material inventory and no finished goods inventory is held, but there will be a small amount of WIP, say one-tenth of a day's production. The system works by the customer triggering the final stage of production, the assembly. As the product is assembled, components are used and this in turn triggers the component stage of production and a small amount of WIP is made ready for the next product. So the cycle goes on until the final trigger requests more raw material from the supplier.

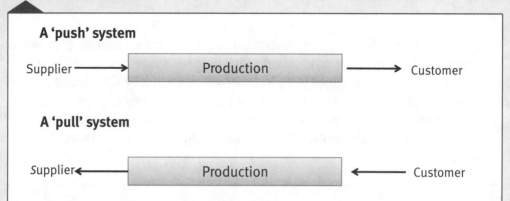

A 'push' system

Supplier ⟶ [Production] ⟶ Customer

A 'pull' system

Supplier ⟵ [Production] ⟵ Customer

If a JIT system is to work satisfactorily, suppliers must deliver several times a day and so when the raw material arrives it may go straight into the factory and be used immediately. This means that the production lead time (i.e. the time from raw materials entering production to the finished goods emerging) should equal the processing time. In many Western organisations in the past it took several months to make a product from start to finish, despite the fact that if worked on continuously it could be made in, say, two days. The difference in time is largely due to WIP waiting to be used in the next process. It will be apparent that value is only added to the product during the actual processing stages. These have been estimated to represent as little as 10 per cent of the total manufacturing lead time in many companies, and thus up to 90 per cent of production time adds costs but no value.

JIT requires the following:

(1) The **labour force must be versatile** so that they can perform any job within reason to keep production flowing as required. Workers in a JIT cell are trained to operate all the machines within it, and perform routine preventive maintenance on them.

(2) Production processes must be **grouped by product line** rather than by function in order to eliminate inventory movements between workstations and to speed flow.

(3) A simple, **infallible information system**. Originally the Japanese used a system based on cards which were called *kanbans*. There would be a small container of components (WIP) between each workstation with a kanban resting on top. When the container was taken for use by the following workstation the card would be taken off and left behind. This would act as a trigger for the previous workstation to produce another container of that component. Nowadays computer systems are likely to be used instead of cards but the basic simplicity of the system should not change.

(4) A **'get it right first time'** approach and an aim of **'zero defects'**. Defects cause breakdowns in the value chain: they stop the flow of production, create expensive rework and lead to late deliveries to customers.

(5) **Strong supplier relationships**. Suppliers must take responsibility for the quality of their goods; the onus is on the supplier to inspect the parts or materials before delivery and guarantee their quality. The considerable savings in inspection costs go happily with the benefits of increased quality to achieve cost reduction – another facet of continuous improvement. This enhanced level of service is obtained by reducing the number of suppliers and increasing the business given to each of them. Longer-term commitments are entered into, assuring the supplier of continuity of demand, and enabling the supplier to plan to meet customers' production schedules. In essence the supplier becomes a key part of the value chain.

An important consequence of the 'pull' system, is that problems in any part of the system will immediately halt the production line, as earlier workstations will not receive the 'pull' signal and later stations will not have their own 'pull' signals answered. This has the powerful effect of concentrating all minds on finding a long-term solution to the problem. JIT exposes problems within a plant, and forces management to address problems and rectify them, rather than simply burying them by holding excess inventory.

The aims of JIT are to produce the required items, at the required quality and in the required quantities, at the precise time they are required.

4 TQM

TQM (Total Quality Management)

TQM is the general name given to programmes which seek to ensure that goods are produced and services supplied of the highest quality. Its origins lie primarily in Japanese organisations and it is argued that TQM has been a significant factor in Japanese global business success.

There are two basic principles of TQM:

(1) **'Get it right, first time**.' TQM considers that the costs of prevention are less than the costs of correction. One of the main aims of TQM is to achieve zero rejects and 100% quality. One aspect of the Japanese management philosophy is a zero-defect target.

(2) **Continuous improvement**. The second basic principle of TQM is dissatisfaction with the status quo. Realistically, a zero-defect goal may not be obtainable. It does however provide a target to ensure that a company should never be satisfied with its present level of rejects. The management and staff should believe that it is always possible to improve and to be able to get more right next time!

There are two approaches to Continuous Improvement : Kaizen Costing (in this chapter) and Target Costing (in the following chapter.)

The costs of quality

Quality costs are divided into compliance costs (or 'conformance costs') and costs of failure to comply ('non-conformance costs').

Conformance costs are further divided into prevention costs (incurred in preventing mistakes from happening) and appraisal costs (incurred in looking for mistakes before a product is manufactured).

[In the PEG November 2012, the Examiner regrets that some candidates were 'not able to select an example of a cost for the four quality cost classifications from the question'.]

Conformance costs

Prevention costs are the costs of ensuring that defects do not occur in the first place. For example:

(1) Routine preventive repairs and maintenance to equipment.

(2) Quality training for operatives to improve skills and efficiency. Training employees works, provided the employee also understand and accept the benefits of such training. Training can occur both inside and outside the workplace. Internal training may include the ideas of team working and quality discussion groups, which are known as quality circles.

(3) Building of quality into the design and manufacturing processes. When a product is designed, its specification should consider factors that will minimise future rectification costs. Production methods should be as simple as possible and use the skills and resources existing within the sphere of knowledge of the organisation and its employees.

(4) Determining whether quality factors have been correctly engineered into the design of products may only be apparent when costs are reported on a 'life cycle' basis. Effective performance management involves monitoring costs and results over the whole life cycle of a product. Just considering production costs over a one-month period (in the form of traditional standard costing and variance analysis) may be of marginal relevance.

Appraisal costs are connected with measuring conformity with requirements and include:

(1) Cost of incoming inspections (note that if suppliers adopt a total quality approach, the cost of incoming inspections can be eliminated)

(2) Cost of set-up inspections

(3) Cost of acquiring and operating the process control and measuring equipment.

Non-conformance costs are divided into 'internal failure' costs, that occur when the units produced fail to reach the set standard; and 'external failure' costs – These arise when the faulty product is not detected until after it reaches the customer.

Non-conformance costs

Internal failure costs include:

(1) Costs of scrap

(2) Reworking costs

(3) Manufacturing and process engineering required to correct the failed process.

As we saw under JIT, it is the aim of total quality management (TQM) programmes to completely eliminate these internal failure costs by working towards a goal of zero defects. It is contended that, in many companies, the costs of internal failure are so great that a total quality programme can be financed entirely from the savings that are made from it – hence the expression *'quality is free'*.

There are several measurable costs of **external failure** to deliver a quality product:

(1) Marketing costs associated with failed products and loss of customer goodwill

(2) Manufacturing or process engineering costs relating to failed products

(3) Compensation/replacement for units returned by customers

(4) Repair costs

(5) Travel costs to visit sites with faulty products

(6) Liability claims.

It is generally accepted that an increased investment in prevention and appraisal is likely to result in a significant reduction in failure costs. As a result of the trade-off, there may be an optimum operating level in which the combined costs are at a minimum. In short, an investment in "prevention" inevitably results in a saving on total quality costs.

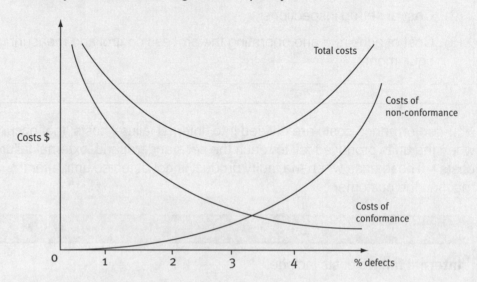

*[In the PEG September 2010, the Examiner explains that candidates were required to **compare and contrast** costs of conformance and costs of non-conformance and that a good answer would have joined the two parts of the question with phrases such as 'in contrast to' or 'as opposed to'. Most candidates appeared to have a good understanding of quality costs but simply failed to put forward answers in line with the question, especially relating to the verbs.*

In the November 2012 PEG, the Examiner again notes that many candidates 'were not able to describe the 'trade-off' between conformance and non-conformance costs, and were not able to discuss its importance for the company.']

Recognising the importance of quality

(1) Accept that the only thing that matters is the customer. The only way to stay in business is to relate everything to customer priorities.

(2) Recognise the all-pervasive nature of the customer/supplier relationship. This includes internal customers. In a transfer environment, passing sub-standard material down to another division just to claim output is not satisfactory. Ultimately, the company must bear the cost of the defective product/service.

(3) Move from relying on inspecting to a predefined level of quality, to actually preventing the cause of the defect in the first place.

(4) Each operative or team of operatives must be personally responsible for defect-free production or service in their domain. This should not just be confined to production staff, it should be extended throughout the organisation. For example, sales, personnel, accounting and the after-sales departments should also ensure that their 'customers' are happy with their service.

(5) In production there should be a move away from acceptable quality levels (AQL) to defect levels measured in parts per million.

(6) Enforce zero defect programmes. These are an obsessive drive to get things right first time. Again this should be enforced throughout all departments.

(7) Quality certification programmes such as BS5750/ISO9002 should be introduced. Although opinion is divided about these programmes, and they are often perceived to be a burden disproportionate to the benefits, the value of a third party audit of control and production procedures to ensure everything is properly controlled has both merit and, in the short term, an influence with customers.

(8) The total cost of quality should be emphasised. Quality does generate savings. For example, better trained operators do not waste material nor do they abuse machines and equipment. Other savings can be achieved by reviewing suppliers, preventive machine maintenance and reduction of scrap and rework.

Commitment to quality

For TQM to bring about improved business efficiency and effectiveness it must be applied throughout the whole organisation. It begins at the top with the managing director, the most senior directors and managers who must demonstrate that they are totally committed to achieving the highest quality standards. The role of middle management is also crucial. They have to understand the importance of TQM and communicate this and their own commitment to quality to the people for whom they are responsible. It is essential that TQM is adopted by all parts of the organisation. Middle management must ensure that the efforts and achievements of their subordinates receive appropriate recognition, attention and reward. This helps secure everyone's full involvement – which is crucial to the successful introduction of TQM.

Quality chains

Throughout and beyond all organisations, whether they are manufacturing concerns, retail stores, universities or hotels, there is a series of quality chains. The ability to meet the customers' requirements is vital, not only between two separate organisations, but within the same organisation. These quality chains may be broken at any point by one person or by one piece of equipment not meeting the requirements of the customer, internal or external.

To achieve quality throughout an organisation, each person in the quality chain must be trained to ask themselves the following questions:

Customers

- Who are my internal customers?
- What are their true requirements?
- How do I find out what the requirements are?
- How can I meet those requirements?

Suppliers

- Who are my internal suppliers?
- What are my true requirements?
- How do I communicate my requirements?
- Do my suppliers have the capability to meet my requirements?

Each person in the organisation must also realise that they must respect their suppliers' needs and expectations if those suppliers are able to fully satisfy their requirements.

Successful implementation of TQM

An organisation should undertake to achieve each of the following to ensure TQM is successful:

- Total commitment throughout the organisation.
- Get close to their customers to fully understand their needs and expectations.
- Plan to do all jobs right first time.
- Agree expected performance standards with each employee and customer.
- Implement a company-wide improvement process.
- Continually measure performance levels achieved.
- Measure the cost of quality mismanagement and the level of firefighting.
- Demand continuous improvement in everything you and your employees do.
- Recognise achievements.
- Make quality a way of life.

Quality circles

A quality circle is a team of four to twelve people usually coming from the same area who voluntarily meet on a regular basis to identify, investigate, analyse and solve work-related problems. The team presents its solutions to management and is then involved in implementing and monitoring the effectiveness of the solutions. The voluntary approach and the process by which the team selects and solves its own problems are key features which give the quality circle a special character: a character which is very different to other problem-solving teams. The problems that circles tackle may not be restricted to quality of product or service topics, but may include anything associated with work or its environment. Items such as pay and conditions and other negotiated items are, however, normally excluded.

Management accounting reports

Management accounting systems can help organisations achieve their quality goals by providing a variety of reports and measures that motivate and evaluate managerial efforts to improve quality – including financial and non-financial measures.

Traditionally, the management accounting systems focused on output, not quality.

Examples:

- the strive to reduce the material price variance often led to the use of inferior quality material

- the costs of normal losses were absorbed by good output.

Non-financial measures include:

- Number of defects at inspection expressed as a percentage of the number of units completed.

- Number of reworked units expressed as a percentage of total sales value.

- Number of defective units delivered to customers as a percentage of total units delivered.

- Number of customer complaints.

- Number of defective units supplied by suppliers.

- Time taken to respond to customer requests.

5 Throughput accounting and the Theory of Constraints

The term throughput is defined by the following equation:

Throughput = Sales revenues less Direct material cost

The aim of throughput accounting is to maximise this measure of throughput. Goldratt and Cox advocate that managers should aim to increase throughput while simultaneously reducing inventory and operational expense.

This goal is achieved by determining what factors prevent the throughput being higher. This constraint is called a bottleneck. A bottleneck may be a machine whose capacity limits the output of the whole production process. The aim is to identify the bottlenecks and remove them or, if this is not possible, ensure that they are fully utilised at all times. Non-bottleneck resources should be scheduled and operated based on the constraints within the system, and should not be used to produce more than the bottlenecks can absorb.

Goldratt and Cox describe the process of identifying and taking steps to remove the constraints that restrict output as the **theory of constraints** (TOC). The process involves five steps:

(1) Identify the system's bottlenecks.

(2) Decide how to exploit the bottlenecks.

(3) Subordinate everything else to the decision in Step 2.

(4) Elevate the system's bottlenecks.

(5) If, in the previous steps, a bottleneck has been broken, go back to Step 1.

The bottleneck is the focus of management's attention. Decisions regarding the optimum mix of products must be undertaken. Step 3 requires that the optimum production of the bottleneck activity determines the production schedule of the non-bottleneck activities. There is no point in a non-bottleneck activity supplying more than the bottleneck activity can consume. This would result in increased work-in-progress (WIP) inventories with no increased sales volume. The TOC is a process of continuous improvement to clear the throughput chain of all the constraints. Thus, step 4 involves taking action to remove, or elevate, the constraint. This may involve replacing the bottleneck machine with a faster one, providing additional training for a slow worker or changing the design of the product to reduce the processing time required on the bottleneck activity. Once a bottleneck has been elevated it will generally be replaced by a new bottleneck elsewhere in the system. It then becomes necessary to return to Step 1.

Constraints on throughput

The idea of constraints is central to the throughput approach. Examples of constraints may include:

- inadequately trained sales force
- poor reputation for meeting delivery dates
- poor physical distribution system
- unreliability of material supplies, delivery and/or quality
- inadequate production resources
- inappropriate management accounting system.

Throughput accounting measures

Throughput = Sales revenues less Direct material cost

The only cost that is deemed to relate to volume of output is the direct material cost. All other costs (including labour costs) are deemed to be fixed. These fixed costs may be called total factory costs (TFC).

The role of the accountant in a throughput environment is to devise measures which will help production staff to achieve a greater volume of throughput. Attention should be drawn to the financial effects of bottlenecks. For example if a bottleneck resource fails to operate for one hour a whole hour's throughput is lost.

Various performance measures have been devised to help measure throughput:

$$\text{Return per factory hour} = \frac{\text{Throughput per unit}}{\text{Product time on the bottleneck resource}}$$

$$\text{Cost per factory hour} = \frac{\text{Total factory costs}}{\text{Total time on the bottleneck resource}}$$

$$\text{Throughput accounting ratio} = \frac{\text{Return per factory hour}}{\text{Cost per factory hour}}$$

The accountant may advise management on how the TA ratio may be maximised.

6 Kaizen costing

Continuous improvement, or 'Kaizen', is an integral part of the just-in-time management philosophy. 'Kaizen' is a Japanese term meaning to improve processes via small, incremental amounts rather than through large innovations. Kaizen costing is a planning method used during the manufacturing cycle that emphasises reducing variable costs of a period below the cost level in the base period. The target reduction rate is the ratio of the target reduction amount to the cost base.

- The organisation should always seek perfection. Perfection is never achieved, so there must always be some scope for improving on current methods and procedures. Improvements should be sought all the time.

- Improvements will be small and numerous rather than occasional and far-reaching.

- Cost reduction targets are set and applied on a more frequent basis than standard costs. Typically these targets are set on a monthly basis whereas standards within a traditional standard costing system are set annually or perhaps semi-annually. The table below *(adapted from Monden and Lee)* points out the differences between the two techniques:

Standard costing concepts	Kaizen costing concepts
Cost **Control** system concepts.	Cost **Reduction** system concepts.
Assume current manufacturing conditions.	Assume Continuous improvement in manufacturing.
Meet cost performance standards.	Achieve cost reduction targets.
Standard cost techniques	**Kaizen costing techniques**
Standards are set annually or semiannually.	Cost reduction targets are set and applied monthly.
Cost variance analysis involving standard costs and actual costs	Continuous Improvement (Kaizen) is implemented during the year to attain target profits or to reduce the gap between target profit and estimated profit.

Investigate and respond when standards are not met.	Cost variance analysis involving target Kaizen costs and actual costs reduction amounts.
	Investigate and respond when target Kaizen amounts are not attained.

[In the PEG September 2010, the Examiner notes that some candidates 'failed to make it clear what Kaizen principles are'].

7 Business Process Re-engineering

The continuous improvement philosophy contrasts sharply with the concept underlying business process re-engineering (BPR). BPR is concerned with making far-reaching one-off changes to improve operations or processes.

Michael Hammer & James Champy define BPR as 'the fundamental rethinking and radical redesign of business processes to achieve dramatic improvements in critical contemporary measures of perfomance such as cost, quality, service and speed.' In other words, BPR focuses on amending existing processes, streamlining processes that are already in place.

Five stages are normally recognised in any BPR project:

- Develop the business vision and process objectives. State which improvements are expected from processes based on some overall business vision of Total Quality Management.

- Identify the processes to be redesigned. Most firms tend to focus on the more important processes, although significant improvements may still be obtained by redesigning inefficient processes in any part of the organisation.

- Understand and measure the existing processes so that a baseline against which to measure improvement is set.

- Identify 'IT levers' that can be used to apply change.

- Design and build a prototype to show which changes are possible, and involve customers before implementing any revised system.

For example, consider a car manufacturing process. Cars are assembled by passing them along a conveyor belt, and adding parts to each one in a predetermined order, to arrive at the finished product. This process can be improved in terms of efficiency by making robots do some of the repetitive and less skilled operations. In this way, the process is being re-designed, to include and enhanced IT element to make it more efficient, and less prone to errors. In other words, BPR is being used to improve the existing process.

Business process re-engineering

A business process consists of a collection of activities that are linked together in a co-ordinated manner to achieve a specific objective. Business process re-engineering involves examining business processes and radically redesigning these processes to achieve cost reduction, improved quality and customer satisfaction. BPR is all about major changes to how business processes operate.

Material handling is an example of a business process and may consist of the following separate activities; material requisitioning, purchase requisitioning, processing purchase orders, inspecting materials, storing materials and paying suppliers. This process could be re-engineered by sending the material requisitions directly to an approved supplier and entering into an agreement which entails delivering high quality material in accordance with the production requirements. This change in business process could result in cost reduction by the elimination of; the administration involved in placing orders, the need for material inspection and storage. By re-engineering the material handling business process the company will reduce costs without compromising the quality of the products delivered to customers.

8 Supply chain management

Supply chain management is often explained with reference to Porter's value chain and value systems. A supply chain is the network of customers and suppliers that a business deals with.

Recent decades have seen an increasing rate of globalisation of the economy and thereby also of supply chains. The days when products were produced and consumed in the same geographical area are long past. In fact it is often the case that the different components of a product come from all over the globe. Such a trend causes longer and more complex supply chains and thus changes the requirements within supply chain management. This, in turn, affects the effectiveness of the IT systems employed within the supply chain. A longer supply chain often results in a lengthening of order-to-delivery lead times.

Supply chain management considers logistics but also relationships between members of the supply chain, identification of end-customer benefit and the organisational consequences of greater inter-firm integration to form 'network organisations'.

Supply chain management may be broken down into several areas:

Purchasing

It is important for a company to work closely with its suppliers. A true partnership will enable a better, faster and more reliable service. Purchasing costs can be reduced by more than 10% when information systems are linked. Day-to-day purchasing, progress chasing and stock control can all be eliminated.

Inventories

Efficient inventory control relies upon accurate customer records, well-managed customer information and effective inventory-control information systems. A close collaboration with suppliers and customers will enable inventory levels to be kept to a minimum. Working more closely with the supply chain partners will require mutual trust and investment in technology, but it will bring benefits to all concerned.

Customer ordering

From the customer's perspective the ordering process should be fast, flexible (meet individual customer needs) and efficient. A satisfied customer is more likely to return for repeat orders. Factors such as price, quality, availability from inventory etc. are important, but a fully automated fulfilment procedure also plays a key part in overall customer satisfaction. On-line ordering is becoming a prerequisite for many customers today.

Orders should be processed smoothly within the firm. Purchasing, inventory control, marketing and accounts should all be linked to the customer-ordering process.

Delivery and logistics

Delivering to the customer is often the culmination of all the business processes. Customers will expect fast, reliable, accurate and predictable delivery schedules. Tracking systems such as radio frequency identification (RFID) enable companies to trace the physical progress of the customer order. With RFID objects are tagged. During manufacturing and delivery the whereabouts of the order can then be traced electronically and remotely (items can be detected up to 100 feet away from the sensor). In the US many large companies such as Wallmart are already requiring their suppliers to use RFID.

Some companies use third party distributors. As technology becomes more complex and sophisticated outsourcing becomes more attractive. Some companies leave distribution to professional logistics companies.

Outsourcing

A significant trend in recent years has been for organisations and government bodies to concentrate on their core competencies. Outsourcing involves the buying in of components, sub-assemblies, finished products and services from outside suppliers rather than supplying them internally. It may be regarded as a management strategy by which an organisation delegates major non-core functions to specialised, efficient service providers.

Traditionally the insourcing/outsourcing decision was focused on a make-or-buy decision for manufacturing functions. However companies are now beginning to apply the decision analysis to nearly all functions and activities.

For example, the following functions are now coming under the outsourcing spotlight: sales; design and development, IT and distribution.

Advantages and disadvantages of insourcing

Advantages	Disadvantages
Higher degree of control over inputs	Requires high volumes
Increases visibility over the process	High investment
Economies of scale/scope to use integration	Dedicated equipment has limited flexibility
	Not a core competence

Advantages and disadvantages of outsourcing

Advantages	Disadvantages
Greater flexibility	Possibility of choosing wrong supplier
Lower investment risk	Loss of visibility and control over process
Improved cash flow	Possibility of increased lead times
Concentrates on core competence	
Enables more advanced technologies to be used without making investment	

Outsourcing to Eastern Europe and the Far East

During recent years foreign investment has begun to pour into Eastern European countries as West European and US companies look for lower-cost manufacturing bases close to the European Union. Today, as these and other countries have joined the EU, the East and Central Europeans themselves are looking in an easterly direction for low-cost manufacturing. As rising wages force them to find ways to become more competitive, some are setting up plants or outsourcing their production to subcontractors in places such as Bosnia, Romania, Russia and the Ukraine. The investment farther east is increasing, and economists and trade experts expect it to increase substantially in the next few years as both living standards and manufacturing costs continue to rise. Taxation is also a major consideration (Russia has attractive tax rates, as low as 13%) but cheaper labour is the major factor.

The UK and other European-based organisations are aware that assembly costs in Eastern European countries are far lower than at home. This fact is leading to the transfer of production to such territories.

Some companies are already looking to China and other parts of Asia, where labour costs are even lower. An organisation which makes sports and leisure gear, now sources 70 to 80% of its production in China, India, Taiwan, Turkey and Vietnam and only uses national manufacturers for sophisticated products and small orders that would be uneconomical to produce in Asia. It is crucial that organisations maintain their ability to compete and thus as production costs in the new EU member states start to approach those in Western Europe, more and more firms could be eastward bound.

Contract manufacturing has always been about cutting costs, and today that means rapid expansion of, for example, the electronic manufacturing services (EMS) industry into China, Eastern Europe and other low-wage areas. At the same time, hand-in-hand with that expansion is contraction, as organisations cut back operations in high-wage areas such as the United States. With original equipment manufacturers (OEMs) increasingly outsourcing printed circuit boards and finished systems, a significant amount of that manufacturing is especially likely to find its way to China. Indeed, it is highly probable that a major trend over the next few years will be the migration to low-cost manufacturing centres, particularly China.

Competitive pressure forces OEMs and contract manufacturers to do all they can to take costs out of their businesses, and consequently many organisations are heading in the direction of Eastern Europe and China in an attempt to do so. As far as China is concerned, not only are costs low but also, in addition to making products there to be sold around the world, firms can entertain the possibility of sales into the Chinese market.

9 Gain-sharing arrangements

In simple terms, gain-sharing is a program that returns cost savings to the employees.

While risk-sharing/gain-sharing arrangements can take different forms, companies typically guarantee their customers that they will achieve a certain amount of cost savings or top-line improvement. If targets are not met, the company commits to making up the difference in cash. If however targets are exceeded, the supplier may also receive a pre-specified percentage of the gains.

These agreements are attractive to companies because they can provide insulation from the cut-throat price competition that characterises today's technology marketplace. Suppliers that guarantee cost savings and top-line improvement can command a price premium in the marketplace. Such risk-sharing agreements are attractive to customers because they reduce the business risk and cost associated with implementing new technologies, systems, and services.

Gain-sharing is an approach to the review and adjustment of an existing contract, or series of contracts, where the adjustment provides benefits to both parties. It is a mutual activity requiring the agreement of both parties to the contract adjustment. Consideration of a gain-sharing proposal will be limited to just that area affected by the proposal.

The sharing of benefits provides an incentive to both parties to a contract to explore gain-sharing possibilities. In the UK, the **Ministry of Defence** is committed to, and industry supports, gain-sharing as one of a number of approaches to improve the efficient use of the defence procurement budget.

Gain-sharing arrangements are popular where there exists the potential to achieve mutual benefit among the parties concerned. The gain, benefit or advantage to be shared might not be financial in nature, though financial benefits are likely to feature strongly. The period of application of the sharing arrangement will need to be agreed. The sharing arrangement may apply only to the current contract; or the effects of the agreement, and the sharing arrangements, may be carried forward into future contracts.

Mutual trust and co-operation between contracting parties is essential since assessment of the financial benefit of a gain-sharing proposal will require both parties to provide each other with access to relevant cost data to provide the basis for the valuation of the benefit and to facilitate the calculation and sharing of that benefit.

Gain-sharing represents a reward for innovative thinking by the contractor; it is important that the nature of any change proposal is agreed at the outset in the light of this principle. Once a gain-sharing proposal is agreed, the concept of sharing the benefits will be fundamental to further discussion and agreement; neither party will seek to secure all the benefits.

A gain-sharing arrangement must possess the following components:

(1) Mutual interdependence and trust between the parties (as opposed to a blame culture).

(2) Identification of common goals for success.

(3) Agreed decision-making and problem-solving procedures.

(4) Commitment to continuous improvement.

(5) Team working down the entire product and supply chain.

(6) Gain-share and pain-share arrangements established in advance.

(7) Open book accounting.

(8) Targets that provide continuous measurable improvements on performance.

Examples:

Public sector	Private sector
The Government Travel Savings Program is a gain-sharing arrangement that rewards federal government employees who save money while on official travel. In general, the cash awards equal 50% of the savings on lodging expenses and/or contract carrier airfare. For example, government employees who stay with relatives or friends and avoid lodging expenses while on official travel receive one-half of the allowed maximum lodging rate. (US)	Gain sharing involves the process by which a hospital and its medical staff identify clinical practices that increase hospital operating costs without improving quality of care, develop initiatives to reduce or eliminate such practices while maintaining quality of care, and share the resulting cost savings directly attributable to the clinical initiatives.

| Gain-sharing in a court might depend on a court unit or program hitting performance targets such as a specific decrease in cost per case, an improvement in trial date certainty or juror utilisation, which positively impacts the bottom line of budgets and balance sheets of the court. A decrease in cost per case might be seen directly in a court's balance sheet, while an improvement in trial date certainty may be seen most significantly in decreased expenditures for witness notification by the prosecution. | A company produces rigid and steering differential axles for tractors. From its records, the company determined that every $1,000,000 of good product output required 10,000 worker hours. Under gain-sharing, the next $1,000,000 of axle output and shipment was produced with only 9,000 hours. If the average wage rate is $10 an hour, the 1,000 hours saved are worth $10,000. That is a gain to be shared equally between the workforce and company. |

10 Practice Questions

Objective Test Question 1: Just-in-Time

The adoption of **JIT** normally requires which one of the following factors to increase?

A   Inventory levels

B   Work-in-progress levels

C   Batch sizes

D   Quality standards

Objective Test Question 2: Quality Costs

Match the cost to the correct cost category:

Costs

(a)   Reliability studies

(b)   Returned material processing and repair

(c)   Quality audits

(d)   Quality control investigations of failures

Cost categories

- Prevention costs
- Appraisal costs
- Internal failure costs
- External failure costs

Objective Test Question 3: TQM

Use the words and phrases in the table provided below to complete the following paragraphs:

quality	output	production problems
Total Quality Management (TQM)	customer goodwill	quality
delays	buffer inventory	

In a company operating on JIT principles, the absence of inventories deprives production of a safety net or '_____'. This exposes the business to production problems or _____ and, ultimately, to lost sales and damaged_____.

In this context, the adoption of a _____ philosophy is key. In this, _____ is a feature rooted in the production process and every individual is responsible for the quality of his/her _____.

This will encourage good quality at all times and therefore minimise_____ that would otherwise occur due to poor _____.

Data Set Question: Throughput accounting

The following data relates to three products manufactured by BJS Ltd:

	Product X	Product Y	Product Z
Selling price per unit	$12	$16	$14
Direct material cost per unit	$3	$10	$7
Maximum demand (units)	15,000	40,000	20,000
Time required on the bottleneck (hours per unit)	3	1.5	7

The firm has 80,000 bottleneck hours available each period, and total factory costs amount to $100,000 in the period.

Task: Calculate the following:

The TPAR (throughput accounting ratio) for Product X

The TPAR (throughput accounting ratio) for Product Y

The TPAR (throughput accounting ratio) for Product Z

The maximum profit achievable by BJS, in $ (this involves a calculation of the optimum product mix).

Integration Style Question – X Ltd

PRE-SEEN MATERIAL

X Ltd manufactures and distributes three types of car (the C1, C2 and C3). Each type of car has its own production line. The company is worried by extremely difficult market conditions, and forecasts losses for the forthcoming year.

Current operations

The budgeted details for next year are as follows:

	C1	C2	C3
	$	$	$
Direct materials	2,520	2,924	3,960
Direct labour	1,120	1,292	1,980
Total direct cost per car	3,640	4,216	5,940
Budgeted production (cars)	75,000	75,000	75,000
Number of production runs	1,000	1,000	1,500
Number of orders executed	4,000	5,000	5,600
Machine hours	1,080,000	1,800,000	1,680,000

Annual overheads

	Fixed	Variable
	$000	$
Set-ups	42,660	13,000 per production run
Materials handling	52,890	4,000 per order executed
Inspection	59,880	18,000 per production run
Machining	144,540	40 per machine hour
Distribution and warehousing	42,900	3,000 per order executed

Proposed JIT system : impact on costs (Source: JIT External Consultants Ltd)

The introduction of the JIT system would have the following impact on costs (fixed and variable):

Direct labour	Increase by 20%
Set-ups	Decrease by 30%
Materials handling	Decrease by 30%
Inspection	Decrease by 30%
Machining	Decrease by 15%
Distribution and warehousing	Eliminated

Task: Email

You receive the following email from the Chief Financial Officer (CFO):

From: Charles Fern Oxley (CFO)
Sent: 04 June, 10.11 a.m.
To: Senior Management Accountant
Subject: JIT

I have attached the executive summary of a report prepared by some external consultants on how we might benefit from switching to JIT.

Please draft me a report that I can submit to the board on the conditions that are necessary for the successful implementation of a JIT manufacturing system.

I would also like your report to identify the potential savings that we might expect if we switch to JIT.

Email attachment reads as follows (extract from report by JIT External Consultants Ltd):

Introducing JIT in your company:

We have lots of experience in introducing Just-In-Time (JIT) measures in businesses similar to X Ltd.

It is our view that many of X Ltd competitors have already introduced this type of JIT measures. We are certain that in order to remain competitive and achieve concrete cost savings, X Ltd should implement JIT measures as a matter of urgency.

Test your understanding answers

Objective Test Question 1: Just-in-Time

Answer D. An increase in quality standards is one of the key factors that allows the other items listed to be reduced.

Objective Test Question 2: Quality Costs

(a) Prevention costs

(b) External failure costs

(c) Appraisal costs

(d) Internal failure costs

Objective Test Question 3: TQM

In a company operating on JIT principles, the absence of inventories deprives production of a safety net or '**buffer inventory**'. This exposes the business to production problems or **delays** and, ultimately, to lost sales and damaged **customer goodwill**.

In this context, the adoption of a **TQM (Total Quality Management)** philosophy is key. In this, **quality** is a feature rooted in the production process and every individual is responsible for the quality of his/her **output**.

This will encourage good quality at all times and therefore minimise **production problems** that would otherwise occur due to poor **quality**.

Data Set Question: Throughput accounting

The TPAR (throughput accounting ratio) for Product X	**2.4**

The TPAR (throughput accounting ratio) for Product Y	**3.2**

The TPAR (throughput accounting ratio) for Product Z	**0.80**

The maximum profit achievable by BJS, in $ (this involves a calculation of the optimum product mix).	**200,000**

Cost per factory hour = $100,000/80,000 = $1.25

	Product X	Product Y	Product Z
Selling price per unit	$12	$16	$14
Direct material cost per unit	($3)	($10)	($7)
Throughput p.u.	$9	$6	$7
Time required on the bottleneck	3	1.5	7
Return per factory hour	**$3**	**$4**	**$1**
T. A. ratio	$3/$1.25	$4/$1.25	$1/$1.25
	= 2.4 : 1	**= 3.2 : 1**	**= 0.80**
Ranking	**2nd**	**1st**	**3rd**

Product	Number of units	Hours per unit	Total hours	Throughput per hour	Total throughput
Y	40,000	1.5	60,000	$4	$240,000
X	6,666	3.0	20,000	$3	$59,994
			80,000		$299,994
Less total factory costs					($100,000)
Total profit					**$199,994**

Integration Style Question – X Ltd

To:	Charles Fern Oxley, X Ltd
From:	Management Accountant
Date:	04 June
Subject:	Successful implementation of JIT

Introduction

The following report includes some calculations on JIT-related savings we can expect in X Ltd. It also explains some of the conditions that are necessary for the successful implementation of a JIT manufacturing system within X Ltd.

Savings:

Original budget

	$000	$000		JIT $000
Set-ups	42,660			
$13,000 × 3,500	45,500	88,160	–30%	61,712
Materials handling	52,890			
$4,000 × 14,600	58,400	111,290	–30%	77,903
Inspection	59,880			
$18,000 × 3,500	63,000	122,880	–30%	86,016
Machining	144,540			
$40 × 4,560,000	182,400	326,940	–15%	277,899
Distribution & warehousing	42,900			
$3,000 × 14,600	43,800	86,700		–
		735,970		503,530

	$000	
Direct material		
($2,520 × 75,000) + ($2,924 × 75,000) ($3,960 × 75,000) + [189,000 + 219,300 + 297,000]	705,300	705,300
Direct labour		
($1,120 × 75,000) + ($1,292 × 75,000) ($1,980 × 75,000) + [84,000 + 96,900 + 148,500]	329,400	395,280
Total costs	1,770,670	1,604,110

$166,560

Conditions that are necessary for the successful implementation of a JIT manufacturing system within X Ltd include:

Supplier relationships

JIT systems require a huge reduction in inventory levels. In order to facilitate this, inventory order sizes must be small. Hence suppliers must be capable of AND willing to deliver small quantities on a regular basis. X Ltd will need to have a good relationship with its accredited suppliers.

JIT systems aim to eliminate raw material inventories. In order to do this suppliers must be capable of achieving all aspects of quality – delivering the correct quantity to the correct location at the correct time. Ideally suppliers should also deliver defect-free items.

Quality issues

For JIT to be effective achieving the highest possible levels of quality is essential. Production scheduling becomes demand-based and in order to meet customers' requirements quality problems need to be eliminated. It is often necessary to implement a quality programme such as Total Quality Management. The aim is to prevent the problems in the first place.

Quality should be considered from several angles:

From suppliers – as mentioned above.

In machinery – equipment should be well-maintained to avoid breakdown and the manufacture of sub-standard output.

In staff – all staff should be appropriately trained and skilled to carry out the task required of them.

Education and training

JIT will only be successful if our employees are willing to make it so. All levels of staff throughout the organisation should be appropriately trained and educated as to the objectives of the new system and the benefits that it will bring to X Ltd.

Work scheduling

Cellular manufacturing or group technology brings great benefits for JIT companies. This is where whole products are made within each manufacturing cell. X Ltd appears to have this system already as each car has its own production line.

Information systems

The new management systems that will be put in place will require new information systems. There will be major changes in the communication line with suppliers and the work scheduling system may need redeveloping in order to cope with the new pull-system.

Financing

Appropriate funds must be available to finance the development and implementation of JIT. Without sufficient funding JIT will fail.

Conclusion

In order to move forward with the JIT proposal we should investigate which of the conditions can be met.

Should you require any further advice, then please do not hesitate to contact me.

AN Accountant

Management Accountant

X Ltd
E: mact@xltd.co.uk
T:0161 233 3434

Costing Techniques

Chapter learning objectives

Syllabus Link

Lead A1: Evaluate techniques for analysing and managing costs for competitive advantage

Component A1c): Discuss techniques for enhancing long-term profits

- Target costing and the determination of target costs from target prices
- Value analysis and quality function deployment
- The value chain and the management of contribution/profit generated throughout the chain
- Life cycle costing and its implications for marketing strategies.

1 Chapter summary

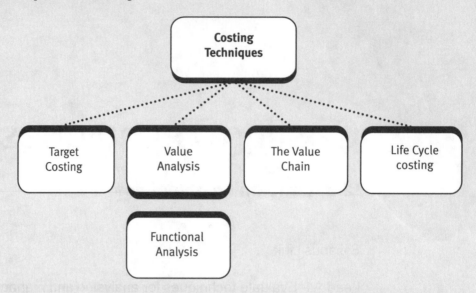

2 Knowledge brought forward

You will already have covered some of these concepts in Paper P1. We will build on this knowledge in P2 with more aspects of some key costing techniques, but make sure you are comfortable with the assumed knowledge, that should have been brought forward as a base, in the following sections.

3 Background

Because traditional overhead absorption was designed for production companies, it dealt with production costs only and, as a consequence, it is less suitable for service or retail organisations. Also, because inventory had to be valued at full production cost only in the published accounts, other costs such as R&D, administration, and marketing have not been related to products.

When traditional absorption costing evolved last century, overheads were only a small part, say, 10 per cent of the cost of production for the average company. Direct labour costs were much higher, say, 50 per cent of the cost of the product. This meant that the absorption method spread 10 per cent of costs on the basis of 50 per cent of costs. Because overheads were such a small part of total costs any inaccuracies in the absorption process were small and insignificant and did not distort product costs.

A few organisations may have this cost structure today, and in such cases traditional absorption costing is perfectly adequate. Most companies, however, now have those percentages reversed and it creates a considerable degree of inaccuracy if 50 per cent of the costs are spread on the behaviour of 10 per cent of the costs. Yet it is vital that an organisation's costing system spreads overheads accurately.

Traditional absorption costing was not designed to make decisions of a short-term nature, and can never be used for this purpose. Marginal costing (variable costing) should be used when short-term decisions on matters such as product/service profitability are required. But if long-term decisions need to be made, an absorption costing system is needed. The system must be accurate and for all the reasons outlined above, total absorption costing is unlikely to produce the required accuracy; alternative costing techniques are needed.

4 Target costing

The target costing approach, a form of life-cycle costing, has recently received some attention. Target costing is driven by external market factors. Marketing managers first estimate the performance characteristics and market price requirements in order to achieve a desired market share for a proposed product. A standard profit margin is then subtracted from the projected selling price to arrive at the target cost for the product. The product development team must then, through its product and process design decisions, attempt to reach the product's target cost.

One of the definitions of target costing reads as follows:

> Target costing is a pro-active cost control system. The target cost is calculated by deducting the target profit from a pre-determined selling price based on customers' views. Functional Analysis, value analysis and value engineering are used to change production methods and/or reduce expected costs so the target is met.

The target profit requirement should be driven by strategic profit planning rather than a standard mark-up. In Japan this is done after consideration of the medium-term profit plans which reflect management and business strategies over that period. Once it is set, the target profit is not just an expectation; it is a commitment agreed by all the people who have any part in achieving it. Therefore the procedures used to derive the target profit must be scientific, rational and agreed by all staff responsible for achieving it, otherwise no-one will accept responsibility for achieving it.

This procedure is just the opposite of that followed by many companies today in which the product is designed with little regard either to the manufacturing process or to its long-run manufacturing cost. With this traditional procedure of first designing the product and then giving the design to process engineers and costs analysts, the product cost is developed by applying standard cost factors to the materials and processes specified for the design. Frequently, this cost may be well above that which can be sustained by market prices and the product is either aborted or, if marketed, fails to achieve desired profitability levels.

Using target cost in the concept and design stages

With the target-cost approach, the new product team, consisting of product designers, purchasing specialists, and manufacturing and process people, works together to jointly determine product and process characteristics that permit the target cost to be achieved. The target cost approach is especially powerful to apply at the design stage, since decisions made at this stage have leverage to affect long-run costs.

The great majority of manufacturing costs become locked in early in the life cycle of the product. Once the product is released into production, it becomes much harder to achieve significant cost reductions. Most of the costs become committed or locked in much earlier than the time at which the major cash expenditures are made.

The target-costing approach is a vital total cost control tool because research has shown that up to 90 per cent of costs are 'built in' at the product's design stage. Below are some examples of costs that become locked in place at the design stage:

- The design specification of the product including extra features

- The number of components incorporated in the product

- Design of components

  These should be designed for reliability in use and ease of manufacture. Wherever possible standard parts should be used because they are proven to be reliable and will help reduce inventory and handling costs. Where new components are required it is important that their manufacturing process is considered before the component is finally designed so that they can be manufactured as cheaply as possible consistent with quality and functionality.

- Type of packaging required

  This includes product packaging and packing per case and per pallet. The aim is to protect the product and to minimise handling costs by not breaking pallets or cases during distribution.

- The number of spare parts that need to be carried

This ties in with the number of components used. Parts must sometimes be held for up to 15 years or so. They may be made while the product is still in production and stored for years, which is costly. The alternative is to disrupt current production to make a small batch of a past component, which is very costly.

Target costing is an iterative process that cannot be de-coupled from design. The pre-production stages can be categorised in a variety of different ways; in the detailed discussion below five different stages are used and the different activities are now listed.

(1) Planning

This includes fixing the product concept and the primary specifications for performance and design. A very brief product concept might be a small, town car for two people with a large amount of easily-accessible luggage space and low fuel consumption – aimed at those in their mid-twenties and so style is important. (In reality the concept would be much fuller.) Value engineering and analysis (VE) could be used to identify new and innovative, yet cost-effective, product features that would be valued by customers and meet their requirements.

Once the concept has been developed a planned sales volume and selling price, which depend on each other, will be set, as well as the required profit discussed earlier. From this the necessary target cost (or allowable cost as it is often known) can be ascertained.

Target cost = Planned selling price – Required profit

(2) Concept design

The basic product is designed. The target cost is now divided into smaller parts reflecting the manufacturing process. See diagram below. First an allowance for development costs and manufacturing equipment costs are deducted from the total. The remainder is then split up into unit costs that will cover manufacturing and distribution, etc. The manufacturing target cost per unit is assigned to the functional areas of the new product. For example, a functional area for a ballpoint pen might be the flow of ink to the tip and a functional area for a car might be the steering mechanism.

The breakdown of target cost

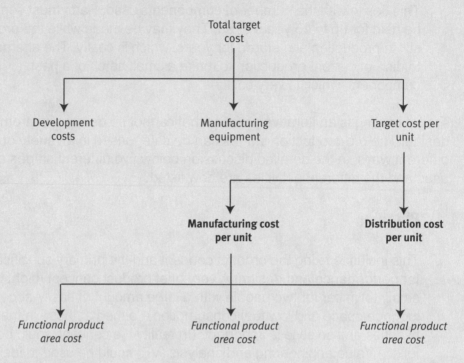

(3) Basic design

The components are designed in detail so that they do not exceed the functional target costs. Value engineering is used to get the costs down to the target. If one function cannot meet its target, the targets for the others must be reduced or the product redesigned.

(4) Detailed design

The detailed specifications and cost estimates are set down from the basic design stage.

(5) Manufacturing preparation

The manufacturing process, including new machines, is designed in keeping with the target cost. Standards for the materials and labour hours that should be used are set. These values are presented to the staff in the factory immediately after they are set so that approval can be given.

The purchasing department negotiates prices for bought-in components.

Target costing for existing products

Cost control is not forgotten once the product goes into production. Manufacturing performance is measured to see if the target is being achieved. The reasons for doing this are:

(1) to see who is responsible for any cost excess and to offer them help; and

(2) to judge whether the cost-planning activities were effective.

If after three months the target cost is missed by a large margin an improvement team is organised which will conduct a thorough value analysis (VA) and will stay in existence for about six months.

Although the Japanese use standard costing to some extent they do not consider it to be suitable for ongoing cost control. They see standard costing as part of budget accounting where the same value is maintained throughout the budget period, whereas they use target costing to control production cost and as a consequence revise it monthly. Monden (1989) expressed the limitations of standard costing this way:

'Since standard costing systems have constraints from a financial perspective, they are inappropriate measures for management. A typical constraint is the infrequency in which quantity standards, such as processing time per production unit or material requirements, are revised.

Normally these standards are maintained at the same level throughout the year.'

Target costing, therefore, continues to be used to control costs throughout the product's life. After the initial start-up stage target costs will be set through budgets, which in Japan tend to be set every six months rather than yearly. This type of target costing is a different technique in the eyes of the Japanese and they call this Genka Kaizen. It is widely used in Japan; about 80 per cent of assembly environments use it. If a manager cannot meet the target cost for a function, a committee will be set up to help achieve it. All costs including both variable and fixed overheads are expected to reduce on a regular basis, usually monthly.

Target costing is widely used among industries in different countries. Mercedes, Toyota, Nissan, and Daihatsu in the car industry, Matsushita, Panasonic and Sharp in the electronics industry, and Apple, Compaq and Toshiba in the personal computer market all use target pricing and target costing.

In summary:

Standard costing	Target costing
A **Push** system: a standard cost per unit (onto which a mark-up is added) is the basis for calculating the selling price.	A **Pull** system that requires understanding of market demand and competition, so that the price required to achieve a target market share or sales level can be set.
An **Internal** tool in mass production environments that do not emphasise continual improvement.	Driven by **External** market prices and may not be attainable in the short term.
A **Cost control** technique.	A **Cost reduction** activity.
A **Reactive** technique – the selling price of a new product will be determined by estimating its standard cost and adding the required profit margin to the cost.	A **Proactive** technique that starts before the design of the product is formalised. Once this target price has been determined, a required long-term profit margin is agreed. It is only once the target cost has been agreed that the design team can begin their work. Our products must be designed with a pre-determined cost ceiling.

Target costs and standard costs

There are some similarities between target costs and standard costs but the significance of a target cost lies in the process of how it is developed. They both provide unit cost targets but here the similarity ends and significant differences include:

- the focus upon what a product should cost in the long term. In constructing the target cost of a new item consideration should first be given to the price at which the product should be sold in order to attract the desired market share. Once this selling price has been determined the required profit margin needs to be deducted in order to arrive at the target cost. A standard cost would tend to be based on attainable standards of efficiency whereas a target cost may incorporate a cost gap which can only be achieved over a longer term.

- A market orientated approach. The use of standard costs which have been derived from target costs ensures that external factors that are related to the marketplace are taken into account. A standard cost is usually based on production cost information only.

- Focus on continual improvement. The target cost may incorporate a series of cost targets which are continuously reduced until the target is achieved. A standard is normally set at the outset of production and may not be reviewed on a regular basis.

- Team approach. Target costing requires that all departments working on the product should be involved in the target costing exercise and should contribute to the target cost being achieved. This includes research and development, marketing and sales as well as production. This contrasts with standard costs which are normally production costs only.

- A target cost will be set before major development costs are incurred. This allows cost reductions to be designed into the product or a decision to be made to abandon the product if the required cost target cannot be achieved. In contrast, standards are set when production commences, by which time 70% to 80% of costs may already be committed.

Kaizen costing and Target costing

Kaizen is the Japanese term for making improvements to a process through small incremental amounts, rather than through large innovations.

Target costing is aimed at reducing the costs incurred because of the way the product is designed, and occurs at the very start of the process.

Kaizen costing is applied during the manufacturing stage of the products life cycle. Kaizen costing therefore focuses on achieving cost reductions through the increased efficiency of the production process. Improvement is the aim and responsibility of every worker in every activity, at all times. Through continual efforts significant reductions in cost can be achieved over time. In order to encourage continual cost reductions an annual (or monthly) Kaizen cost goal is established. Actual results are then compared with the Kaizen goal and then the current actual cost becomes the base line for setting the new Kaizen goal the following year. It should be noted however that as the products are already at the production stage the cost savings under Kaizen costing are smaller than target costing. Because cost reductions under target costing are achieved at the design stage where 80–90% of the product costs are locked in, more significant savings can be made.

5 Value analysis/Value engineering

Value analysis/value engineering is an activity which helps to design products which meet customer needs at a lower cost while assuming the required standard of quality and reliability. **Value analysis** relates to existing products, whereas **Value engineering** relates to products that have not yet been produced. CIMA's *Official Terminology* definitions read as follows:

> *Value analysis* is 'the systematic interdisciplinary examination of factors affecting the cost of a product or service, in order to devise means of achieving the specified purpose most economically at the required standard of quality and reliability'.

> *Value engineering* is 'the redesign of an activity, product or service so that value to the customer is enhanced while costs are reduced or at least increased by less than the resulting price increase).

The **purpose** of value analysis is to identify any unnecessary cost elements within the components of goods and services. It is more comprehensive than simple cost reduction, because it examines the purposes or functions of the product and is concerned with establishing the means whereby these are achieved. Any cost data that do not add value to the product or service should be eliminated.

Types of value

Cost value: this is the cost incurred by the firm producing the product.

Exchange value: the amount of money that consumers are willing to exchange to obtain ownership of the product, i.e. its price.

Use value: this is related entirely to function, i.e. the ability of a product to perform its specific intended purpose. A basic small car provides personal transport at a competitive price and is reasonably economic to run.

Esteem value: this relates to the status or regard associated with ownership. Products with high esteem value will often be associated with premium or even price-skimming prices.

Value is a function of both use and esteem. Value analysis aims to maintain the esteem value in a product, but at a reduced cost value. The result of value analysis is to achieve an improved value/cost relationship.

Method of value analysis

- Determine the function of the product and each component that is used within the product.

- Determine the existing costs associated with individual components.

- Develop alternative solutions to the needs met by the components. This may involve design changes, manufacturing method, materials used, etc.

- When analysing a components a questioning attitude should be adopted. Some of these points may be considered:

  - How does this component contribute to the value of the product?

  - How much does it cost?

  - Are all its features and specifications absolutely necessary?

  - Is there another similar part that may be used?

  - Can an alternative part be used?

  - Will an alternative design perform the same function?

- Evaluate the alternatives and their anticipated effect.

- Implement the recommendations.

Value analysis will often lead to the reduction of components used in a product, the use of alternative, cheaper components and the standardisation of parts across several product lines.

6 Functional analysis

Functional analysis is defined in CIMA's *Official Terminology* as an analysis of the relationships between product functions, their perceived value to the customer and their cost of provision.

Functional analysis uses the functions of a product as the cost object and is used either in initial designs or in the review of existing products. It can be extended to services, overhead expenses, and organisation structure and even to the overall strategy of the company (Innes et al, Contemporary Cost Management).

The central theme of functional analysis is, like value analysis, **customer focus**. An important aspect when gathering information is to identify the functions of the product that customers' value and identify alternative ways of achieving these functions. So, for example, a newsletter sent out by an accounting company may have the functions of advertising services, keeping clients up to date with new developments, providing details of social events and networking opportunities. There may be many ways of achieving these functions, e.g. by sending out letters, by sending emails or by posting information on a website. Analysis will be carried out to find out which alternative achieves the required function at the least cost.

Once an alternative has been chosen this must be implemented and performance measured to assess the degree to which the objective has been achieved. Lessons may be learned to help in future functional analyses.

Functional analysis

In functional analysis, the company will first break down the product into its many functions. For example, a mobile phone may offer an MP3 player, a voice-recording feature, a camera and an internet browser in addition to the ability to make and receive calls and texts.

Research is also carried out to identify the importance the customer attaches to each feature. This information may be obtained from a mixture of past purchasing patterns and customer interviews and questionnaires. Research will also be carried out into the amount the customer would be willing to pay for the final product – this can be used to find the overall target cost for the product by deducting an appropriate profit margin.

The company will then calculate the target cost of providing each of these functions. This is calculated as a percentage of the overall target cost based on the relative importance of each feature to the customer.

The next step will be to compare the expected cost to provide each function with the target cost. If the expected cost of the function exceeds the target (i.e. has a value ratio of less than one) then the function should be either modified, re-evaluated and an alternative found or eliminated.

---

7 The value chain

The value chain is a linked set of value-creating activities starting from basic raw material sources or component suppliers through to the ultimate end-use product or service delivered to the customer. Co-ordinating the individual parts of the value chain together creates conditions to improve customer satisfaction, particularly in terms of cost efficiency, quality and delivery. A firm which performs the value chain activities more efficiently, and at a lower cost, than its competitors will gain competitive advantage.

The value chain was designed by Professor Michael Porter of the Harvard Business School (1985).

Porter's value chain

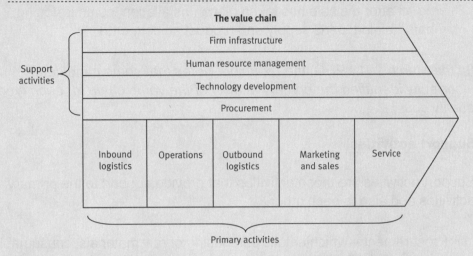

It is necessary to understand how value chain activities are performed and how they interact with each other. The activities are not just a collection of independent activities but a system of interdependent activities in which the performance of one activity affects the performance of other activities.

The activities which comprise the value chain are as follows:

[In the PEG for the March 2013 exam, the Examiner notes that, although both the value chain and aspects of quality costs sit within the P2 syllabus, many candidates seem confused when the two topics are linked together.].

Primary activities

These are the activities which involve the physical movement of raw materials and finished products, production of goods and services, marketing sales and subsequent services to outputs of a business unit.

(1) Inbound logistics – which entail receiving, storing, materials handling, warehousing, inventory control, vehicle scheduling, returns to suppliers.

(2) Operations – which entail transferring inputs into final product form (e.g. machining, packaging, assembly, equipment maintenance, testing, printing and facility operations).

(3) Outbound logistics – which entail distributing the finished product (e.g. finished goods warehousing, material handling, operation of delivery vehicles, order processing and scheduling).

(4) Marketing and sales – which entail inducing and facilitating buyers to purchase the product (e.g. advertising, activities of sales personnel, preparation of quotations, channel selection, channel relations, pricing of goods and services).

(5) Service – which entails maintaining or enhancing the value of the product after the sale has taken place (installation, commissioning, repair, training, parts supply and product adjustment.)

[In the March 2013 PEG, the Examiner notes that some candidates incorrectly identified the primary activity of the value chain for each type of quality cost.]

Support activities

Support activities are those activities that provide support to the primary activities and also to each other.

(1) Procurement – which entails purchasing of raw materials, consumable items and capital items.

(2) Technology development – which entails the use of know how, procedures to be applied and the technological inputs required in every activity which forms part of the value chain.

(3) Human resource management – which entails the selection, retention and promotion of staff, the appraisal of staff and performance-rewards linkage, management development and employee relations.

(4) Firm infrastructure – which entails general management, accounting and finance, quality management and planning activities.

Each activity within the value chain provides inputs which after processing constitute added value to the output, which the customer ultimately receives in the form of a product or service or as the aggregate of values at the end of the value chain.

Each primary and support activity has the potential to contribute to the competitive advantage of the business unit by enabling it to produce, market and deliver products or services which meet or surpass the value expectations of purchasers in comparison with those resulting from other value chains.

Focusing on each of the nine activities enables management to see how each creates value that may be understood as the difference between cost and revenue.

According to Porter, an organisation can develop sustainable competitive advantage by following one of two strategies:

(1) **Low-cost strategy**. Essentially this is a strategy of cost leadership, which involves achieving a lower cost than competitors via, for example, economies of scale and tight cost control.

(2) **Differentiation strategy**. This involves creating something that customers perceive as being unique via brand loyalty, superior customer service, product design and features.

Shank and Govindarajan (1993) advocate that a company should evaluate its value chain relative to the value chains of its competitors or the industry. They suggest the following methodology:

(1) Identify the industry's value chain and then assign costs, revenues and assets to the value activities. These activities are the building blocks with which firms in the industry created a product that buyers find valuable.

(2) Diagnose the cost drivers regulating each value activity.

(3) Develop sustainable cost advantage, either through controlling cost drivers better than competitors or by reconfiguring the chain value. By systematically analysing costs, revenues and assets in each activity, a firm can achieve low cost. This is achieved by comparing the firm's value chain with the value chains of a few major competitors and identifying actions needed to manage the firm's value chain better than competitors manage their value chains.

[In the March 2013 PEG, the Examiner notes that some candidates submit impractical ideas on how to reduce cost e.g. 'cut out the number of inspections' or 'tell the warehouse staff to be more careful'.]

8 Life-cycle costing

Life-cycle costing is the accumulation of costs for activities that occur over the entire life cycle of a product, from inception to abandonment.

According to Berliner and Brimson (1988), companies operating in an advanced manufacturing environment are finding that about 90% of a product's life-cycle cost is determined by decisions made early in the cycle. In many industries a large fraction of the life-cycle costs consists of costs incurred on product design, prototyping, programming, process design and equipment acquisition. This has created a need to ensure that the tightest controls are at the design stage, because most costs are committed or 'locked-in' at this point in time. Management accounting systems should therefore be developed that aid the planning and control of product life-cycle costs and monitor spending and commitments at the early stages of a product's life-cycle.

Product life-cycle costing

There are a number of factors that need to be managed in order to maximise a product's return over its life cycle. These are:

- design costs out of the product
- minimise the time to market
- maximise the length of the life cycle itself

These factors will be considered in turn.

Design costs out of the product

It was stated earlier that between 80% and 90% of a product's costs were often incurred at the design and development stages of its life. That is decisions made then committed the organisation to incurring the costs at a later date, because the design of the product determines the number of components, the production method, etc. It is absolutely vital therefore that design teams do not work in isolation, but as part of a cross-functional team in order to minimise costs over the whole life cycle.

Minimise the time to market

In a world where competitors watch each other keenly to see what new products will be launched, it is vital to get any new product into the marketplace as quickly as possible. The competitors will monitor each other closely so that they can launch rival products as soon as possible in order to maintain profitability. It is vital, therefore, for the first organisation to launch its product as quickly as possible after the concept has been developed, so that it has as long as possible to establish the product in the market and to make a profit before competition increases. Often it is not so much costs that reduce profits as time wasted.

Maximise the length of the life cycle itself

Generally the longer the life cycle the greater the profit that will be generated, assuming that production ceases once the product goes into decline and becomes unprofitable. One way to maximise the life cycle is to get the product to market as quickly as possible because this should maximise the time in which the product generates a profit. Another way of extending a product's life is to find other uses, or markets, for the product. Other product uses may not be obvious when the product is still in its planning stage and need to be planned and managed later on. On the other hand, it may be possible to plan for a staggered entry into different markets at the planning stage.

Many organisations stagger the launch of their products in different world markets in order to reduce costs, increase revenue and prolong the overall life of the product. A current example is the way in which new films are released in the USA months before the UK launch. This is done to build up the enthusiasm for the film and to increase revenues overall. Other companies may not have the funds to launch worldwide at the same moment and may be forced to stagger it.

Skimming the market is another way to prolong life and to maximise the revenue over the product's life. This was discussed in the unit on pricing.

Customer life cycle costing

Not all investment decisions involve large initial capital outflows or the purchase of physical assets. The decision to serve and retain customers can also be a capital budgeting decision even though the initial outlay may be small. For example a credit card company or an insurance company will have to choose which customers they take on and then register them on the company's records. The company incurs initial costs due to the paperwork, checking creditworthiness, opening policies, etc. for new customers. It takes some time before these initial costs are recouped. Research has also shown that the longer a customer stays with the company the more profitable that customer becomes to the company.

Thus it becomes important to retain customers, whether by good service, discounts, other benefits, etc. A customer's 'life' can be discounted and decisions made as to the value of, say, a 'five-year-old' customer. Eventually a point arises where profit no longer continues to grow; this plateau is reached between about five years and 20 years depending on the nature of the business. Therefore by studying the increased revenue and decreased costs generated by an 'old' customer, management can find strategies to meet their needs better and to retain them.

Many manufacturing companies only supply a small number of customers, say between six and ten, and so they can cost customers relatively easily. Other companies such as banks and supermarkets have many customers and cannot easily analyse every single customer. In this case similar customers are grouped together to form category types and these can then be analysed in terms of profitability.

For example, the UK banks analyse customers in terms of fruits, such as oranges, lemons, plums, etc. Customers tend to move from one category to another as they age and as their financial habits change. Customers with large mortgages, for example, are more valuable to the bank than customers who do not have a large income and do not borrow money. Banks are not keen on keeping the latter type of customer

The life cycle cost budget

The application of life cycle costing requires the establishment of a life cycle cost budget for a given product which in turn necessitates identification of costs with particular products. Actual costs incurred in respect of the product are then monitored against life cycle budget costs.

A company is in a weak position if all its products are at the same phase of the life cycle. If they are all in the growth phase there are problems ahead; if they are all in one of the other phases there are immediate difficulties.

Companies try to overcome this problem by introducing new products that are growing as the old products are declining and by having products with life cycles of different lengths.

In applying life cycle costing a supplier will recognise that the life of the product commences prior to its introduction to the marketplace. Indeed up to 90% of costs result from decisions made prior to its 'launch' concerning issues such as functions, materials, components and manufacturing methods to be adopted.

Life cycle costs may be classified as follows:

- development costs
- design costs
- manufacturing costs
- marketing costs, and
- distribution costs.

A pattern of costs will emerge over the life cycle of the product. Invariably the absolute level of costs will rise and this trend should 'track' the pattern of sales of the product. The supplier will always be monitoring relevant costs and revenues in an attempt to ensure that the rise in resultant sales revenues is greater than the rise in the attributable costs of the product.

Moreover, the supplier will expect reductions to occur in the unit cost of a product as a consequence of economies of scale and learning and experience curves. In order to maximise the profits earned by a product over its life cycle management need to give consideration to minimising the time required to get the product to the marketplace. This may enable an organisation to 'steal a march' on its competitors who will invariably attempt to launch a rival product at the earliest available opportunity. Hence 'time to market' assumes critical significance since it affords an organisation that is first to the marketplace with an opportunity to make profits prior to arrival of competitor products.

Once the product has reached the marketplace management attention should be focused upon maximising the length of the product's life cycle. In this regard 'time to market' is also critical since by definition the earlier a product reaches the marketplace the longer will be its resultant life cycle.

Management should always be searching for other potential uses of the product and/or finding alternative markets for the product. Whilst it may be difficult to envisage other potential uses for product at the planning stage it may be possible for an organisation to draw up a plan which involves the staggered entry of the product into geographically separate markets with the resultant effect of increasing the overall life cycle of the product. A major benefit of this staggered approach which is often adopted by global players lies in the fact that the income streams from one market may be used to fund the launch of the product into another market.

The application of life cycle costing requires management to consider whether the anticipated cost savings that were expected to be achieved via the application of cost reduction techniques, both prior to and following the product's introduction, have actually been achieved. Its use may also assist management in allocating resources to non-production activities. For example, a product which is in the mature stage may require less marketing support than a product which is in the growth stage.

9 Practice Questions

Objective Test Question 1: Target costing

The selling price of product Z is set at $250 for each unit and sales for the coming year are expected to be 500 units.

If the company requires a return of 15% in the coming year on its investment of $250,000 in product Z, the target cost for each unit for the coming year is:

A $145

B $155

C $165

D $175

E $185

Objective Test Question 2: Value analysis

Casabee was established in 2010 and manufactures a range of kitchen utensils, which it makes from material purchased from a number of suppliers. The recently appointed Managing Director has expressed increasing concern about the trends in falling sales volumes, rising costs and hence declining profits over the last two years.

There is general agreement amongst the managers of Casabee that these trends are the result of the increased intense competition that has emerged over the last two years. Casabee continues to have a reputation for high quality, but this quality is now being matched by the competition.

The competitors are taking Casabee's share of the market by selling equivalent products at lower prices. It is thought that in order to offer such low prices, the production costs of the competitors must be lower than Casabee's. Its MD is now proposing the following to improve sales volumes, costs sand profits:

(i)   We must enter a Value Analysis exercise. Value Analysis is a cost reduction and problem solving technique that analyses an existing product, in order to identify and reduce or eliminate any costs which do not contribute to value or performance.

(ii) We must enter a Value Analysis exercise. Value Analysis focuses on the value to the customer of each function of the product, and consequently allocates resources to those functions from which the customer gains the most value.

(iii) We also must enter a Functional Cost Analysis exercise. Functional cost analysis is a method that can be applied to examine the component costs of a product or service, in relation to the value as perceived by the customer. Functional cost analysis can be applied to new products, and breaks the product down into its component parts. For example, a kitchen utensil may have the function to be dishwasher- and microwave-safe, and therefore require less manual cleaning.

(iv) Both value analysis and functional cost analysis have potential to help Casabee, but Value Analysis is likely to be a more useful technique, because kitchen utensils are products that are sold more on the basis of their use value, rather than their esteem value.

Which of the foregoing arguments are valid?

A   (i), (iii) and (iv)

B   (i), (ii), (iii) and (iv)

C   (i) and (iii)

D   (ii) and (iv)

Objective Test Question 3: Life cycle costing

A company has carried out extensive product research and, as a result, has just launched a new innovative product unlike anything else that is currently available on the market. The company has launched this product using a market skimming pricing policy, i.e. charging very high prices initially.

The market in which it operates is highly competitive and historically success has been achieved by being the first to market with new products. Only a small number of companies have survived in the market, and those that remain are constantly aiming to develop new products either by improving those already in the market, or by extensive product research.

Select ALL that apply:

- In the introduction stage, the product is unique and therefore the company can charge a high price.

- In the introduction stage, competitors will buy the product to carry out reverse engineering and see how the product works, so that they can develop their own similar, but different product.

- In the introduction phase, the company will seek to avoid this competition by maintaining its selling price at the end of the introduction stage.

- In the growth stage, the company will adopt a lower selling price to continue to attract new purchasers of the product.

- In the growth stage, if the product cannot be differentiated in other ways, the company may need further reductions in selling price to maintain growth.

- The growth stage is the ideal time to offer short term one-off offers or discounts for multiple purchases.

- In the maturity stage, the selling price of the product becomes unstable and the product is not financially viable anymore.

- In the decline stage, the product may continue to be sold, provided its margin is positive.

- If the product's margin is not positive in the decline phase, the product may be bundled with other products or sold for less than its unit cost in order to clear the company's inventory of what has become an obsolete product.

Data Set Question: Target costing and cost gap

Company S is a specialist car manufacturer and intends to produce a new, limited edition 'Compact Executive' car in 2016. The car will be called the S2016. The production will be limited to 1,000 units of the S2016 car.

Company S is considering using a target costing approach and has conducted market research to determine the features that consumers require in a car of that type. Based on this market research and knowledge of competitors products, Company S has decided to price the S2016 at $19,950. Company S requires an operating profit margin of 25% of the selling price of the car. Company S uses activity-based costing principles to assign overhead costs to units of production, and details for the forthcoming year are as follows:

Forecast direct costs for a S2016 car : Labour $5,000, Material $9,500.

Forecast annual overhead costs: Production line costs $4,630,000 (see note 1) and transportation costs $1,800,000 (see note 2).

Note 1: The production line that would be used for S2016 has a capacity of 60,000 machine hours per year. The production line time required for one S2016 is 6 machine hours per car. This production line will also be used to make other cars and will be working at full capacity.

Note 2: Some models of cars are delivered to showrooms using car transporters. 60% of the transportation costs are related to the distance travelled.

The car transporters are forecast to make a total of 640 deliveries in the year, and carry 10 cars each time. The car transporter will always carry its maximum capacity of 10 cars.

The total annual distance travelled by car transporters is expected to be 225,000 kms. 50,000 kms of this is for the delivery of the S2016 only. All 1,000 S2016 cars that will be produced will be delivered in the year using the car transporters.

Task: Calculate the following:

The production line cost per S2016 car

The transportation cost per S2016 car

The total overhead cost per S2016 car

The full product cost for a S2016 car (forecast)

The target cost of a S2016 car

The current cost gap for a S2016 car

PRE-SEEN MATERIAL

AVN designs and assembles electronic devices to allow transmission of audio/visual communications between the original source and various other locations within the same building. Many of these devices require a wired solution but the company is currently developing a wireless alternative.

The company produces a number of different devices depending on the number of input sources and the number of output locations, but the technology used within each device is identical. AVN is constantly developing new devices which improve the quality of the audio/visual communications that are received at the output locations.

Task: Briefing note

You receive the following email from the Managing Director:

From: Michael Drake, Managing Director
Sent: 03 June, 10.23 a.m.
To: Senior Management Accountant
Subject: The extended Value Chain

I have just returned from a conference on World Class Manufacturing in London. The workshop I enjoyed the most was entitled 'The extension of the Value Chain to include suppliers and customers'.

Please help – may I have a briefing note on all this? What are the components of the extended Value Chain? And how can we, in AVN, apply each of these components?

Test your understanding answers

Objective Test Question 1: Target costing

(4)   Answer: D

	$
Sales revenue 500 units @ $250	125,000
Return on invst. required 15% × 250,000	37,500
	————
Total cost allowed	87,500
Target cost per unit	175

Objective Test Question 2: Value analysis

A.

(ii)   defines Functional Cost Analysis.

Objective Test Question 3: Life cycle costing

- In the introduction stage, the product is unique and therefore the company can charge a high price. **TRUE**

- In the introduction stage, competitors will buy the product to carry out reverse engineering and see how the product works, so that they can develop their own similar, but different product. **TRUE**

- In the introduction phase, the company will seek to avoid this competition by maintaining its selling price at the end of the introduction stage. **FALSE:** the company will seek to avoid this competition by lowering it selling price towards the end of the introduction stage, to deter competitors from entering the market and also to make its product more affordable to the wider market.

- In the growth stage, the company will adopt a lower selling price to continue to attract new purchasers of the product. **TRUE**

- In the growth stage, if the product cannot be differentiated in other ways, the company may need further reductions in selling price to maintain growth. **TRUE**

- The growth stage is the ideal time to offer short term one-off offers or discounts for multiple purchases. **FALSE**: the maturity stage is the ideal time for this.

- In the maturity stage, the selling price of the product becomes unstable and the product is not financially viable anymore. **FALSE**

- In the decline stage, the product may continue to be sold, provided its margin is positive. **TRUE**

- If the product's margin is not positive in the decline phase, the product may be bundled with other products or sold for less than its unit cost in order to clear the company's inventory of what has become an obsolete product. **TRUE**

Data Set Question: Target costing and cost gap

The production line cost per S2016 car	**$463**
The transportation cost per S2016 car	**$328.75**
The total overhead cost per S2016 car	**$791.75**
The full product cost for a S2016 car (forecast)	**$15,291.75**
The target cost of a S2016 car	**$14,962.50**
The current cost gap for a S2016 car	**$329.50**

Workings

$4,630,000/60,000 annual production line machine hours = $77.17 per machine hour, $77.17 × 6 machine hours for a S2016 = $463

Transportation cost
60% delivery related = $1,080,000
40% distance travelled related = $720,000

$1,080,000/640 deliveries = $1,687.50 per delivery
$1,687.5/10 cars = $168.75 per car

$720,000/225,000km = $3.20 per km travelled
$3.20 × 50,000km = $160,000
$160,000/1,000 cars = $160 per car

Target selling price $19,950
Profit margin 25%
Target cost $14,962.50
Forecast cost $15,291.75
Cost gap $329.25

Test your understanding – Case Style Question-AVN

To:	Michael Drake, MD
From:	Management Accountant
Date:	21 November 2014
Subject:	Value chain – Briefing note

The value chain refers to the sequence of processes through which value is added to an organisation's products and services. The components of the value chain include research and development, design, production, marketing, distribution and customer services. The extended value chain refers to the extension of this sequence outside of the organisation to include suppliers and customers.

The objective of the value chain is to focus the organisation on achieving value to the customer. Profit can then be optimised by finding the most effective processes to deliver the required product. The value chain should therefore begin with the customer. Clear requirements should be identified and communicated to departments within AVN.

The role of research and development will be to develop new products that meet customer requirements but are not necessarily constrained by currently available technology. It may be useful to carry out a functional analysis to identify what the customer requires the product to do rather than how it is to be done. In this way R and D may be able to develop new technology which will result in competitive advantage.

The role of design will be to take a new idea and produce a cost-effective design. Target costing may be useful to determine the expected market price of the product and, after deducting the required profit margin, find the target cost for which the product must be produced. The design department will try to reduce the cost of the product by using standard components and layouts. It will need to liaise with production, distribution and marketing to ensure that the design is cost effective, feasible and will deliver the product at the required quality to the customer.

At this stage supplies may be involved to help develop new sources of material and components.

The production department must then produce the product efficiently. AVN should have determined the price that customers would be prepared to pay for different levels of quality. If the strategy is for high quality/high price products, then AVN may invest heavily in appraisal and prevention activities such as training and inspections to prevent internal and external quality failure costs.

Production must also be aware of when the customer requires the product. Customers should be able to receive the product as required. This may mean that inventories of finished goods are held and the relative costs and benefits of these inventories should be considered.

Marketing has an important role in informing potential customers of new products. This may involve identifying target markets and the most effective marketing policy to adopt. Distribution must ensure that products reach the customer as required.

AVN may have to decide whether to sell directly to the customer or via retailers or wholesalers. The additional costs of a direct sales force and installation teams may have to be weighed against the benefit of remaining in control of the quality of the process and remaining in close contact with customers to be able to develop new improved products.

Customer services may be a vital link in obtaining feedback from customers which may be important in generating repeat sales. It may also be possible to assess the extent to which customers' requirements have been met.

AN Accountant

Management Accountant
X Ltd

E: mact@avn.co.uk
T: 0191 253 3434

Learning Curves

Chapter learning objectives

Lead A1: Evaluate techniques for analysing and managing costs for competitive advantage

Component A1d): Apply learning curves to estimate time and cost for activities, products and services

- Learning curves and their use in predicting product/service costs, including derivation of the learning rate and the learning index.

1 Chapter summary

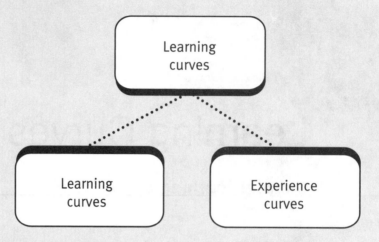

2 Knowledge brought forward

There is no knowledge brought forward from Papers C01 and P1, but you will need to be comfortable with the maths concept of logarithms, covered below.

3 Introduction

It has been observed in some industries that there is a tendency for labour time per unit to reduce in time. As more of the units are produced, workers become more familiar with the task.

See the graph below:

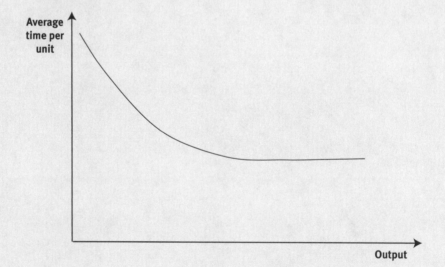

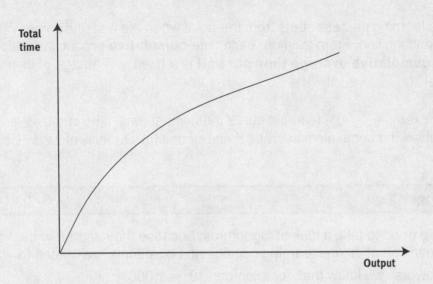

From the experience of aircraft production during World War II, aircraft manufacturers found the rate of improvement was so regular that it could be reduced to a formula, and the labour hours required could be predicted with a high degree of accuracy from a **learning curve**.

The first time a new operation is performed, both the workers and the operating procedures are untried. As the operation is repeated, the workers become more familiar with the work, labour efficiency increases and the **labour cost per unit declines.**

Wright's Law states that as cumulative output doubles, the cumulative average time per unit falls to a fixed percentage (the **'learning rate'**) of the previous average time.

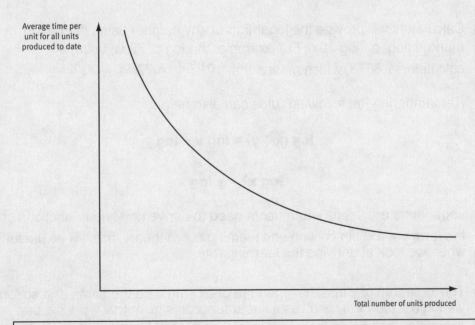

CIMA's *Official Terminology* defines the learning curve as '*The mathematical expression of the commonly observed effect that, as complex and labour-intensive procedures are repeated, unit labour times tend to decrease.*'

The learning process starts from the point when the first unit comes off the production line. From then on, each time **cumulative** production is doubled, the **cumulative average time per unit** is a fixed percentage of its previous level.

For example, a 90% learning curve means that each time cumulative output doubles the cumulative average time per unit falls to 90% of its previous value.

Logarithms

We need to take a look at logarithms, because they appear in the definition of **'b'**, the learning coefficient. Logarithms are related to powers : we know that, for example, $10^3 = 1,000$.

This is the same as $10^3 = 10 \times 10 \times 10$.

So, if you had wanted to solve the equation $10^n = 1,000$, you would know that the answer is x = 3.

However, what if the equation were $10^n = 2.5$?

If you want to rearrange an equation with powers, then you will have to use **log** functions:

$$10^n = 2.5 \text{ is equivalent to } n = \log_{10} 2.5 = 0.39794\ldots$$

This is read 'log 2.5 to base 10'.

Calculators will provide the logarithm of any number using the button marked 'log' or 'log 10x'. For example, the log of 72 is, using a calculator, 1.8573, which means that $10^{1.8573} = 72$.

Remembering the following rules can also help :

$$\log (x * y) = \log x + \log y$$

$$\log x^y = y \log x$$

Logarithms are useful when users need to derive non-linear functions of the form $y = ax^n$. In costing and learning curve theory, this will be useful when we look at deriving the learning rate.

The logarithm of y and the logarithm of ax^n must be the same and so log y = log a + nlog x. This gives a linear function similar to y = a + nx, the only difference being that in place of x and y, the logarithms of x and y must be used.

A value for 'n' and a value for 'log a' can be deduced using simultaneous equations. The value of 'log a ' can be translated into a 'nice' number using antilogs i.e. the button 10^x on your calculator.

For example, suppose the relationship between x and y can be described by the function $y = ax^n$, and that the following applies:

If x = 500, y = 50,250
If x = 1,000, y = 42,750

Substitute these values into log y = log a + nlog x and we find that:

Equation (1): $50{,}250 = a{\times}500^n$ gives Log 50250 = loga +nlog500, i.e. 4.7011 = loga +2.69897n

Equation (2): $42750 = a \times 1000^n$ gives Log42750 = log a + nlog1000, i.e. 4.6309 = loga + 3n

Equation (1) – Equation (2): 0.0702 = –0.30103n, so n = –0.2332

Then, replacing 'n' with '–0.2332' in Equation (1), we find that 4.7011 = loga +2.69897 × (–0.2332)

log a = 5.3305 therefore a = $10^{5.3305}$ i.e. **a = 214,042** and our function is $y = 214{,}042x^{-0.2332}$

[In the PEG March 2011, the Examiner regrets that some candidates are 'unable to use logs' and in November 2012, 'unable to apply a logarithmic approach to solving the Learning Curve']

Consider the following example of the time taken to make the first four units of a new product:

Serial number of units	Time to make the unit concerned (hours)
01	10 hours
02	8 hours
03	7.386 hours
04	7.014 hours

While it is clear that we are getting quicker, it is not obvious how the times to make successive units are related. However, a pattern becomes apparent if we look at the cumulative average time per unit instead:

Serial number of unit	Time to make the unit concerned (hours)	Total cumulative time to make all units so far	Cumulative average time per unit	
01	10.000	10.000	10.000	× 90%
02	8.000	18.000	9.000	
03	7.386	25.386	8.462	× 90%
04	7.014	32.400	8.100	

In this example, Wright's Law is verified as the cumulative average decreases to 90% of the previous average every time we double the cumulative output, such as from 1 to 2 or from 2 to 4 units. We therefore say that the process demonstrates a **90% learning rate**.

All learning curve calculations use this idea of a cumulative average, so imagine all units having serial numbers so you can see how they fit into the cumulative picture.

For example, how long would it take to make a further 4 units, doubling the cumulative total to 8? The order of calculations is very important:

Step 1: Calculate the cumulative average time for the target production. Here, the cumulative average for the first 8 units = 8.100 × 90% = 7.290 hours per unit

Step 2: Calculate the total cumulative time. The total cumulative time for the first 8 units = 7.290 × 8 = 58.320 hours

Step 3: Time to make the next 4 units = the time to make 8 in total – the time to make the first 4

Time to make next 4 units = 58.320 – 32.400 = **25.920 hours**.

Or, shown as a table:

Serial number of unit	Total cumulative time	Cumulative average time	
04	32.400	8.100	× 90%
08	58.320	7.290	

[In the PEG for the March 2013 exam, the Examiner warns against the dangers of incorrect rounding and rounding too early.]

A new product will take 100 hours for the first unit. An 80% learning curve applies.

Required:

Complete the table.

Cumulative			Incremental		
Units	Average time per unit	Total time	Units	Total time	Average time per unit

Solution:

Cumulative			Incremental		
Units	Average time p.u.	Total time	Units	Total time	Average time p.u.
1	100	100	1	100	100
2	80	160	1	60	60
4	64	256	2	96	48
8	51.2	409.6	4	153.6	38.4
16	40.96	655.36	8	245.76	30.72

The problem with total doubling is that we cannot calculate averages for all levels of production. For example, to calculate how long the fifth unit should take to make, we need to use the following formula:

$$Y = a * x^{\,b}$$

The learning curve table shown above is useful if output keeps doubling, but for intermediate output levels such information could be obtained graphically or by formula.

$$Y_x = a.x^b \qquad \textbf{GIVEN}$$

where
- y = average labour hours per unit
- a = number of labour hours for first unit
- x = cumulative number of units
- b = the learning coefficient

$$b = \frac{\text{Log learning curve rate}}{\text{Log 2}}$$

For example an 80% learning curve:

$$b = \frac{\text{Log } 0.8}{\text{Log 2}} = -0.3219$$

Note: the value of 'b' may be given in exam questions.

[In the PEG November 2010 exam, the Examiner notes that 'some candidates are unable to use the Learning Curve formula].

In our first example, where

$$a = 10 \text{ hours}$$

$$b = \frac{\log 0.9}{\log 2} = -0.152$$

$$X = 5$$

$$Y_x = aX^b = 10 \times 5^{-0.152} = 7.830 \text{ hours}$$

The table can then be completed in the order above:

Serial number of unit	Time to make the unit concerned	Total cumulative time	Cumulative average time
04	7.014	32.400	8.100
05	6.750 ⟸	39.150 ⟸	7.830

The first unit of a new product is expected to take 100 hours. An 80% learning curve is known to apply.

Calculate:

(a) the average time per unit for the first 16 units

(b) the average time per unit for the first 25 units

(c) the time it takes to make the 20th unit.

Solution:

(a) a $\quad\quad\quad$ = $\quad$ 100 $\quad\quad\quad\quad\quad$ b = –0.3219 $\quad\quad$ x = 16

$\quad$ y $\quad\quad\quad\quad$ = $\quad 100.16^{-0.3219}$

$\quad\quad\quad\quad\quad\quad$ = $\quad$ 40.96 hours

(b) x $\quad\quad\quad\quad$ = $\quad$ 25

$\quad$ y $\quad\quad\quad\quad$ = $\quad 100.25^{-0.3219}$

$\quad\quad\quad\quad\quad\quad$ = $\quad$ 35.48 hours

(c) We will find the value for the 20th unit by finding the total time for 20 units, and subtract the total time for 19 units.

$\quad$ x $\quad\quad\quad\quad$ = $\quad$ 20

$\quad$ y $\quad\quad\quad\quad$ = $\quad 100.20^{-0.3219}$

$\quad\quad\quad\quad\quad\quad$ = $\quad$ 38.12 hours

Total time for $\quad$ = $\quad$ 762.48
20 units =
38.12 × 20

$\quad$ x $\quad\quad\quad\quad$ = $\quad$ 19

$\quad$ y $\quad\quad\quad\quad$ = $\quad 100.19^{-0.3219}$

$\quad\quad\quad\quad\quad\quad$ = $\quad$ 38.76 hours

Total time for $\quad$ = $\quad$ 736.44
19 units =
38.76 × 19

$\quad\quad\quad\quad\quad\quad$ = $\quad$ 762.48 – 736.44

$\quad\quad\quad\quad\quad\quad$ = $\quad$ **26.04 hours**

A firm produces 100 units and the average time per unit is 5.32 hours. A 90% learning curve applies.

Required:

(a) Find the average time per unit if 500 units are produced.

(b) Find the average time per unit for the next 250 units.

Solution:

(a) x = 100 units y = 5.32 hours b = $\dfrac{\text{Log } 0.9}{\text{Log } 2}$ = –0.1520

$y = a.x^b$

$5.32 = a.100^{-0.1520}$

∴ a = 10.71 hours

when x = 500 units

$y = 10.71 \times 500^{-0.1520}$

y = 4.16 hours per unit

Average time per unit is 4.16 hours

(b) Cumulative output = 750 units

Therefore

When x = 750,

$y = 10.71 \times 750^{-0.1520}$

= 3.915 hours per unit

Total hours for 750 units	= 3.915 × 750	= 2,936.25 hours
Total hours for 500 units	= 4.16 × 500	= 2,080 hours
Total hours for last 250 units	= 2,936.25 – 2,080	= 856.25
Therefore, time per unit	= 856.25 ÷ 250	= **3.43 hours per unit**

4 The steady state

Eventually, the learning effect will cease and the time to make each successive unit stabilises at a constant time per unit. This is because there is a limit to manual dexterity and/or other limiting factors come into play such as a limit on how quickly materials can be supplied.

5 Learning curves and management accounting

Knowledge of the learning curve for a new product can be very useful when applying management accounting techniques, such as budgeting, pricing decisions and work scheduling.

Budgeting and standard setting

While the learning curve can be used for a number of purposes as it predicts time reduction, it is normally associated with budgeting: this is because budgets and standards will only provide reliable benchmarks to measure actual performance against if account is taken of the learning effect.

Therefore, it is difficult to set labour standards where a learning curve applies. Standards should not be set until the 'steady state' has been achieved.

Consequently, **cash budgets** should take into account the effect of the reduction in variable costs.

[In the PEG May 2010, the Examiner insists on the necessity of an 'understanding of Learning curves and their interaction with budgets']

Pricing

The initial cost estimates for a new product may be very high, but if they fall through the learning curve, it may allow the company to sell at a lower and hence more competitive price.

For example, it is estimated that the cost of the first unit of a new product is $650, but an 80% learning curve is expected to apply. It is estimated that the company will make and sell 2,000 units during the first year. The average cost per unit for the first 2,000 units can be calculated as follows:

(80% learning/experience)

$b = -0.3219$

$Y = \$650 \times 2000^{-0.3219} = \$56.27$ per unit

This means that the selling price can be set at far below the cost of the first unit and make the company more competitive.

[In the PEG for the March 2013 exam, the Examiner notes that, when prices are examined in a Learning Curve question, candidates 'submit answers that are not realistic' i.e. far too low or far above the limits imposed by its lifecycle phase.].

Work scheduling

Understanding the learning curve allows correct scheduling of labour and enables deliveries to take place on time. Also, when a company plans to recruit new employees to help with increasing production, the learning curve or steady state assumptions will have to be reviewed.

6 General conditions for a LC to apply

The Learning Curve theory will apply in practice when the following conditions are present:

(1) The activity should be labour intensive, rather than in a highly automated or mechanised environment.

(2) The process should be repetitive for each unit.

(3) Labour turnover should be low, and there should be no prolonged breaks between production.

[In the PEG for the November 2010 exam, the Examiner notes that 'Candidates are not appreciating and explaining that the Learning Curve is only prevalent in labour intensive situations'.].

7 Experience curves

Experience curves are very similar to learning curves but they cover all costs, not just labour costs. For example:

(1) **Material costs** may decrease slightly with quantity discounts, etc. but will not decrease by a large amount.

(2) **Variable overheads** often follow the pattern of direct labour and so may decrease in a similar way.

(3) **Fixed overheads** will decrease per unit as more units are made.

8 Practice Questions

Objective Test Question 1: The learning curve rate

Average unit times for product Alpha have been tabulated as follows:

Unit number	Average time per unit Y_x	Total time
1	120 minutes	
2		
4		
8		
16		1,375.52

Required:

What is the Learning Curve rate?

Objective Test Question 2: The learning curve rate

Average unit times for product X have been tabulated as follows:

Unit number	Average time per unit Y_x
1	20 minutes
2	17.2 minutes
4	14.792 minutes
8	12.72 minutes

Required:

What is the Learning Curve rate?

Objective Test Question 3: The learning curve rate

Manufacturing the first unit of product Beta took 50 hours; and 42 hours to manufacture the second unit.

Required:

What is the Learning Curve rate?

Objective Test Question 4: Units of production

Department F assembles widgets by hand. A new product line commenced last week. The first widget produced took five hours. The labour hours were fully utilised making 2,000 widgets in the first week of production. No additional labour hours are available in the short term.

Note: the department bases its learning curve calculations on the model:

$$y = a.x^{-0.23}$$

How many units were produced in the second week?

Test your understanding – Data set

You are the management accountant of a new small company that has developed a new product using a labour-intensive production process. You have recently completed the budgets for the company for next year and, before they are approved by the Board of Directors, you have been asked to explain your calculation of the labour time required for the budgeted output. In your calculations, you anticipated that the time taken for the first unit would be 40 minutes and that a 75% learning curve would apply for the first 30 units.

(a) **The expected time for the 6th unit of output is _____ minutes.**

(**Note:** 2 decimal places please. The learning index for a 75% learning curve is −0.415.)

(b) **Use the words and phrases in the table provided below to complete the following paragraphs:**

doubled	cumulative	less
labour intensive	reduction	fall
doubled	constant	doubled

It has been observed in some industries, particularly where skilled labour predominates such as in aircraft manufacture, that as more of the same units are produced, there is a _____ in the time taken to manufacture them until the learning process is complete.

A learning curve is the mathematical expression of the phenomenon that when complex and _____ _____ procedures are repeated, unit labour times tend to decrease at a _____ rate.

The learning curve phenomenon states that each time the number of units produced is _____, the cumulative average time per unit is reduced by a constant percentage. If this constant reduction is 20%, this is referred to as an 80% learning curve, and a 10% reduction as a 90% learning curve. This is an important phenomenon that has been empirically observed. The _____ average time is the average time per unit for all units produced up to the present time, including right back to the very first unit made.

If, for instance, there is a 60% learning curve, the cumulative average time per unit of output will _____ to 60% of what it was before, every time output is _____.

The importance of the learning effect

If the product enjoys a learning effect, but the effect is ignored, then the planned unit cost estimated will be too high, since the fact that the products will take progressively _____ labour will have been ignored. Budgeted costs must therefore take into account any expected learning curve when they are being formulated.

Test your understanding – Integration style question

You are the Senior Management Accountant working for Z plc. Z plc is about to start producing a product called the Vadenough.

In your company, recent industrial action has revealed that production line staff are widely dissatisfied with current working conditions. Production stoppages are frequent, and labour turnover is high.

The Production Manager has recently suggested that all production lines in Z plc should become largely automated. Currently, the Vadenough is produced in batches of 10 units. The first batch of 10 units is expected to take 15 labour hours.

There will be a 95% learning curve that will continue until 64 batches have been produced.

You have received the following email:

From: Ani Patel, Financial Director
Sent: 03 June, 10.23 a.m.
To: Senior Management Accountant
Subject: Learning curve effects – Vadenough

At a conference the other day, I overheard a conversation where someone was saying that 'The learning curve is a simple mathematical model but its application to management accounting problems requires careful thought.'

I am not very clear on this, and I am worried about the current problems we have had with the labour force. Please could you prepare a briefing note for me? Would the learning curve theory apply for us, when we start production on the Vadenough? I would like to be as prepared for this as we can – what conditions must exist in the production process for the Learning Curve to be realised?

Test your understanding answers

Objective Test Question 1: The learning curve rate

The total time for 16 units is 1,375.52 minutes.

This means that the average time per unit is 1,375.52 minutes/16 units = 85.97 minutes per unit.

Making the first unit takes 120 minutes on average. Making 16 units takes 85.97 minutes on average per unit.

Between 1 unit and 16 units, the output has doubled **four** times:

(i)   From 1 unit to 2 units

(ii) From 2 units to 4 units

(iii) From 4 units to 8 units

(iv) From 8 units to 16 units.

The learning curve rate can therefore be expressed as r^4

and we can write 120 minutes × r^4 = 85.97 minutes

So r^4 = 85.97 minutes/120 minutes

r^4 = 0.71641 so r=

$\sqrt[4]{0.7164}$

r = 0.92 or **92%**

Objective Test Question 2: The learning curve rate

20 minutes x r^3 = 12.72 minutes

r^3 = 12.72/20

r^3 = 0.636 so r=

$\sqrt[3]{0.636}$

r = 0.86 or **86%**

Objective Test Question 3: The learning curve rate

Y_1 = 50 hours (or average time at first unit is 50 hours)

Y_2 = (50 hours + 42 hours)/2

Y_2 = 46 (or average time after second unit is unit is 46 hours)

(46/50) * 100% = **92%**

r = 0.92 or **92%**

Objective Test Question 4: Units of production

a	=	5
x	=	2,000
b	=	−0.23
y	=	$5.2000^{-0.23}$
	=	0.8704 hours per unit
Total labour hours available each week	= 2,000 × 0.8704	= 1,740.857 hours
Cumulative hours after two weeks	= 1,740.857 × 2	= 3,481.71 hours

Let 'x' be total production in two weeks

$$y = a \cdot x^b$$

$$\frac{3{,}481.71}{x} = 5 \cdot x^{-0.23}$$

$$\frac{3{,}481.71}{5} = x^1 \cdot x^{-0.23}$$

When multiplying the two x terms together, it is necessary to add the powers, i.e. $1 + - 0.23 = + 0.77$

$696.34 \quad = x^{0.77}$

$^{0.77}\sqrt{696.34} = x$

$4,920.12 \quad = x$

Total production after two weeks = 4,920 units

Therefore production in the second week = 4,920 – 2,000 = 2,920 units

Test your understanding – Data set

(a) From the formula sheet, the learning curve formula is given by $Y_x = ax_b$

Where:

Y_x = the cumulative average time per unit to produce X units

a = the time required to produce the first unit of output

x = the cumulative number of units

b = the index of learning

Here $Y_x = 40x^{-0.415}$

Expected time for 6th unit is difference between the total time to produce 6 units and the total time for 5 units.

Cumulative average time for 5 units $= 40 \times 5^{-0.415} = 20.51$ minutes

Total time for first 5 units $= 5 \times 20.51 = 102.56$ minutes

Cumulative average time for 6 units $= 40 \times 6^{-0.415} = 19.02$ minutes

Total time for first 6 units $= 6 \times 19.02 = 114.12$ minutes

Expected time to produce 6th unit $= 114.12 - 102.56 = 11.56$ minutes

(b) It has been observed in some industries, particularly where skilled labour predominates such as in aircraft manufacture, that as more of the same units are produced, there is a **reduction** in the time taken to manufacture them until the learning process is complete.

A learning curve is the mathematical expression of the phenomenon that when complex and **labour intensive** procedures are repeated, unit labour times tend to decrease at a **constant** rate. The learning curve phenomenon states that each time the number of units produced is **doubled,** the **cumulative** average time per unit is reduced by a constant percentage. If this constant reduction is 20%, this is referred to as an 80% learning curve, and a 10% reduction as a 90% learning curve. This is an important phenomenon that has been empirically observed. The **cumulative** average time is the average time per unit for all units produced up to the present time, including right back to the very first unit made.

If, for instance, there is a 60% learning curve, the cumulative average time per unit of output will **fall** to 60% of what it was before, every time output is **doubled**.

The importance of the learning effect

If the product enjoys a learning effect, but the effect is ignored, then the planned unit cost estimated will be too high, since the fact that the products will take progressively **less** labour will have been ignored. Budgeted costs must therefore take into account any expected learning curve when they are being formulated.

Test your understanding – Integration style question

Briefing note

- In order for the learning curve effect to be realised at Z plc, a number of conditions must be satisfied.

- The Production Manager is favouring automation, but the production process must be labour intensive for the learning effects to be felt. The Vadenough's production process should have direct involvement from our labour force, rather than be largely automated.

- The production process should also be complex in its composition; complicated production processes will allow scope for learning. This seems to be the case for the Vadenough, with the first batch expected to take 15 hours.

- It is also important that the production process should be continuous, without extended stoppage periods. The reduction in production time stated by the learning curve effect can only be achieved if production occurs without significant breaks; at the moment, in our business, this does not seem to be the case. The current prolonged stoppages in production risks the learning from previous units being lost, and production time increasing back towards the time for the first batch, that was 15 hours.

- Finally, for the learning effect to apply, there should be a low turnover of production labour. Yet again, we must try and improve this. A high number of production line operatives leaving the organisation will mean that we must keep employing new staff. These new individuals will have no experience of the production in Z plc, and consequently take a longer time to produce units than more experienced employees. The steady state production time per unit of Vadenough will be achieved once all production staff have sufficient experience to realise the learning effect.

Responsibility Centres

Chapter learning objectives

Syllabus Link

Lead B1: Discuss decision making in responsibility centres

Component B1a): Discuss the information needed for decision making in different organisational structures

- Relevant cost information for cost centre managers: controllable and uncontrollable costs and budget flexing.

- Relevant revenue and cost information for profit and investment centre managers: cost variability, attributable costs, controllable costs and identification of appropriate measures of profit centre 'contribution'.

Syllabus Link B2c): Discuss the criticisms and behavioural aspects of budgeting in responsibility centres.

- Behavioural issues in budgeting: participation in budgeting and its possible beneficial consequences for ownership and motivation; participation in budgeting and its possible adverse consequences for 'budget padding' and manipulation; setting budget targets for motivation; implications of setting standard costs, etc.

- Criticisms of budgeting and the arguments for and against 'beyond budgeting'.

1 Chapter summary

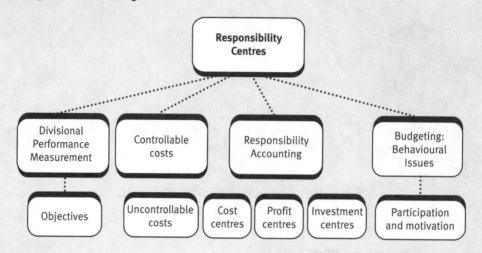

2 Decentralisation

Decentralisation, which is also known as divisionalisation, seeks to overcome the problem of managing a large organisation by creating a structure based on several autonomous decision-making units.

Objectives

(1) Ensure goal congruence

(2) Increase motivation of management

(3) Reduce head office bureaucracy

(4) Provide better training for junior and middle management.

The major disadvantage of decentralisation is the potential for dysfunctional decision making, i.e. where divisions make decisions **in their own best interests**, but which are not good from the overall company point of view.

The problem can be overcome by introducing a suitable system of performance evaluation, that has the following objectives:

(1) Promote goal congruence

(2) Encourage initiative and motivation

(3) Provide feedback to management

(4) Encourage long-term rather than short term views

These objectives can only be achieved with the introduction of **responsibility centres.**

3 Cost, profit and investment centres

In **responsibility accounting**, a specific manager is given the responsibility for a particular aspect of the budget, and within the budgetary control system, he or she is then made accountable for actual performance. Managers are therefore made accountable for their area of responsibility.

The area of operations for which a manager is responsible is called a responsibility centre. Within an organisation, there could be a hierarchy of responsibility centres.

- If a manager is responsible for a particular aspect of operating costs, the responsibility centre is a **cost centre:** 'a production or service location, function, activity or item of equipment for which costs are accumulated.' A cost centre could be large or small, such as an entire department or the activities associated with a single item of equipment.

- If a manager is responsible for revenue as well as costs, the responsibility centre is a **profit centre**, and the manager responsible is held accountable for the profitability of the operations in his or her charge.

There could be several cost centres within a profit centre, with the cost centre managers responsible for the costs of their particular area of operations, and the profit centre manager responsible for the profitability of the entire operation.

- If a manager is responsible for investment decisions as well as for revenues and costs, the responsibility centre is an **investment centre**. The manager is held accountable not only for profits, but also for the return on investment from the operations in his or her charge. There could be several profit centres within an investment centre.

Each cost centre, profit centre and investment centre should have its own budget, and its manager should receive regular budgetary control information relating to the centre, for control and performance measurement purposes.

4 Responsibility accounting and controllability of costs

If the principle of controllability is applied, a manager should be made responsible and accountable only for the costs (and revenues) that he or she is in a position to control. A controllable cost is a cost 'which can be influenced by its budget holder'. Controllable costs are generally assumed to be **variable** costs, and **directly attributable fixed costs**. These are fixed costs that can be allocated in full as a cost of the centre.

It is important to make managers responsible and accountable for costs they can control. Without accountability, managers do not have the incentive to control costs and manage their resources efficiently and effectively.

If the principle of controllability is applied, control reports would make managers responsible for the variable costs and directly attributable costs of the centre.

A common assumption in management accounting is that controllable costs consist of variable costs and directly attributable fixed costs. Uncontrollable costs are costs that cannot be influenced up or down by management action.

This assumption is not entirely correct, and it should be used with caution.

Some items treated as variable costs cannot be influenced or controlled in the short term. Direct labour costs are treated as a variable cost, but in reality, the direct labour work force is usually paid a fixed wage for a minimum number of working hours each week. Without making some employees redundant, and unless there is overtime working, the direct labour cost cannot be reduced or increased in the short term because it is really a fixed cost item.

An item that is **uncontrollable** for one manager could be controllable by another. In responsibility accounting, it is important to identify areas of responsibility. In the long term, all costs are controllable. At senior management level, control should be exercised over long-term costs as well as costs in the short term.

A useful distinction can be made between **committed** fixed costs, which are costs that are uncontrollable in the short term, but are controllable over the longer term; and **discretionary** fixed costs, which are costs treated as fixed cost items that can nevertheless be controlled in the short term, because spending is subject to management discretion.

Examples are advertising expenditure, and executive travel and subsistence costs.

Controllable and uncontrollable costs

A summarised report for the profit centres of an organisation might be:

	Centre A $	Centre B $	Centre C $	Total $
Revenue	300,000	260,000	420,000	980,000
Variable costs	170,000	100,000	240,000	510,000
Directly attributable costs	70,000	120,000	80,000	270,000
Controllable costs	**240,000**	**220,000**	**320,000**	**780,000**
Attributable gross profit	60,000	40,000	100,000	200,000
Other overhead costs				**(180,000)**
Net profit				20,000

A criticism of the controllability accounting principle is that managers are not encouraged to think about costs for which they are not responsible. In the example above, there are $180,000 of costs not attributable to any profit centre. These might be head office costs, for example, or marketing overheads.

- Within a system of responsibility accounting, there should be cost centre managers accountable for these costs.

- Even so, these overhead costs might be caused to some extent by the demands placed on head office administration or marketing services by the profit centre managers.

- When these costs are high, a further problem is that profit centre profits need to be large enough to cover the general non-allocated overhead costs.

An argument could therefore be made that profit centre managers should be made accountable for a share of overhead costs that are not under their control, and a share of these costs should be charged to each profit centre. Profit reporting would therefore be as follows:

	Centre A $	Centre B $	Centre C $	Total $
Revenue	300,000	260,000	420,000	980,000
Variable costs	170,000	100,000	240,000	510,000
Directly attributable costs	70,000	120,000	80,000	270,000
Controllable costs	**240,000**	**220,000**	**320,000**	**780,000**
Attributable gross profit	60,000	40,000	100,000	200,000
Other overhead costs	(50,000)	(50,000)	(80,000)	**(180,000)**
Net profit	10,000	(10,000)	20,000	20,000

5 Pros and cons

The advantages of this approach to responsibility accounting are:

- profit centre managers are made aware of the significance of other overhead costs

- profit centre managers are made aware that they need to earn a sufficient profit to cover a fair share of other overhead costs.

The disadvantages of this approach are that:

- profit centre managers are made accountable for a share of other overhead costs, but they can do nothing to control them

- the apportionment of other overhead costs between profit centres, like overhead apportionment generally, is usually a matter of judgement, lacking any economic or commercial justification.

Responsibility centres and internal markets (extract)

Bob Scarlett, Financial Management, April 2007

An objective must be set for an autonomous responsibility centre. Determining how far that objective has been achieved provides a performance measure for the centre. The system must be adapted to priorities and circumstances in each case. Accordingly, responsibility centres may be grouped under three main headings:

(1) **Cost centre (CC)**

This is a responsibility centre to which costs are attributed, but not earnings or capital.

CCs can be designed in two alternative ways: either (a) the CC is given a fixed quantity of inputs and be required to maximise outputs, or (b) a required level of outputs is specified for the CC which must be achieved with minimum inputs.

An example of (a) is a public relations department, which is given a fixed budget to spend and has to use this to achieve the best possible result. An example of (b) is a cleaning department, which is given certain areas to clean and has to do this at minimum cost. In both cases, the CC manager is allowed a degree of autonomy in making decisions on how the operation is run. But the system guides the manager to act in a manner which is consistent with the interest of the organisation.

However, the CC offers one particular weakness insofar as it relies on the measurement of financial spend to assess performance. There is no direct incentive for the manager to enhance the quality of output. Costs can always be contained by reducing quality. In the case of a CC, quality reduction is not identified by the use of financial performance metrics.

Many organisations treat their IT departments as cost centres. This often has unfortunate consequences.

The idea that IT is a cost centre and carries no profit or loss is dangerous and should be opposed wherever it is encountered, according to Simon Linsley, head of consultancy, IT and development at Philips. Will Hadfield, Computer Weekly, 30 May 2006

This CW article describes how IT system installation projects were usually completed on time and within budget at the electronics firm Philips. However, the manner in which system projects were implemented often gave rise to serious disruption at the operational level, causing stress to the staff of client departments and degraded customer service.

(2) Profit centres (PC)

This is a responsibility centre to which costs and revenues are attributed, but not capital.

In the case of a CC, the manager has autonomy as regards either (a) outputs or (b) inputs – but not both together. In the case of the PC, the manager has autonomy over both inputs and outputs. The objective of a PC is to maximise profit or achieve a profit target. The manager of the PC is allowed to make decisions concerning both the resources used and output (in terms of both quantity and price) achieved.

In the case of a PC, reliance on financial performance measures does not provide any incentive to lower quality. Lowering quality will impact on sales quantity and/or selling price, which will impact on profit. The PC may also induce other behaviour which is in the interests of an organisation. For example, unit costs within a CC may be minimised by use of long continuous production runs and this pattern of production may be favoured accordingly. But, it is a pattern of production which will result in high inventory holding and/or lowered response levels to individual customer requirements. These last features will adversely impact on profit and, therefore, a sub-optimum pattern of production is less likely to be induced within a PC.

An IT department within an organisation may be organised as a profit centre. Typically, this will involve invoicing client departments for its services and inviting competition from outside consultants for system installation projects.

IT directors should push for the IT function in their organisation to be treated as a profit centre rather than a cost to the business. This was the key message from Glenn Martin, managing director and chief technology officer at financial services firm Cazenove, speaking to the City IT financial services technology forum last week. Christian Annesley, Computer Weekly, 15 November 2005

Rather than forcing through system installations in a manner which minimises costs, IT managers are now incentivised to allow for the full operational requirements of client departments when organising projects.

The logic behind responsibility centres suggests that an organisation should be split into decoupled internal components with decision rights in each given to its own management, within certain parameters. Each component trades its services with the others on an arms length basis, giving rise to an 'internal market'.

This concept was applied widely in the British public sector in the 1990s. The BBC under Director General John Birt introduced an internal market amongst its different components – Technology, Production, News and so on. The development of an internal market has also been a feature of NHS reform, whereby different units within the NHS have the character of buyers and providers of services.

So much for the theory. Practical experience has introduced organisations to a concept known as 'failure of the internal market'. For example, the BBC Gramophone Library was rated as the greatest sound archive in the world and it was traditionally run as a cost centre. During the reforms of the 1990s, it became a profit centre and was required to charge user departments in the BBC for the issue of recordings.

Music that was previously provided free by the Library now came with a charge and it wasn't cheap. Which is why all the music shops in Oxford Street were busy with BBC researchers buying far cheaper commercial CDs. At the prestigious Radio 4 daytime current affairs programmes, The World at One and PM, staff were barred from using any material from the BBC's gramophone library because the cost was too high. Netribution, 'BBC axes Producer Choice', March 2006

The BBC's internal market was deeply unpopular and produced unintended effects in the way that managers behaved. It has been largely abandoned in recent years. The reality was that the BBC's Gramophone Library was a vital resource that had to be seen as a cost centre and nothing other than that.

Responsibility centres and internal markets have much to offer. But insensitivity in their use, or their use in inappropriate circumstances, can result in them doing more harm than good.

6 Behavioural aspects of budgeting

It is often accepted that **participation in the budget setting process** will improve motivation, which in turn will improve the quality of budget decisions and the efforts of individuals to achieve their budget targets.

In a divisionalised structure, there are two ways in which a budget can be set:

(1) From the top down (imposed budget), that is set without allowing the ultimate budget holder to have the opportunity to participate in the budgeting process, or

(2) From the bottom up (participatory budget), whereby budget holders (heads of departments, for example) have the opportunity to participate in setting their own budgets.

Imposed style

An imposed/top-down budget is **'a budget allowance which is set without permitting the ultimate budget holder to have the opportunity to participate in the budgeting process'**

CIMA Official Terminology

Advantages of imposed style

There are a number of reasons why it might be preferable for managers not to be involved in setting their own budgets:

(1) Involving managers in the setting of budgets is more time consuming than if senior managers simply impose the budgets.

(2) Managers may not have the skills or motivation to participate usefully in the budgeting process.

(3) Senior managers have a better overall view of the company and its resources and may be better-placed to create a budget which utilises those scarce resources to best effect.

(4) Senior managers also are aware of the longer term strategic objectives of the organisation and can prepare a budget which is in line with that strategy.

(5) Managers may build budgetary slack or bias into the budget in order to make the budget easy to achieve and themselves look good.

(6) Managers cannot use budgets to play games which disadvantage other budget holders.

(7) By having the budgets imposed by senior managers, i.e. someone outside the department, a more objective, fresher perspective may be gained.

(8) If the participation is only pseudo-participation and the budgets are frequently drastically changed by senior management, then this will cause dissatisfaction and the effect will be to demotivate staff.

[In the PEG November 2012, the Examiner notes that some candidates are 'incorrectly describing a top-down budget.']

Participative budgets

Participative/bottom up budgeting is **'a budgeting system in which all budget holders are given the opportunity to participate in setting their own budgets'**

CIMA Official Terminology

[In the PEG November 2012, the Examiner regrets that some candidates are 'failing to define or describe a participative budget'.]

Advantages of participative budgets

(1) The morale of the management is improved. Managers feel like their opinion is listened to, that their opinion is valuable.

(2) Managers are more likely to accept the plans contained within the budget and strive to achieve the targets if they had some say in setting the budget, rather than if the budget was imposed upon them. Failure to achieve the target that they themselves set is seen as a personal failure as well as an organisational failure.

(3) The lower level managers will have a more detailed knowledge of their particular part of the business than senior managers and thus will be able to produce more realistic budgets.

7 Behavioural aspects of budgetary control

Another very important aspect of budgetary control systems is its impact on the human beings who will operate and be judged by those systems.

It is only comparatively recently that the results of years of study of personal relationships in the workplace have percolated into the field of management accounting. It is now recognised that failure to consider the effect of control systems on the people affected could result in a lowering of morale and a reduction of motivation. Further, those people may be induced to do things that are not in the best interests of the organisation.

Specific behavioural issues encountered in budgeting include the following:

Motivation and co-operation

To be fully effective, any system of financial control must provide for motivation and incentive. If this requirement is not satisfied, managers will approach their responsibilities in a very cautious and conservative manner. It is often found that adverse variances attract investigation and censure but there is no incentive to achieve favourable variances. Failure to distinguish controllable from uncontrollable costs in budgetary control can alienate managers from the whole process.

Personal goals and ambitions are, in theory, strongly linked to organisational goals. These personal goals may include a desire for higher income and higher social standing. To simultaneously satisfy the goals of the organisation and the goals of the individual there must be 'goal congruence'. That is, the individual manager perceives that his or her own goals are achieved by his or her acting in a manner that allows the organisation to achieve its goals. The problem is that reliance on budgetary control systems does not always result in goal congruence.

The success of a budgetary control system depends on the people who operate and are affected by it. They must work within the system in an understanding and co-operative manner. This can only be achieved by individuals who have a total involvement at all stages in the budget process. However, it is often found that

(1) A budget is used simply as a pressure device. If the budget is perceived as 'a stick with which to beat people', then it will be sabotaged in all sorts of subtle ways, and

(2) The budgeting process and subsequent budgetary control exercises induce competition between individual departments and executives. Managers may be induced to do things in order to 'meet budget' that are not in the best interests of the business as a whole.

Failure of goal congruence

It has been seen that an essential element in budgetary control is performance evaluation. Actual results are compared with budget or standard in order to determine whether performance is good or bad. What is being evaluated is not just the business operation but the managers responsible for it. The purpose of budgetary control is to induce managers to behave in a manner that is to the best advantage of the organisation. Compliance with budget is enforced by a variety of negative and positive sanctions.

When adverse variances are reported for operations then this implies poor performance by the managers of the operations. If they are unable to correct or explain away the adverse variances, then they may suffer negative sanctions. They may forgo salary increases, or they may be demoted to a less prestigious post. Other more subtle negative sanctions are possible that anyone who has ever worked for a large organisation will be aware of.

Positive inducements may be offered to encourage managers to avoid adverse variances. A manager who meets budget may be granted a performance-related salary bonus, promotion, a new company car or use of the executive dining room.

Consequently, the manager has a considerable incentive to ensure that the department or operation he is responsible for achieves its budgeted level of performance. However, there are a variety of ways of doing this that might not be to the advantage of the organisation as a whole.

For example, the manager of a production line can cut costs and hence improve its reported performances by reducing quality controls. This may result in long-term problems concerning failure of products in service, loss of customer goodwill and rectification costs – but these are not the concern of the production line manager. This is a clear failure of goal congruence.

The control system is capable of distorting the process it is meant to serve – or 'the tail wags the dog'. The enforcement of a budgetary control system requires sensitivity if this is not to happen.

The budget as a pot of cash

In some environments managers may come to consider the budget as a sum of money that has to be spent. This arises particularly in service departments or public sector organisations, the performance of which is gauged mainly through comparison of actual and budget spending.

The manager of a local authority 'street cleaning' department may be given an annual budget of £120,000 to clean the streets. The manager knows that she will be punished if she spends more than £120,000 in the year. She also knows that if she spends less than £120,000 in the year then her budget will probably be reduced next year. Such a reduction will involve a personal loss of status in the organisation and will make her job more difficult in the next year.

In order to ensure that she does not overspend her annual budget in the current year the manager may spend at a rate of £9,000 per month for the first 11 months of the year. This can be achieved by reducing the frequency of street cleaning and using poor-quality materials. It allows a contingency fund to be accumulated in case of emergencies.

However, in the final month of the year the manager has to spend £21,000 if she wishes to ensure that her whole budget is fully used. She might achieve this by using extra labour and high-quality materials.

Does this behaviour make sense? Of course it does not. The whole pattern of behaviour is distorted by the control system. It means that local residents have a substandard service for 11 months of the year and money is wasted in the 12th month.

It is, however, a fact that suppliers to government departments and local councils often experience a surge in orders towards the end of the financial year. This surge is caused by managers placing orders at the last moment in order to ensure that their full budget for the year is committed.

Budget negotiation

Budgets are normally arrived at by a process of negotiation with the managers concerned. A budget may actually be initiated by departmental managers and then corrected as a result of negotiation with the budget officer.

Clearly, a manager has an incentive to negotiate a budget that is not difficult to achieve. This produces a phenomenon known as 'padding the budget' or 'budgetary slack'. A manager will exaggerate the costs required to achieve objectives. This has the following results:

(1) If the manager succeeds in padding his budget, then the whole control exercise is damaged. Comparison of actual with budget gives no meaningful measure of performance and the manager is able to include inefficiencies in his operation if he wishes.

(2) A successful manager becomes one who is a hard negotiator. The problem with this is that the negotiations in question are between colleagues and not with customers. 'Infighting' may become entrenched in the management process.

(3) A great deal of time and energy that could be directed to the actual management of the business is distracted by what are essentially administrative procedures.

These are all examples of a control system distorting the processes they are meant to serve.

Influence on accounting policies

Any management accountant who has been engaged in the preparation of financial control reports will be familiar with attempts by managers to influence the accounting policies that are used. For example, the apportionment of indirect costs between departments often contains subjective elements. Should security costs be apportioned on the basis of floor space or staff numbers?

The manner in which the indirect costs are apportioned can have a considerable impact on how the performance of individual departments is perceived. This position creates the scope and incentive for managers to argue over accounting policies.

If a manager perceives that her department's performance is falling below budget, then she may sift through the costs charged to her department and demand that some be reclassified and charged elsewhere. The time and energy that goes into this kind of exercise has to be diverted from that available for the regular management of the business.

Budget constrained management styles

When the performance of a manager is assessed by his ability to meet budget, then he is likely to adopt a conservative approach to new business opportunities that appear. The immediate impact of new business ventures is likely to be a rise in capital and operating costs – with an adverse impact on current period profit. The benefits of such ventures may only be felt in the long term. Hence, when a new opportunity appears, the manager evaluating it may only perceive that its acceptance will result in below-budget performance in the current period – and turn it down on this ground alone. Another consideration is that reliance on budgetary control is an approach to management that involves sitting in an office and reading financial reports. Such an approach (in conjunction with features such as executive dining rooms) may result in an unsatisfactory corporate culture based on hierarchies and social divisions. Large organisations that rely heavily on budgetary control systems often take on an 'ossified' character.

Yet another consideration is that a reliance on budgetary planning may induce managers to favour projects and developments that are most amenable to the construction of budgets. Projects that involve little uncertainty and few unknowns are easy to incorporate in budgets and hence managers may be more inclined to adopt such projects than the alternatives. Projects that involve significant uncertainties may be attractive if they incorporate some combination of high expected returns and low cost interim exit routes – but a budget constrained manager may be disinclined to adopt such projects simply because they are difficult to incorporate in budgets. Some writers suggest that the budgetary approach may be particularly inappropriate in a dynamic and turbulent business environment.

The general conclusion concerning this and previous points is that good budgetary control can offer certain benefits. However, when budgetary control is enforced in a rigid or insensitive manner it may end up doing more harm than good.

Budgets and motivation

Much of the early academic work on budgets concerned the extent to which the 'tightness' or looseness' of a budget acted as an incentive or disincentive to management effort. This was the issue of 'budget stretch'. Seminal works in this general area included studies by A.C. Stedry (see his 1960 text 'Budget Control and Cost Behaviour') and G.H. Hofstede (see his 1968 text 'The Game of Budget Control').

The main thrust of the findings that emerged from these studies was:

(1) Loose budgets (i.e. ones easily attainable) are poor motivators

(2) As budgets are tightened, up to a certain point they become more motivational

(3) Beyond that point, a very tight budget ceases to be motivational.

The role of budget participation and the manner in which aspirations and objectives are stated was also explored in certain studies. It was suggested that the participation of managers in budget setting was a motivational factor – but see earlier discussion concerning budget padding and negotiation.

8 Practice Questions

Objective Test Question 1: Non-controllable costs

Bitluns is a holiday company, that operates more than 100 all-inclusive resorts. The performance of the manager of each resort is evaluated using financial measures.

Many of the resort managers are not very happy, because their profit reports, that they are assessed on, include a share of head office costs and other costs that they cannot control.

Use the words and phrases in the table provided below to complete the following paragraphs:

controllable	costs	unfair
control	performance	profit
uncontrollable	fair	responsibility

Uncontrollable costs may be included in the performance report of a _____ centre so that the report shows the final_____ of that centre. This is sometimes done to make the manager aware of the other _____ involved in running the business.

However, from a performance measurement perspective, if it is the _____ of the manager that is being measured, then it is _____ to measure their performance on results that include items that are beyond their _____.

The solution to this is to include the _____ items in a separate section of the report, and to measure the manager's performance based only on the _____ items.

Data Set Question: Participation

A school is preparing its budget for 2015. In previous years, the Headmaster has prepared the school budget without the participation of senior staff (heads of departments), and presented it to the Board of Governors for approval.

In 2013, the Board of Governors criticised the Headmaster over the lack of participation of his senior staff in the preparation of the 2014 budget, and requested that for the 2015 budget, the senior staff were to be involved.

Task: Answer 'TRUE' or 'FALSE' to the following:

Involvement would encourage heads of department to be motivated to achieve their targets, because they would take ownership of their budget.

The participative process is not time consuming, so there is no risk of the availability of the budget for 2015 being delayed.

Heads of departments may agree among themselves to include unnecessary expenditure (budgetary slack) so that it is easier for them to achieve the cost targets they have set.

Even with involvement, heads of departments would not feel that they are being respected for the value that their experience brings to the running of the school.

Case style question

PRE-SEEN MATERIAL

You have recently been appointed as a company's Assistant Management Accountant. The company is large and runs a well-developed cost centre system. On joining the company, you got introduced to its different types of divisions:

- Those divisions, such as the IT support department, that incurs costs but have no revenue streams

- Those divisions where the manager has no authority to alter the level of investment in the division, but is responsible for both costs and revenues

- Those divisions in which the manager does have the authority to invest in new assets or dispose of existing ones.

You have just received the following email:

From: Fiona Dalton, Finance Director
Sent: 03 June, 10.23 a.m.
To: Senior Management Accountant
Subject: Responsibility Centres

I am considering the introduction of profit centres throughout the organisation, where appropriate – but I need technical advice and assistance for the proposed scheme.

Please prepare a report for me to present to the Board on Monday. I would be grateful if you would:

1. describe the main characteristics and objectives of profit centres and investment centres;
2. explain what conditions are necessary for the successful introduction of such centres;
3. describe the main behavioural and control consequences which may arise if such centres are introduced.

Test your understanding answers

Objective Test Question 1: Non-controllable costs

Uncontrollable costs may be included in the performance report of a **responsibility** centre so that the report shows the final **profit** of that centre. This is sometimes done to make the manager aware of the other **costs** involved in running the business.

However, from a performance measurement perspective, if it is the **performance** of the manager that is being measured, then it is **unfair** to measure their performance on results that include items that are beyond their **control**.

The solution to this is to include the **uncontrollable** items in a separate section of the report, and to measure the manager's performance based only on the **controllable** items.

Data Set Question: Participation

Involvement would encourage heads of department to be motivated to achieve their targets, because they would take ownership of it at their budget.	**TRUE**
The participative process is not time consuming, so there is no risk of the availability of the budget for 2015 being delayed.	**FALSE**
Heads of departments may agree among themselves to include unnecessary expenditure (budgetary slack) so that it is easier for them to achieve the cost targets they have set.	**TRUE**
Heads of departments would not feel that they are being respected for the value that their experience brings to the running of the school.	**FALSE**

REPORT

To: Fiona Dalton, Finance Director

From: Assistant Management Accountant

Subject: Responsibility centres

Date: XX-May

Introduction

Please find a report that briefly explains the concepts linked with implementing profit centres and/or investment centres throughout an organisation.

(i) **Main characteristics and objectives of profit centres and investment centres**

The CIMA definition of a profit centre is 'a segment of the business entity by which both revenues are received and expenditure are caused or controlled, such revenues and expenditure being used to evaluate segmental performance. This may also be called a business centre, business unit or strategic business unit, depending upon the concept of management responsibility prevailing in the entity concerned.

An investment centre is defined as 'a profit centre in which inputs are measured in terms of expenses and outputs in terms of revenues, and in which assets are also measured, the excess of revenue over expenditure then being related to assets.'

In our case, the conversion of cost centres into profit and investment centres will have necessitated the delegation of responsibility for investment decisions. The objective of profit and investment centres will be to earn as high profits as possible either in absolute terms or, in some way, relative to the level of investment.

The objective behind setting up these centres (decentralising or divisionalising) is to improve the overall profitability of the large organisation. It is hoped that this is achieved, since divisional managers will be motivated to perform well.

[Tutorial note: you would also have got credit for mentioning the reasons behind a decision to decentralise: size, specialisation, geographical, fiscal, etc.]

(ii) Conditions necessary for the successful introduction of profit centres and investment centres

Successful introduction is likely to be achieved if those managers responsible for cost centres currently can be encouraged to propose the idea themselves rather than have it imposed on them by senior executives. Taking the process one stage further, it is likely to be a success if:

- The activities of the cost centres are dissimilar
- The cost centres are more or less independent from each other
- It is possible to control the new profit and investment centres so that a centre cannot adversely affect the overall profit of the organisation by a decision aimed to increase its own profit.

In practice, these three conditions are unlikely to hold.

Once the new structure is introduced, policies must be adopted which achieve the three-fold aims of:

- Motivation
- Independence
- Goal congruence.

(iii) Behavioural and control consequences

The obvious consequence of the system proposed will be a greater need to delegate decisions and to control those making those decisions. Whereas formerly senior management made investment decisions these are now to be passed down to management committees of investment centres. Senior management may be reluctant to let loose the reins, while middle management may not be adequately prepared to make the decisions.

A major problem will be the need to achieve goal congruence. The new divisions will aim to maximise their own individual profitability; this has to be achieved without adversely affecting the overall performance of the organisation. This can only be achieved by central monitoring of divisional decisions with the consequent loss of divisional independence, and possibly a reduction in the motivation of divisional managers.

New performance measures will have to be introduced. It is important that managers feel that they can make decisions which allow them to affect the profit of their divisions. In circumstances such as this, it is often the case that one former cost centre's performance depends purely on the performance of those other divisions that they serve To this end the transfer pricing policy must be fair, and they must have a full say in investment decisions.

One potential problem is that decisions may be made that present a healthy picture of a division, although decisions are taken which adversely affect long-term profitability. Managers may try to 'fiddle the system', for example by cutting down on investment. Controls over items such as training and maintenance may have to be introduced.

Motivation is likely to be enhanced if good performance is rewarded in some way. However, such bonus schemes will exacerbate the dangers outlined above and also should not be an excuse for providing inadequate basic remuneration.

Conclusion

I hope that the above report clarifies the basic concepts linked with responsibility accounting and I look forward to providing more assistance and technical advice on the proposed scheme.

Signed: Assistant Management Accountant

6

Performance Measures and Budgetary Control

Chapter learning objectives

Syllabus Link

Lead B1: Discuss decision making in responsibility centres

Component B2a): Prepare reports for the evaluation of projected and actual performance

- Key metrics for the assessment of financial consequences including profitability, liquidity and asset turnover ratios, return on investment, residual income and economic value.

- Analysis of reporting by dimension (e.g. segment, product, channel.)

1 Chapter summary

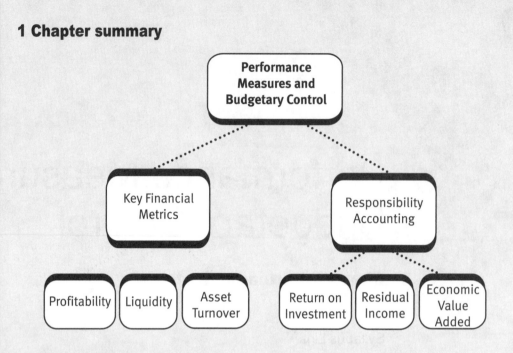

2 Knowledge brought forward

You will need to be comfortable with some basic financial analysis concepts covered in previous papers. We will use this knowledge in P2 with more advanced ratios, so make sure you are comfortable with the assumed knowledge, that should have been brought forward as a base.

3 Key metrics in the budget

An organisation should have certain targets for achievement. Targets can be expressed in terms of key metrics. The term 'metric' is now in common use within the context of measurement of performance. It is a basis for analysing performance (both budgeted and actual).

A budget should not be approved by senior management unless budgeted performance is satisfactory, as measured by the key metrics. Actual performance should then be assessed in comparison with the targets. The term 'key performance indicators' might be used.

Key areas of financial performance are:

- profitability
- liquidity
- asset turnover.

Profitability

A key metric for profitability might be the **profit/sales ratio** (profit margin), or the contribution/sales ratio (contribution margin).

Senior management might set a target for a minimum profit/sales ratio for the budget period, and refuse to authorise a budget unless this minimum target is met in the plan.

Three key profitability indicators recently examined are the Return on Capital Employed (ROCE) the asset turnover and the profit/sales percentage. These can be explained by the use of a diagram and a simply worked example.

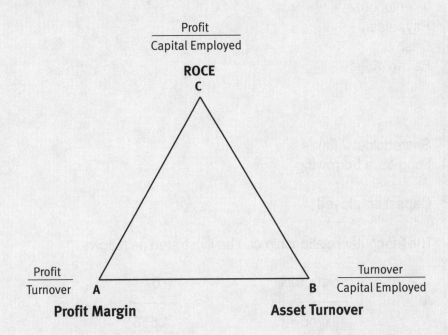

There is a direct relationship between the three figures; All figures are used twice, meaning $A \times B = C$

$$\frac{\text{Profit}}{\text{Turnover}} \times \frac{\text{Turnover}}{\text{Capital employed}} = \frac{\text{Profit}}{\text{Capital employed}}$$

Profit margin   ×   Asset turnover   =   ROCE

Capital employed = equity + long-term finance

Triangulation [DuPont model of measurement]

Extracts from the accounts of The Beta Company read as follows:

The Beta Company

Income Statement extracts $000

Sales/Revenue	1,556
Net profit	**67**

Statement of Financial Position extracts $000

Non-current assets	1,380
Inventories	241
Payables	201
Cash	–
Receivables	(301)
	1,521
Shareholders' funds	1,021
Long-term borrowing	500
Capital employed	**1,521**

The triangular relationship can be illustrated as follows:

$$A \quad \frac{\text{Net profit}}{\text{Turnover}} = \frac{67}{1,556} = 4.306\%$$

$$B \quad \frac{\text{Turnover}}{\text{Capital employed}} = \frac{1,556}{1,521} = 1.023 \text{ times}$$

$$C \quad \frac{\text{Net profit}}{\text{Capital employed}} = \frac{67}{1,521} = 4.405\%$$

[In the PEG November 2011, the Examiner notes that 'most candidates were not aware that the three ratios/percentages being requested were interlinked and the figures triangulated. Common errors included using different capital employed and profit figures in each ratio].

Liquidity

Liquidity means having cash, or ready access to cash. Liquid assets are therefore cash and short-term investments that can be readily sold if the need arises. In addition, liquidity is improved by unused bank borrowing facilities.

Liquidity is improved through efficient cash management, and an important element of good cash management is control over inventory, trade receivables and trade payables.

A key metric for liquidity might therefore be the **current ratio** (which is the ratio of current assets to current liabilities), or the **quick ratio** or acid test ratio (which is the ratio of current assets excluding inventories to current liabilities).

$$\text{Current ratio} = \frac{\text{Current assets}}{\text{Current liabilities}}$$

$$\text{Quick ratio (acid test)} = \frac{\text{Current assets} - \text{inventory}}{\text{Current liabilities}}$$

A low liquidity ratio could indicate **poor liquidity and a risk of cash flow difficulties**. The appropriate minimum value for a liquidity ratio varies from one industry to another, because the characteristics of cash flows vary between different industries. As a broad rule, however, a current ratio below 2.0 times and a quick ratio below 1.0 times might be considered low.

Within a budgeting system, senior management might set a target for liquidity, in the form of a maximum and minimum acceptable current ratio and/or quick ratio. A current ratio or quick ratio that declines from one year to the next could indicate deteriorating liquidity and greater risk.

On the other hand, a business can have **excessive liquidity, with too much capital tied up in working capital.** The current ratio and quick ratio should therefore not be expected to rise above a maximum acceptable level.

We have seen also that an important element of good cash management is control over the various parts of working capital, in particular inventory, trade receivables and trade payables. We have seen also that an important element of good cash management is control over the various parts of working capital, in particular inventory, trade receivables and trade payables.

4 Investment centres and performance measures

Return on Investment (ROI/ROCE)

$$\text{ROI/ROCE} = \frac{\text{Divisional earnings before interest and tax}}{\text{Capital employed}} \times 100\%$$

Profit, or 'earnings', can be measured in relation to the financial resources they use, the 'Capital Employed'. ROCE is common at the overall corporate level, whereas ROI is more commonly used for investment appraisal and for divisional performance.

Advantages

(1) Widely used and accepted

(2) As a relative measure it enables comparisons to be made with divisions or companies of different sizes

(3) It can be broken down into secondary ratios for more detailed analysis.

[In the PEG March 2011, the Examiner regrets that some candidates do not know that 'pre-tax profit %' and 'asset turnover' are secondary ratios to the ROCE].

Disadvantages

(1) May lead to dysfunctional decision making, e.g. a division with a current ROCE of 30% would not wish to accept a project offering an ROCE of 25%, as this would reduce its current figure.

(2) Different accounting policies can confuse comparisons

(3) ROCE increases with age of asset if NBVs are used, thus giving managers an incentive to hang on to possibly inefficient, obsolete machines.

[From the PEG November 2010: Candidates were asked to calculate the ROI for the last three years and discuss the performance of the division using the data provided; a good answer would have related to the scenario, whereas a poor answer would have provided a generic explanation of performance measures.

It is also patently obvious that many candidates do not understand that area of the syllabus and had not included it in their revision programme. (...) The presentation of figures for parts (b) and (c) was particularly poor, with markers not being able to award marks on many occasions due to figures being set down at random, and figures appearing with no explanation and no workings to support them.]

5 Residual income

Residual income is profit less an imputed interest charge for invested capital.

> **Residual income RI = Profit – (Capital Employed × Cost of capital)**

The imputed interest charge is the amount of capital employed times the cost of capital.

Advantages

(1) It reduces ROCE's problem of rejecting projects with a ROCE in excess of the company's target, but lower than the division's current ROCE.

(2) The cost of financing a division is brought home to divisional managers.

Disadvantages

(1) Does not facilitate comparisons between divisions.

(2) Does not relate the size of a division's profit to the assets employed in order to obtain that profit.

Residual Income vs. ROI

An investment centre has capital employed of $800,000, and made profits before interest of $160,000. The notional cost of capital is 12%. An opportunity has arisen to invest in a new project costing $100,000. The project would have a four-year life, and would make cash profits of $40,000 each year.

It is assumed that depreciation is charged on a straight line basis.

Required:

(a) What would be the average ROI with and without the investment? Would the investment centre manager wish to undertake the investment if performance is judged on ROI in Year 1?

(b) What would be the average annual residual income with and without the investment? Would the investment centre manager wish to undertake the investment if performance is judged on residual income in Year 1?

To calculate ROI and residual income, use the value for capital employed as at the start of Year 1.

Solution:

(a) It is assumed that depreciation is charged on a straight line basis at $25,000 each year, so that the increase in annual profit with the investment will be $15,000 ($40,000 – $25,000).

	Without the investment	With the investment
Profit	$160,000	$175,000
Capital employed	$800,000	$900,000
ROI	20%	19.4%

ROI would be lower; therefore the centre manager will not want to make the investment.

(b) Residual income

	Without the investment	With the investment
Profit	$160,000	$175,000
Notional interest	($800,000 × 12%) $96,000	($900,000 × 12%) $108,000
Residual income	$64,000	$67,000

The investment centre manager will want to undertake the investment because it will increase residual income. This is because the accounting return on the new investment is 15% in year 1 ($15,000/$100,000), which is higher than the notional cost of interest.

6 Economic value added (EVA®)

Economic value added (EVA) is a measure of performance similar to residual income, except the profit figure used is the ECONOMIC profit and the capital employed figure used is the ECONOMIC capital employed. It is argued that the profit and capital employed figures quoted in the financial statements do not give the true picture and that the accounting figures need to be adjusted to show the true underlying performance.

The basic concept of EVA is that the performance of a company as a whole, or of investment centres within a company, should be measured in terms of the value that has been added to the business during the period. It is a measure of performance that is directly linked to the creation of shareholder wealth.

The measurement of EVA is conceptually simple. In order to add to its economic value, a business must make an economic profit in excess of the cost of the capital that has been invested to earn that profit.

EVA Summary:

(1)	**PAT is adjusted to give the Net Operating Profit after tax (NOPAT)**	**X**
	then	
(2)	**Deduct the economic value of the capital employed x cost of capital**	**(X)**
		X

In more detail:

(1)	**NOPAT is calculated from PAT**	**X**
	Add back items that are non cash, such as:	
	Accounting depreciation	Note 1 XX
	Provision for doubtful debts	Note 2 XX
	Non cash expenses	Note 3 XX
	Interest paid net of tax	Note 4 XX
	Add back items that add value, such as:	
	Goodwill amortised	Note 5 XX
	Development costs	Note 6 XX
	Operating leases	Note 7 XX
	Take off:	
	Economic depreciation	Note 8 (X)
	Any impairment in the value of goodwill	
	= NOPAT in cash flow terms	XX

(2) Deduct the charge for the cost of capital

Capital employed
Add adjustments to allow for the net replacement cost of
tangible non current assets
= Capital invested

(3) Multiply capital invested by the cost of capital x%
= Charge for the cost of capital   (XX)

= EVA   **X**

More on EVA

Note 1 – Accounting depreciation: We add this back to PAT, because EVA is calculated after profits have been charged with economic depreciation (not accounting depreciation)

Note 2 – Provision for doubtful debts: Where a company had made a provision for doubtful debts, this should be reversed. Any adjustment in the income statement for an increase or decrease in the provision for doubtful debts should be reversed.

Note 3 – Non cash expenses: These were charged to profit, but must be added back because we want NOPAT in cash flow terms. Examples of non-cash expenses include depreciation and capitalised development costs .

Note 4 – Interest paid net of tax: if tax is at 35%, take interest payments and multiply by 0.65.

Adding this back results in earnings that would have been reported had all the companies capital requirements been financed with ordinary shares. A charge for interest and the tax effect of actual gearing are incorporated into the weighted average cost of capital (so if we leave the interest charge within the NOPAT number it will be double counted). It is the **net** interest i.e. interest after tax that is added back to reported profit because interest will already have been allowed as an expense in the computation of the taxation liability.

Note 5 – Goodwill: Goodwill is a measure of the price paid for a business in excess of the current cost of the net separable assets of the business. Payments in respect of goodwill may be viewed as adding value to the company. Therefore any amounts in respect of goodwill amortisation appearing in the income statement are added back to reported profit since they represent part of the intangible asset value of the business.

Note 6 – Development costs: Spending by the company on development costs should not be charged in full against profit in which the expenditure occurs. Instead, it should be capitalised because it has added value to the economic value of capital employed. The adjustment can be made by:

- Increasing NOPAT by the net increase in capitalised development costs, and

- Increasing the economic value of capital employed by the same amount.

Note 7 – Leases

All leases should be capitalised. Finance leases will have already been capitalised but operating leases should be capitalised too. The economic value of the capital employed increased to include the current value of the operating lease. The capitalised cost should then be amortised. The value of NOPAT should be increased by the operating lease charge and reduce by the amortisation charge. The net effect to increase NOPAT by the implied interest cost of the operating lease.

Note 8 – Economic depreciation

Considered to be a measure of the economic use of assets during a year. Involves a process of valuation. It is the period by period change in the market value of the asset.

Advantages of EVA

The advantages of EVA are as follows.

- It is a performance measure that attempts to put a figure to the increase (or decrease) that should have arisen during a period from the operations of a company or individual divisions within a company.

- Like accounting return and residual income, it can be measured for each financial reporting period.

- It is easily understood by non-accountants.

- It is based on economic profit and economic values of assets, not accounting profits and asset values.

Measuring and using EVA

The principle underlying EVA can be stated as follows.

- The objective of a company is to maximise shareholder wealth.

- The value of a company depends on the extent to which shareholders expect future economic profits to exceed the cost of the capital invested.

- A share price therefore depends on expectations of EVA.

- Current performance (EVA) is reflected in the current share price, so in order to increase the share price a company must achieve a sustained increase in EVA.

Peter Drucker has written: 'Until a business returns a profit that is greater than its cost of capital, it operates at a loss. Never mind that it pays taxes as if it had a genuine profit. The enterprise still returns less to the economy than it devours in resources…. Until then, it does not create wealth, it destroys it.'

Measuring EVA

The difficulties in applying EVA in practice arise from the problem of establishing the economic profit in a period, and the economic value of capital employed. These values are estimated by making adjustments to accounting profits and accounting capital employed.

- Accounting profits are based on the accruals concept of accounting, whereas NOPAT for EVA is based on cash flow profits. Adjustments have to be made to convert from an accruals basis to a cash flow basis.

- **Depreciation** of non-current assets is a charge in calculating EVA as well as accounting profit. Economic depreciation is the fall in the economic value of an asset during the period.

  - It might be assumed that the accounting charge for depreciation is a good approximation of the economic cost of depreciation, in which case no adjustment to accounting profit is necessary.

  - Alternatively, it might be assumed that the economic value of the assets are their net replacement cost, in which case economic depreciation will be based on replacement cost. An adjustment to accounting profit should then be made for the amount by which economic depreciation exceeds the accounting charge for depreciation.

- Similarly, an adjustment might be necessary for intangible non-current assets such as goodwill.

- Where a company had made a provision for doubtful debts, this should be reversed. Any adjustment in the income for an increase or decrease in the provision for doubtful debts should be reversed, and NOPAT increased or reduced accordingly.

- Spending by the company on development costs should not be charged in full against profit in the year the expenditure occurs. Instead, it should be capitalised because it has added to the economic value of capital employed, and it should then be amortised over an appropriate number of years. In practice, the adjustment can be made by:

  - increasing NOPAT by the net increase in capitalised development costs, and

  - increasing the economic value of capital employed by the same amount.

- All leases should be capitalised. Finance leases will have been capitalised already, but operating leases should be capitalised too, and the economic value of capital employed increased to include the current value of operating leases. Stern Stewart amortise this capitalised cost over five years. In adjusting from accounting profit to NOPAT, the value of NOPAT should be increased by the operating lease rental charge, and reduced by the amount of the amortisation charge. (The net effect is to increase NOPAT by the implied interest cost of the operating lease.)

Using EVA

Economic value added can be used to:

- set targets for performance for investment centres (divisions) and the company as a whole

- measure actual performance

- plan and make decisions on the basis of how the decision will affect EVA.

When EVA is used to measure performance, Stern Stewart have recommended that divisional managers should be:

- given training to understand the principles of EVA. Stern Stewart have found than non-accountants find the concept of EVA fairly easy to understand, and they see the link between EVA and changes in shareholder value

- informed about the interest cost that will be applied for the capital charge

- taught how to calculate EVA for decision-making purposes

- given a pay incentive based on a bonus for achieving or exceeding a target EVA.

- EVA can also be used for control purposes, by encouraging managers to:
    - identify products and services that provide the greatest EVA, and concentrate resources on those

    - identify customers who provide the greatest EVA, and give priority to serving them

    - identify and eliminate activities that do not add to EVA

    - identify capital that is not providing a sufficient return to cover its capital cost (such as excess equipment) and seek to reduce the capital investment.

7 Practice Questions

Objective Test Question 1: ROCE and decision making

Nielsen Ltd has 2 divisions with the following information:

	Division A	Division B
	$	$
Profit	90,000	10,000
Capital employed	300,000	100,000
ROCE	30%	10%

Division A has been offered a project costing $100,000 and giving returns of $20,000. Division B has been offered a project costing $100,000 and giving returns of $12,000. The company's cost of capital is 15%. Divisional performance is judged on ROCE and the ROCE-related bonus is sufficiently high to influence the managers' behaviour.

Which of the following statements are TRUE? Select ALL that apply.

- Both divisional managers should accept the project offered to them.

- If he/she acts in the best interests of their own division, only the manager of Division A will want to accept the project offered to him/her.

- If he/she acts in the best interests of their own division, only the manager of Division B will want to accept the project offered to him/her.

- ROCE is a good decision-making method and in this case, will guarantee that the correct decision will be made by both divisional managers.

- If managers want to act in the best interests of the business as a whole, only the manager of Division A should accept the project offered to him/her.

Objective Test Question 2: Controllable RI

The manager of a trading division has complete autonomy regarding the purchase and use of non-current assets. The division operates its own credit control policy in respect of customers but the group operates a central purchasing function through which the division places all orders with suppliers and invoices are paid by head office.

Inventories of goods for sale are kept in central stores, from which local divisions call off requirements for local sales on a monthly basis into a local inventory.

Divisional performance is assessed on the basis of controllable Residual Income. The company requires a rate of return of 'R'.

Using the following symbols:

Divisional non-current assets	N
Apportioned net book value of central stores	S
Divisional working capital	
Receivables	D
Local Inventory	I
Bank	B
Payables	(P)
	___
	W
	___
Divisional net assets	T
	___
Divisional contribution	C
Controllable fixed costs	(F)
Head Office charges	(H)
	___
Divisional net income	G
	___

Which ONE of the following formulae calculates the division's **controllable residual income?**

(i) $[C - F] - [(N + D + B) \times R]$

(ii) $[C - F] - [(N + D + I + B) \times R]$

(iii) $C - [(N + D) \times R]$

(iv) $G - (T \times R)$

A   (i) only

B   (ii) only

C   (iii) only

D   (i) and (iv) only

Objective Test Question 3: EVA

A division has a reported annual profit of $27m. This was after charging $6m for the development and launch costs of a new product which is expected to have a life of 3 years.

The division has a risk adjusted cost of capital of 10% per annum, but it has a large bank loan, which incurs annual interest charges of 8%.

The net book value of the division's net assets is $85m. The replacement cost of the assets is estimated to be $96m.

Ignore the effects of taxation. The Division's EVA is:

$m [   ]

Data Set Question: Key metrics and depreciation

Tweedle Ltd has two divisions, Division Dee and Division Dum. Tweedle founded Dee on 1 January 2013. Dum was an independent business that had been formed some years before. Tweedle purchased Dum as a going concern in August 2013. Tweedle's directors are keen to benchmark the two divisions, because they produce similar products.

Details for the two companies for the year ended 31 December 2013 are as follows (in $000):

	Dee	Dum
Revenue	1,650	1,000
Cost of sales:		
Variable production costs	400	400
Fixed production costs (including depreciation, see note 2)	800	390
	1,200	790
GROSS PROFIT	**450**	**210**
Administration costs (fixed)	120	80
OPERATING PROFIT	**330**	**130**
Non-current assets:		
Cost	2,500	2,000
Depreciation	500	1,367
	2,000	633
Net current assets	200	150
Capital employed	2,200	783

Performance measures

	Dee	Dum
Return on Capital Employed (ROCE)	15.0%	16.6%
Operating profit margin	20.0%	13.0%
Asset turnover	0.8	1.3

Notes

(1) Dee and Dum use different depreciation policies. Dee depreciates its non-current assets using straight-line depreciation, at the rate of 20% of cost with no residual value. Dum uses the reducing balance method of depreciation at the rate of 25% per annum.

(2) Included in the fixed element of cost of sales for the year ended 31 December 2013 is depreciation of $500,000 for Dee and $200,000 for Dum.

(3) Dee's assets are newer.

Tweedle's management team in charge of Dee have argued that it is unfair to compare them with Dum, because the two entities have different depreciation policies and Dum's assets are newer.

The parent company directors have agreed to restate Dee's results so that the assets are assumed to be the same age as Dum's, and the depreciation policy is the same.

After aligning Dee's operating profits and capital employed, as well as its performance measures, restate, for Dee:

Its operating profit, in $.

Its capital employed, in $.

Its (revised) ROCE, in %.

Its (revised) operating profit margin, in %.

Its (revised) asset turnover.

Integration Style Question: Liquidity, profitability

PRE-SEEN MATERIAL

You work as the Senior Management Accountant in Nordic plc. Its chairman, Lars Johansson, has recently been quoted in the press as saying:

'Nordic is doing so well. We have always been a profitable company. However, we are following a high growth strategy based on low prices, and this has put pressure on cash flows. We have a number of new clients signed up, and we believe the future is bright.'

You have also been looking at the first draft budget from the budget planners. Compared with the previous budget period, operating costs are expected to be higher. The initial draft budget shows a current ratio of 1.10 at the end of the budget period, and a contribution to sales ratio for the year of 51%.

You have just received the following email:

> **From:** Lars Johansson, Financial Director
> **Sent:** 03 June, 10.23 a.m.
> **To:** Senior Management Accountant
> **Subject:** Profitability and Liquidity
>
> As you know, we have always set a target minimum current ratio of 1.25 times as a liquidity performance metric, and a minimum contribution/sales ratio target of 55% as a profitability performance metric.
>
> So this draft budget really won't do!!! Why are our liquidity and profitability indicators so low?
>
> Please draft me a report I can pass on to the Budget Planners, that explains the situation, and suggests steps they should now consider to improve the budget!
>
> Thanks
> Lars

Test your understanding answers

Objective Test Question 1: ROCE and decision making

- If he/she acts in the best interests of their own division, only the manager of Division B will want to accept the project offered to him/her.

- If managers want to act in the best interests of the business as a whole, only the manager of Division A should accept the project offered to him/her.

Workings:

	Division A	Division B
	$000	$000
Old ROCE		
Profit	90	10
	———	———
Capital employed	300	100
Old ROCE	30%	10%
New ROCE	90 + 20	10 + 12
Profit	———	———
	300 + 100	100 + 100
New ROCE	27.5%	11%
Will manager want to accept project?	No	Yes

The manager of division A will not want to accept the project as it lowers the divisional ROCE from 30% to 27.5%. The manager of division B will like the new project as it will increase their ROCE from 10% to 11%. Although the 11% is bad, it is better than before.

Looking at the whole situation from the group point of view, we are in the ridiculous position that the group has been offered 2 projects, both costing $100,000. One project gives a profit of $20,000 and the other $12,000. Left to their own devices then the managers would end up accepting the project giving only $12,000. This is because ROCE is a defective decision making method and does not guarantee that the correct decision will be made.

There are a number of different ways of making the correct decision. The simplest way is to calculate the ROCE of the project itself.

ROCE of project

Profit	20	12
	———	———
Capital employed	100	100
Old ROCE	20%	12%
Should manager accept project?	Yes	No

Now the correct decision has been made. Division A will accept the project giving a return of 20% as it the cost of capital is only 15%, but division B will reject its project as it only gives a return of 12%.

Objective Test Question 2: Controllable RI

Answer B (ii) only

Objective Test Question 3: EVA

Calculation of NOPAT

	$m
Accounting operating profit	27
Add back development and launch costs	6
Less one year's amortisation of development and launch costs	(2)
	——
	31
	——

Calculation of value of capital employed

	$m
Replacement cost of net assets	96
Add back increase in capitalised launch and development costs	4
	——
	100
	——

Calculation of EVA

The correct figure to use for calculating the capital charge is the cost of capital, i.e. the 10%. The 8% is a distracter.

	$m
NOPAT	31
Capital charge (10% × $100m)	10
	——
EVA	21
	——

Data Set Question: Key metrics and depreciation

Its operating profit, in $.	$566,000
Its capital employed, in $.	$991,000
Its revised ROCE, in %.	57.15%
Its revised operating profit margin, in %.	34.32%
Its revised asset turnover.	1.66

Approach:

First, we have to recalculate Dee's operating profit if the depreciation charge contained in the fixed production costs had been calculated using a reducing balance method, which is the method used by Dum.

At the moment, depreciation for Dee is $500,000 using straight line depreciation at 20%. This means $500,000 depreciation charge every year for 5 years, and the assets were originally $2.5 m = the assets in Dee are only 1 year old.

Calculating the age of assets in Dum:

In Dum, accumulated depreciation is $1,367,000. This represents 4 years worth of depreciation.(W1), and Dum's assets are therefore 4 years old.

We then need to 'pretend' that Dee's assets are also 4 years old in order to align their age with that of Dum's assets. At the moment, depreciation of $500,000 is included in the fixed element of the cost of sales.

What would Dee's depreciation charge for the year be if we used a reducing balance method of depreciation at the rate of 25% per annum?

	Depreciation charge for the year @ 25%	NBV	Accumulated depreciation
Year 1	625	1,875	625
Year 2	469	1,406	1,094
Year 3	352	1,055	1,445
Year 4	**264**	791	1,709

Dee's depreciation charge for the year be if we used a reducing balance method of depreciation at the rate of 25% per annum would be **$264,000**. At the moment, the depreciation charge amounts to $500,000. The difference of $236,000 comes to inflate the operating profit for Dee, which becomes $330,000 + $236,000 = $566,000.

The divisional Fixed Assets will also change their value. Instead of an accumulated depreciation charge of $500,000, we now have an accumulated depreciation of $1,709,000. Therefore, the value of fixed assets becomes $791,000 and not $2m as per the question.

This represents a reduction in fixed assets value of $1,209,000, and capital employed becomes $991,000.

Therefore, ROCE = ($566,000/$991,000) = 57.15%

Operating profit margin = ($566,000/$1,650,000) = 34.32%

Asset turnover = ($1,650,000/$991,000) = 1.66

Working 1 (in $000)

	Depreciation charge for the year @ 25%	NBV	Accumulated depreciation
Year 1	500	1,500	500
Year 2	375	1,125	875
Year 3	281	844	1,156
Year 4	211	633	**1,367**

Integration Style Question: Liquidity, profitability

From: AN Accountant

To : Lars Johansson

Date: 29 July 2014

Subject: Profitability and liquidity

The first step by the budget planners should be to consider why liquidity and profitability are not as good in the draft budget as the minimum targets. There are several possible reasons.

- The budget allows for higher operating costs, but there is no plan to increase sales prices. This will reduce profit margins and cash balances, and explain, fully or in part, the unsatisfactory performance ratios for profitability and liquidity.

- The targets of 1.25 for current ratio and 55% for the contribution/sales ratio might be unrealistic, and should therefore be re-considered.

- There could be padding (slack) in the budget estimates for expenditure.

Please do not hesitate to contact me if I can be of further assistance.

AN

Alternative measures of performance

Chapter learning objectives

Syllabus Link

Lead B2: Discuss issues arising from the use of performance measures and budgets for control

Component B2a): Prepare reports for the evaluation of projected and actual performance

- Benchmarking.

Component B2b): Discuss traditional and non-traditional approaches to performance measurement

- Non-financial performance indicators
- Balanced Scorecard.

Syllabus Link B2c): Discuss the criticisms and behavioural aspects of budgeting in responsibility centres.

- Criticisms of budgeting and the arguments for and against 'Beyond Budgeting'.

1 Chapter summary

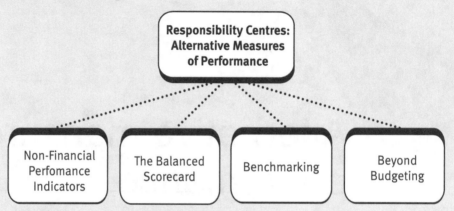

2 Knowledge brought forward

There is no knowledge brought forward from previous papers, but you will need to be comfortable with some basic financial analysis concepts. We will use this knowledge in P2 with more advanced ratios, so make sure you are comfortable with the assumed knowledge, that should have been brought forward as a base.

3 Shortcomings of financial indicators

The use of traditional financial performance metrics is widespread, but the practice has its problems. For example:

(1) They only tell what has happened over a limited period in the immediate past.

(2) They give no indication of what is going to happen in the future.

(3) They are vulnerable to manipulation and to the choice of accounting policy on matters such as depreciation and inventory valuation.

(4) They do not relate to the strategic management of the business and may induce 'short-termism', at the expense of motivation, quality and efficiency.

4 Non-Financial Performance Indicators

So, if we wish to obtain a fuller evaluation of performance, then we have to turn to a range of non-financial performance indicators (NFPIs).

Non-financial performance indicators are **'measures of performance based on non-financial information that may originate in, and be used by, operating departments to monitor and control their activities without any accounting input.'**

CIMA Official Terminology

Non-financial performance measures may give a more timely indication of the levels of performance achieved than financial measures do, and may be less susceptible to distortion by factors such as uncontrollable variations in the effect of market forces on operations.

Certain academic writers have developed models of performance evaluation for strategic advantage. The general thrust behind these is that performance indicators should be developed that relate to the long-term strategic development of the organisation. This follows the principle advocated by management guru/writer Tom Peters: **'What gets measured gets done'.**

The performance indicators adopted for a given business or business segment should relate to its key success factors – those things that are most likely to determine its success or failure. NFPIs can be expressed in either quantitative or qualitative terms. For example, it might be reported that we have a 5 per cent market share (a quantitative measure) and we are first supplier of preference to almost all our established customers (a qualitative measure).

Let us consider a number of NFPIs, how they might be expressed and relevant information relating to them might be gathered.

Competitiveness

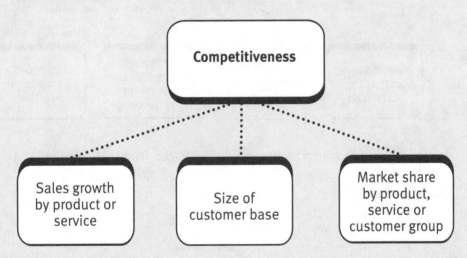

Regular market surveys drawing on both internal and external sources of information can be used to compile reports.

Activity level

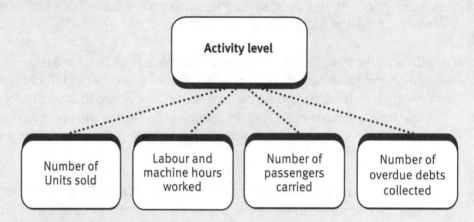

Relevant information could be drawn mainly from internal sources, with appropriate checks to ensure accuracy.

Productivity

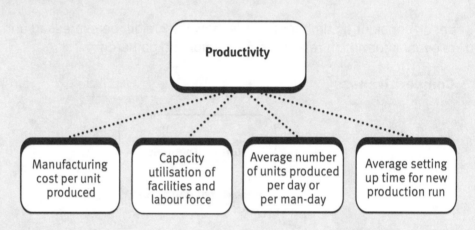

Again, most of this information could be drawn from **internal** sources.

Quality of service

Again, most relevant information would be available from internal sources but this could be reinforced by periodic customer surveys.

Customer satisfaction

Relevant information would have to come mainly from customer surveys although some internal sources could be selectively used. Customer surveys can be carried out on a regular structured basis or on an occasional informal basis. If a sample of customers is being used to compile information, then care has to be taken that the sample is significant in size and representative in structure.

Quality of staff experience

Some information could be taken from internal sources but much would have to come from colleges and external trainers. Exit interviews and confidential staff opinion surveys could also be used.

Innovation

Innovation

Number of new products or services brought to market

Proportion of Sales relating to new products

Technical lead relative to competitors

Lead time to bring new products to market

This kind of information would have to be taken from a variety of internal and external sources. The slightly subjective nature of what constitutes a 'new product' is such that this may be an area where an external assessor or consultant might be used to prepare the report.

These sort of performance indicators have the advantage of being 'forward looking'. That is, they are likely to address factors that relate to how well or badly the business will perform in the future.

For example, a service business with a high staff turnover rate is at a disadvantage. If experienced and qualified staff are constantly leaving and being replaced, then this may not contribute to the quality of service being offered to customers. We have all experienced visits to a shop, travel agent or garage where we have been served by an inexperienced and obviously new member of staff – who is unfamiliar with our account history and appears to have limited knowledge of the products that he or she is trying to sell. We find it much more satisfactory to be served by an experienced member of staff who knows his or her customers and products.

Yet, a deterioration in the standard of staff being employed (as evidenced by the indicators listed above under quality of staff experience) would not impact greatly on current period ROCE. A focus on current ROCE might actually induce a business to make greater use of poorly paid, junior staff in order to minimise operating costs. The impact of this on the business might be felt only in the long term.

As with any performance indicator, an NFPI has to be viewed in some context in order to be most meaningful. A good control report will express indicators in terms of a deviation from plan, relative to an industry benchmark or as part of a trend analysis covering comparable earlier periods.

Further, it is best to consider performance indicators as part of a package giving a multi-dimensional impression of how the organisation is performing.

BAA

One example of the use of NFPIs frequently reported in management literature is that of BAA plc (formerly the British Airports Authority). This is the case of a service company that attempts to evaluate its own performance in terms of the quality it is able to offer to customers.

It has identified about 12 key success factors which include access, aesthetics, cleanliness, comfort, staff competence, staff courtesy, reliability, responsiveness and security. These take on board the factors that customers appreciate when using an airport – short distances to walk from point of arrival to point of departure, safety from attack or robbery, easy availability of luggage trolleys and wheel chairs and so on.

BAA carries out regular surveys involving interviews with customers, consultant reports, analysis of operational data, and monitoring customer feedback. Appropriate indicators for each factor are reported and studied through comparison between different airports and trend analysis over time. For example, if airport A persistently reports a higher level of theft from customers than other airports – then this might prompt the introduction of additional security measures at airport A. If complaints about staff courtesy at airport D have been on a persistent upward trend over time, then this might prompt enquiries into staff supervision at that site and/or additional staff training.

A customer survey might include a question as follows:

'Your impression of the service available in the cafeterias at Airport B is best described as

A   Most satisfactory

B   Satisfactory

C   Acceptable

D   Less than acceptable

E   Unsatisfactory.

Answering this involves a qualitative judgement on the part of the customer, but the survey results can be reported and evaluated in quantitative terms. For example, if 80% of customers offered A or B answers to this question, then the impression given is that the standard of service at Airport B cafeterias is not a problem– and it may even serve as a model of best practice for other airports.

This line of discussion leads us into the more modern models of performance evaluation which fall broadly under the 'Beyond Budgeting' heading encountered in the previous chapter.

5 Benchmarking

Benchmarking is a technique that is increasingly being adopted as a mechanism for continuous improvement. CIMA's *Official Terminology* reads as follows:

> The establishment, through data gathering, of targets and comparators, that permit relative levels of performance (and particular areas of underperformance) to be identified. The adoption of identified best practices should improve performance.

It is a continuous process of measuring a firm's products, services and activities against other best-performing organisations, either internal or external to the firm. The idea is to ascertain how the processes and activities can be improved. Ideally, benchmarking should involve an external focus on the latest developments, best practice and model examples that can be incorporated within various operations of business organisations. It therefore represents the ideal way of moving forward and achieving high competitive standards.

In addition to monitoring performance through variance analysis, or as an alternative to variance reporting, organisations might use benchmarking to monitor their performance, and set targets for improved performance.

The basic idea of benchmarking is that performance should be assessed through a comparison of the organisation's own products or services, performance and practices with 'best practice' elsewhere.

The reasons for benchmarking may be summarised as:

- To receive an alarm call about the need for change
- Learning from others in order to improve performance
- Gaining a competitive edge (in the private sector)
- Improving services (in the public sector).

Different types of benchmarking

It is important to remember that in order to use benchmarking, it is necessary to gather information about best practice. This leads on to the problem of how much information is available and where it can be obtained.

Benchmarking can be categorised according to what is being benchmarked and whose performance is being used for comparison (as 'best in class').

- **Internal benchmarking**. With internal benchmarking, other units or departments in the same organisation are used as the benchmark. This might be possible if the organisation is large and divided into a number of similar regional divisions. Internal benchmarking is also widely used within government. In the UK for example, there is a Public Sector Benchmarking Service that maintains a database of performance measures. Public sector organisations, such as fire stations and hospitals, can compare their own performance with the best in the country.

- **Competitive benchmarking.** With competitive benchmarking, the most successful competitors are used as the benchmark. Competitors are unlikely to provide willingly any information for comparison, but it might be possible to observe competitor performance (for example, how quickly a competitor processes customer orders). A competitor's product might be dismantled in order to learn about its internal design and its performance: this technique of benchmarking is called reverse engineering.

- **Functional benchmarking**. In functional benchmarking, comparisons are made with a similar function (for example selling, order handling, despatch) in other organisations that are not direct competitors. For example, a fast food restaurant operator might compare its buying function with buying in a supermarket chain.

- **Strategic benchmarking**. Strategic benchmarking is a form of competitive benchmarking aimed at reaching decisions for strategic action and organisational change. Companies in the same industry might agree to join a collaborative benchmarking process, managed by an independent third party such as a trade organisation. With this type of benchmarking, each company in the scheme submits data about their performance to the scheme organiser. The organiser calculates average performance figures for the industry as a whole from the data supplied. Each participant in the scheme is then supplied with the industry average data, which it can use to assess its own performance.

'Benchmarking', by Bob Scarlett

CIMA Insider, October 2003

Benchmarking is the process of improving performance by continuously identifying, understanding (studying and analysing), and adapting outstanding practices and process found inside and outside the organisation and implementing the results' (American Productivity and Quality Centre, 1997)

Benchmarking is an approach to performance management that starts with the premise that whatever the process (supply, production, sales or services), performance can best be measured and managed by comparing that process with an appropriate outside entity that is already achieving world-class performance. The outside entity used to provide the benchmark need not operate within the same sector as our process. Further the benchmark can be from either another organisation (an 'external' benchmark) or a different segment within the same organisation (an 'internal' benchmark).

A benchmark provides a standard of excellence against which to measure and compare. Benchmarks are performance measures – How many? (e.g. 'customers served per staff member per hour') How quickly? (e.g. 'delivery time to customer') How high? (e.g. 'proportion of sales giving rise to repeat business') How low? (e.g. 'proportion of output being defective'). To be meaningful, a benchmark should relate to a 'key performance indicator', that is something within the business process that has a major influence on results. Establishing benchmarks is a necessary part of benchmarking but itself does not provide an understanding of best practices nor does knowledge of the benchmarks necessarily lead to improvement. Benchmarking is the learning of lessons about how best performance is achieved. Rather than merely measuring performance, benchmarking focuses on how to improve any given business process by exploiting 'best practices' by discovering the specific practices responsible for high performance, understanding how these practices work and adapting and applying them to the organisation. A benchmarking exercise may take the form of a process comparison which does not involve the use of metrics.

Some writers identify three distinct approaches to benchmarking:

(1) **Metric benchmarking**. The practice of comparing appropriate metrics to identify possible areas for improvement

(2) **Process benchmarking**. The practice of comparing processes with a partner as part of an improvement process

(3) **Diagnostic benchmarking**. The practice of reviewing the processes of a business to identify those which indicate a problem and offer a potential for improvement.

The Xerox corporation is often cited as the pioneer in benchmarking practice. When it wanted to improve performance in its warehousing and distribution operation it did not go down the then conventional road of process redesign. Rather, it identified the business which was acknowledged as being the very best at warehousing and distribution – the L.L. Bean catalogue merchant. L.L. Bean agreed to undertake a co-operative benchmarking project. Over a period the two exchanged data on various aspects of their inventory handling and processing of orders. As a result of this, Xerox identified those areas in its own operation which were performing at below Bean's standards and acted to implement improvements. One critical point to note is that Xerox did not adopt another office equipment business as its model – it adopted a business operating in a different sector altogether.

Benchmarking in all its varied forms is becoming increasingly widespread in industry, services and the public sector. In particular, it is perceived to offer a more sophisticated tool in performance management than more traditional approaches such as standard costing. The general thrust behind this idea is that standard costing belongs in the era when goods were produced in long continuous production runs and a high proportion of costs were 'product specific'. In the new economy, goods tend to be highly customised, contain a significant service element and are produced in short discontinuous production runs on a JIT basis. A large proportion of product costs are determined at the design stage or are 'customer specific', that is they relate to the manner in which the goods are provided to the customer. Efficiency is therefore very much a function of product engineering, the flexibility of the production operation and customer relationship management. It is argued that the traditional budgetary control report based on standard costing simply does not address these issues.

A comprehensive system of benchmarking can provide a much fuller impression of how well or badly an operation is performing. And, it is more likely to give an indication of those areas in the operation that are amenable to improvement. That said, benchmarking has its critics. For example:

Benchmarking relies on competitive data that isn't readily available. When the data is available, it may be neither accurate nor timely. Moreover, it allows a comparison at only one point in time and does not provide a way to continually improve performance. (John Pucket, Boston Consulting Group (quoted from 1997)).

That is fair comment, but the discussion above indicates some of the ways in which such criticism might be answered. For one thing, benchmarking need not rely on competitive data. As with most business techniques, benchmarking has to be carried out well if it is to yield results.

6 Kaplan and Norton – The balanced scorecard

The joke

You're at the airport and there's a little while to your flight. You have a drink to pass the time and a person in uniform comes and sits next to you at the bar and after a while you get chatting and you find out that she is the pilot of the aeroplane that you are about to catch. You say that it must be very difficult flying an aeroplane with all those dials and knobs and switches and meters and things, and she says, 'No, not really. All I look at is the speedometer and I figure that if I get my speed right then things are fine.' You look at her a bit funny and you say, 'Well, what about the fuel gauge? Isn't that important?' She says, 'Yes, you're right, it is important and I used to look at it, but now I just look at the speedometer'. Then you say, 'Well what about the altimeter? Surely that's important?' She replies, 'Well, yes it is, but I try and focus on one thing at a time. Once I'm happy with my airspeed then in a few flights' time I might concentrate on altitude'

The question Kaplan and Norton now ask is would you catch that aeroplane?

The point that Kaplan and Norton are trying to make (in the unlikely event that you missed it) is that you cannot fly an aeroplane with only one instrument. Nor can you run a business by looking at one performance measure. Kaplan and Norton's Balanced Scorecard focuses on four different perspectives.

The balanced scorecard

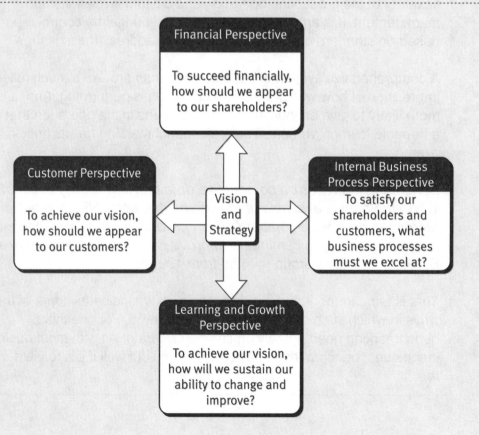

Robert Kaplan and David Norton published the original article (The Balanced Scorecard – Measures That Drive Performance) in the Harvard Business Review in January/February 1992. It has become one of the most requested HBR reprints.

The traditional performance measure for a business is of course financial, but one problem is that the financial measures relate to the past. Another is that the financial accounting model does not adequately consider the value to a company of its intangible assets such as a happy and loyal customer base, well motivated, well trained and efficient staff and good quality products or services. The Balanced Scorecard incorporates non-financial measures of the drivers of future performance as well as financial measures of past performance.

In their 1996 book Kaplan and Norton state that 'Several critics have advocated scrapping financial measures entirely to measure business unit performance. They argue that in today's technologically and customer-driven global competition, financial measures provide poor guidelines for success. They urge managers to focus on improving customer satisfaction, quality, cycle times, and employee skills and motivation. According to this theory, as companies make fundamental improvements in their operations, the financial numbers will take care of themselves.' Kaplan and Norton reply that the use of financial measures still serves a purpose as it is not enough to improve quality and customer satisfaction and generate new products, etc, in the end these improvements have to be converted to financial advantage.

Kaplan and Norton also ask in their 1996 book are 4 perspectives sufficient? They answer their own question by saying that there is no rule that says that every organisation in the world should use exactly the 4 perspectives, and nothing else, but that in general across a variety of companies and industries the 4 perspectives do seem to work. They say that some companies do incorporate extra perspectives such as an environmental perspective, but they have yet to see a company use less than 4.

It can be seen from the diagram above that a vital part of the Balanced Scorecard is the company strategy and the starting point for the creation of a Balanced Scorecard is a company's mission statement or vision.

Measures for the balanced scorecard

The following lists give examples of possible measures:

Financial perspective

Goals would be set in terms of 3 main areas and the measures would relate to those areas.

- Survival   Cash flow, gearing

- Success   Monthly or quarterly sales growth and operating income

- Prosperity Increase in market share and ROI

Customer perspective

- Customer profitability
- Customer retention
- Customer satisfaction
- Customer acquisition
- Market share
- Percentage of sales from new products
- Percentage of on-time deliveries
- Preferred supplier status
- Lead time from receipt of order to delivery
- No of customer complaints

Internal business process perspective

- Percentage of sales from new products
- Percentage of sales from proprietary products
- New product introduction versus competitors also new product introduction versus plan
- Manufacturing process capabilities
- Time to develop next generation of products
- Cycle time
- Unit cost
- Efficiency

Learning and growth perspective

- Employee satisfaction
- Employee retention
- Employee productivity
- Time to market
- Percentage of products giving 80% of sales

[In the March 2013 PEG, the Examiner notes that 'a significant number of candidates encountered difficulties when applying the balanced scorecard to the scenario. Common errors include:

(1) *Putting forward performance measures that do not relate to the company's objectives*

(2) *Putting forward unrealistic objectives e.g. 'to become the best pathology laboratory in the world'*

(3) *Putting forward weak objectives for which it is difficult to establish a performance measure, e.g. 'we need to find out if customers/employees are happy' or 'we need to measure how quickly patients get better'*

(4) *Labelling the perspectives incorrectly*

(5) *Putting forward performance measures that did not relate to the scenario'.]*

Performance evaluation in the not-for-profit sector

An NFP organisation exists to achieve certain objectives and an evaluation of its performance in achieving those objectives must have regard to a combination of efficiency and effectiveness factors. The organisation should achieve the maximum output from the resources at its disposal (efficiency) and at the same time it should organise those resources in a manner that achieves a given result by the cheapest route (effectiveness).

Many of the performance indicators considered above can be applied to NFPs. For example, in evaluating the performance of a local authority one might consider:

(1) Cost per km of road maintained

(2) Cost per child in school

(3) Cost per square metre of grass verge mown

(4) Cost per tonne of sewage disposed of.

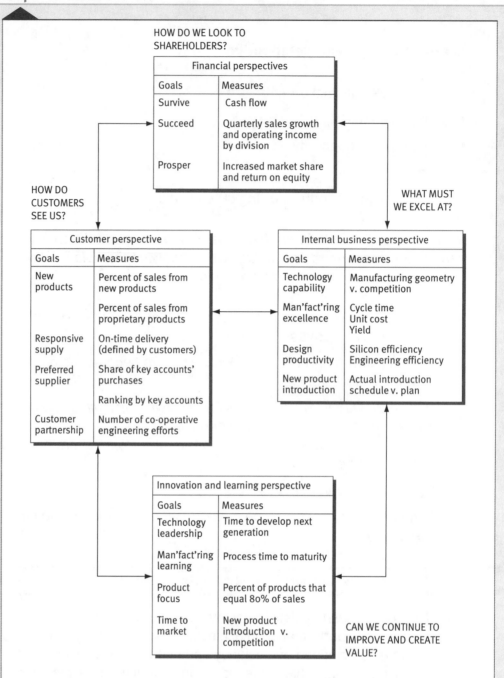

These are all quantitative measures and care should be taken in their interpretation. For example, town A's sewage disposal cost might be half that of town B. Does that mean that A is more efficient than B? Not necessarily, because A might be pumping raw sewage direct into the sea whereas B treats sewage and transports it for disposal. If A is a resort town then its 'efficiency' in disposing of sewage might have a variety of adverse knock-on effects. In considering performance one has to consider qualitative factors. A variety of qualitative indicators might also be considered in tandem with the quantitative ones listed above:

• Number of claims made by motorists arising from pot holed roads

- Number of local children obtaining 2 A level GCEs or equivalent

- Rating of local road system by the Automobile Association

- Number of complaints from visitors concerning smell/taste of sea water.

Benchmarking is probably the most important recent innovation in performance evaluation in the NFP sector. The standard benchmarking practice can be used to:

- Study processes in the organisation and select which are to be benchmarked

- Secure suitable benchmark partners

- Compare appropriate figures and indicators with partners

- Adopt and implement 'best practices'.

A benchmark partner for one local authority need not necessarily be another local authority. For example, if the activity being benchmarked is 'office costs', then one could bench-mark against an insurance company or a mail order company. However, while such benchmark partners might give a local authority an idea about its efficiency in certain areas, they would offer little guidance on effectiveness. If the authority is seeking guidance on the appropriate combination of spend on police, social services, housing and so on in order to provide a certain level of welfare for elderly residents (a quest for effectiveness), then the appropriate benchmark partners would have to be other authorities providing a similar service.

In the United Kingdom, benchmarking and its associated concept of 'best practice' are now widely used in public sector performance evaluation. The Department of the Environment rates all local authorities on the basis of periodic reviews. The use of appropriate performance indicators are a central element in these reviews. Such indicators have regard to both quantitative and qualitative factors.

As with all performance evaluation exercises, it must be appreciated that the calculation of a particular indicator will probably mean little unless it is set in some sort of context. Calculating the value of a particular indicator means little, until it is **compared with** a budget, set in a trend or set against a best practice benchmark.

One final comment in this area should be made. You are reminded of the **Peter** principle – *'What gets measured gets done'*.

If a performance evaluation is based on an incorrect or incomplete range of metrics, then the system can induce the wrong things to get done. For example, in the late 1990s the performance of hospitals was judged on the length of their waiting lists. Specifically, the average time taken for a referred patient to have a first consultation was adopted as a key performance indicator. It is claimed that this induced hospitals to concentrate on patients with minor illnesses since they could be treated quickly and cleared off the list. The small number of patients requiring major treatments often had to wait longer than was the case before the performance indicator was adopted.

Hospital waiting lists were reduced, but not in a wholly neutral manner. Some people gained and some lost as a result of the system. That was never the intention.

7 Beyond Budgeting

The whole concept of budgeting turns around the idea that the operation of an organisation can be meaningfully planned for in some detail over an extended period into the future. Further, that this plan can be used to guide, control and co-ordinate the activities of numerous departments and individuals within the organisation.

The traditional budgeting concept has its critics:

In one division with 300 employees and $100 m in annual costs, their operating budget was more than four inches thick and involved over 100 business units. They completed the budget six months into the current fiscal year with managers and directors under great pressure to revise the budget to meet corporate goals. But each revision was just an editorial exercise in changing the numbers, not in revising operating activities. These were only changes in a lengthy and cumbersome document that few understood. Budget complexity drives out meaning and relevance.

Bruce Neumann, *Streamlining Budgeting in the New Millennium* (Strategic Finance 12/2001)

The modern economic environment is associated with a **rapidly changing environment, flexible manufacturing, short product life-cycles and products/services which are highly customised**. The 'lean business' and the 'virtual business' are responses to this. Such businesses own limited assets of the traditional kind but assemble resources as and when needed to meet customer demand. The keys to their operation are flexibility and speed of response. They are able to move quickly to exploit opportunities as they arise and do not operate according to elaborate business plans.

In an age of discontinuous change, unpredictable competition, and fickle customers, few companies can plan ahead with any confidence – yet most organisations remain locked into a 'plan-make-and-sell' business model that involves a protracted annual budgeting process based on negotiated targets and that assumes that customers will buy what the company decides to make. Such assumptions are no longer valid in an age when customers can switch loyalties at the click of a mouse.

J Hope and R Fraser. *Beyond Budgeting* (Strategic Finance 10/2000)

'Beyond Budgeting' (BB) is the generic name given to a body of practices intended to replace budgeting as a management model. The core concept is the need to move from a business model based on centralised organisational hierarchies to one based on devolved networks.

> *Beyond Budgeting* is defined in CIMA's *Official Terminology* as 'the idea that companies need to move *beyond budgeting* because of the inherent flaws in budgeting especially when used to set incentive contracts. It is argued that a range of techniques, such as rolling forecasts and market-related targets, can take the place of traditional budgets.'

Beyond Budgeting Round Table (BBRT)

BB is identified with the 'Beyond Budgeting Round Table' (BBRT). The latter is. . . *at the heart of a new movement that is searching for ways to build lean, adaptive and ethical enterprises that can sustain superior competitive performance. Its aim is to spread the idea through a vibrant community'. (*BBRT website)

BBRT is a research consortium which was set up in 1998 to promote research into and the adoption of BB. At its centre is the eight strong 'BBRT team', the best known of whom are Robin Fraser and Jeremy Hope. The full round table community consists of the team, business and academic associates and the member businesses.

Budgeting is a pervasive exercise that provides the administrative basis for organisational planning and control in many traditionally run organisations. The vision of the Chief Executive is translated into a plan which is expressed in the form of a budget. Once that budget is adopted, then the management function becomes one of securing compliance. Budgeting is a core management process which provides stability and reduces risk. This becomes a cultural phenomenon reflecting a hierarchical approach to management whereby subordinate managers are judged on how far they succeed in complying with orders. It is an approach which has been linked to some high-profile business failures. For example, managers at WorldCom claimed that working life was all about satisfying the demands of CEO Bernie Ebbers and a small group of his associates:

'You would have a budget and he would mandate that you had to be 2 percent under budget. Nothing else was acceptable'

BBRT advances the idea that budgeting should be abolished and an alternative business model should be substituted in its place. BB is a 'responsibility model' whereby managers are given goals which are based on benchmarks linked variously to world class performance, peers, competitors and/or earlier periods. This requires an adaptive approach whereby authority is devolved to managers. An organisation run in this manner will be more a network than a hierarchy. The whole spectrum of modern management techniques and aids should be incorporated in an implementation of the BB model. IT networks provide easy communication between different component parts of an organisation together with its customers, associates and suppliers. Quality programmes (TQM), process engineering (BPR), supply chain management (SCM), balanced scorecards and activity accounting all have a role. Advocates of BB claim that it does not provide a softer environment for management than budget compliance. Both individual and team performance should have a high visibility in a devolved management environment.

Illustration

For example, a performance control report based on the scorecard principle might appear as follows:

XYZ Ltd, Performance Control Report for Quarter 4 Scorecard

	Actual	Target	Var (%)
Financials			
Revenue ($)	18,360,000	17,500,000	4.91
Income/Expenditure	1.055	1.040	1.44
Earnings ($)	181,900	170,000	7.00
Market capitalisation ($)	190,800,000	200,000,000	(4.60)
Customers			
Customer satisfaction (points)	8.731	9.00	(2.99)
Returns (%)	2.89	2.00	(44.50)
Processes			
Delivery errors (%)	0.86	0.90	4.44
Design errors (points)	1.976	2.000	1.20
Design-delivery time (days)	94	90	(4.44)
Staff			
Staff satisfaction (points)	7.310	8.00	(8.63)
Training hours per FTE staff member	4.217	3.500	20.49

That gives a fuller impression of performance than a straight actual-budget comparison and the approach can be refined much further. Results can be reported using graphics and trends. It is possible to adopt industry averages or trend analysis based projections as the relevant benchmarks instead of fixed targets.

8 Beyond Budgeting – 6 principles

A BB implementation should incorporate the following six main principles:

(1) An organisation structure with **clear principles and boundaries**; a manager should have no doubts over what he/she is responsible for and what he/she has authority over; the concept of the internal market for business units may be relevant here.

(2) Managers should be given goals and targets which are based on **relative success** and linked to shareholder value; such targets may be based on key performance indicators and benchmarks following the balanced scorecard principle.

(3) Managers should be given a **high degree of freedom** to make decisions; this freedom is consistent with the total quality management and business process reengineering concepts; a BB organisation chart should be 'flat'.

(4) Responsibility for decisions that generate value should be placed with **'front line teams'**; again, this is consistent with TQM and BPR concepts.

(5) Front line teams should be made responsible for **relationships** with customers, associate businesses and suppliers; direct communication between all the parties involved should be facilitated; this is consistent with the SCM concept.

(6) Information support systems should be transparent and ethical; an activity based accounting system which reports on the activities for which managers and teams are responsible is likely to be of use in this regard.

BB is essentially an approach that places modern management practices within a cultural framework.

'The process of management is not about administering fixed budgets, it is about the dynamic allocation of resources'

Lord Browne, former CEO of BP

9 Benefits of Beyond Budgeting

All the cases studied are different, but the following general benefits for BB are claimed:

(1) **Faster response time** – operating within a flexible organisational network and with strategy as an 'adaptive process' allows managers to respond quickly to customer requests.

(2) **Better innovation** – managers working within an environment wherein performance is judged on the basis of team and business unit results encourages the adoption of new innovations. Relations with customers and suppliers through SCM may facilitate the adoption of new working methods and technologies.

(3) **Lower costs** – in the context of BB managers are more likely to perceive costs as scarce resources which have to be used effectively than as a budget 'entitlement' that has to be used. BB is also likely to promote an awareness of the purposes for which costs are being incurred and thereby the potential for reductions.

(4) **Improved customer and supplier loyalty** – the leading role of front line teams in dealing with customers and suppliers is likely to deepen the relevant relationships.

As with many innovations in management practice, BB was a creature of its time. It appeared in the mid-1990s at a time when globalisation and advances in IT were tending to speed up the business environment. In particular, customers had greater choice and expected faster service. The key competitive constraint in most business situations is no longer land, labour or capital. For example, if labour is locally scarce then work can be outsourced to India or manufacturing can be relocated to China. In many practical business situations the key competitive factor is likely to be intellectual and knowledge based in character.

The BB model appeared as a set of information-age best practices which was attuned to the new situation. BB is intended to be an exercise in mobilising competent managers, skilled workers and loyal customers. However, traditional budgeting still has its defenders. Such defenders claim that while budgeting may be associated with a 'command and control' management style, it is the management style that is the problem and not budgeting.

Svenska Handelsbanken

Researchers have explored the history of BB implementations to determine whether or not these have delivered improved results. BBRT has reported several case studies, the best known of which is that of **Svenska Handelsbanken**.

This Swedish bank abandoned budgeting in 1972 and switched to delegation model (involving 600 autonomous work units) that avoids formal planning and target setting. Branch managers run their own businesses and are able to decide how many staff they need, where they obtain support services from and what products they market to which customers. Branch performance is assessed using measures such as customer profitability, customer retention and work productivity.

The Svenska Handelsbanken model might indicate a higher level of corporate risk with all that would imply for cost of money and market capitalisation. However, it is claimed that the model favours flexibility. In the absence of a fixed plan, products and projects are designed to allow easy modification and exit routes. This view suggests that the model invites a different approach to risk management rather than the acceptance of higher risk.

10 Practice Questions

Objective Test Question 1: Balanced scorecard

Suggest performance indicators to include in the Balanced Scorecard of a credit card company.

Financial indicators of performance:	'Customers' indicators of performance:
Learning and growth indicators of performance:	**Internal processes indicators of performance:**

Data Set Question: Faster Pasta

Faster Pasta is an Italian fast food restaurant that specialises in high quality, moderately priced authentic Italian pasta dishes and pizzas. The restaurant has recently decided to implement a balanced scorecard approach and has established the following relevant goals for each perspective:

Perspective	Goal
Customer perspective	• To increase the number of new and returning customers
	• To reduce the % of customer complaints
Internal	• To reduce the time taken between taking a customer's order and delivering the meal to the customer.
	• To reduce staff turnover
Innovation and learning	• To increase the proportion of revenue from new dishes
	• To increase the % of staff time spent on training
Financial	• To increase spend per customer
	• To increase gross profit margin

The following information is also available for the year just ended and for the previous year.

	20X8	20X9
Total customers	11,600	12,000
– of which are new customers	4,400	4,750
– of which are existing customers	7,200	7,250
Customer complaints	464	840
Time between taking order and customer receiving meal	4 mins	13 mins
% staff turnover	12%	40%
% time staff spend training	5%	2%
Revenue	$110,000	$132,000
– revenue from new dishes	$22,000	$39,600
– revenue from existing dishes	$88,000	$92,400
Gross profit	$22,000	$30,360

Task: Answer 'TRUE' or 'FALSE' to the following assertions that Faster Pasta has achieved its goals of:

Increasing the number of new and returning customers

Decreasing the % customer complaints

Reducing the time taken between taking the customer's order and delivering the meal to the customer

Reducing staff turnover

Increasing the proportion of revenue from new dishes

Increasing the % of staff time spent on training

Increasing the spend per customer

Increasing gross profit margin

Case Style question – Benchmarking

PRE-SEEN MATERIAL

You work as Financial Controller for E5E. E5E is a charity concerned with heart disease. Its mission statement is as follows:

'To fund world class research into the biology and the causes of heart disease; To develop effective treatments and improve the quality of life for patients; To reduce the number of people suffering from heart disease; To provide authoritative information on heart disease.'

E5E obtains funding from voluntary donations from both private individuals and companies, together with government grants. Much of the work it does, in all departments, could not be achieved without the large number of voluntary workers who give their time to the organisation and who make up approximately 80% of the workforce.

E5E does not employ any scientific researchers directly, but funds research by making grants to individual medical experts employed within universities and hospitals. In addition to providing policy advice to government departments, the charity's advisors give health educational talks to employers and other groups.

You have just received the following email from the Board's spokesperson:

From: Pablo Perez, Managing Director
To: A.N. Accountant
Date: 02.07.2014
Subject: Benchmarking

The Board recognises the need to become more professional in the management of the organisation. It feels that this can be best achieved by conducting a benchmarking exercise. However, it recognises that the introduction of this process may make some members of the organisation, particularly the volunteers, unhappy.

Could you prepare a report for us, that discusses the advantages and disadvantages of benchmarking for E5E? We would also welcome advice on the stages in conducting a benchmarking exercise in the context of E5E , and on how those implementing the exercise should deal with the concerns of the staff, particularly the volunteers.

Thank you

Test your understanding answers

Objective Test Question 1: Balanced scorecard

Financial indicators of performance:	'Customers' indicators of performance:
Increase market share year-on-year	Wean businesses off cheque books
Increase cardholder's spending	Get banks to switch cards
Increase % fee	Focus on big spenders
Reduce debt	Issue more cards
	Maintain image
	Add reward programmes
Learning and growth indicators of performance:	**Internal processes indicators of performance:**
Outsource IT jobs	Increased marketing spend
Acquire other companies	Offer more products
Improve staff training levels	Achieve economies of scale

Data Set Question: Faster Pasta

Increasing the number of new & returning customers	TRUE

Measure: The number of new customers has increased year on year from 4,400 to 4,750. This is an 8.0% increase. The number of returning customers has also increased slightly from 7,200 to 7,250, i.e. a 1.0% increase.

Comment: The company has achieved its goal of increasing the number of new and existing customers. It is worth noting that the proportion of customers who are returning customers has fallen slightly from 62.1% to 60.4% of the total customers. This could indicate a small drop in the level of customer satisfaction.

Decreasing the % customer complaints	FALSE

Measure: The percentage of customer complaints has increased from 4% (464 ÷ 11,600) to 7% (840 ÷ 12,000).

Comment: Faster Pasta should investigate the reasons for the increase in customer complaints and take the required action immediately in order to ensure that it can meet this goal in the future.

Reducing the time taken between taking the customer's order and delivering the meal to the customer	FALSE

Measure: The time taken has more than tripled from an average of 4 minutes in 20X8 to an average of 13 minutes in 20X9.

Comment: Customers may place a high value on the fast delivery of their food. The increase in time may be linked to the increased number of customer complaints. If this continues customer satisfaction, and therefore profitability, will suffer in the long-term. The restaurant should take steps now in order to ensure that this goal is achieved going forward.

Reducing staff turnover	FALSE

Measure: This has risen significantly from 12% to 40% and hence the business has not achieved its goal.

Comment: The reasons for the high staff turnover should be investigated immediately. This may be contributing to longer waiting times and the increase in customer complaints. This will impact long-term profitability.

Increasing the proportion of revenue from new dishes	TRUE

Measure: This has increased year on year from 20% ($22,000 ÷ $110,000) in 20X8 to 30% ($39,600 ÷ $132,000) in 20X9. Therefore, the restaurant has achieved its goal.

Comment: This is a favourable increase and may have a positive impact on long-term profitability if the new products meet the needs of the customers.

Increasing the % of staff time spent on training	**FALSE**

Measure: This has fallen significantly from 5% to only 2% and hence the company is not achieving its goal.

Comment: Staff may be unsatisfied if they feel that their training needs are not being met. This may contribute to a high staff turnover. In addition, staff may not have the skills to do the job well and this would impact the level of customer satisfaction.

Increasing the spend per customer	**TRUE**

Measure: Spend per customer has increased from $9.48 ($110,000 ÷ 11,600) to $11.00 ($132,000 ÷ 12,000), i.e. a 16.0% increase.

Comment: This is a favourable increase. However, the issues discussed above must be addressed in order to ensure that this trend continues.

Increasing gross profit margin	**TRUE**

Measure: The gross profit margin has increased year on year from 20% ($22,000 ÷ $110,000) to 23% ($30,360 ÷ $132,000).

Comment: This is a favourable increase. However, the issues discussed above must be addressed in order to ensure that this trend continues.

Case Style question – Benchmarking

REPORT

From: A.N.A.

To: Pablo Perez, The Board

Date: 02.07.2014

Subject: Benchmarking

It is undeniable that in practice, differences between charities and their aims make benchmarking principles difficult to apply.

However, advantages of benchmarking for a charity like ours may be listed as follows:

- A better understanding of the charity's position
- Highlights particular areas that need changing
- Can identify problem areas in advance
- Can be integrated into target-setting, performance appraisal and bonuses
- Could highlight areas where other charities are much more effective so perhaps E5E should stop those activities
- Can be used to overcome complacency
- Should be particularly useful in improving economy and, to some extent, efficiency – all charities have financial constraints and benchmarking would highlight areas for improvement
- Enables better information to be provided to stakeholders – particularly useful in supporting applications for government funds.

However, some **disadvantages** are also present:

- Time consuming and expensive to implement
- Finding suitable comparisons can be difficult
- Not so useful in improving effectiveness as the stated objectives are very difficult to measure:
  - 'To fund world class research into the biology and the causes of heart disease.' What is 'world-class'?
  - 'To develop effective treatments and improve the quality of life for patients.' How do you measure 'quality of life'?
  - 'To reduce the number of people suffering from heart disease.' Cause and effect can be difficult to match – can reductions in mortality rates be traced directly to E5E's work?

- 'To provide authoritative information on heart disease.' How to measure what is 'authoritative'?

- Not a competitive industry – does it matter if another charity is more effective in certain areas?

- Danger of information overload

- Problems gathering information when so many staff are volunteers – there may be a need for extra training here as well

- Can be de-motivating if the organisation fails to meet benchmarks.

In summary benchmarking may help the charity become more economic and efficient but will not aid effectiveness.

Stages in conducting a benchmarking exercise

There is no universally agreed set of steps to follow when conducting a benchmarking exercise – the following is just one suggested answer.

E5E could use the following steps to conduct a benchmarking exercise:

(1) **Planning**

- Decide what you wish to benchmark – for example, fund raising, % of funds passed on to recipients, % of funds raised from government, % of staff who are volunteers, funds raised per person, etc.

- Decide against whom you want to benchmark – this could include internal benchmarks (difficult), competitive benchmarks (e.g. other health research charities such as cancer research), activity benchmarks (e.g. universities to assess the educational aspects of E5E) and generic benchmarks (e.g. other communications organisations such as newspapers).

- Identify outputs required – e.g. a breakdown of funds collected, feedback on talks given.

- Determine data collection methodologies – e.g. should volunteers record information, should standard forms be prepared for talks, etc.

(2) **Data collection**

- Secondary/background research – getting comparators.

- Primary research – from the benchmark.

(3) **Analysis**

- Of the gaps – are they significant?

- Of the factors that create the gaps (enablers) – E5E would need to discuss findings with the relevant staff to understand why there are differences. For example, the benchmarking charity may have been much larger than E5E.

(4) **Implementation of improvement programmes**

- Implementation planning – for example, visiting best in class and observing their methods.

- Roll-out of new modus operandi (changes) – for example, setting up new training programmes for volunteer staff, designing new advertising, training speakers, etc.

(5) **Monitoring results**

- The process should be continuous.

Dealing with the concerns of staff

In each of the above stages the concerns of voluntary staff should be taken into account:

- E5E should have meetings to explain to staff why benchmarking is being introduced, its benefits and potential problems.

- Staff should be reassured of senior management commitment to the process.

- They should be consulted when deciding what to benchmark and what measures to use.

- They should be asked to help design new forms if they will be using them.

- They should be asked if they have any experience of benchmarking – just because they are volunteers does not mean that they have not had jobs where such experience may be gained.

- Emphasis should be on improvements of the processes rather than criticising staff.

I trust the above helps.

With regards

AN.

Transfer Pricing

Chapter learning objectives

Syllabus Link

Lead B2: Discuss issues arising from the use of performance measures and budgets for control

Component B3a): Discuss the likely behavioural consequences of performance measurement within an organisation

- The behavioural consequences of performance management and control in responsibility centres.
- The behavioural consequences arising from divisional structures: internal competition and internal trading.

Component B3b): Discuss transfer pricing systems

- The theory of transfer pricing, including perfect, imperfect and no market for the intermediate good.
- Negotiated, market, cost-plus and variable cost-based transfer prices. 'Dual' transfer prices and lump sum payments as means of addressing some of the issues that arise.

Syllabus Link B3c): Evaluate the effects of transfer prices

- The motivation of divisional management.
- Divisional and group profitability.
- The autonomy of individual divisions.

1 Chapter summary

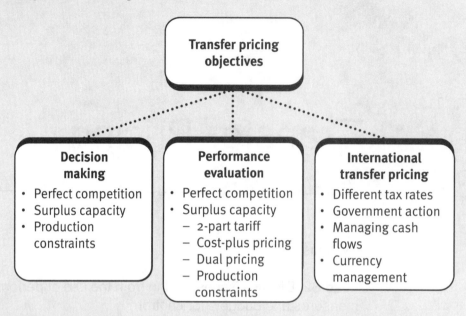

2 Performance management: behavioural consequences

When an organisation is structured into profit centres or investment centres, authority is delegated to the profit centre or investment centre managers. These managers are given the authority to take decisions at a local level, without having to wait for instructions from head office.

Control is applied from head office through performance measurement: centre managers are held accountable for the profits or returns that they make.

The purposes of decentralisation should be to:

(1) give autonomy to local centre managers in decision-making

(2) motivate centre managers to improve performance: with profit centres and investment centres, this includes motivating them to increase profitability

(3) through performance enhancement at a profit centre level, to achieve better results for the organisation as a whole.

Decentralisation can create tension between local centre managers and head office management.

The performance of the managers of profit centres and investment centres will be assessed, and the managers themselves will be rewarded, on the basis of the results of their particular centre. Profit centre managers will therefore be motivated to optimise the results of their own division, regardless of other profit centres and regardless of the organisation as a whole.

When head office management believe that a profit centre manager is taking decisions that improve the profit centre performance, but are damaging for the interests of the organisation as a whole, they might want to step in and either:

(1) alter the decisions that have been made at profit centre level, or

(2) make new decisions for the profit centre.

However, if head office interferes in decision-making at profit centre level, local autonomy in decision making is lost.

3 Transfer pricing

In an organisation with profit centres and investment centres, there will almost certainly be some inter-connection between different centres. Some profit centres will supply goods and services to others.

When *inter-divisional* (inter-company) trading takes place between profit centres, the centre providing the goods or services to the other will want to earn income from the transfer. Unless it receives income from the transfer, it will make a loss on the transaction.

For example, if Division A provides items to Division B that cost $10 each to make, Division A must earn at least $10 from the transfer, otherwise it will make a loss. If decision making is delegated to profit centre management, the manager of Division A would refuse to supply Division B unless it is allowed to earn income of at least $10 for each unit.

Inter-divisional transfers must therefore be priced. The price of the transfer is the **transfer price**.

- The transfer is treated as an internal sale and an internal purchase within the organisation. It provides sales income to the supplying division and is a purchase cost for the receiving division.

- The sales income of one division is offset by the purchase cost of the other division. The transfer therefore affects the profits of the two divisions individually, but has no effect on the profit of the organisation as a whole.

Setting a transfer price: Inter-divisional trading policy

The transfer price for inter-divisional transactions is significant because:

- it determines how the total profit is shared between the two divisions, and

- in some circumstances, it could affect decisions by the divisional managers about whether they are willing to sell to or buy from the other division.

Both divisions must benefit from the transaction if inter-divisional sales are to take place.

- A selling division will not agree to sell items to another division unless it is profitable for the selling division to do so.

- Similarly, a buying division will not wish to purchase items from another division unless it is profitable for the division.

Transfer prices have to be established and agreed. They could be decided either centrally or locally.

- They could be imposed by head office.

- Alternatively, they could be decided by commercial negotiation between the profit centre managers.

- If decentralisation is to allow the power of decision making to profit centre managers, they should have the authority to agree transfer prices by discussion or negotiation between themselves.

Inter-divisional trading should take place within a broad company policy, that:

- for a 'selling division', given the choice between making a sale to an external customer or supplying goods or services to another division within the group, **the preference should be to sell internally**

- for a 'buying division', given the choice between purchasing from an external supplier or from another division within the company, the **preference should be to purchase internally**.

However, a division should be allowed to sell externally rather than transfer internally, or buy externally rather than internally, if it has a good commercial reason. Good commercial reasons would include an external customer offering a higher price, or an external supplier offering a lower price.

Example 1 – Inter-divisional trading

A company has two profit centres, Centre A and Centre B. Centre A supplies Centre B with a part-finished product. Centre B completes the production and sells the finished units in the market at $35 per unit.

Budgeted data for the year:

	Division A	Division B
Number of units transferred/sold	10,000	10,000
Materials costs	$8 per unit	$2 per unit
Other variable costs	$2 per unit	$3 per unit
Annual fixed costs	$60,000	$30,000

Required:

Calculate the budgeted annual profit of each profit centre and the organisation as a whole if the transfer price for components supplied by Division A to Division B is:

(a) $20

(b) $25

Inter divisional trading

A company has two profit centres, Centre A and Centre B. Centre A supplies Centre B with a part-finished product. Centre B completes the production and sells the finished units in the market at $35 per unit.

Budgeted data for the year:

	Division A	Division B
Number of units transferred/sold	10,000	10,000
Materials costs	$8 per unit	$2 per unit
Other variable costs	$2 per unit	$3 per unit
Annual fixed costs	$60,000	$30,000

Required:

Calculate the budgeted annual profit of each profit centre and the organisation as a whole if the transfer price for components supplied by Division A to Division B is:

(a) $20

(b) $25

(a) If the transfer price is $20:

	Division A	Division B	Company as a whole
	$000	$000	$000
External sales	0	350	350
Inter-divisional transfers	200	0	0
	200	200	200
Costs			
Inter-divisional transfers	0	200	0
Other material costs	80	20	100
Other variable costs	20	30	50
Fixed costs	60	30	90
Total costs	160	280	240
Profit	40	70	110

(b) If the transfer price is $25:

	Division A	Division B	Company as a whole
	$000	$000	$000
External sales	0	350	350
Inter-divisional transfers	250	0	0
	250	350	350
Costs			
Inter-divisional transfers	0	250	0
Other material costs	80	20	100
Other variable costs	20	30	50
Fixed costs	60	30	90
Total costs	160	330	240
Profit	90	20	110

Conclusions from the example:

- The choice of transfer price does not affect the profit of the organisation as a whole, provided that there is agreement on the quantity of transfers.

- However, the choice of transfer price affects the profitability of the individual profit centres.

4 Objectives of transfer pricing

(1) Goal congruence

Within a divisionalised company, divisional managers will have responsibility for and will be judged on their division's performance. They will act independently, autonomously and selfishly in the best interests of their own division. They neither know nor care what is happening in other divisions.

It is the task of the management accounting system in general and the transfer pricing policy in particular to ensure that what is good for an individual division is good for the company as a whole.

(2) Performance measurement

The transfer pricing system should result in a report of divisional profits that is a reasonable measure of the managerial performance.

(3) Maintaining divisional autonomy

One of the purposes of decentralisation is to allow managers to exercise greater autonomy. There is little point in granting additional autonomy and then imposing transfer prices that will affect the profitability of the division.

(4) Minimising the global tax liability

When a divisionalised company operates entirely within one tax regime the transfer pricing policy will have a minimal impact on the corporate tax bill. However multinational companies can and do use their transfer pricing policies to move profits around the world and thereby minimise their global tax liabilities.

(5) Recording the movement of goods and services

In practice, an extremely important function of the transfer pricing system is simply to assist in recording the movement of goods and services.

(6) A fair allocation of profits between divisions

Most of the advantages claimed for divisionalisation are behavioural. Insofar as transfer pricing has a material effect on divisional profit it is essential that managers perceive the allocation of corporate profit as being fair if the motivational benefits are to be retained.

Needless to say, a number of these objectives can conflict with each other, and prove difficult to achieve in practice. It is highly unlikely that any one method would meet all the firm's requirements in all circumstances the best that can be hoped for is a reasonable compromise.

Bases for setting a transfer price

In broad terms, there are three bases for setting a transfer price:

(1) market-based prices

(2) cost-based prices

(3) negotiated prices.

A market-based transfer price might be agreed when there is an intermediate market for the transferred item. An intermediate market is a term to describe an external market for the goods or services of the selling division. The selling division can therefore make its profits either by transferring the goods or services internally, or selling them in the external market.

A **market-based** transfer price could be:

- the price for the item in the external market ('intermediate market'), or at a discount to the external market price, to allow for a share of the savings in selling costs that the selling division enjoys by transferring internally rather than selling externally. For example, packaging, distribution and warranty costs may be saved by transferring internally.

A **cost-based** transfer price could be:

- the marginal cost to the selling division of making the product or providing the service
- the selling division's marginal cost plus a mark-up for profit
- the full cost to the selling division of making the product, or
- the selling division's full cost plus a mark-up for profit.

When a transfer price is based on cost, it could be actual cost or budgeted cost. The most suitable basis would be budgeted cost (or standard cost).

- Standard costs or budgeted costs are known in advance; therefore transfers can be priced as they occur. The selling division can invoice the buying division immediately for all items transferred.

- Actual costs are not known until after the end of the accounting period. There would consequently be a delay in pricing transfers and issuing invoices.

- If transfers are at standard or budgeted cost, the selling division's manager could be motivated to improve profits by keeping actual costs below the standard or budgeted amount.

The intermediate market

The intermediate market for the products or services of a selling division could be:

- perfect
- imperfect, or
- non-existent.

A perfect intermediate market

If the intermediate market is perfect, all suppliers to the market are able to sell all their output at the prevailing market price. There are no restrictions on sales demand at that price, and no individual supplier dominates market supply.

When a selling division has a perfect external market for its output, it is therefore able to:

- sell all its output on the external market at the market price, and
- provided that it can sell at a price above its marginal cost, the only limitation on profitability from external sales is the output capacity of the division.

An imperfect intermediate market

An intermediate market is imperfect when the selling division is unable to sell all its output externally at the same market price. This can happen when the division is a dominant influence in the market, and monopoly or oligopoly conditions apply. In order to sell larger volumes of output in the intermediate market, the division is therefore required to reduce the sales price.

When there is an imperfect intermediate market, the problem of identifying a suitable transfer price for inter-divisional sales becomes fairly complex.

It might be possible to establish for the intermediate market a 'demand curve', showing the volume of sales demand at different prices. Demand curves are difficult to establish in practice, although some companies do use them. However, demand curves are common in the academic literature on transfer pricing and there could be examination questions on the topic.

A demand curve

The rule of market prices is that the total market demand for an item varies with the sales price. If the relationship between sales price and sales demand is linear, a demand curve could be expressed by the formula:

$P = a + bQ$

where

P is the sales price for all items sold

Q is the quantity of items sold

Values can be established for a and b. When the price is a, Q should be zero.

Example

Division X in Tropp Group has an imperfect intermediate market for its product B55. The demand curve for B55 is:

$P = 100 - 0.005Q$

This demand curve shows that:

- the maximum sales price is 100, but at this price sales demand would be zero

- for each reduction in price of 0.005, sales demand will increase by 1 unit

- at a price of 0, sales demand will be 20,000 units (= 100/0.005).

Marginal revenue

Marginal revenue is the extra revenue that will be earned by selling one additional unit in the market. In a perfect market, the marginal revenue for a company is always the market price of the item, because all output can be sold at the prevailing market price.

When the market is imperfect, marginal revenue is always lower than the market price.

If you are familiar with differentiation, you will no doubt know how to calculate marginal revenue from a demand curve. If you are not familiar with differentiation, the following rules should be learned:

- The demand curve gives a value for P: $P = a + bQ$

- Total revenue = $P \times Q$

- Substituting, we get: Total revenue = $(a + bQ) \times Q$

Total revenue = $aQ + bQ^2$

- Marginal revenue is found by differentiating $aQ + bQ^2$

Without going into the details of the arithmetic:

Marginal revenue (MR) = $a + 2bQ$

Example

The demand curve for product B55 is: $P = 100 - 0.005Q$

Total revenue (TR) from selling B55 = $(100 - 0.005Q) \times Q$

TR = $100Q - 0.005 Q^2$

The marginal revenue from selling each extra unit of B55 is:

MR = 100 − (2 × 0.005)Q

MR = 100 − 0.010Q

Maximising profit

In an imperfect market, profits are maximised by selling output up to a volume where marginal revenue = marginal cost.

The profit-maximising rule of MR = MC comes from economics and, in economics, cost includes an element for normal profit. However, the same rule can be applied in accounting, where marginal cost does not include a profit element.

This rule might have to be applied in order to determine the profit-maximising output for a company as a whole, and for a profit centre within the company.

5 Decision-making

The general rule for decision-making is that all goods and services should be transferred at **opportunity cost**.

[In the PEG 2012, the Examiner regrets that too many candidates are 'presuming that 'marginal cost' is another name for 'opportunity cost' and are 'unable to describe an opportunity cost approach to Transfer Pricing'.]

There are 3 possible situations.

(1) **Where there is a perfectly competitive market for an intermediate product**

A perfect market means that there is only one price in the market, there are no buying or selling costs and the market is able to absorb the entire output of the primary division and meet all of the requirements of the secondary division.

OPTIMUM TP (DM) = MARKET PRICE + ANY SMALL ADJUSTMENTS

TP in a perfect intermediate market

Perfect intermediate market and no variable selling costs

Division A of the Robin Group makes a product A22, which it sells externally and to another division in the Group, Division B. Division B uses product A22 as a component in product B46, which it sells externally. There is a perfect external market for both A22 and B46.

Costs and sales prices are as follows:

	Division A Product A22	Division B Product B46
Variable production cost	$12 per unit	
Further variable costs		$15 per unit
Fixed costs	$200,000	$300,000
Sales price	$20 per unit	$45 per unit

Division A can either sell product A22 externally for $20, or transfer the product internally to Division B. Unless the transfer price is $20 or more, Division A will prefer to sell externally, in order to maximise its profit.

Division B can either buy product A22 from external suppliers at $20, or buy internally from Division A. If the transfer price exceeds $20, Division B will prefer to buy externally, in order to minimise its costs and so maximise its profit.

Conclusions

- The only transfer price at which Division A and Division B will be willing to trade with each other is $20, the **external market price**.

- At a transfer price of $20, each division would produce and sell up to its capacity. Each division would maximise its profit by making and selling as much as possible, and the total company profit would be maximised. Goal congruence would be achieved.

- In both Divisions A and B, the manager should be motivated to make and sell as much as possible, and to keep costs under control, in order to maximise profit.

- This price would probably be negotiated freely between the managers of Divisions A and B, without head office interference.

- The performance of each profit centre would be measured on a fair basis.

- If company policy is to encourage inter-divisional sales unless there is a good commercial reason for selling or buying externally, the two divisions should trade internally up to the output capacity of the lower-capacity division.

Another way of stating the ideal transfer price is:

	$
Marginal cost in Division A	12
Opportunity cost: contribution forgone from external sale by transferring a unit to Division B: ($20 – $12)	8
Ideal transfer price (= market price)	20

It can be seen that, in these circumstances, setting the transfer price as the market price satisfies all of the objectives of a transfer pricing system.

Perfect intermediate market, but with variable selling costs

If there are variable selling costs or buying costs in the intermediate market:

- it will cost the selling division more to sell externally than to transfer internally, or

- it will cost the buying division more to purchase from an external supplier than to buy internally.

It is therefore cheaper and more profitable to transfer internally than to sell or buy externally. The cost savings can be reflected in an adjustment to the transfer price, so that both divisions share the benefit.

Example

The example of divisions A and B of the Robin Group will be used again, except that the costs and sales prices are as follows:

	Division A Product A22	Division B Product B46
Variable production cost	$12 per unit	
Variable selling cost in the external market	$3 per unit	
Further variable costs		$15 per unit
Fixed costs	$200,000	$300,000
Sales price	$20 per unit	$45 per unit

Division A can either sell product A22 externally for $20 to earn a contribution of $5 per unit ($20 – $15) or transfer the product internally to Division B to earn a contribution of $8. The manager of Division A would prefer to sell to Division B because it is cheaper and more profitable. The lowest transfer price that Division A would accept is $17.

	$
External selling price	20
External variable selling cost	(3)
Minimum transfer price (= market price)	17

Division B can either buy product A22 from external suppliers at $20, or buy internally from Division A. If the transfer price exceeds $20, Division B will prefer to buy externally, in order to minimise its costs and so maximise its profit.

Conclusions

- There is **a range** of ideal transfer prices, between $17 and $20, at which Division A and Division B will be willing to trade with each other.

- If the transfer price is set between $17 and $20, each division would produce and sell up to its capacity. Each division would maximise its profit by making and selling as much as possible, and the total company profit would be maximised. Goal congruence would be achieved.

- In both Divisions A and B, the manager should be motivated to make and sell as much as possible, and to keep costs under control, in order to maximise profit.

- This price would probably be negotiated freely between the managers of Divisions A and B, without head office interference. However, the manager of Division B might need to be aware that Division A is saving costs by selling internally, in order to extract a price concession in negotiations on the transfer price.

- The performance of each profit centre would be measured on a fair basis.

- If company policy is to encourage inter-divisional sales unless there is a good commercial reason for selling or buying externally, the two divisions should trade internally up to the output capacity of the lower-capacity division.

It can be seen that there is a range of prices which will satisfy the general objectives of a transfer pricing system.

(2) **Where there is surplus capacity**

A situation might arise where a profit centre has an intermediate market for its output, and also sells internally, but:

 – there is a limit to the amount that it can sell externally, and

 – it has spare capacity.

In such a situation, the opportunity cost of transferring units internally would be nil, and the ideal transfer price would be based on cost, not the external market price. The opportunity cost of transferring units internally is nil because the selling division can meet external demand in full, and still have excess capacity for making inter-divisional sales. The ideal transfer cost would therefore be marginal cost.

OPTIMUM TP (DM) = MARGINAL COST

(3) **Where there are production constraints**

The shadow price is the opportunity cost of the lost contribution from the other product or it is the extra contribution that would be earned if more of the scarce resource were available.

OPTIMUM TP (DM) = MARGINAL COST + SHADOW PRICE

Example 2 – Relevant costs

AB Ltd has two Divisions – A and B. Division A manufactures a product called the aye and Division B manufactures a product called the bee. Each bee uses a single aye as a component. A is the only manufacturer of the aye and supplies both B and outside customers. Details of A's and B's operations for the coming period are as follows:

	Division A	Division B
Fixed costs	$7,500,000	$18,000,000
Variable costs per unit	$280	$590 (*)
Capacity – Units	30,000	18,000

Note: exclude transfer costs

Market research has indicated that demand for AB Ltd's products from outside customers will be as follows in the coming period:

- the aye: at unit price $1,000 no ayes will be demanded but demand will increase by 25 ayes with every $1 that the unit price is reduced below $1,000

- the bee: at unit price $4,000 no bees will be demanded, but demand will increase by 10 bees with every $1 that the unit price is reduced below $4,000.

Required:

(a) Calculate the unit selling price of the bee (accurate to the nearest $) that will maximise AB Ltd's profit in the coming period.

(b) Calculate the unit selling price of the bee (accurate to the nearest $) that is likely to emerge if the Divisional Managers of A and B both set selling prices calculated to maximise Divisional profit from sales to outside customers and the transfer price of ayes going from A to B is set at 'market selling price'.

(c) Explain why your answers to parts (a) and (b) are different, and propose changes to the system of transfer pricing in order to ensure that AB Ltd is charging its customers at optimum prices.

6 Performance evaluation

The aim is to set a transfer price that will give a fair measure of performance in each division, i.e. profit.

(1) **Where there is a perfectly competitive market for an intermediate product**

When transfers are recorded at market prices, divisional performance is more likely to represent the real economic contribution of the division to total company profits.

If the supplying division did not exist, the intermediate product would have to be purchased on the outside market, at the current market price. Alternatively, if the receiving division did not exist, the intermediate product would be sold on the outside market at the current market price. Divisional profits are therefore likely to be similar to the profits that would be calculated if the divisions were separate organisations.

OPTIMUM TP (DM) = MARKET PRICE + ANY SMALL ADJUSTMENTS

This is fair.

(2) Where there is surplus capacity

OPTIMUM TP (DM) = MARGINAL COST

The problem is that transferring at marginal cost is unlikely to be 'fair' to the supplying division.

Possible solutions:

(i) 2 part tariff

The transfer price is marginal cost, but in addition a fixed sum is paid per annum or per period to the supplying division to go at least part of the way towards covering its fixed costs, and possibly even to generate a profit.

Archer Group

Archer Group has two divisions, Division X and Division Y. Division X manufactures a component X8 which is transferred to Division Y. Division Y uses component X8 to make a finished product Y14, which it sells for $20. There is no external market for component X8.

Costs are as follows:

	Division X Component X8	Division Y Product Y14
Variable production cost	$5 per unit	$3 per unit*
Annual fixed costs	$40,000	$80,000

Excluding the cost of transferred units of X8.

Under a two-part tariff transfer pricing arrangement, Division Y would pay:

(1) a fixed fee of $40,000 each year plus possibly a negotiated mark up for profit, plus

(2) $5 for each unit of component X8 transferred.

A two-part tariff should ensure that the selling division would not make a loss, and would make a profit if its actual costs are less than the agreed transfer price fixed fee and/or a profit mark up has been allowed for in the fixed fee.

However, there is no incentive for the manager of Division X to produce more output, and a two-part tariff has a number of disadvantages:

- It may not provide motivation to the selling division manager.

- The measurement of the performance of the selling division may not be fair.

- The negotiation process may be time consuming and a fair profit may have to be imposed by head office.

(ii) Cost-plus pricing

The transfer price is the marginal cost or full cost plus a mark-up.

(iii) 'Dual pricing'

Dual pricing is where one transfer price is recorded by the supplying division and a different transfer price is recorded by the buying division.

An adjustment account in the HQ books holds the differences between the divisions.

Fern Group

Fern Group has two divisions, Domestic and Business. Business Division manufactures computer desks for business customers. Its annual capacity is 15,000 desks, but currently annual demand is only 10,000 desks.

The marginal cost of making a desk in Business Division is $600, and the desks sell for $800. Fixed costs in the Business Division are $1,500,000.

Domestic Division makes and sells furniture items for retail customers. Its manager has seen an opportunity to make some alterations and additions to the Business Division computer desk, and sell it to retail customers as an IT desk for the home.

The extra cost of amending and improving the Business Division desk would be $200 per desk. The Domestic Division manager believes he could sell 5,000 desks for the home each year at $880 each. However, he would not want to pay Business Division more than $560 for each desk.

Required:

How might a dual transfer price arrangement help to reach an agreement between the two divisions?

Solution:

The first step with any transfer pricing problem is to establish what is in the best interests of the company as a whole.

In this example, it is in the interests of the company for Domestic Division to make and sell the 5,000 IT desks for the home.

Selling price	$880
Marginal cost in Business Division	$600
Marginal cost in Domestic Division	$200
Total marginal cost for each unit	$800
Contribution for each unit sold	$80
Total increase in annual contribution (5,000 units)	$400,000

The company should want the Domestic Division to make and sell the IT desks, and Business Division has sufficient spare capacity to meet the demand without affecting its own external sales of computer desks.

However, Business Division will not agree to a transfer price below marginal cost. At a transfer price of $560, it would lose $40 for each unit transferred.

Head office could try to persuade the manager of Domestic Division to agree to a transfer price at marginal cost plus. A transfer price between $600 and $680 would share the marginal profits between the two divisions.

If head office suggested a price above $600, the Domestic Division manager might decide to drop the plan to make and sell the IT desks, since the hoped-for extra profit might not be sufficient to justify the risk of offering a new product to the market. To get round the problem, head office might decide on **dual transfer prices:**

(1) Domestic Division should buy desks from Business Division at $560 per unit.

(2) Business Division should be paid in excess of marginal cost for supplying desks to Domestic Division. A transfer price of $610 might be offered.

(3) The difference $50 ($610 – $560) between the two transfer prices would be a charge to head office.

(4) With this arrangement, Business Division would supply 5,000 desks to Domestic Division.

(5) Business Division would make additional annual profits of $10 per desk ($50,000 in total).

(6) Domestic Division would make a contribution of $120 per desk sold ($880 – $200 – $560) and so increase annual profits by $600,000.

(7) Head office would take a charge of $50 per desk or $250,000 in total.

(8) The company as a whole would benefit by $50,000 + $600,000 – $250,000 = $400,000.

(3) **Where there are production constraints**

OPTIMUM TP (DM) = MARGINAL COST + SHADOW PRICE

Whether the transfer price is fair for performance evaluation purposes depends on what the shadow prices reflect.

There are 2 possibilities:

(i) Where internal demand has to be met by foregoing external sales of another product, the shadow prices reflect contribution foregone on that other product. The resulting TP (DM) is also suitable for performance evaluation.

(ii) Where the supplying division makes only one product which is only sold internally, the shadow price must now reflect contribution from the final production. The TP (DM) builds that contribution into the supplying division's revenue.

Therefore all contribution will appear in the supplying division's books (and none in the buying division's).

The problem is that the optimum TP (DM) is unfair to the buying division.

Possible solutions:

(a) 2-part tariff
(b) Cost-plus pricing
(c) Dual pricing

Example 3 – Dual Pricing: Pool Group

Pool Group has two divisions that operate as profit centres. Each centre sells similar products, but to different segments of the market:

- Division P makes product P29 which it sells to external customers for $150. Variable costs of production are $45 per unit. The maximum annual sales demand for P29 is 5,000 units, although Division P has capacity for 7,000 units. Increasing output from 5,000 to 7,000 each year would result in additional fixed cost expenditure of $8,000.

- The manager of Division L has seen an opportunity to sell an amended version of Product P29 to its own customers, and is interested in buying 2,000 units each year to re-sell externally at $90 per unit. The costs of amending Product P29, for sale as Product L77, would be $25 per unit. However, the manager of Division L will not pay more than $40 per unit of Product P29. He argues that Division P will benefit from lower fixed costs per unit by working at full capacity. The manager of Division P refuses to sell at a price that does not cover the division's incremental costs.

Required:

Suggest a dual transfer pricing arrangement that might overcome the disagreement between the two divisional managers.

Transfer pricing: Behavioural considerations

Transfer prices tend to vary over the product life cycle according to Cats-Baril et al. (1988). During the introductory phase, they suggest a cost plus fixed fee or cost plus a profit share. During the growth phase, they suggest a price related to the closest substitute and during maturity a price based on identical products. This is common sense to a large extent. It is probably only during the maturity stage that identical substitutes exist and during the introductory phase there may be no basis other than cost on which to base the price.

Using any actual cost or cost plus as a transfer price does not motivate the supplying division to act in the interest of the group. Standard or predetermined costs should always be used in place of actual cost. If actual cost is used, the supplying division is not encouraged to be efficient, and control costs as inefficiencies are passed on to the receiving division by way of a higher transfer price. It is even worse if a mark-up is used because the selling division is encouraged to push up the actual cost as this will increase the mark-up, and increase the division's profit. Standard costs are at least subject to scrutiny when they are set once a year and the receiving division has a chance to challenge them. If standard cost is used, the selling division has an incentive to control actual costs below that level and so increase its own profits.

It is usual to imagine transfer pricing taking place in vertically integrated manufacturing organisations. This is not the norm today. Transfer pricing takes place in many different types of organisation and it can have a profound effect on behaviour. For example, a garage carries out a number of different activities that are linked to the activities of another section. The activities include selling new cars, selling old cars, servicing cars sold, general repairs, repairing and servicing used cars accepted in part payment, providing financing and so on. A transfer price is used to transfer a used car accepted in part-payment for a new car between the new car sales and used car sales divisions. A transfer price will also have to be established for transferring the cost of servicing and repairing these cars for sale between the servicing division and the used car sales division. These prices will have considerable implications for the profitability of the different sections and on the actions of the employees when making sales deals. If performance measurement and assessment is to be fair, transfer prices need to be set carefully.

Transfer prices can also be used to deter competitors. If a vertically integrated company concentrates profits at the stage of production where there is least competition, competitors may be attracted to enter. On the other hand, competitors operating at the other stages may be disadvantaged by the low profits the vertically integrated company is taking and they may not be able to achieve a satisfactory return if they are only operating in a limited area of the value chain. Neghandhi (1987) cites cases of US oil companies and Japanese trading and manufacturing companies doing this.

7 International transfer pricing

Transfers within an international group will often be cross-border, between divisions in different countries. With international transfers and international transfer pricing, the issues already described in this chapter still apply. In addition, other factors need to be considered.

8 Different tax rates

A multinational company will seek to minimise the group's total tax liability. One way of doing this might be to use transfer pricing to:

- reduce the profitability of its subsidiaries in high-tax countries, and
- increase the profitability of its subsidiaries in low-tax countries.

Changes in the transfer price can redistribute the pre-tax profit between subsidiaries, but the total pre-tax profit will be the same. However, if more pre-tax profit is earned in low-tax countries and less profit is earned in high-tax countries, the total tax bill will be reduced.

[In the PEG September 2010, the examiner regrets that candidates are not considering the consequences of using an inflated transfer price to reduce the overall tax burden of the company.]

Taxation and transfer pricing

International and intra-group trading is a very important part of business today. One-third of the UK's exports to Europe are intra-group transactions. Foreign-owned assets in Europe and the USA increased considerably during the 1980s and 1990s. During the 1980s, foreign-owned assets in the USA tripled, but the tax paid changed very little, as more than half the companies involved reported no taxable income (Pear, 1990).

International intra-group transfer pricing has its own special considerations, and so a multinational organisation will have matters other than behavioural ones to consider when it sets its transfer prices. There is a natural inclination to set transfer prices in order to minimise tax payments.

Taxation

If a group has subsidiaries that operate in different countries with different tax rates, the overall group corporation tax bill could be reduced by manipulating the transfer prices between the subsidiaries.

For example, if the taxation rate on profits in Country X is 25 per cent and in Country Y it is 60 per cent, the group could adjust the transfer price to increase the profit of the subsidiary in Country X and reduce the profit of the subsidiary in Country Y.

Thus, if the subsidiary in Country X provides goods or services to the subsidiary in Country Y, the use of a very high transfer price would maximise the profits in the lower-tax country, and minimise the profits in the higher-tax country.

There is also a temptation to set up marketing subsidiaries in countries with low corporation tax rates and transfer products to them at a relatively low transfer price. When the products are sold to the final customer, a low rate of tax will be paid on the difference between the two prices.

According to a survey by Ernst and Young (1995), more than 80 per cent of multinational companies viewed transfer pricing as a major international tax issue, and more than half of those companies saw it as the major issue. The taxation authorities in most countries monitor transfer prices in an attempt to control the situation and in order to collect the full amount of taxation due. Double taxation agreements between countries mean that companies pay tax on specific transactions in one country only. However, if the company sets an unrealistic transfer price in order to minimise tax, and the tax authority spots this, the company will pay taxation in both countries, that is, double taxation. This additional payment can amount to millions of pounds and, as a result, is quite an effective deterrent. On the other hand, the gains of avoiding taxation may be even greater.

There have been many cases of transfer price fixing for one reason or another over the years. One of the most notorious of UK transfer pricing cases was that of Hoffman La Roche, as it was then called. Hoffman La Roche had developed the drugs of Librium and Valium. The products were imported into the UK at prices of $437 and $979 per kilo, respectively. The UK tax authority accepted the prices; however, the Monopolies Commission sprang into life and questioned the prices on the grounds that the same chemical ingredients, which were unbranded, could be obtained from an Italian company for $9 and $28 per kilo. Hoffman La Roche argued on two grounds: (1) that the price was not set on cost but on what the market would bear, and (2) they had incurred the research and development costs and so had to recover those in the price. However, this was not accepted and they were fined $1.85 m in 1960.

More recently in the UK in 1992, Nissan was caught for unpaid tax of $237 m for falsely inflated invoices that were used to reduce profits. The freight charges were inflated by 40–60 per cent by a Norwegian company. The next year Nissan was required to pay $106 m in unpaid tax in the USA because the authorities felt that part of their USA marketing profits were being transferred to Japan as transfer prices on imports of cars and trucks were too high. Interestingly, the Japanese tax authorities took a different view and returned the double tax, which is a very rare occurrence.

Most countries now accept the Organisation for Economic Co-operation and Development's (OECD) 1995 guidelines. These guidelines were produced with the aim of standardising national approaches to transfer pricing as part of the OECD's charter to encourage the freedom of world trade. They provide guidance on the application of 'arm's length' principles. They state that where necessary transfer prices should be adjusted using an 'arm's length' price, that is, a price that would have been arrived at by two unrelated companies acting independently. There are three methods the tax authorities can use to determine an arm's length price.

The first is the comparable price method. This is the most widely used and involves setting the arm's length price by using the prices of similar products, that is, the market price or an approximation to one. The method is known as using comparable uncontrolled prices (CUPS) and is the preferred method wherever possible. This may seem a straightforward basis but as most international trade is carried out between related companies meaningful comparisons are hard to find. For example, in the UK in the 1980s, it was possible to use independent car distributorships to find a CUP but now that car manufacturers have developed their own dependent distributor networks, finding arm's length comparability is much more difficult.

Where a CUP cannot be found, or is inappropriate, one of two gross margin methods should be used. These involve a review of gross margins in comparable transactions between uncontrolled organisations. The resale price method is used for the transfer of goods to distributors and marketing operations where goods are sold on with little further processing. The price paid for a final product by an independent party is used and from this a suitable mark-up (to allow for the seller's expenses and profit) is deducted. The second gross margin method is the cost-plus method. Here an arm's length gross margin is established and applied to the seller's manufacturing cost.

These methods are of little help when attempting to establish an arm's length price for intangible property such as a patent right or trade name. Also, much of the data needed may not be in the public domain and so setting fair transfer prices is not easy. In the past, this did not matter so much but today it is often up to the taxpayer to 'prove' the price.

For example, the US section 482 regulations on transfer pricing cover 300 pages and the onus is on the taxpayer to support the transfer price with 'timely' documentation. If this is not done, a non-deductible penalty of up to 40 per cent of the arm's length price may be levied. In the past in the UK, it was up to the tax authorities to detect cases of inappropriate transfer pricing. This left the UK vulnerable to a certain amount of tax leakage. But now under the self-assessment regulations, the onus has switched to the taxpayer to provide correct information. Failure to demonstrate a reasonable attempt at an arm's length price in the tax return will give rise to a penalty of 100 per cent of any tax adjustment. Other European countries are also tightening their regulations in response to the USA and OECD's moves.

To safeguard the position, the taxpayer may enter into an Advanced Pricing Agreement (APA) with the relevant two tax authorities involved. This is a new approach and is done in advance to avoid any dispute and the costly penalty of double taxation and penalty fees. According to the Ernst and Young (1995) survey referred to earlier, more than 60 per cent of companies intend to do or are doing this.

Example 4 – Seacross

Seacross Group has two subsidiaries, UKD in the UK and GD in Germany.

UKD makes and sells Product S99. The variable cost of manufacture in the UK is £200 per unit and annual fixed costs are £210,000. Product S99 sells for £500 per unit in the UK market and annual demand is 800 units.

GD in Germany buys 400 units of S99 from UKD each year, adapts them for the German market, and sells them for the equivalent of £700 per unit. The variable costs of adapting the product and selling it in Germany are £50 per unit. The cost of shipping the 400 units to Germany is £6,000 and these are paid by GD. Fixed costs in GD are £24,000 each year.

The rate of taxation on company profits is 30% in the UK and 50% in Germany.

Required:

What would be the annual after-tax profits of the group if the transfer price for S99 is:

(a) its UK market price, £500

(b) its variable cost of manufacture, £200?

9 Government action on transfer prices

Governments are aware of the effect of transfer pricing on profits, and in many countries, multinationals are required to justify the transfer prices that they charge. Multinationals could be required to apply 'arm's length' prices to transfer prices: in other words, they might be required under tax law to use market-based transfer prices, to remove the opportunities for tax avoidance.

It is also possible, on the other hand, that some countries wishing to attract business might have tax laws that are very favourable to business. A country with the status of a 'tax haven' might offer:

• a low rate of tax on profits

• a low withholding tax on dividends paid to foreign holding companies

- tax treaties with other countries
- no exchange controls
- a stable economy
- good communications with the rest of the world
- a well-developed legal framework, within which company rights are protected.

Multinationals might set up subsidiary companies in tax havens, trade through these companies, and hope to reduce their total tax liabilities.

10 Transfer pricing to manage cash flow

Some governments might place legal restrictions on dividend payments by companies to foreign parent companies.

In this situation, it would be tempting for a multinational to sell goods or services to a subsidiary in the country concerned from other divisions in other countries, and charge very high transfer prices as a means of getting cash out of the country.

This tactic is not possible, however, when the country's tax laws require that transfer prices should be set on an arm's length basis.

11 International transfer pricing and currency management

When inter-divisional transfers are between subsidiaries in different countries or currency zones, a decision has to be made about the currency to select for transfer pricing.

Exchange rates, even for strong currencies, can be very volatile and subsidiaries could make unexpected profits or losses from movements in an exchange rate.

Example: A UK subsidiary sells goods to a US subsidiary for $12.80 per unit. The exchange rate was £1 = $1.60 when the transfer price was agreed, and the cost of making each unit in the UK and shipping it to the US is £6.

When the exchange rate is $1.60, the sterling equivalent value of the $12.80 transfer price is £8, and the UK subsidiary makes a profit of £2 per unit transferred.

However, if the dollar weakened in value, and the exchange rate moved to $2.00, the sterling value of the transfer price would fall to £6.40, and the profit per unit would fall to £0.40.

The implications for an international group of currency risk in transfer prices are as follows:

(i) With inter-divisional trading between subsidiaries in different currency zones, one subsidiary or the other (or possibly both, if the transfer price is set in a third currency) will be exposed to a risk of losses from adverse movements in the exchange rate.

(ii) When one subsidiary makes a loss on an adverse exchange rate movement, the other will make a profit.

(iii) The company as a whole should manage its exposures to currency risks. This might be the responsibility of either the profit centre managers or a treasury department.

(iv) When it is fairly certain which way an exchange rate might move in the future, a multinational company might be tempted to set transfer prices in a currency such that any currency losses arise in the subsidiary in the high-tax country, and currency profits arise in the country with the lower tax rate.

Example 5 – Multinational computer manufacturer

A multinational computer manufacturer has a number of autonomous subsidiaries throughout the world. Two of the group's subsidiaries are in America and Europe. The American subsidiary assembles computers using chips that it purchases from local companies. The European subsidiary manufactures exactly the same chips that are used by the American subsidiary but currently only sells them to numerous external companies throughout Europe. Details of the two subsidiaries are given below:

America

The American subsidiary buys the chips that it needs from a local supplier. It has negotiated a price of $90 per chip. The production budget shows that 300,000 chips will be needed next year.

Europe

The chip production subsidiary in Europe has a capacity of 800,000 chips per year. Details of the budget for the forthcoming year are as follows:

Sales: 600,000 chips

Selling price	$105 per chip
Variable costs	$ 60 per chip

The fixed costs of the subsidiary at the budgeted output of 600,000 chips are $20 million per year, but they would rise to $26 million if output exceeds 625,000 chips. The maximum external demand is 600,000 chips per year and the subsidiary has no other uses for the current spare capacity.

Group directive

The Managing Director of the group has reviewed the budgets of the subsidiaries and has decided that, in order to improve the profitability of the group, the European subsidiary should supply chips to the American subsidiary. She is also thinking of linking the salaries of the subsidiary managers to the performance of their subsidiaries but is unsure which performance measure to use. Two measures that she is considering are 'profit' and the 'return on assets consumed' (where the annual fixed costs would be used as the 'assets consumed').

The Manager of the European subsidiary has offered to supply the chips at a price of $95 each. He has offered this price because it would earn the same contribution per chip that would be earned on external sales (this is after adjusting for increased distribution costs and reduced customer servicing costs).

Required:

(a) Assume that the 300,000 chips are supplied by the European subsidiary at a transfer price of $95 per chip. Calculate the impact of the profits on each of the subsidiaries and the group.

(5 marks)

(b) Calculate the minimum unit price at which the European subsidiary would be willing to transfer the 300,000 chips to the American subsidiary if the performance and salary of the Manager of the subsidiary is to be based on:

(i) the profit of the subsidiary (currently $7 million)

(ii) the return on assets consumed by the subsidiary (currently 35%).

(9 marks)

(c) Write a report to the Managing Director of the group that discusses issues raised by the directive and the introduction of performance measures. (You should use your answers to parts (a) and (b), where appropriate, to illustrate points in your report.)

(10 marks)

(d) Briefly explain how multinational companies can use transfer pricing to reduce their overall tax charge and the steps that national tax authorities have taken to discourage the manipulation of transfer prices.

(6 marks)

(Total: 30 marks)

12 Practice Questions

Objective Test Question 1: Transfer pricing

A professional firm has two divisions, a computer consultancy division (CSD) and a management advisory division (MAD). Each division provides consultancy and advisory services to clients and in the year just ended, the fees earned by CSD were $500,000 and the fees earned by MAD were $700,000. Establishment costs were $400,000 for the year in CSD and $500,000 for the year in MAD.

In providing services to their clients, each division obtains supporting services from the other division. During the year, CSD provided 5,000 hours of services to MAD and MAD provided 2,000 hours of services to CSD.

It has been agreed that the transfer prices for services should be $20 per hour for work done by CSD and $30 per hour for services provided by MAD.

Required:

The profit for the year reported by CSD was:

A $60,000

B $100,000

C $140,000

D $200,000

Objective Test Question 2: Transfer pricing

Hock Group has two divisions, Division P and Division Q. Division P manufactures an item that is transferred to Division Q. The item has no external market, and 60,000 units produced are transferred internally each year. The costs of each division are as follows:

	Division P	Division Q
Variable cost	$10 per unit	$12 per unit
Fixed costs each year	$120,000	$90,000

Head office management decides that a transfer price should be set that provides a profit of $30,000 to Division P. What should the transfer price per unit be?

Objective Test Question 3: Transfer pricing

An international group operates in four countries, the US, France, the UK and Malaysia. Its divisions in each country trade with each other. There are large differences between the countries in rates of taxation on corporate profits.

The company's management is reasonably confident that for the next year or so, it can predict which of its operating currencies (US dollars, euros, sterling and ringgitts) will rise in value against the others and which will fall.

Required:

In which currencies might the group's management wish to price inter-company sales within the group?

Data Set Question: Division A and Division B

Division A transfers 100,000 units of a component to Division B each year. The market price of the component is $25. Division A's variable cost is $15 per unit, and A's divisional's fixed costs are $500,000 each year.

What price would be credited to Division A for each component that it transfers to Division B under:

Dual pricing (based on marginal cost and market price)?

Two-part tariff pricing (where the Divisions have agreed that the fixed fee will be $200,000)?

Integration Style Question: Transfer Pricing

PRE-SEEN MATERIAL

Division A of a large divisionalised organisation manufactures a single standardised product. Some of the output is sold externally whilst the remainder is transferred to Division B where it is a sub-assembly in the manufacture of that division's product. The unit costs of division A's product are as follows:

Direct material	$4
Direct labour	$2
Direct expense	$2
Variable manufacturing overheads	$2
Fixed manufacturing overheads	$4
Selling and packing expenses – variable	$1
	$15

Annually, 10,000 units of the product are sold externally at the standard price of $30.

In addition to external sales, 5,000 units are transferred annually to Division B at an internal transfer price of $29 per unit. This transfer price is obtained by deducting variable selling and packing expense from the external price since these costs are not incurred on internal transfers.

Division B incorporates the transferred in goods into a more advanced product. The unit costs of this product are as follows:

Transferred in item (from Division A)	$29
Direct material and components	$23
Direct labour	$3
Variable overheads	$12
Fixed overheads	$12
Selling and packing expenses – variable	$1
	$80

You work as the Company's Management Accountant and you have just received the following email from the Manager of Division B:

From: Tomasina Goic, Manager, Division B
To: A.N. Accountant
Date: 02.07.2014
Subject: Transfer Pricing

I disagree with the basis used to set the transfer price. Transfers should be made at variable cost plus an agreed (minimal) mark-up, because Division B is taking output that Division A would be unable to sell at a price of $30.

Partly because of this disagreement, a study of the relationship between selling price and demand has recently been made for each division by the company's sales director. The resulting report contains the following table:

Customer demand at various selling prices:

	Selling price	Demand
Division A	$20	15,000
	$30	10,000
	$40	5,000
Division B	$80	7,200
	$90	5,000
	$100	2,800

You then get the following email:

From:	Tomasina Goic, Manager, Division B
To:	A.N. Accountant
Date:	03.07.2014
Subject:	Transfer Pricing

This study supports my case, does it not? I suggest that a transfer price of $12 would give Division A a reasonable contribution to its fixed overheads while allowing my Division B to earn a reasonable profit.I also believe that it would lead to an increase in output and an improvement in the overall level of company profits.

Email a reply to Tomasina Goic, in which you will have established the maximum contribution that can be earned by the company and the effect that the current transfer pricing system will have; Your email should also establish the likely effect on profits of adopting the manager of Division B's suggestion of a transfer price of $12.

Test your understanding answers

Example 1 – Inter-divisional trading

(a) If the transfer price is $20:

	Division A	Division B	Company as a whole
	$000	$000	$000
External sales	0	350	350
Inter-divisional transfers	200	0	0
	200	200	200
Costs			
Inter-divisional transfers	0	200	0
Other material costs	80	20	100
Other variable costs	20	30	50
Fixed costs	60	30	90
Total costs	160	280	240
Profit	40	70	110

(b) If the transfer price is $25:

	Division A	Division B	Company as a whole
	$000	$000	$000
External sales	0	350	350
Inter-divisional transfers	250	0	0
	250	350	350
Costs			
Inter-divisional transfers	0	250	0
Other material costs	80	20	100
Other variable costs	20	30	50
Fixed costs	60	30	90
Total costs	160	330	240
Profit	90	20	110

Conclusions from the example:

- The choice of transfer price does not affect the profit of the organisation as a whole, provided that there is agreement on the quantity of transfers.

- However, the choice of transfer price affects the profitability of the individual profit centres.

Example 2 – Relevant costs

(a)

Division A	*Division B*
Capacity 30,000	Capacity 18,000
Marginal cost = $280	Marginal cost = $590
Fixed cost = $7.5 million	Fixed cost = $18 million
P = 1,000 – 0.04Q	P = 4,000 – 0.1Q
MR = 1,000 – 0.08Q	MR = 4,000 – 0.2Q

To maximise group profits from sales of bee;

Marginal revenue from bee	= Marginal cost of bee
4,000 – 0.2Q	= 280 + 590
Q	= 15,650
P	= 4,000 – 0.1 × 15,650
	= $2,435

Conclusion

A unit selling price of $2,435 per bee will maximise AB Ltd's profit in the coming period.

(b) Division A: Division A; for external sales of aye the division will ensure that:

Marginal revenue from aye	= Marginal cost of aye
1,000 – 0.04Q	= $280
Q	= 9,000
P	= 1,000 – 0.04 × 9,000
	= $640

This now becomes the internal transfer price and as such forms part of Division B's divisional marginal cost.

Division B; for sales of bee they will ensure their division MR = divisional MC

$$4,000 - 0.2Q = 640 + 590$$
$$Q = 13,850$$

$$P = 4,000 - 0.1 \times 13,850$$
$$= \$2,615$$

This now becomes the internal transfer price and as such forms part of Division B's divisional marginal cost.

(c) In part (a) of the question we establish that the group should sell 15,650 units of bee at $2,435 in order to maximise group profits. Under part (b) of the question the manager of A is not using a transfer price that will bring about this decision (goal congruency).

As the divisions are acting autonomously, it is understandable that the manager of A will aim to earn a divisional contribution from internal sales of aye. As he sells externally at a price of $640 he may consider that this seems to be a fair price for internal sales.

However, this internal transfer price then forms part of Division B's marginal costs. The divisional marginal costs at this point ($640 + $590) are NOT the same as the true marginal cost of a bee ($280 + $590). The manager of B ensures his divisional profits are maximised, however, this does not coincide with the group objective as the wrong cost data is essentially being used.

To overcome this problem, Head Office could impose a transfer price. Given the surplus capacity at A, the TP to guarantee goal congruency should be the Marginal Cost of an aye, that is $280. At this transfer price the manager of B will record a divisional marginal cost of $870 ($280 + $590) and will happily operate at the optimum level, selling 15,650 bees at $2,435.

However, at a TP of marginal cost the manager of A is likely to become demotivated as his division receives no reward or benefit for work on internal transfers. Additionally, if divisional profit is used as a performance indicator, the system will fail to measure the performance of division A adequately.

So, as an alternative to the relevant cost being used for the TP, a cost based price could be used. Three methods may be employed;

- cost plus price. Here a mark-up could be added to the marginal cost

- two part tariff. This is where the marginal cost is used as the UNIT price of an aye, but a fixed fee is paid to Division A from Div B each period

- dual pricing system could be implemented. Division A sells ayes internally recording one TP (say $640 – the external market price of an aye) and Division B records purchases of aye at a different transfer price. Div B could use a TP of $280 – the MC of an aye. Under this system Division B would operate at the optimum level for the group, and Division A would earn a contribution on internal sales. Head office would reconcile the discrepancies with a reconciliation account.

Example 3 – Dual Pricing: Pool Group

It is in the interests of Pool Group for the additional units to be made and sold as Product L77.

The contribution per unit will be $90 – $45 – $25 = $20. The contribution from selling 2,000 units each year ($40,000) exceeds the additional fixed costs of $8,000.

To cover the incremental costs in Division P, the transfer price needs to be $45 + $(8,000/2,000 units) = $49.

Division L will not pay more than $40.

A dual transfer pricing arrangement that might win the agreement of both divisional managers is for Division P to receive $49 per unit of P29 and for Division L to pay $40. The difference of $9 per unit or $18,000 in total for the year would be a charge to head office.

Example 4 – Seacross

[*Note: This example shows that when two profit centres are in different countries, it would be in the interests of the company as a whole to set transfer prices that keep a larger proportion of the total profit in the low-tax country.*

In this example, the higher transfer price gives more profit to the UK division and less profit to the German division. The total pre-tax profit remains the same, but total tax charges are lower, giving a higher-total post-tax profit for the group.]

(a) **Transfer price = £500**

	UKD	GD	Company as a whole
	£	£	£
External sales	400,000	280,000	680,000
Inter-divisional transfers	200,000	0	0
	600,000	280,000	680,000
Costs			
Inter-divisional transfers	0	200,000	0
Other variable costs	240,000	20,000	260,000
Shipping costs	0	6,000	6,000
Fixed costs	210,000	24,000	234,000
Total costs	450,000	250,000	500,000
Pre-tax profit	150,000	30,000	180,000
Tax (30%:50%)	(45,000)	(15,000)	(60,000)
After-tax profit	105,000	15,000	120,000

(b) **Transfer price = £200**

	UKD	GD	Company as a whole
	£	£	£
External sales	400,000	280,000	680,000
Inter-divisional transfers	80,000	0	0
	480,000	280,000	680,000
Costs			
Inter-divisional transfers	0	80,000	0
Other variable costs	240,000	20,000	260,000
Shipping costs	0	6,000	6,000
Fixed costs	210,000	24,000	234,000
Total costs	450,000	130,000	500,000
Pre-tax profit	30,000	150,000	180,000
Tax (30%:50%)	(9,000)	(75,000)	(84,000)
After-tax profit	21,000	75,000	96,000

Example 5 – Multinational computer manufacturer

(a) Without the transfer the European subsidiary would make a profit of:

$$(\$105 - \$60) \times 600,000 - \$20m = \$7m$$

With the transfer the profit would increase to:

$$\$45 \times 800,000 - \$26m = \$10m$$

The internal transfer would lead to an increase in cost for the American subsidiary of

$$300,000 \times \$5 = \$1.5m$$

The net impact on profit for the group would be:

European subsidiary	American subsidiary	Group
Increase of $3m	Reduction of $1.5m	Increase of $1.5m

(b) (i) Let TP = transfer price required.

Maximum capacity is 800,000 units so to supply the American subsidiary with 300,000 units only 500,000 units can be sold externally.

Contribution per unit on external sales = $105 − $60 = $45

If contribution remains the same when the transfer price is $95 then the variable cost per unit relating to internal transfers must be $95 − $45 = $50

$300,000 \times (TP − 50) + 500,000 \ \$45 − \$26m = \$7m$

$TP − 50 = \$7m + \$26m − \$22.5m/300,000 = \$35$

So TP = $85

(ii)

$$\frac{300,000 \times (TP − 50) + 500,000 \times \$45 − \$26m}{\$26m} \times 100 = 35\%$$

$300,000 \times (TP − 50) = 35\% \times \$26m − 500,000 \times \$45 + \$26m$
$= \$12.6m$

$TP − 50 = \$12.6m/300,000 = \$42$

So TP = $92

(c)

REPORT

To: Managing Director

From: Management Accountant

Date: XX.XX.XX

Subject: Group Directive

This report discusses issues raised by the directive and the introduction of performance measures.

Internal transfer of chips

The European subsidiary has 200,000 units of spare capacity and should, in principle, be prepared to supply these at any price which exceeds incremental costs. For 200,000 units this would be $50 + $6m/200,000 = $80 per unit. (Note that the variable cost of internal transfers is lower than that of external sales – see part b). The American subsidiary would be prepared to accept any price under $90, the price at which the chips can be purchased from a local supplier. For the first 200,000 units there is a range of possible transfer prices which would be acceptable to both subsidiaries of $80 to $90.

The American subsidiary requires 300,000 units however and the additional 100,000 units could only be supplied by reducing the supply to external customers. The minimum transfer price acceptable to the European subsidiary would be $95 as this would earn the same contribution per chip as external sales. At this price the American subsidiary would be paying $5 per chip more than from the external market and so would not be motivated to buy internally.

An average price for all 300,000 units could be set using $80 for the first 200,000 units and $95 for the remaining 100,000 units.

200,000 × $80 + 100,000 × $95/300,000 = $85.

It has already been seen in part (b) that this is the minimum price the European subsidiary would consider if performance was measured on profit. The American subsidiary would be saving $5 per chip.

A better solution may be to transfer 200,000 chips internally and purchase the remaining 100,000 chips from the external supplier. Assuming the transfer price is set at $80 this would result in a profit for the European subsidiary of 600,000 × $45 + 200,000 × $30 – $26m = $7m. The American subsidiary would reduce costs by 200,000 × $15 = $3m. Group profits would increase by $3m, an increase of $1.5m compared to using a transfer price of $95 (see part a).

At $80 all of the profit increase was in the American subsidiary. Depending on where the transfer price is set in the range $80 to $90 the increase in profit can be divided more equitably between the two divisions.

Performance measures

If performance is measured using profit then any price above $85, (for 300,000 units), but below $90 would allow both subsidiaries to increase profits. If return on assets is used however the minimum price that would be acceptable to the European subsidiary would be $92 (part b). The American subsidiary would be unwilling to trade at that price. It would be impossible to set a transfer price that would be acceptable to both divisions.

Conclusion

It would be beneficial for the group if 200,000 chips were transferred internally rather than the current practise of external purchase. Providing the external supplier is willing to supply only 100,000 chips at $90 per unit this is the preferred option. A performance measurement system based on profit allows a transfer price to be set which would be acceptable to both subsidiaries. This is not the case if return on assets consumed is used.

(d) Multi-nationals may have some companies located in countries with high rates of corporate tax and others with lower rates. To reduce the overall tax charge the aim will be to keep profit as low as possible in high tax rate countries. This can be achieved by charging high transfer prices to companies in high tax countries purchasing goods and set low transfer prices for those companies in high tax countries supplying goods.

National tax authorities have taken action to discourage manipulation of profits. Internal transfers are examined closely and are expected to be at market prices, or where this is not possible, at cost. Heavy fines are imposed on companies suspected of deliberately manipulating transfer prices to avoid tax.

Objective Test Question 1: Transfer pricing

[Tutorial note: Only the profit reported by CSD is required. Total profit is shown here for information.]

	Company	*MAD*	*Company*
External sales	500,000	700,000	1,200,000
Internal transfers: 5,000 × $20	100,000	–	–
Internal transfers: 2,000 × $30	–	60,000	–
	600,000	760,000	1,200,000
Costs			
Transfers	60,000	100,000	0
Establishment costs	400,000	500,000	900,000
	460,000	600,000	900,000
Profit	**140,000**	**160,000**	**300,000**

The answer is C.

Objective Test Question 2: Transfer pricing

Target profit for Division P	$30,000
Fixed costs of Division P	120,000
Target contribution of Division P	$150,000

	$per unit
Target contribution per unit (÷ 60,000)	$2.50
Variable cost	$10.00
Transfer price required	**$12.50**

Objective Test Question 3: Transfer pricing

Provided the arrangements are permitted by the tax regulations, the group should want to increase the chances of higher profits in lower-tax countries and lower profits in the higher-tax countries. The companies might agree prices for the year and:

- sales from a division in a higher-tax country might be priced in the weaker currency

- sales from a division in a lower-tax country might be priced in a stronger currency.

If exchange rates move as expected, profits of the companies in the higher-tax countries will be reduced and the companies in the lower-tax country will obtain the matching benefit.

Data Set Question: Division A and Division B

Dual price transfer price from division A's point of view is market price $25. This ensures that the supplying division can earn a profit.

The two-part tariff transfer price per unit is marginal cost $15.

Integration Style Question: Transfer Pricing

EMAIL

To: Tomasina Goic

From A.N. Accountant

Date: 04.07.2014

Subject: Transfer pricing

(a) A first step is to calculate the contribution that Division A could earn by selling its product on the intermediate external market.

Division A

Unit price ($)	$20	$30	$40
Demand	15,000	10,000	5,000
Revenue	$300,000	$300,000	$200,000
Variable costs (at $11 per unit)	($165,000)	($110,000)	($55,000)
Contribution	$135,000	$190,000	$145,000

The optimal policy would be to sell 10,000 units on the intermediate market at $30.

Assuming that Division A does not have any capacity constraints, the next step is to calculate how profits would be maximised from sales to the end market. For selling to the end market, the variable cost to the company is $49 per unit (= $10 in Division A, since there is no variable selling cost with a transfer, and $39 in Division B).

Division B

Unit price ($)	$80	$90	$100
Demand	7,200	5,000	2,800
Revenue	$576,000	$450,000	$280,000
Variable costs (at $49 per unit)	($352,800)	($245,000)	($137,200)
Contribution	$ 223,200	$205,000	$142,800

The optimal policy is to sell 7,200 units at a price of $80. The optimal contribution is therefore:

	$
Contribution from sales in intermediate market	190,000
Contribution from sales in end market	223,200
Total achievable contribution	**413,200**

At the current transfer price of $29, the maximum contribution might not be achieved. In Division B, if the transfer price is $29, the total variable cost of sale for Division B would be $68 (= variable cost $39 + transfer price $29).

The profits for Division B at each of the possible selling prices would be:

Division B

Unit price ($)	$80	$90	$100
Demand	7,200	5,000	2,800
Revenue	$576,000	$450,000	$280,000
Variable costs (at £68 per unit)	($489,600)	($340,000)	($190,400)
Contribution	$86,400	$110,000	$89,600

The manager of Division B would choose to sell 5,000 units at a price of $90, in order to maximise the division's profit. This would not achieve goal congruence, and the total company profit would not be maximised.

	Division A	Division B	Total
Maximum contribution obtainable	$190,000	$223,200	$413,200
Contribution if transfer price is $29	$190,000	$205,000	$395,000

Shortfall in profit due to transfer price policy $18,200

(b) Transfer price = $12

The decision about what to sell in the intermediate market would not be affected. For Division B, the variable cost of sale, including the transfer price, would be $51 (= $39 + $12).

Division B

Unit price (£)	$80	$90	$100
Demand	7,200	5,000	2,800
Revenue	$576,000	$450,000	$280,000
Variable costs (at £51 per unit)	($367,200)	($255,000)	($142,800)
Contribution	$208,800	$195,000	$137,200

The Division B manager will now choose to sell 7,200 units at $80 each, in order to maximise profit.

The total contribution for the company, and for each division, will be:

Division A

External market sales	$190,000
Internal transfers (7,200 × (12 – 10))	$14,400
	$204,400
Division B (see above)	$208,800
Company as a whole	**$413,200**

Goal congruence is achieved with a transfer price of $12.

Investment appraisal techniques

Chapter learning objectives

Syllabus Link

Lead C1: Evaluate information to support project appraisal

Component C1a): Analyse information for use in long-term decision-making (including consideration of tax, inflation and other factors).

- Relevant cash flows taking into account of tax, inflation and other factors, and the use of perpetuities to derive 'final' project value where appropriate.

- The identification and integration of non-financial factors in long-term decisions.

Component C1b): Discuss the financial consequences of dealing with long-run projects, in particular the importance of accounting for the 'time value of money'.

- The process of investment decision making, including origination of proposals, creation of capital budgets, go/no go decisions on individual projects (where judgements on qualitative issues interact with financial analysis).

- Discounting, including the use of annuities in comparing projects with unequal lives and the profitability index in capital rationing situations.

- Capital investment real options (i.e. to make follow-on investment, abandon or wait.)

Component C1c): Evaluate investment appraisal techniques and explain their results.

- The strengths and weaknesses of payback, discounted payback, accounting rate of return (ARR), Net Present Value (NPV), Internal Rate of Return (IRR) and modified internal rate of return, (based on a project's terminal value).

- Prioritisation of projects that are mutually exclusive, and/or are subject to single-period capital rationing, have unequal lives.

1 Chapter summary

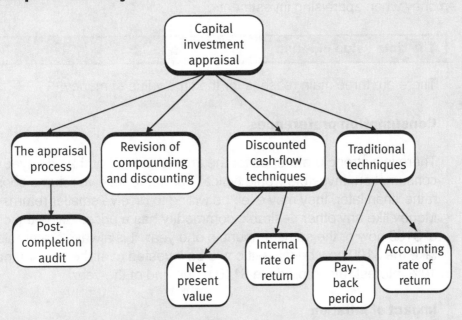

Introduction

Capital investment decisions normally represent the most important decisions that an organisation makes, since they commit a substantial proportion of a firm's resources to actions that are likely to be irreversible. Many different investment projects exist including; replacement of assets, cost-reduction schemes, new product/service developments, product/service expansions, statutory, environmental and welfare proposals, etc.

One characteristic of all capital expenditure projects is that the cash flows arise over the long term (a period usually greater than 12 months). Under this situation it becomes necessary to carefully consider the time value of money.

2 The time value of money

Money received today is worth more than the same sum received in the future, i.e. it has a **time value.**

For example, if offered the choice between a certain sum of $100 now or the expectation of $100 in a year's time, then most (all) people will prefer the $100 now. However, what if the choice is between $100 now and $105 in one year or $110 or...?

Suppose you are indifferent between $100 now or the expectation of $112 in one year – this would indicate that your time value of money can be expressed as an interest rate of 12% per annum.

Discounted cash flow (DCF) techniques take account of this time value of money when appraising investments.

The time value of money

There are three main reasons for the time value of money:

Consumption preferences

There is a strong preference for the immediate rather than delayed consumption. Investors would typically prefer to receive returns sooner rather than later. they may even be willing to receive smaller returns now. Money like any other desirable commodity has a price. Given the choice of $100 now or the same amount in one year, it is always preferable to take the $100 now because it could be invested over the next year at say 10% interest rate to produce $110 at the end of the year.

Impact of inflation

In most countries, in most years prices rise as a result of inflation. Therefore funds received today will buy more than the same amount a year later, as prices will have risen in the meantime. The funds are subject to a loss of purchasing power over time.

Risk

The earlier cash flows are due to be received, the more certain they are – there is less chance that events will prevent payment. Earlier cash flows are therefore considered to be less risky.

3 Compound interest

A sum invested today will earn interest. Compounding calculates the future (or **terminal value**) of a given sum invested today for a number of years.

To compound a sum, the figure is increased by the amount of interest it would earn over the period.

FORMULA FOR COMPOUNDING

$$V = X(1 + r)^n$$

Where
V = Future value
X = Initial investment (present value)
r = Interest rate (expressed as a decimal)
n = Number of time periods

Compounding

$100 is invested in an account for five years. The interest rate is 10% per annum.

The value of the account after five years can be calculated as follows:

$V = 100 (1.10)^5 = \$161.05$

Similarly, if your time value of money is 10% per annum, then you would be indifferent between receiving $100 now or $161.05 in five years' time. They would have the same value to you.

Test Your Understanding: Compounding

$450 is invested in an account earning 6.25% interest p.a. Calculate the fund value after 12 years.

4 Discounting

Discounting performs the opposite function to compounding. Compounding finds the future value of a sum invested now, whereas discounting considers a sum receivable in the future and establishes its equivalent value today. This value in today's terms is known as the **Present Value (PV).**

In potential investment projects, cash flows will arise at many different points in time. Calculating the present value of future flows is a key technique in investment appraisal decisions.

FORMULAE FOR DISCOUNTING

Present value = Future value x discount factor **LEARN**

Where: Discount factor $= \dfrac{1}{(1+r)^n}$ or $(1+r)^{-n}$ **GIVEN**

where: r is the interest rate expressed as decimal

n is the number of time periods

$(1 + r)^{-n}$ can be looked up in discounting tables. It is known as the discount factor.

Illustration: Discounting

$5,000 is required in 10 years. $x is invested in an account earning 5% interest p.a.

The value of $x may be established as follows:

$$x \quad = \quad \frac{5,000}{1.05^{10}} \quad = \quad \$3,070$$

Test Your Understanding: Discounting

Calculate the present value of $25,000 receivable in six years' time, if the interest rate is 10% p.a.

Test Your Understanding: Discounting II

Calculate how much should be invested now in order to have $250 in eight years' time? The account pays 12% interest per annum.

The cost of capital

In the above discussions we referred to the rate of interest. There are a number of alternative terms used to refer to the rate a firm should use to take account of the time value of money:

- cost of capital
- discount rate
- required rate of return.

Whatever term is used, the rate of interest used for discounting reflects the cost of the finance that will be tied up in the investment.

5 Capital investment appraisal

> **Initial assumptions**
>
> (1) All cash inflows and outflows are known with certainty.
> (2) Sufficient funds are available to undertake all profitable investments.
> (3) There is zero inflation.
> (4) There is zero taxation.
>
> These assumptions are all considered in the next session.

Appraisal methods

There are four widely used appraisal methods:

(1) Net present value (NPV).
(2) Internal rate of return (IRR).
(3) The payback period.
(4) Accounting rate of return (ARR).

The NPV and IRR both consider the time value of money. They are discounted cash flow (DCF) techniques.

6 Net present value (NPV)

The net benefit or loss of benefit in present value terms from an investment opportunity.

NPV is the 'difference between the sum of the projected discounted cash inflows and outflows attributable to a capital investment or other long-term project' (Official CIMA Terminology).

The NPV represents the surplus funds (after funding the investment) earned on the project. This means that it tells us the impact on shareholder wealth. Therefore:

Decision criteria

- Any project with a positive NPV is viable.
- Projects with a negative NPV are not viable.
- Faced with mutually-exclusive projects, choose the project with the highest NPV.

Note: the NPV is a surplus. If the NPV is zero or tiny then the project is still providing the required rate of return. A positive NPV is desirable and the bigger it is the better, but it doesn't have to be more than zero.

What does the NPV actually mean?

NPV is defined as the:

difference between the sum of the projected discounted cash inflows and outflows attributable to a capital investment or other long-term project.

(CIMA Official Terminology)

However, it is often easier to understand it as the surplus of funds available to the investor.

Suppose, in an investment problem, we calculate the NPV of certain cash flows at 12% to be – $97, and at 10% to be zero, and yet at 8% the NPV of the same cash flows is + $108. Another way of expressing this is as follows.

- If the company's cost of capital is 12% the investor would be $97 out of pocket – i.e. the investment earns a yield below the cost of capital.

- If the company's cost of capital is 10% the investor would break even – i.e. the investment yields a return equal to the cost of capital.

- If the company's cost of capital is 8% the investor would be $108 in pocket – i.e. the investment earns a return in excess of the cost of capital.

In other words, an NPV of zero indicates that the project generates an acceptable rate of return and is, therefore, worth accepting because shareholder wealth is being maintained. A positive NPV indicates that the rate offered exceeds the required rate and so shareholder wealth increases. A negative NPV indicates that the project does not earn an acceptable rate of return and so it would reduce shareholder wealth.

Assumptions used in NPV & IRR

- All cash flows occur at the start or end of a year.

Although in practice many cash flows accrue throughout the year, for discounting purposes they are all treated as occurring at the start or end of a year. Note also that if today (T_0) is 01/01/20X0, the dates 31/12/20X1 and 01/01/20X2, although technically separate days, can be treated for discounting as occurring at the same point in time, i.e. at T_1.

- Initial investments occur at once (T_0), other cash flows start in one year's time (T_1).

In project appraisal, the investment needs to be made before the cash flows can accrue. Therefore, unless the examiner specifies otherwise, it is assumed that investments (including any working capital requirement) occur in advance. The first cash flows associated with running the project are therefore assumed to occur one year after the project begins, i.e. at T_1.

Example 6 – PROJECT APPRAISAL

Mickey Ltd is considering two mutually-exclusive projects with the following details:

Project A

Initial investment	$450,000				
Scrap value at the end of year 5	$20,000				

Year:	1	2	3	4	5
Annual cash flows ($000)	200	150	100	100	100

Project B

Initial investment	$100,000				
Scrap value at the end of year 5	$10,000				

Year:	1	2	3	4	5
Annual cash flows ($000)	50	40	30	20	20

Assume that the initial investment is at the start of the project and the annual cash flows are at the **end** of each year.

Required:

Calculate the Net Present Value for Projects A and B if the relevant cost of capital is 10%.

Year	Discount factor 10%	Project A		Project B	
		Net cash flow $000	PV $000	Net cash flow $000	PV $000
0					
1					
2					
3					
4					
5					

Calculate which project has the highest NPV.

Advantages	Disadvantages
• Does consider the time value of money	• Fairly complex
	• Not well understood by non-financial managers
• It is a measure of absolute profitability	• It may be difficult to determine the cost of capital
• Considers cash flows	
• It considers the whole life of the project	
• A company selecting projects on the basis of NPV maximisation should maximise shareholders wealth	

Advantages and disadvantages of NPV

When appraising projects or investments, NPV is considered to be superior (in theory) to most other methods. This is because it:

- considers the time value of money – discounting cash flows to PV takes account of the impact of interest, inflation and risk over time. (See later sessions for more on inflation and risk.) These significant issues are ignored by the basic methods of payback and accounting rate of return (ARR)

- is an absolute measure of return – the NPV of an investment represents the actual surplus raised by the project. This allows a business to plan more effectively. Neither ARR nor payback is an absolute measure

- is based on cash flows not profits – the subjectivity of profits makes them less reliable than cash flows and therefore less appropriate for decision making.

- considers the whole life of the project – methods such as payback only consider the cash flows prior to the payback. NPV takes account of all relevant cash flows

- should lead to maximisation of shareholder wealth. If the cost of capital reflects the investors' (i.e. shareholders') required return, then the NPV reflects the theoretical increase in their wealth. For a company, this is considered to be the primary objective of the business.

However, there are some potential drawbacks:

- It is difficult to explain to managers. To understand the meaning of the NPV calculated requires an understanding of discounting. The method is not as intuitive as techniques such as payback.

- It requires knowledge of the cost of capital. The calculation of the cost of capital is, in practice, more complex than identifying interest rates. It involves gathering data and making a number of calculations based on that data and some estimates. The process may be deemed too protracted for the appraisal to be carried out.

- It is relatively complex. For the reasons explained above, NPV may be rejected in favour of simpler techniques.

Note: some of the advantages and disadvantages refer to the ARR and payback techniques which are covered later in the chapter. These issues may therefore need to be reviewed after studying those techniques.

7 Internal rate of return (IRR)

This is the rate of return at which the project has a NPV of zero.

Decision criteria

- If the IRR is greater than the cost of capital the project should be accepted. If the IRR is less than the cost of capital the project should be rejected.

Further explanation of IRR

Using the NPV method, PVs are calculated by discounting cash flows at a given cost of capital, and the difference between the PV of costs and the PV of benefits is the NPV. In contrast, the IRR method of analysis is to calculate the exact rate of return that the project is expected to achieve.

If an investment has a positive NPV, it means it is earning more than the cost of capital. If the NPV is negative, it is earning less than the cost of capital. This means that if the NPV is zero, it will be earning exactly the cost of capital.

Conversely, the percentage return on the investment must be the rate of discount or cost of capital at which the NPV equals zero. This rate of return is called the IRR and if it is higher than the target rate of return then the project is financially worth undertaking.

Calculating the IRR (using linear interpolation)

The steps in linear interpolation are:

(1) Calculate two NPVs for the project at two different costs of capital

(2) Use the following formula to find the IRR:

 FORMULA FOR IRR

$$IRR = L + \frac{N_L}{N_L - N_H} \times (H - L)$$

where:

L = Lower rate of interest

H = Higher rate of interest

N_L = NPV at lower rate of interest

N_H = NPV at higher rate of interest.

Accuracy of the formula

The formula makes an approximation of the IRR by assuming that the NPV will move downward in a straight line. In reality the NPV line is curved and therefore there will be an element of error in the IRR estimation. The choice of rates to estimate the IRR can effect the answer provided by the formula.

Ideally you should aim to satisfy two criteria:

- do not use rates which are too far apart. A 5% difference should be sufficient. The further the rates are away from each other then the greater the amount of error in the IRR calculation.

- try to have one discount rate which gives a positive NPV, and another which gives a negative NPV. If we use two positive NPV's then we are likely to under-estimate the IRR, whilst the use of two negatives is likely to over-estimate the IRR. So having one positive and one negative is likely to give a slightly more accurate estimate.

Example 6 – CONTINUED 1

(a) Calculate the internal rate of return of Project A.

| Year | Discount factors at ?% | Project A | |
		Net cash flow $000	PV $000
0		(450)	
1		200	
2		150	
3		100	
4		100	
5		120	

(b) Calculate the internal rate of return of Project B.

You are given the following:

At 10% the NPV was $33,310
At 20% the NPV is $8,510
At 30% the NPV is – $9,150

Calculating the IRR using a graph

The IRR may be calculated by a linear interpolation, i.e. by assuming a linear relationship between the NPV and the discount rate. Plotting a graph would give an approximate IRR, but the same point can also be found using a formula.

Step 1   Calculate two NPVs for the project at two different costs of capital. You can choose any costs of capital and get a fair result. However, it helps to find two costs of capital for which the NPV is close to 0, because the IRR will be a value close to them. Ideally, you should use one cost of capital where the NPV is positive and the other cost of capital where the NPV is negative, although this is not essential. You should not waste time in the exam.

Step 2   Once the two NPVs have been calculated, they and their associated costs of capital can be used to calculate the IRR. In other words, we can estimate the IRR by finding the point where a line joining these points would cross the x-axis (the point where the NPV is zero) in a graph plotting the project NPV against various discount rates.

To calculate the exact IRR requires a more complex technique, best carried out using an Excel spreadsheet. This will not be expected in the exam.

IRR where there are annuities/perpetuities

(**Note:** This section should only be reviewed after annuities and perpetuities have been studied later in this chapter)

Calculating the IRR of a project with even cash flows

There is a simpler technique available, using annuity tables, if the project cash flows are annuities i.e. where it equal annual cash flows from year 1 onwards.

(1) Find the cumulative discount factor, Initial investment ÷ Annual inflow

(2) Find the life of the project, n.

(3) Look along the n year row of the cumulative discount factor until the closest value is found.

(4) The column in which this figure is found is the IRR.

Illustration – Calculating IRR of a project with even cash flows

Find the IRR of a project with an initial investment of $1.5 million and three years of inflows of $700,000 starting in one year.

Solution

NPV calculation:

		Cash flow	DF (c) %	PV
		$000		$000
Time				
0	Investment	(1,500)	1	(1,500)
1–3	Inflow	700	(b)	(a)
NPV				Nil

- The aim is to find the discount rate (c) that produces an NPV of nil.

- Therefore the PV of inflows (a) must equal the PV of outflows, $1,500,000.

- If the PV of inflows (a) is to be $1,500,000 and the size of each inflow is $700,000, the DF required (b) must be 1,500,000 ÷ 700,000 = 2.143.

- The discount rate (c) for which this is the 3-year factor can be found by looking along the 3-year row of the cumulative discount factors shown in the annuity table.

- The figure of 2.140 appears under the 19% column suggesting an IRR of 19% is the closest.

Calculating the IRR of a project where the cash flows are perpetuities

$$\text{IRR of a perpetuity} = \frac{\text{Annual inflow}}{\text{Initial investment}} \times 100$$

Illustration – Calculating IRR where cash flows are perpetuities

Find the IRR of an investment that costs $20,000 and generates $1,600 for an indefinitely long period.

Solution

$$\text{IRR} = \frac{\text{Annual inflow}}{\text{Initial investment}} \times 100 = \frac{\$1,600}{\$20,000} \times 100 = 8\%$$

Advantages	Disadvantages
• Does consider the time value of money	• It is not a measure of absolute profitability
• As a percentage return it is easily understood by non-financial managers	• Interpolation only provides an estimate of the true IRR
• Considers cash flows	• Fairly complicated to calculate – although spreadsheets now have built-in programs
• It considers the whole life of the project	• Basing decisions on the IRRs of projects may conflict with looking at NPVs. If this occurs the NPV must take precedence
• It can be calculated without reference to the cost of capital (but the cost of capital is necessary in applying the decision criteria)	
• A company selecting projects where the IRR exceeds the cost of capital will normally increase shareholders' wealth	

Advantages and disadvantages of IRR

Advantages:

- IRR considers the time value of money. The current value earned from an investment project is therefore more accurately measured. As discussed above this is a significant improvement over the basic methods.

- IRR is a percentage and therefore easily understood. Although managers may not completely understand the detail of the IRR, the concept of a return earned is familiar and the IRR can be simply compared with the required return of the organisation.

- IRR uses cash flows not profits. These are less subjective as discussed above.

- IRR considers the whole life of the project rather than ignoring later flows (which would occur with payback).

- The IRR can be calculated when the cost of capital is unknown (say, if finance for a project has yet to be determined). It therefore may provide a useful benchmark for appraising potential sources of capital.

- IRR a firm selecting projects where the IRR exceeds the cost of capital would normally increase shareholders' wealth. This holds true provided the project cash flows follow the typical pattern of an outflow followed by a series of inflows, as in the investment examples above.

However there are a number of difficulties with the IRR approach:

- It is not a measure of absolute profitability. A project of $1,000 invested now and paying back $1,100 in a year's time has an IRR of 10%. If a company's required return is 6%, then the project is viable according to the IRR rule but most businesses would consider the absolute return too small to be worth the investment.

- Interpolation only provides an estimate (and an accurate estimate requires the use of a spreadsheet programme). The cost of capital calculation itself is also only an estimate and if the margin between required return and the IRR is small, this lack of accuracy could actually mean the wrong decision is taken.

  For example if the cost of capital is found to be 8% (but is actually 8.7%) and the project IRR is calculated as 9.2% (but is actually 8.5%) the project would be wrongly accepted. Note that where such a small margin exists, the project's success would be considered to be sensitive to the discount rate (see session 12 on risk).

- Non-conventional cash flows may give rise to no IRR or multiple IRRs. For example a project with an outflow at T0 and T2 but income at T1 could, depending on the size of the cash flows, have a number of different profiles on a graph (see below). Even where the project does have one IRR, it can be seen from the graph that the decision rule would lead to the wrong result as the project does not earn a positive NPV at any cost of capital.

For example, a project with an immediate outflow of $10m, followed by an inflow of $90m in one year's time and a final outflow of $100m would have the following NPVs:

Discount rate	NPV ($m)
10%	−10.8
29.85%	0
60%	7.2
670.5%	0
1000%	−2.64

The NPV starts off negative, then at rates above 30% will become positive, before becoming negative again at rates above 670.5%. This could be represented by the dark line in the diagram/graph below

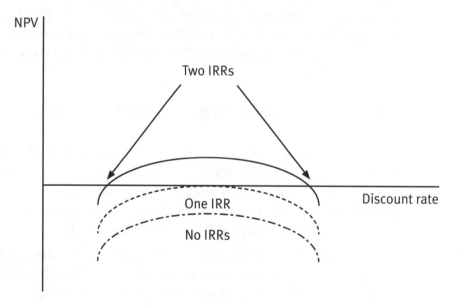

As the size of the project flows reduce the NPV would likewise reduce and the NPV line fall (as in the lower dashed lines). It can therefore be seen that there might only be one NPV (if the line just touches the zero NPV point) or no IRR's at all if the project has negative NPVs at all discount rates.

Note: multiple IRRs are usually associated with two or more periods when the project has an outflow. The problem doesn't arise if there is a traditional project with an initial investment, followed by annual inflows. It is also highly unlikely to arise if the second outflow is small and/or in the very distant future. For example, a project might have very small closure costs at the end, in which case it is still unlikely that there will be more than one IRR.

8 NPV versus IRR

Both NPV and IRR are investment appraisal techniques which discount cash flows and are superior to the basic techniques discussed in the previous session. However only NPV can be used to distinguish between two mutually-exclusive projects, as the diagram on the next page demonstrates.

Explanation of the principle

NPV and IRR may sometimes give conflicting advice and recommend different projects.

Consider the following two projects:

	Initial investment ($m)	Year 1 flow ($m)	Year 2 flow ($m)	NPV ($m) @ 10%	IRR
Project A	(10)	0	25	10.7	58.1%
Project B	(10)	10	12	9.0	70.4%

Project A has the higher NPV but the lower IRR. The choice of project appraisal method would therefore affect the choice of project.

The NPV of these projects could be represented diagrammatically as follows:

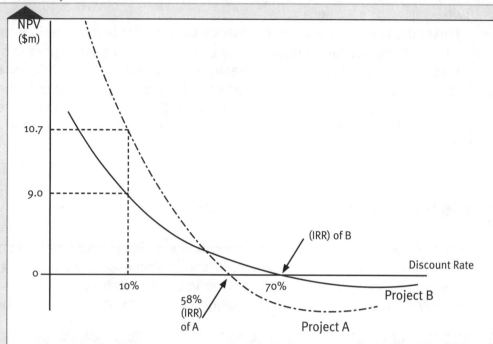

It can be seen that the NPV curves cross. But the vital piece of information is the firm's cost of capital. This is the actual cost of financing the project (i.e. it is the cost that the company will have to pay for financing the initial $10m investment). Once this cost is met, the remaining project surplus (the NPV) can be returned to shareholders. It is therefore the NPV information which will be of more concern to investors or shareholders.

The IRR is not an actual cost of capital. It instead tells us the cost of capital at which the project will break even. This cost of capital might never arise.

The IRR is a useful piece of information when we are examining one project. It allows us to determine the highest acceptable cost of capital. But when comparing one project to another, the NPV figure is based on a more appropriate cost of capital. Therefore the NPV of projects should be used when deciding which project in which to invest.

The advantage of NPV is that it tells us the absolute increase in shareholder wealth as a result of accepting the project, at the current cost of capital. The IRR simply tells us how far the cost of capital could increase before the project would not be worth accepting.

Attitudes to risk

The general decision rule in DCF analysis is that where mutually exclusive projects are being considered, the one with the highest NPV is preferred. However, some caution should be exercised in the use of this rule. Our earlier exploration of attitude to risk indicated that a low-risk project with a lower expected NPV may be preferred to a high risk project with a higher NPV.

IRR is normally reported as part of a project appraisal. However, since it is a relative measure which lacks an element of scale it should not be used to select between alternatives. A large project with a high NPV will normally be preferred to a small project with a lower NPV but a higher IRR. A tiny project can have a very high IRR. But IRR can still be informative since it offers insights into the return that alternative uses for capital offer and this can be a guide to future strategy and decision-making.

9 The Modified IRR

A more useful measure is the modified internal rate of return or MIRR.

This measure has been developed to counter the above problems since it:

- is unique
- gives a measure of the return from a project
- is a simple percentage.

It is therefore more popular with non-financially minded managers, as a simple rule can be applied:

MIRR = Project's return

If Project return > company cost of finance ⇒ Accept project

The interpretation of MIRR

MIRR measures the economic yield of the investment under the assumption that any cash surpluses are reinvested at the firm's current cost of capital.

Although MIRR, like IRR, cannot replace net present value as the principle evaluation technique it does give a measure of the maximum cost of finance that the firm could sustain and allow the project to remain worthwhile. For this reason it gives a useful insight into the margin of error, or room for negotiation, when considering the financing of particular investment projects.

Calculation of MIRR

There are several ways of calculating the MIRR, but the simplest is to use the following formula:

$$MIRR = [PVR/PVI]^{1/n}(1+r_e) - 1$$

where

PVR = the present value of the "return phase" of the project

PVI = the present value of the "investment phase" of the project

r_e = the firm's cost of capital.

Student Accountant article

Read Bob Ryan's April 2008 article in Student Accountant magazine for more details on MIRR.

Test your understanding 1

A project with the following cash flows is under consideration:

$000	T_0	T_1	T_2	T_3	T_4
	(20,000)	8,000	12,000	4,000	2,000

Cost of capital 8%

Required:

Calculate the MIRR.

10 The payback period

The payback period is the time a project will take to pay back the money spent on it. It is based on expected cash flows and provides a measure of liquidity and risk (the quicker that an investor can recover the initial investment the quicker they can reinvest it elsewhere and the lower the risk of this particular investment).

This is the time which elapses until the invested capital is recovered. It considers cash flows only. Unlike DCF techniques, it is assumed that the **cash flows** occur evenly during the year.

Decision criteria

- Compare the payback period to the company's maximum return time allowed and if the payback is quicker the project should be accepted.

- Faced with a choice between mutually-exclusive projects, choose the project with the quickest payback (provided it meets the company's target payback period).

Calculation – Constant annual flows

$$\text{Payback period} \quad = \quad \frac{\text{Initial investment}}{\text{Annual cash inflow}}$$

A payback period may not be for an exact number of years. To calculate the payback in years and months you should multiply the decimal fraction of a year by 12 to the number of months.

Illustration: Payback

An expenditure of $2 million is expected to generate net cash inflows of $500,000 each year for the next seven years.

The payback period for the project may be calculated as follows:

Calculation – constant annual flows

$$\text{Payback period} \quad = \quad \frac{\$2m}{\$500,000}$$

$$\text{Payback period} \quad = \quad 4 \text{ years}$$

Calculations – Uneven annual flows

However, if cash inflows are uneven (a more likely state of affairs), the payback has to be calculated by working out the cumulative cash flow over the life of a project

Example 6 – CONTINUED 2

Which project should the company select, if the objective is to minimise the payback period?

Discounted payback

One of the major criticisms of using the payback period is that it does not take into account the time value of money. The discounted payback technique attempts to overcome this criticism by measuring the time required for the **present values** of the cash inflows from a project to equal the present values of the cash outflows.

The techniques are identical but the present value of the cash flows is used to calculate the cumulative cash flow and to determine the payback period.

Advantages	Disadvantages
• Simple to understand	• Is not a measure of absolute profitability
• Selecting projects on the basis of payback may help reduce the risk of liquidity problems	• Ignores the time value of money. **Note:** A discounted payback period may be calculated to overcome this problem
• Uses cash flows, not subjective accounting profits	• Does not take into account cash flows beyond the payback period
• Emphasises the cash flows in the earlier years	

Advantages and disadvantages of payback

Advantages

• Simplicity

As a concept, it is easily understood and is easily calculated.

• Improving investment conditions

When investment conditions are expected to improve in the near future, attention is directed to those projects that will release funds soonest, to take advantage of the improving climate.

• Payback favours projects with a quick return

It is often argued that these are to be preferred for three reasons.

- Rapid project payback leads to rapid company growth – but in fact such a policy will lead to many profitable investment opportunities being overlooked because their payback period does not happen to be particularly swift.

- Rapid payback reduces the risk of liquidity problems – but liquidity problems are best dealt with separately, through cash forecasting.

- Cash flows

  Cash flows are much more objective than accounting figures such as profit. Profit figures are easily manipulated using accounting policies, whereas this is not possible for cash flows.

Disadvantages

- Project returns may be ignored – In particular, cash flows arising after the payback period are totally ignored.

- Timing ignored – Cash flows are effectively categorised as pre-payback or post-payback, but no more accurate measure is made. In particular, the time value of money is ignored. This problem can be overcome if the discounted payback method is used.

- Lack of objectivity – There is no objective measure as to what length of time should be set as the minimum payback period. Investment decisions are therefore subjective.

- Project profitability is ignored – Payback takes no account of the effects on business profits and periodic performance of the project, as evidenced in the financial statements. This is critical if the business is to be reasonably viewed by users of the accounts.

11 Accounting rate of return (ARR)

The ARR method calculates a percentage return provided by the *accounting* profits of the project.

The most common formula is:

$$ARR = \frac{\text{Average annual profit}}{\text{Average value of investment}}$$

LEARN

Important notes to the formula:

- The 'average annual profit' is after depreciation.
- Net cash flow is normally equivalent to 'profit before depreciation'.

Average annual profit = Net cash flow less depreciation

- The average value of the investment represents the average capital employed over the life of the project.

    Average value of investment $= \dfrac{\text{Initial investment plus residual value}}{2}$ **LEARN**

Decision criteria

- The ARR for a project may be compared with the company's target return and if higher the project should be accepted.

- Faced with a choice of mutually-exclusive investments, the project with the highest ARR should be chosen (provided it meets the company's target return).

Example 6 – CONTINUED 3

Project A

Initial investment	$450,000
Scrap value in year 5	$20,000

Year:	1	2	3	4	5
Annual cash flows ($000)	200	150	100	100	100

Project B

Initial investment	$100,000
Scrap value in year 5	$10,000

Year:	1	2	3	4	5
Annual cash flows ($000)	50	40	30	20	20

Required:

Calculate the ARR for each project, and indicate which project should be chosen.

Advantages	Disadvantages
• Simple to understand	• Ignores the time value of money
• Widely used and accepted	• Is not a measure of absolute profitability
• It considers the whole life of the project	• Does not consider cash flows. Uses subjective accounting profits, which include depreciation

Advantages and disadvantages of ARR

Advantages

- Simplicity – As with the payback period, it is easily understood and easily calculated.

- Link with other accounting measures – Return on capital employed, calculated annually to assess a business or sector of a business (and therefore the investment decisions made by that business), is widely used and its use for investment appraisal is consistent with that. The ARR is expressed in percentage terms with which managers are familiar. However, neither this nor the preceding point necessarily justify the use of ARR.

Disadvantages

There are a number of specific criticisms of the ARR.

- It fails to take account of either the project life or the timing of cash flows (and time value of money) within that life. For example, a project with a very long life which has a high ARR might be accepted before a project with a shorter life and marginally lower ARR. The NPV of the shorter project may actually be higher. In example 6, it can be seen that Project B has a much higher ARR but that Project A has a much higher NPV. Project A is the project that should be accepted by management on a financial basis.

- It will vary with specific accounting policies, and the extent to which project costs are capitalised. Profit measurement is thus 'subjective', and ARR figures for identical projects could vary from business to business depending on the accounting policies used.

- Like all rate of return measures, it is not a measurement of absolute gain in wealth for the business owners.

- There is no definite investment signal. The decision to invest or not remains subjective in view of the lack of an objectively set target ARR.

- It is concluded that the ARR does not provide a reliable basis for project evaluation.

12 NPV and IRR with equal cash flows

Discounting annuities
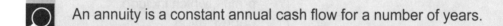

An annuity is a constant annual cash flow for a number of years.

When a project has equal annual cash flows the annuity factor may be used to calculate the NPV (and hence the IRR).

The **annuity factor** (AF) is the name given to the sum of the individual DF.

The PV of an annuity can therefore be quickly found using the formula:

PV = Annual cash flow × AF

As when calculating a discount factor, the annuity factors (AF) can be found using an annuity formula or annuity tables (cumulative present value tables).

Annuity factor formula

The formula is:

$$AF = \frac{1 - (1+r)^{-n}}{r}$$

Where

r = cost of capital

n = the number of periods

For example, for a six-year annuity at 10%:

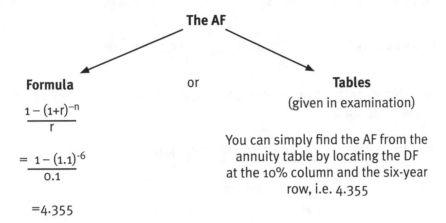

The AF

Formula

$$\frac{1 - (1+r)^{-n}}{r}$$

$$= \frac{1 - (1.1)^{-6}}{0.1}$$

$$= 4.355$$

or

Tables
(given in examination)

You can simply find the AF from the annuity table by locating the DF at the 10% column and the six-year row, i.e. 4.355

Note: there is a small difference due to roundings.

Note: annuity tables are titled cumulative present value tables in the exam.

Illustration: Annuities

Pluto Ltd has been offered a project costing $50,000. The returns are expected to be $10,000 each year for seven years. Cost of capital is 10%.

To decide whether the project be accepted:

Year	Cash flow $	Discount factor	Present value $
0	(50,000)	1.000	(50,000)
1–7	10,000	4.868	48,680
			(1,320)

The project should therefore be rejected.

The IRR of the project may be calculated as follows:

$10,000 × annuity factor = $50,000

Annuity factor = 5

Using tables and a life of seven years, the closest annuity factor to 5 is 5.033. This means the IRR is approximately 9%

Discounting perpetuities

A perpetuity is an annual cash flow that occurs forever.

It is often described by examiners as a cash flow continuing 'for the foreseeable future'.

The PV of a perpetuity is found using the formula:

$$PV = \frac{\text{cashflow}}{r}$$

'r' in the formula is the company's required rate of return (or cost of capital).

or

$$PV = \text{cashflow} \times \frac{1}{r}$$

$\dfrac{1}{r}$ is known as the perpetuity factor.

Illustration: Perpetuities

An investment of $50,000 is expected to yield $5,670 per annum in perpetuity.

The net present value of the investment opportunity if the cost of capital is 9% can be calculated as follows:

NPV = ($50,000) + $5,670 ÷ 0.09 = $13,000

Annuities/perpetuities in advance

The use of annuity factors and perpetuity factors both assume that the first cash flow will be occurring in one year's time. If this is not the case, you will need to adjust your calculation.

Advanced annuities and perpetuities

Some regular cash flows may start now (at T_0) rather than in one years time (T_1).

Calculate the PV by ignoring the payment at T_0 when considering the number of cash flows and then adding one to the annuity or perpetuity factor.

Illustration – Advanced annuities and perpetuities

A 5-year $600 annuity is starting today. Interest rates are 10%. Find the PV of the annuity.

Solution

This is essentially a standard 4-year annuity with an additional payment at T_0. The PV could be calculated as follows:

	T_0	T_1	T_2	T_3	T_4
CF	600	600	600	600	600
PV	600 +		$600 \times$ 4-year 10% AF		

PV = 600 + 600 × 3.17 = 600 + 1902 = $2,502

The same answer can be found more quickly by adding 1 to the AF:

PV = 600 × (1 + 3.17) = 600 × 4.17 = $2,502.

Illustration – Advanced perpetuities

A perpetuity of $2,000 is due to commence immediately. The interest rate is 9%. What is the PV?

Solution

This is essentially a standard perpetuity with an additional payment at T_0. The PV could be calculated as follows:

T_0		T_1	T_2	T_3		T_4 ....
2,000		$2,000 \rightarrow \infty$				

PV (2000) + (2000 × 9% perpetuity formula)

Again, the same answer can be found more quickly by adding 1 to the perpetuity factor.

$$2000 \times \left(1 + \frac{1}{0.09}\right) = 2000 \times 12.11 = \$24,222$$

Annuities/perpetuities in arrears

Delayed annuities and perpetuities

Some regular cash flows may start later than T_1.

These are dealt with by:

(1) applying the appropriate factor to the cash flow as normal

(2) discounting your answer back to T_0.

Illustration – Delayed annuities and perpetuities

What is the PV of $200 incurred each year for four years, starting in three year's time, if the discount rate is 5%?

Solution

Method: A four-year annuity starting at T_3
                        (1 – 4)

T_0	T_1	T_2	T_3	T_4	T_5	T_6
			200	200	200	200
PV	2.					
		1.				

Step 1.   Discount the annuity as usual

200 × 4 yr 5% AF = 200 × 3.546 = 709.2

Note that this gives the value of the annuity at T_2

Step 2. Discount the answer back to T_0

709.2 × 2 yr 5% DF = 709.2 × 0.907 = $643

Annuity or perpetuity factors will discount the cash flows back to give the value one year before the first cash flow arose. For standard annuities and perpetuities this gives the present (T_0) value since the first cash flow started at T_1.

However for delayed cash flows, applying the factor will find the value of the cash flows one year before they began, which in this example is T_2. To find the PV, an additional calculation is required – the value must be discounted back to T_0.

Care must be taken to discount back the appropriate number of years. The figure here was discounted back two years because the first step gave the value at T_2. It can help to draw a timeline as above and mark on the effect of the first step (as shown with a 1. here) to help you remember.

13 Changing discount rates

Throughout this chapter we have assumed that a company will have a constant discount rate. This allows us to use the tables of discount rates that are provided in the exam. However, in reality discount rates might change from year to year. For example, in the next chapter we will see that inflation affects discount rates, and because inflation is not constant discount rates will not be constant.

Therefore in these instances we cannot use the tables that we are provided with and instead must calculate each year's discount factor individually using the discounting formula from the start of this chapter.

Illustration

A company is considering a four year investment. Its cost of capital during this period is expected to rise each year as interest rates and inflation rates rise in the economy. It expects its cost of capital to be as follows:

Year 1	10%
Year 2	12%
Year 3	15%
Year 4	16%

Calculate the discount rate that should be used for each year.

Answer

Because the cost of capital is changing each year we cannot use the tables that we are provided with. Instead we have to calculate the discount rate for each year individually.

The best way to do this is to divide the discount factor for the previous year by (1 + the cost of capital for the year in question). This can be shown as follows:

	Calculation	Discount factor
Year 0		1.000
Year 1	1.000/1.10	0.909
Year 2	0.909/1.12	0.812
Year 3	0.812/1.15	0.706
Year 4	0.706/1.16	0.608

These are the discount factors that would be used in any NPV calculation employed by the company.

Note: this means that the cash flow in year 3, say, has to be discounted on the basis that we need a 10% return for year 1, followed by 12% for year 2, followed by 15% for year 3.

This technique can be very important when dealing with inflation in the next chapter.

14 Dealing with non annual periods

In some instances we may have to deal with cash flows which are not in annual terms – for example, costs might be paid in 6 monthly blocks. In these cases we need to pro-rate the discount rate to match the period of the cash flows.

Illustration

If, say, we are given an annual discount rate of 10% but cashflows are received in non-annual instalments, in order to calculate the appropriate cost of capital to use for calculations we would need to pro-rate the 10% as follows:

Cashflows are in...	Pro-rata formula	Calculation	Appropriate discount rate
Quarters	$(1+i)^{1/4} -1$	$(1.10)^{1/4} -1$	2.41% per quarter
6 monthly periods	$(1+i)^{1/2} -1$	$(1.10)^{1/2} -1$	4.88% per 6 months
Months	$(1+i)^{1/12} -1$	$(1.10)^{1/12} -1$	0.8% per month
2 yearly instalments	$(1+i)^2 -1$	$(1.10)^2 -1$	21% per two years

This technique will be particularly useful in calculating the cost of receivables and payables later in the syllabus.

15 The capital investment process

A decision making model for capital expenditure decisions is shown below:

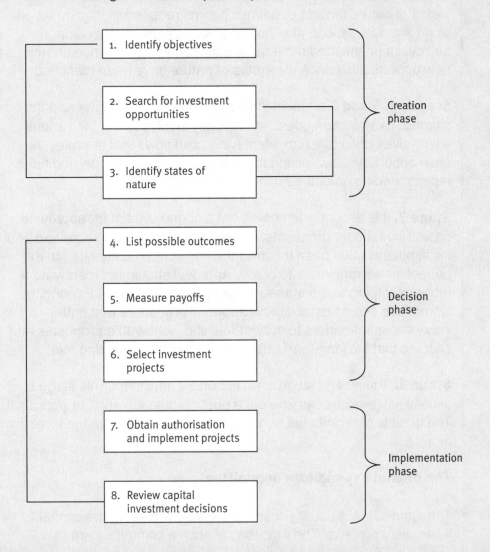

Notes to the diagram

Stage 1 indicates the objectives or goals of the organisation. Most organisations pursue a variety of goals, for example maximisation of profits, maximisation of sales, survival of the firm, achieving satisfactory profits and obtaining the largest share of the market. Achieving profit maximisation in the long term will ensure maximisation of the market value of the shareholders' wealth. The capital investment process seeks to achieve maximisation of wealth by maximising the net present value of future net cash inflows.

Stage 2 involves the search for investment opportunities. Without a proactive, deliberate search for creative projects and opportunities, even the most sophisticated evaluation techniques are worthless. A firm's prosperity is dependent upon its ability to create investment opportunities.

Stage 3 requires data to be gathered about possible future environments that may affect the outcomes of the project. Examples of states of nature include economic booms/recessions, high inflation, world shortages etc. It may be necessary to amend the company objectives (in the medium term at least) and/or to continue searching for new opportunities once the states of nature have been identified.

Stages 4, 5 and 6 are considered in detail in this chapter and the next chapter. Examination questions typically involve listing the various alternatives open to a firm, identifying cash flows that are relevant to each opportunity, evaluating the value of these cash flows and finally recommending an optimum investment strategy.

Stage 7. It is essential to implement a sound system for approving capital investment proposals. Once approval has been obtained and initial outlays have been incurred the firm is often committed to the project for several years to come. Approval should not merely be a rubberstamping of the managers' proposals. A Capital Expenditure Committee should establish an approval procedure that both encourages managers to submit realistic, achievable proposals and ensures that the long-term objectives of the firm are being met.

Stage 8. The review stage is an important final step. This stage is usually achieved by carrying out a post-completion audit or appraisal. The audit is often initiated approximately 12 months into the investment project.

The capital expenditure committee

The Committee is usually responsible for overseeing the capital investment process. The functions of such a committee are to:

- co-ordinate capital expenditure policy

- appraise and authorise capital expenditure on specific projects

- review actual expenditure on capital projects against the budget (see next section).

In many organisations, multidisciplinary teams, or working parties, are set up to investigate individual proposals and report back to top management on their findings.

Such a team might comprise:

- project engineer

- production engineer

- management accountant

- relevant specialist, e.g. personnel officer, for a project involving sports facilities or canteens, safety officers, etc.

16 Post-completion audit

The post-completion appraisal of projects provides a mechanism whereby experience gained from current and past projects can be fed into the organisation's decision-making process to aid decisions on future projects. In other words, it aids organisational learning. A post-completion appraisal reviews all aspects of an ongoing project in order to assess whether it has fulfilled its initial expectations. It is a forward-looking rather than a backward-looking technique. The task is often carried out by the Capital Expenditure Committee, or an appointed sub-committee.

Further discussion on post-completion audits

Benefits of post-completion audit

(1) If managers know in advance that projects are going to be subject to a post-completion appraisal they ensure that assumptions and plans for the project are more accurate and realistic.

(2) If an appraisal is carried out before the project life ends, and it is found that the benefits have been less than expected because of management inefficiency, then steps can be taken to improve efficiency.

(3) It might identify weaknesses in the forecasting techniques and the estimating techniques used to evaluate the project. The discipline and quality of forecasting for future investments can be improved.

(4) Managers may be motivated to achieve the forecast results if they are aware of a pending post-completion appraisal.

(5) The appraisal reveals the reliability and quality of contractors and suppliers involved in the project.

(6) The appraisal may highlight the reasons for success or failure in previous projects – thereby providing a learning experience for managers to aid better decision making in the future.

Problems with post-completion audits

(1) It may not be possible to identify separately the costs and benefits of any particular project.

(2) It can be a time-consuming and costly exercise.

(3) Applied punitively, post-completion appraisal may lead managers to becoming over-cautious and risk averse.

(4) The strategic effects of a capital investment project may take years to materialise and it may never be possible to identify and quantify them correctly.

(5) There are many uncontrollable factors in long-term investments. A post-completion appraisal will not help managers change these factors in the future.

Role of post-appraisal in project abandonment

Those intimately involved with a project may be reluctant to admit, even to themselves, that early problems with a project are likely to continue. When problems are being experienced in project implementation, those involved may be tempted to try to resolve the situation in one of two ways. They can make a change in the original plans and/or incur further expenditure in order to meet the original objective.

Whether either of these responses is appropriate will depend on the particular circumstances of the project but any significant changes or deviations should not be undertaken without the formal approval of higher management. The control systems in place will normally require changes of scope to be documented and approved before they are undertaken. It is usually the responsibility of the engineers associated with the project to ensure that this is done.

Expected project cost overruns should be highlighted by the routine monitoring of project expenditure by accounting staff, and formal approval should be obtained for the anticipated overspend. A prerequisite of approval by top management will often be the provision of the same level of detailed justification as was required when the initial funds were sanctioned. These controls ensure that significant changes to the character of a project cannot be made without top management's approval. However, they do not, of themselves, ensure that the option to terminate a project is considered, although it would be unlikely that management would fail to consider this possibility.

Some companies require an audit on all projects that need additional funds. The request for further funding would then be considered alongside the audit report. Routine monitoring of projects tends to focus almost exclusively on costs. An audit will review both costs and revenues, and, most importantly, focuses on the future. By checking the continuing validity of both forecast costs and revenues, the post-audit team is in a position to prepare a report to advise management on the wisdom of continuing with the project.

17 Project abandonment

During a post-completion appraisal it may be realised that the project is not likely to be so profitable as first thought and the possibility of abandoning it or terminating it early should be considered. Past cash flows are, of course, irrelevant to the decision – only future cash flows need to be considered. Abandoning the project is only necessary when the net discounted expected future cash flow of the project becomes negative.

Example project abandonment decisions

Case I

A project, P, has expected cash flows as follows:

Year	Cash flow	DF @ 10%	PV
$			$
0	(3,500)	1.000	(3,500)
1	2,000	0.909	1,818
2	2,000	0.826	1,652
3	2,000	0.751	1,502
NPV			+ 1,472

The initial investment of $3,500 in project P represents the purchase of a customised machine, the price of which is known with certainty. Because it is a customised machine its resale value is low; it can only be sold for $1,000 immediately after purchase. Once the machine is bought, therefore, the expected value of abandoning the project would be $1,000 (1.0 × $1,000). This must be compared with the expected value of continuing with the project, which is $4,972 ($1,818 + $1,652 + $1,502). In this case the expected benefits of continuing with the project far outweigh the returns from abandoning it immediately.

Case II

The decision to abandon a project will usually be made as a result of revised expectations of future revenues and costs. These revisions may be consistent with the data on which the original investment decision was based, or represent an alteration to earlier expectations. If the decision is consistent with the original data, the possibility, but not the certainty, that the project might have to be abandoned would have been known when the project was accepted. In these circumstances, project abandonment is one of a known range of possible outcomes arising from accepting the project.

In Case I, the cashflows for the project were based on expected value techniques. The expected cash flows and probabilities were as follows:

Year 0		Year 1		Year 2		Year 3
$	p	$	p	$	p	$
3,500	0.33	3,000	0.33	3,000	0.33	3,000
	0.33	2,000	0.33	2,000	0.33	2,000
	0.33	1,000	0.33	1,000	0.33	1,000
		_____		_____		_____
Expected value		2,000		2,000		2,000

In year 0, the expected net cash inflow in each year of project P's 3-year life is $2,000. The actual outcome of any of the 3 years is unknown at this point, and each of the three possible outcomes is equally likely. The factors that will cause any one of these results to occur may differ each year, or they may be the same each year. In some instances, a particular outcome in the first year may determine the outcome of years 2 and 3 with certainty. For example, the outcome of $3,000 in year 1 may mean that this same outcome will follow with certainty in years 2 and 3. Similarly outcomes of $2,000 and $1,000 in year 1 may be certain to be repeated in years 2 and 3. In year 0, the investor can only calculate the expected net cash flow in years 2 and 3, but with perfect correlation of flows between years these future flows are known with certainty at the end of year 1. If the year 1 inflow is either $3,000 or $2,000, perfect correlation between years will ensure that the actual NPV of the project will be positive. But if the first year's outcome is $1,000, the investment will have a negative NPV of $1,014, that is ($[3,500] + $1,000 × 2.486).

Should the project be abandoned? The information is now certain and so the decision on whether to abandon should be made using a risk-free interest rate and not the company's normal cost of capital. If we assume that the risk-free rate is 5 per cent, the present value of *continuing* at the end of year 1 will be:

Year	Cash flow	DF @ 5%	PV
$			$
0	(1,000)	1.000	(1,000)
1	1,000	0.952	952
2	1,000	0.907	907

PV of continuing	after 1 year		+ 859

Clearly the project should not be abandoned.

Case III

Consider another project, Project X with the following expected cash flows:

Year	Discounted cash flow
	$m
1	(8)
2	(16)
3	(24)
4	55

NPV	+ 7

The company experienced great difficulty in implementing the project in year 1, and the actual costs incurred during that year were $16 m. The company must then ask itself whether the actual outcome in year 1 necessitates any revision in the expected outcomes of later years. If no revision is required, further costs of $40 m (year 0 values) must be incurred to secure inflows of $55 m (year 0 values). The expected net present value of continuing with project X beyond year 1 will thus be $15 m (year 0 values). (Note that adjusting the figures to year 1 values would increase the expected NPV slightly, strengthening the case for continuation.)

The overall result of the investment would, of course, be negative by $1m, if years 2 – 4 costs and revenues are as forecast. The excess spend of $8m in year 1 is greater than the $7 m net present value originally predicted. However, at the end of year 1 the $16 m is a sunk cost and does not influence a decision on termination made at that time.

18 Practice questions

Objective Test Question 1: NPV

An organisation is considering a capital investment in new equipment. The estimated cash flows are as follows.

Year	Cash flow
	$
0	(240,000)
1	80,000
2	120,000
3	70,000
4	40,000
5	20,000

The company's cost of capital is 9%.

Calculate the NPV of the project to assess whether it should be undertaken.

Objective Test Question 2: Multiple Choice

A company is considering a project with a three-year life producing the following costs and revenues:

	$
Cost of machine	100,000
Depreciation of machine (for three years)	20,000 p.a.
Residual value of machine	40,000
Annual cost of direct labour	20,000
Annual charge for foreman (10% apportionment)	5,000
Annual cost of components required	18,000
Annual net revenues from machine	80,000
Cost of capital	20%

Identify which of the following is closest to the net present value of the machine:

A   ($13,000)

B   ($11,380)

C $11,610

D $22,370

Objective Test Question 3: IRR

A potential project's predicted cash flows give a NPV of $50,000 at a discount rate of 10% and – $10,000 at a rate of 15%.

Calculate the internal rate of return (IRR).

Objective Test Question 4: IRR Multiple Choice

Identify the correct explanation of the internal rate of return – it is the interest rate that equates the present value of expected future net cash flows to:

A   the initial cost of the investment outlay

B   the depreciation value of the investment

C   the terminal (compounded) value of future cash receipts

D   the firm's cost of capital

Objective Test Question 5: IRR and decision making

A business undertakes high-risk investments and requires a minimum expected rate of return of 17% pa on its investments. A proposed capital investment has the following expected cash flows:

Year	$
0	(50,000)
1	18,000
2	25,000
3	20,000
4	10,000

State, on financial grounds alone, whether this project should go ahead.

Note: you should calculate the NPV of the project at a cost of capital of 15% and 20%.

Objective Test Question 6: Payback

$50,000 is to be spent on a machine having a life of five years and a residual value of $5,000. Operating cash inflows will be the same each year, except for year 1 when the figure will be $6,000. The accounting rate of return (ARR) is measured as average annual profit as a percentage of the initial investment. If the ARR is 30% then identify the payback period:

A   2.75 years

B   2.15 years

C   1.85 years

D   2.54 years

Objective Test Question 7: IRR and Payback

A project has a normal pattern of cash flows (i.e. an initial outflow followed by several years of inflows).

Identify what would be the effects of an increase in the company's cost of capital on the internal rate of return (IRR) of the project and its discounted payback period (DPP)?

	IRR	DPP
A	Decrease	Decrease
B	Decrease	Increase
C	No change	Increase
D	No change	Decrease

(2 marks)

Objective Test Question 8: Target Payback

A business is considering a project which would last 5 years and have an initial investment of $40,000 in machinery. At the end of the project the machinery would have a scrap value of $4,000. The project would provide annual net cash inflows as follows:

Year	Net cashflow ($000)
1	16
2	20
3	12
4	12
5	10

The company has a target payback period of 2.5 years and new projects must also provide and average accounting rate of return of at least 15% p.a.

Advise the company on whether this project meets the company's targets.

Objective Test Question 9: Present Value, annuities, perpetuities

Calculate the present value of the following cash flows:

(1) A fifteen year annuity of $300 starting at once. Interest rates are 6%.

(2) A perpetuity of $33,000 commencing immediately. Interest rates are 22%.

Objective Test Question 10: IRR, perpetuities

Calculate the IRR of an investment of $50,000 if the inflows are:

(a) $5,000 in perpetuity

(2 marks)

(b) $8,060 for eight years.

(2 marks)

Data Set Question: NPV

The financial director of A Co has prepared the following schedule to enable her to appraise a new project. Interest rates are 10%. She wants to calculate the PV of the cash flows using two different assumptions regarding the project duration.

The assumptions are as follows:

A   That the real annual cash flow will be $250,000 from Year 4 for the foreseeable future.

B   That the real annual cash flow will be $250,000 from Year 4 to Year 18.

Year	T_0	T_1	T_2	T_3	Assumption (A) T_4 onwards	Assumption (B) T_4–T_{18}
	$000	$000	$000	$000	$000	$000
Net cash flow	(2,000)	(440)	363	399	250	250

Required:

Calculate the NPV from the project under

Assumption A

Assumption B

Integration Style question: MN plc

PRE-SEEN MATERIAL

MN plc has a rolling programme of investment decisions. One of these investment decisions is to consider mutually-exclusive investments A, B and C. The following information has been produced by the investment manager.

	Investment decision A $	Investment decision B $	Investment decision C $
Initial investment	105,000	187,000	245,000
Cash inflow for A: years 1 to 3	48,000		
Cash inflow for B: years 1 to 6		48,000	
Cash inflow for C: years 1 to 9			48,000
Net present value (NPV) at 10% each year	14,376	22,040	31,432
Ranking	3rd	2nd	1st
Internal rate of return (IRR)	17.5%	14%	13%
Ranking	1st	2nd	3rd

You have just received the following email from MN's Managing Director:

> **From:** Mahmood Al-Hiri, Managing Director
> **To:** A.N. Accountant
> **Date:** 03.07.2014
> **Subject:** Investment appraisal
>
> I trust you were shown the information produced by John, our investment manager. Time to make a decision! Please could you prepare a report for me, we need advice on which project should be selected. In your report, please include a graph showing the sensitivity of the three investments to changes in the cost of capital?
>
> Also, why does John's info show differences between NPV and IRR rankings? If this is a problem, one of the directors has suggested using payback to assess the investments. Would that do?

Test your understanding answers

Test Your Understanding: Compounding

$$V = 450(1.0625)^{12} = \$931.45$$

Test Your Understanding: Discounting

$$PV = 25,000 \times 0.564 = \$14,100$$

Test Your Understanding: Discounting II

$$\times = 250 \times 0.404 = \$101$$

Example 6 – PROJECT APPRAISAL

Year	Discount factor	Project A		Project B	
		Cash flow $000	Present value $000	Cash flow $000	Present value $000
0		(450)	(450)	(100)	(100)
1	0.909	200	181.8	50	45.45
2	0.826	150	123.9	40	33.04
3	0.751	100	75.1	30	22.53
4	0.683	100	68.3	20	13.66
5	0.621	120	74.52	30	18.63
		NPV =	73.62	NPV =	33.31

Example 6 – CONTINUED 1

(a)

		Project A	
Year	Discount factors at 20%	Net cash flow $000	PV $000
0	1.000	(450)	(450)
1	0.833	200	167
2	0.694	150	104
3	0.579	100	58
4	0.482	100	48
5	0.402	120	48
		NPV @ 20% =	(25)

$$IRR = L + \frac{N_L}{N_L - N_H} \times (H - L)$$

$$IRR = 10 + \frac{74}{74 - (-25)} \times (20 - 10)$$

$$IRR = 10 + \frac{74}{99} \times (10)$$

$$IRR = 10 + (0.747 \times 10)$$

IRR = 17.5%

(b) **Project B**

At 10% the NPV was $33,310
At 20% the NPV is $8,510
At 30% the NPV is – $9,150

$$IRR = 20 + \frac{8,510}{8,510 - (-9,150)} \times (30 - 20)$$

$$IRR = 20 + \frac{8,510}{17,660} \times (10)$$

$$IRR = 20 + (0.482 \times 10)$$

IRR = 24.8%

Test your understanding 1

PVR = 22,340 (this is the present value of the year 1-4 cash flows).

PVI = 20,000

$1 + MIRR = (1+re) \times (PVR/PVI)^{1/n} = 1.08 \times (22,340/20,000)^{1/4} = 1.1103$, giving MIRR = 11% pa.

Example 6 – CONTINUED 2

Project A	Cashflow	Cumulative cash flow
Year 0	(450)	(450)
Year 1	200	(250)
Year 2	150	(100)
Year 3	100	0

Payback period = 3 years

Project B		
Year 0	(100)	(100)
Year 1	50	(50)
Year 2	40	(10)
Year 3	30	20

Payback period = 3 years

Note:

The question states that cashflows only arise at year ends. If they were to arise evenly throughout the year then a more accurate payback period would be 2 years and 4 months.

Example 6 – CONTINUED 3

	Project A	Project B
	$000	$000
Total profit before depreciation (total operating cash)	650	160
Less total depreciation	(430)	(90)
Total profit after depreciation	220	70
÷ number of years	5	5
Average annual profit	44	14
Average value of investment	235	55
Accounting rate of return	18.7%	25.5%

Conclusion: the firm should select project B

Overall summary for the projects:

Project A NPV: $73,620
IRR: 17.5%
Payback period: 3 years
Discounted payback period: just over 4 years
ARR: 18.7%

Project B NPV: $33,310
IRR: 24.8%
Payback period: 2 years and 4 months
Discounted payback period: just under 3 years
ARR: 25.5%

It can be seen that different methods recommend different projects. All of the methods except NPV would recommend Project B. Yet the NPV method should prevail and Project A is the project which will provide the most wealth for shareholders and most closely achieve the organisation's goals. More on the conflict between NPV and IRR is covered later in the chapter.

Objective Test Question 1: NPV

Year	Cash flow	DF at 9%	PV
	$		$
0	(240,000)	1.000	(240,000)
1	80,000	0.917	73,360
2	120,000	0.842	101,040
3	70,000	0.772	54,040
4	40,000	0.708	28,320
5	20,000	0.650	13,000
NPV			+ 29,760

The PV of cash inflows exceeds the PV of cash outflows by $29,760, which means that the project will earn a DCF return in excess of 9%, i.e. it will earn a surplus of $29,760 after paying the cost of financing. It should therefore be undertaken.

Objective Test Question 2: Multiple Choice

Revenue – components – labour = $80,000 – $18,000 – $20,000 = $42,000

Year	Cash flow $000		Discount factor	Present value
0	Initial cost	(100)		(100)
1 – 3	Annual cash	42	2.106	88.452
3	Residual	40	0.579	23.16
				11.612

Net present value = $11,612

Answer C

Objective Test Question 3: IRR

$$IRR = 10\% + \frac{50,000}{50,000 - (-10,000)} \times (15\% - 10\%) = 14.17\%$$

Objective Test Question 4: IRR Multiple Choice

At the IRR, PV of future net cash flows = initial capital outlay.

Answer A

Objective Test Question 5: IRR and decision making

Year	Cash flow	DF @ 15%	PV @ 15%	DF @ 20%	PV @ 20%
	$		$		$
0	(50,000)	1.000	(50,000)	1.000	(50,000)
1	18,000	0.870	15,660	0.833	14,994
2	25,000	0.756	18,900	0.694	17,350
3	20,000	0.658	13,160	0.579	11,580
4	10,000	0.572	5,720	0.482	4,820
NPV			+ 3,440		(1,256)

The IRR is above 15% but below 20%.

Using the interpolation method:

(1)   The NPV is + 3,440 at 15%.

(2)   The NPV is − 1,256 at 20%.

(3)   The estimated IRR is therefore:

$$IRR = 15\% + \frac{3,440}{(440 - (-1,256))} \times (20 - 15)\%$$

$$= 15\% \quad + 3.7\%$$

$$= 18.7\%$$

The project is expected to earn a DCF return in excess of the target rate of 17%, so on financial grounds (ignoring risk) it is a worthwhile investment.

Objective Test Question 6: Payback

Average annual profit = $50,000 × 30%	$15,000
	× 5 yrs
Total profit	$75,000
Add back depreciation	$45,000
Total cash	$120,000
Less year 1 cash flow	(6,000)
	$114,000
Cash per annum (yrs 2–5) 114/4	$28,500
Outlay	$50,000
Cash inflow after 2 years 6,000 + 28,500	$34,500
Still required	$15,500
Proportion of year 3 to gain balance of cash =	15,500 ÷ 28,500 = 0.54
Hence payback period =	2.54 years

Answer D

Objective Test Question 7: IRR and Payback

The IRR will be unaffected by the cost of capital. As the discount rate increases future cash flow reduce in present value terms, therefore the discounted payback period will increase.

Answer C

Objective Test Question 8: Target Payback

Payback period

After two years $36,000 of the initial $40,000 of the investment has been recovered. It will take one third of year 3 ($4,000 required/$12,000 received in year 3) to recover the remaining investment.

So the payback period is 2.33 years, which satisfies the target of 2.5 years.

Accounting rate of return

Average annual profit $= \dfrac{\text{Total net cashflows} - \text{Total depreciation}}{\text{Life of the project}}$

$= \dfrac{\$70,000 - \$36,000}{5 \text{ years}}$

$= \$6,800$

Average investment $= \dfrac{\text{Initial investment} + \text{Scrap value}}{2}$

$= \dfrac{\$40,000 + \$4,000}{2}$

$= \$22,000$

ARR $= \dfrac{\$6,800}{\$22,000}$

ARR = 30.9% p.a.

This is above the target return of 15%.

Overall

The investment satisfies both target measures and should therefore be accepted.

Objective Test Question 9: Present Value, annuities, perpetuities

(1) This is a standard 14-year annuity with one additional payment at T_0.

Step 1: Look up the 14-year AF ⇨

AF = 9.295

Step 2: Add 1 ⇨ 9.295 + 1 = 10.295

Step 3: Calculate the PV ⇨ 300 × 10.295 = $3,088.50

(2) This is simply a standard perpetuity with one additional payment at T_0.

Step 1: Calculate the perpetuity factor ⇨ 1/0.22 = 4.545

Step 2: Add 1 ⇨ 4.545 + 1 = 5.545

Step 3: Calculate the PV ⇨ 33,000 × 5.545 = $182,982

Objective Test Question 10: IRR, perpetuities

$$\text{(a) IRR} = \frac{\text{Annual inflow}}{\text{Initial investment}} \times 100 = \frac{\$5,000}{\$50,000} \times 100 = 10\%$$

(b) NPV calculation

Time		Cash flow $	DF(c) %	PV $
0	Investment	(50,000)	1	(50,000)
1–8	Inflow	8,060	(b)	(a)
			NPV	Nil

- The aim is to find the discount rate (c) that produces an NPV of nil.

- Therefore the PV of inflows (a) must equal the PV of outflows, $50,000.

- If the PV of inflows (a) is to be $50,000 and the size of each inflow is $8,060, the DF required must be 50,000 ÷ 8,060 = 6.20.

- The discount rate (c) for which this is the 8-year factor can be found by looking along the 8-year row of the cumulative DFS shown in the annuity table.

- The figure of $6.210 appears under the 6% column suggesting an IRR of 6% is the closest.

Data Set Question: NPV

Year	T_0	T_1	T_2	T_3	Assumption (A) T_4 onwards	Assumption (B) T_4-T_{18}
	$000	$000	$000	$000	$000	$000
Net cash flow	(2,000)	(440)	363	399	250	250
Perpetuity factor (here discounts the cash flow to T_3)					1 ÷ 0.1 = 10	
AF (here discounts the cash flow to T_3)						15-yr 10% AF =7.606
DFs @ 10%	1.000	0.909	0.826	0.751	0.751	0.751
PV	(2,000)	(400)	300	300	1,878	1,428
NPV (A)					78	
NPV (B)						(372)

Integration Style question: MN plc

To: M. Al-Hiri

From: The Management Accountant

Subject: Investment projects A, B and C

Date: xx.xx.xx

The investment manager has analysed three mutually-exclusive investment opportunities A, B and C. The financial benefits from these opportunities are illustrated below in diagrammatical form.

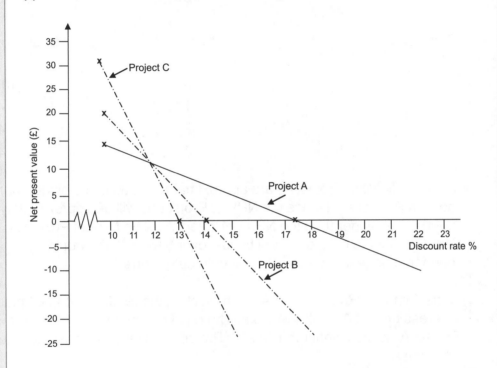

Reasons for differences between NPV and IRR rankings

There are two main reasons that NPV and IRR rankings differ:

(1) The magnitude of the cash flows.

(2) The timing of the cash flows.

Magnitude of cash flows

Imagine we were faced with a choice between the following two projects:

Project A₁	Year	Cash flow $
	0	(105,000)
	1	48,000
	2	48,000
	3	48,000

Project A₂	Year	Cash flow $
	0	(105)
	1	49
	2	49
	3	49

The cash flows in Project A_1 are approximately 1,000 times bigger than those in Project A_2. Hence the NPV of Project A_1 will be approximately 1,000 times bigger than the NPV of Project A_2. The NPV of Project A_1 is $14,376, but the NPV of A_2 will be just over $16.86. NPV would therefore suggest that Project A_1 should be preferred.

Consider the IRRs of A_1 and A_2. In project A_2 the return is $48,000 p.a., whereas project A_2 yields $49 p.a. The relative percentage return from Project A_2 is thus higher than that of Project A_1. Hence A_2 has a greater IRR than A_1.

The inconsistency in ranking has been caused by the magnitude of the figures.

Timing of cash flows

The actual time periods when the cash is generated can produce conflicting results.

Again consider two projects.

Project A₁	Year	Cash flow $
	0	(105,000)
	1	48,000
	2	48,000
	3	48,000

Project A$_2$	Year	Cash flow
		$
	0	(105,000)
	1	130,000
	2	0
	3	0

The NPV of Project A$_2$ is $13,170 (130 × 0.909 – 105).

This NPV is lower than the NPV of Project A$_1$.

The magnitude of the cash sums is very similar in both projects.

If we consider how the NPVs of the two projects reduce as the discount rate rises.

The NPV of A$_1$ will fall rapidly as the cash flows in the years 2 and 3 very quickly reduce in present value terms. The NPV of this project becomes zero at a 17.5% discount rate.

The cash in Project A$_2$ is all received in the first year. This cash sum is only $130,000, compared to cash in flows of $144,000 in Project A$_1$. However the value of the year 1 cash flow remains strong even as the discount rate rises.

Indeed, at a discount rate of 17.5% the NPV of A$_2$ is still positive at $5,630 (130 × 1/1.175 – 105).

Hence the IRR of Project A$_2$ MUST be greater than 17.5%.

Again there has been a conflict in the rankings, this time because of the timing of the cash flows.

These examples should illustrate that it is just as important to consider WHEN the cash flows arise as to consider HOW MUCH the cash flows are. It is very important to obtain cash in the early years of a project whilst it holds a high present value.

Comparison of opportunities A, B and C

The capital outlay in Project C is much greater than the other two projects. Cash inflows are generated for 9 years.

At a low cost of capital this project is worth the most to the company. The cash in years 6–9 maintains a high value when discount rates are low.

However, this project is very sensitive to increases in discount rates. As the cost of capital rises the NPV of Project C declines rapidly. This is illustrated in the graph at the beginning of the report.

Project A is less sensitive to increases in discount rates. All its cash is received in years 1 to 3. These maintain a strong value as the discount rate increases. Project A could be said to be the least risky of the three choices if interest rates are volatile.

Which project should be selected?

The company has a cost of capital of 10%. At this rate Project C produces an NPV of $31,432. This is of higher benefit to MN plc than either projects A or B. Hence this project should be selected.

Assumptions: cash flows are known and certain. The cost of capital is known. Taxation and inflationary aspects have been ignored.

If MN plc is very risk averse, Project A may be considered as its NPV is more robust to increases in the cost of capital than projects B or C.

Payback

The payback period is the time that elapses before the initial cash outlay is recovered.

The paybacks in the example are:

	Assuming even cash flows	Assuming year end cash flows
Project A:	2 years 2 months	3 years
Project B:	3 years 10 months	4 years
Project C:	5 years 1 month	6 years

Advantages of payback

(1) *Exposure to risk.* It is widely recognised that long-term forecasting is less reliable than short-term forecasts. Projects with short paybacks tend to be less risky than projects with long paybacks. A project with a one-year payback is less risky than a project with a 10-year payback. Management can have very little confidence in forecasts of events ten years from now.

(2) *Liquidity*. Investment opportunities often require significant capital outlay. It may be important to recover this capital expenditure quickly for the company to maintain a strong position. Payback illustrates how quickly the capital can be recovered.

(3) *Simple measure*. The payback period is not a complicated measure. Technical expertise is not required to understand the meaning of payback.

(4) *Not subjective*. Payback period uses cash flows. Some investment appraisal methods use the rather more subjective measure of accounting profit (the accounting rate of return).

Disadvantages of payback

(1) The time value of money is ignored. Each of the projects being considered by MN plc generates $48,000. Payback period fails to recognise that as time elapses the present value of this cash diminishes. It would be possible to overcome this problem by calculating a discounted payback period.

(2) Cash flows after the payback are ignored. Option C has a payback of a little over five years. This information does not reveal that Project C continues to generate cash for four further years.

(3) Not a measure of absolute profitability. Payback fails to indicate HOW MUCH each project is worth. It seems naïve to select a project on the basis of payback without considering the amount of benefit received.

In the example Project A has a payback of just over two years, however its NPV is only $14,376.

Project C yields an NPV of $31,432 – more than double A's NPV. Payback period ignores this fact.

If you require any further information on this matter, please do not hesitate to contact me.

Signed: Management Accountant

10

Further aspects of investment appraisal

Chapter learning objectives

Syllabus Link

Lead C1: Evaluate information to support project appraisal

Component C1a): Analyse information for use in long-term decision-making (including consideration of tax, inflation and other factors).

- Relevant cash flows taking into account of tax, inflation and other factors, and the use of perpetuities to derive 'final' project value where appropriate.
- The identification and integration of non-financial factors in long-term decisions.

Component C1b): Discuss the financial consequences of dealing with long-run projects, in particular the importance of accounting for the 'time value of money'.

- The process of investment decision making, including origination of proposals, creation of capital budgets, go/no go decisions on individual projects (where judgements on qualitative issues interact with financial analysis).
- Discounting, including the use of annuities in comparing projects with unequal lives and the profitability index in capital rationing situations.
- Capital investment real options (i.e. to make follow-on investment, abandon or wait.)

Component C1c): Evaluate investment appraisal techniques and explain their results.

- The strengths and weaknesses of payback, discounted payback, accounting rate of return (ARR), Net Present Value (NPV), Internal Rate of Return (IRR) and modified internal rate of return (MIRR), (based on a project's terminal value).

- Prioritisation of projects that are mutually exclusive, and/or are subject to single-period capital rationing, and have unequal lives.

Lead D1: Analyse information to assess its impact on long-term decisions

Component D1a): Apply sensitivity analysis

- Sensitivity analysis to identify the input variables that most affect the chosen measure of project worth (payback, ARR, NPV or IRR).

1 Chapter summary

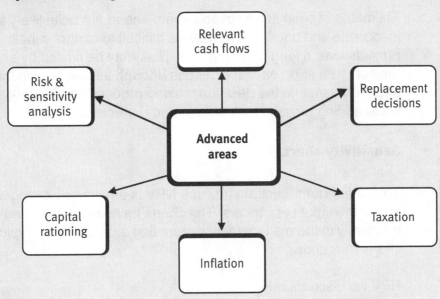

2 Dealing with risk in investment appraisal decisions

Investment appraisal often involves a degree of uncertainty and risk. This may be dealt with in a number of ways:

- Adding a risk premium to the discount rate in order to compensate for risk
- Calculating the payback period to give an indication of risk
- Sensitivity analysis – explored further here
- Using probability distributions to give an indication of risk
- Monte Carlo Simulation – a computerised system that extends sensitivity analysis

Further details

- **Adding a risk premium to the discount rate**

  A premium may be added to the usual discount rate to provide a safety margin. The premium may vary from project to project to reflect the different levels of risk.

- **Payback period**

  Estimates of cash flows several years ahead are quite likely to be inaccurate and unreliable. It may be difficult to control capital projects over a long period of time. Risk may be limited by selecting projects with short payback periods (though this might also induce short-termism into the decision making process and longer-term value-adding projects may be rejected unnecessarily).

- **Sensitivity charts**

  These diagrams illustrate how the NPV is affected by changes in one of the input parameters. The charts have been examined frequently in the management accounting examinations. Typical charts may show:

  NPV vs. discount rate,

  NPV vs. level of activity,

  NPV vs. change in variable cost per unit,

  NPV vs. change in selling price.

  The NPV should be plotted on the y-axis and the other parameter on the x-axis. Calculate two NPVs at two different levels (e.g. low demand and high demand) and then plot the two points. Draw the relationship assuming linearity.

- **Probability distribution**

  A probability distribution of expected cash flows may be determined and hence the expected NPV may be found together with risk analysis, e.g. best possible outcome, worst possible outcome, probability of a negative NPV, etc. A more sophisticated measure of risk is to calculate the standard deviation. This considers the degree of dispersion of the different possible NPVs around the expected NPV. The greater the spread of outcomes around the expected NPV, the higher the potential risk. The coefficient of variation should be calculated to compare projects. This was considered in an earlier Lesson.

• Monte Carlo simulation

Simulation is a modelling technique that shows the effect of more than one variable changing at the same time.

It is often used in capital investment appraisal.

The Monte Carlo simulation method uses random numbers and probability statistics. It can include all random events that might affect the success or failure of a proposed project - for example, changes in material prices, labour rates, market size, selling price, investment costs or inflation.

The model identifies key variables in a decision : costs and revenues, say. Random numbers are then assigned to each variable in a proportion in accordance with the underlying probability distribution. For example, if the most likely outcomes are thought to have a 50% probability, optimistic outcomes a 30% probability and pessimistic outcomes a 20% probability, random numbers, representing those attributes, can be assigned to costs and revenues in those proportions.

A powerful computer is then used to repeat the decision repeatedly (thousands or even millions of times), until the outcome starts to 'settle down' and give management a view of the likely range and level of outcomes. Depending on the management's attitude to risk, a more informed decision can be taken.

This helps to model what is essentially a one-off decision using many possible repetitions. It is only of any real value, however, if the underlying probability distribution can be estimated with some degree of confidence.

Monte Carlo Illustration 1 – MP Organisation

The MP Organisation is an independent film production company. It has a number of potential films that it is considering producing, one of which is the subject of a management meeting next week. The film which has been code named CA45 is a thriller based on a novel by a well respected author.

The expected revenues from the film have been estimated as follows: there is a 30% chance it may generate total sales of $254,000; 50% chance sales may reach $318,000 and 20% chance they may reach $382,000.

Expected costs (advertising, promotion and marketing) have also been estimated as follows: there is a 20% chance they will reach approximately $248,000; 60% chance they may get to $260,000 and 20% chance of totalling $272,000.

In a Monte Carlo simulation, these revenues and costs could have random numbers assigned to them:

Sales Revenue	Probability	Assign Random Numbers (assume integers)
$254,000	0.30	00–29
$318,000	0.50	30–79
$382,000	0.20	80–99

Costs		
$248,000	0.20	00–19
$260,000	0.60	20–79
$272,000	0.20	80–99

A computer could generate 20-digit random numbers such as 98125602386617556398. These would then be matched to the random numbers assigned to each probability and values assigned to 'Sales Revenues' and 'Costs' based on this. The random numbers generated give 5 possible outcomes in our example:

Random number	Sales revenue in $000	Random Number	Costs in $000	Profit
98	382	12	248	134
56	318	02	248	70
38	318	66	260	58
17	254	55	260	(6)
63	318	98	272	46

NPV and standard deviation

In order to measure the risk associated with a particular project, it is helpful to find out how wide ranging the possible outcomes are. The conventional measure is the standard deviation explained in a previous chapter. The standard deviation compares all the actual outcomes with the expected value (or mean outcome). It then calculates how far on average the outcomes deviate from the mean. It is calculated using a formula.

If we have two probability distributions with different expected values their standard deviations are not directly comparable. We can overcome this problem by using the coefficient of variation (the standard deviation divided by the expected value) which measures the relative size of the risk.

Expected values, standard deviations or coefficient of variations are used to summarise the outcomes from alternative courses of action.

However it must be remembered that they do not provide all the relevant information to the decision maker. The probability distribution will provide the decision maker with all of the information they require. It would be appropriate to use expected values, standard deviations or coefficient of variations for decision making when there are a large number of alternatives to consider i.e. where it is not practical to consider the probability distributions for each alternative.

Sensitivity analysis

Sensitivity analysis in NPV questions typically involves posing 'what if' questions. The NPV is recalculated under different conditions, e.g. what would happen if demand fell by 10%, how would the result be affected if variable costs are 5% higher, etc.

Alternatively, we may wish to discover the maximum possible change in one of the parameters before the opportunity becomes non-viable.

This maximum possible change is often expressed as a percentage:

$$\text{Sensitivity margin} = \frac{\text{NPV}}{\text{PV of flow under consideration}}$$

LEARN

This formula works for total cash flows. It cannot be used for individual units, selling prices, variable cost per unit, etc. Have a go at the following example.

Example 1 – SENSITIVITY ANALYSIS

BJS Ltd is considering investing $120,000 in equipment that has a life of 15 years. Its final scrap value is $25,000.

The equipment will be used to produce 15,000 deluxe pairs of rugby boots per annum, generating a contribution of $2.75 per pair. Specific fixed costs are estimated at $18,000 per annum. The firm has a 15% cost of capital.

Required:

(a) Calculate the NPV of the project.

(b) Calculate the sensitivity of your NPV to the:
   (i)   initial investmen
   (ii) annual contribution
   (iii) annual fixed costs.

(c) Identify the minimum annual sales required to ensure that the project at least breaks even.

Pros and cons of sensitivity analysis

Strengths of sensitivity analysis

- No complicated theory to understand.

- Information will be presented to management in a form which facilitates subjective judgement to decide the likelihood of the various possible outcomes considered.

- Identifies areas which are crucial to the success of the project. If the project is chosen, those areas can be carefully monitored.

- Indicates just how critical some of the forecasts which are considered to be uncertain are.

Weaknesses of sensitivity analysis

- It assumes that changes to variables can be made independently, e.g. material prices will change independently of other variables. This is unlikely. If material prices went up the firm may be able to increase selling price at the same time and there would be little effect on NPV. A technique called simulation (discussed earlier) allows us to change more than one variable at a time.

- It only identifies how far a variable needs to change. It does not look at the probability of such a change. In the above analysis, sales volume appears to be the most crucial variable, but if the firm were facing volatile raw material markets a 65% change in raw material prices would be far more likely than a 29% change in sales volume.

- It is not an optimising technique. It provides information on the basis of which decisions can be made. It does not point directly to the correct decision.

3 Relevant cash flows

Investment decisions, like all other decisions, should be analysed in terms of cash flows that can be directly attributable to them. This has many implications:

Sunk costs

A sunk cost has already been incurred and therefore will not be relevant to the investment decision.

Opportunity cost

As in all decision making, opportunity costs are relevant, and should be included in investment decisions.

Fixed costs

Should be treated as a whole, and only where relevant. This means that fixed overheads that are "absorbed"/ "charged"/ "allocated"/ "apportioned" to a project should be ignored. Only extra/incremental changes in fixed overheads should be included in discounted cash flow calculations.

Depreciation

Depreciation is not a cash flow, and so should **never** be included in a discounted cash-flow calculation. The only investment appraisal technique that will include depreciation is ARR.

Example 2

As part of a new product development a company has employed a building consultant to perform an initial survey. This initial survey has cost $40,000. But there will be an ongoing need for her services if the company decides to proceed with the project. This work will be charged at a fixed rate of $20,000 per annum.

What relevant cost should be included for the building consultants services in the first year when considering whether the project should proceed?

A $0

B $20,000

C $40,000

D $60,000

Further details

Relevant costs are those which will be affected by the decision being taken. All relevant costs should be considered in management decision-making. If a cost will remain unaltered regardless of the decision being taken, then it is called a non-relevant cost or irrelevant cost.

Non-relevant costs

Costs that are not usually relevant in management decisions include the following:

(a) Sunk or past costs. This is a 'cost that has been irreversibly incurred or committed and cannot therefore be considered relevant to a decision. Sunk costs may also be termed irrecoverable costs' (CIMA Official Terminology). An example of a sunk cost is expenditure that has been incurred in developing a new product. The money cannot be recovered even if a decision is taken to abandon further development of the new product. The cost is therefore not relevant to future decisions concerning the product.

(b) Absorbed fixed overheads that will not increase or decrease as a result of the decision being taken. The amount of overhead to be absorbed by a particular cost unit might alter because of the decision; however, this is a result of the company's cost accounting procedures for overheads. If the actual amount of overhead incurred by the company will not alter, then the overhead is not a relevant cost.

(c) Expenditure that will be incurred in the future, but as a result of decisions taken in the past that cannot now be changed. These are known as committed costs. They can sometimes cause confusion because they are future costs. However, a committed cost will be incurred regardless of the decision being taken and therefore it is not relevant. An example of this type of cost could be expenditure on special packaging for a new product, where the packaging has been ordered and delivered but not yet paid for. The company is obliged to pay for the packaging even if they decide not to proceed with the product; therefore it is not a relevant cost.

(d) Historical cost depreciation. Depreciation is an accounting adjustment but does not result in any future cash flows. They are merely the book entries that are designed to spread the original cost of an asset over its useful life.

(e) Notional costs such as notional rent and notional interest. These are only relevant if they represent an identified lost opportunity to use the premises or the finance for some alternative purpose.
In these circumstances, the notional costs would be opportunity costs. This explanation will become clearer when you learn more about opportunity costs later in this chapter.

Conclusion

It is essential to look to the future when deciding which costs are relevant to a decision. Costs that have already been incurred or that will not be altered in the future as a result of the decision being taken are not relevant costs.

Opportunity costs

An opportunity cost is a special type of relevant cost. An opportunity cost can be defined as 'the value of the benefit sacrificed when one course of action is chosen in preference to an alternative. The opportunity cost is represented by the foregone potential benefit from the best rejected course of action' *(CIMA Official Terminology).*

With opportunity costs we are concerned with identifying the value of any benefit forgone as the result of choosing one course of action in preference to another.

Examples of opportunity costs

The best way to demonstrate opportunity costs is to consider some examples.

(a) A company has some obsolete material in stock that it is considering to use for a special contract. If the material is not used on the contract it can either be sold back to the supplier for $2 per tonne or it can be used on another contract in place of a different material that would usually cost $2.20 per tonne.

The opportunity cost of using the material on the special contract is $2.20 per tonne. This is the value of the next best alternative use for the material, or the benefit forgone by not using it for the other contract.

(b) Chris is deciding whether or not to take a skiing holiday this year. The travel agent is quoting an all-inclusive holiday cost of $675 for a week. Chris will lose the chance to earn $200 for a part-time job during the week that the holiday would be taken.

The relevant cost of taking the holiday is $875. This is made up of the out-of-pocket cost of $675, plus the $200 opportunity cost, that is the part-time wages forgone.

Notional costs and opportunity costs

Notional costs and opportunity costs are often similar. This is particularly noticeable in the case of notional rent. The notional rent could be the rental that the company is forgoing by occupying the premises itself, that is it could be an opportunity cost. However, it is only a true opportunity cost if the company can actually identify a forgone opportunity to rent the premises. If nobody is willing to pay the rent, then it is not an opportunity cost.

If an examination question on relevant costs includes information about notional costs, read the question carefully and state your assumptions concerning the relevance of the notional cost.

Avoidable, differential and incremental costs

There are two other types of relevant cost that you will need to know about: avoidable costs and differential/incremental costs.

Avoidable costs

CIMA defines avoidable costs as 'the specific costs of an activity or sector of a business which would be avoided if that activity or sector did not exist'.

For example, if a company is considering shutting down a department, then the avoidable costs are those that would be saved as a result of the shutdown. Such costs might include the labour costs of those employed in the department and the rental cost of the space occupied by the department. The latter is an example of an attributable or specific fixed cost. Costs such as apportioned head office costs that would not be saved as a result of the shutdown are unavoidable costs. They are not relevant to the decision.

Differential/incremental costs

CIMA defines a differential/incremental cost as 'the difference in total cost between alternatives. This is calculated to assist decision making'.

For example, if the relevant cost of contract X is $5,700 and the relevant cost of contract Y is $6,200, we would say that the differential or incremental cost is $500, that is the extra cost of contract Y is $500.

Using incremental costs

Incremental costs can be useful if the cost accountant wishes to highlight the consequences of taking sequential steps in a decision. For example, the accountant might be providing cost information for a decision about whether to increase the number of employees in a department.

Instead of quoting several different total-cost figures, it might be more useful to say 'the incremental cost per five employees will be $5,800 per month'.

Remember that only relevant costs should be used in the calculations.

Incremental revenues

Just as incremental costs are the differences in cost between alternatives, so incremental revenues are the differences in revenues between the alternatives. Matching the incremental costs against the incremental revenue will produce a figure for the incremental gain or loss between the alternatives.

Cash flows to include

The cash flows that should be included are those which are specifically incurred as a result of the acceptance or non-acceptance of the project. In some cases, these may be opportunity costs.

When deciding what figure should be included in any DCF calculation it sometimes helps to tabulate for a particular element of cost.

| Cash flow if project accepted | – | Cash flow if project rejected | = Relevant cash flow |

Example 3

Activity 1

A mining operation uses skilled labour costing $4 per hour, which generates a contribution, after deducting these labour costs, of $3 per hour.

A new project is now being considered that requires 5,000 hours of skilled labour. There is a shortage of the required labour. Any used on the new project must be transferred from normal working. Calculate the relevant cost of using the skilled labour on the project. Calculate the contribution cash flow that is lost if the labour is transferred from normal working

Activity 2

Suppose the facts about labour are as above, but there is a surplus of skilled labour already employed (and paid) by the business which is sufficient to cope with the new project. The presently idle men are being paid full wages.

Calculate the contribution cash flow that is lost if the labour is transferred to the project from doing nothing.

More on opportunity costs

If there are scarcities of resources to be used on projects (e.g. labour, materials, machines), then consideration must be given to revenues that could have been earned from alternative uses of the resources.

For example, the skilled labour that is needed on the new project might have to be withdrawn from normal production causing a loss in contribution. This is obviously relevant to the project appraisal. The cash flows of a single department or division cannot be looked at in isolation. It is always the effects on cash flows of the whole organisation that must be considered.

Example

A new contract requires the use of 50 tons of metal ZX81. This metal is used regularly on all the firm's projects. There are 100 tons of ZX81 in stock at the moment that were bought for $200 per ton. The current purchase price is $210 per ton, and the metal could be disposed of for net scrap proceeds of $150 per ton. With what cost should the new contract be charged for the ZX81?

Solution

The use of the material in stock for the new contract means that more ZX81 must be bought for normal workings. The cost to the organisation is therefore the money spent on purchase, no matter whether existing stock or new stock is used on the contract. Assuming that the additional purchases are made in the near future, the relevant cost to the organisation is current purchase price, i.e.:

$$50 \text{ tons} * \$210 = \$10,500$$

Example

Suppose the organisation has no use for the ZX81 in stock. What is the relevant cost of using it on the new contract?

Solution

Now the only alternative use for the material is to sell it for scrap. To use 50 tons on the contract is to give up the opportunity of selling it for:

$$50 * \$150 = \$7,500$$

The contract should therefore be charged with this amount.

Example

Suppose that there is no alternative use for the ZX81 other than a scrap sale, but that there is only 25 tons in stock.

Solution

The relevant cost of the 25 tons in stock is $150 per ton. The organisation must then purchase a further 25 tons, and assuming this is in the near future, it will cost $210 per ton.

The contract must be charged with:

	$
25 tons @ $150	3,750
25 tons @ $210	5,250
	9,000

Relevant costs and the decision to abandon

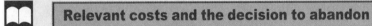

During our initial consideration of project appraisals, it was noted that past costs were irrelevant to any decision regarding the future of a project. This remains true for those occasions when the company has already started a project and wishes to establish whether it should continue with it, or whether it should abandon the project part way through its life.

The only relevant costs are future costs: these will be compared with future revenues to decide the viability of abandonment. Management is often reluctant to take a decision to abandon a project half-way through, as it is often considered to reflect a poor past decision; however true this may be, it would be even worse to compound the error by making another poor decision. Projects must, therefore, be kept constantly under review.

Factors in the decision to abandon

The following considerations must be taken into account in deciding whether to continue or abandon a project:

- future cash outflows associated with the project
- future cash inflows associated with the project
- revenues/costs that would arise if the project were abandoned
  - other projects, which may be:
    alternatives to the project under consideration
    more profitable uses of funds tied up in the project under review.

Each of these factors must be consciously assessed at each stage of the project's life and, if it is seen that abandoning the project would be more beneficial than proceeding with it, then an abandonment decision must be made.

4 Dealing with taxation

There are two tax effects that we need to deal with in investment appraisal, which are the effects of corporation tax, and the impact of tax depreciation (also known as capital allowances).

Typical assumptions are that the taxable profits will be **the net cash flows from the project less any tax depreciation** (explored later).

We also make assumptions about the timing of the payments: in exam questions, corporation tax is usually paid in two instalments. half the tax is payable in the year in which it arises, the balance is paid in the following year.

The corporation tax rate will be given in the question.

The impact of taxation on cash flows

Taxation may have a significant impact on the viability of a capital investment project. Taxation payments and savings in tax payments are clearly cash flows associated with the project. They are relevant, and should be considered in a DCF analysis.

Taxation has the following effects on an investment appraisal problem:

- Project cash flows will give rise to taxation which itself has an impact on project appraisal. Normally we assume that tax is paid in two instalments, where half the tax is payable in the year in which it arises, and the balance is paid in the following year. However, it is possible for alternative assumptions to be made and so you should read any examination question carefully to ascertain precisely what assumptions are made in the question.

- Organisations benefit from being able to claim tax depreciation (also known as capital allowances) – a tax deductible alternative to depreciation. The effect of these is to reduce the amount of tax that organisations are required to pay. Again it is important to read any examination question carefully in order to identify what treatment is expected by the examiner. A common assumption is that tax depreciation is available on a 25% reducing balance basis.

Note that the **tax depreciation is not a cash flow** and to calculate the tax impact we have to multiply each year's tax depreciation by the corporation tax rate. The effect of tax depreciation is on the amount of tax payable, which is the relevant cash flow.

In dealing with these tax effects it is always assumed that:

- where a tax loss arises from the project, there are sufficient taxable profits elsewhere in the organisation to allow the loss to reduce any relevant (subsequent) tax payment (and it may therefore be treated as a cash inflow) and that the company has sufficient taxable profits to obtain full benefit from tax depreciation.

In practice, the effects of taxation are more complex, and are influenced by a number of factors including the following:

- the taxable profits and tax rate
- the company's accounting period and tax payment dates
- whether assets qualify for tax depreciation
- losses available for set-off

A detailed knowledge of tax is not required for this paper. Assumptions and simplifications will be made. These will usually be set out clearly in each examination question. It is important to follow the instructions for the treatment of tax in the question being attempted. Any assumptions that you make must also be clearly stated.

Tax depreciation

Tax depreciation is used to reduce taxable profits, and the consequent reduction in a tax payment should be treated as a cash saving arising from the acceptance of the project. In this examination tax depreciation is generally allowed on the cost of plant and machinery at the rate of 25% on a reducing balance basis. It may also be possible to claim tax depreciation on the costs of installation, such as labour and overhead costs of removing an old machine and levelling the area for the new machine.

Balancing allowance (or charge)

When the plant is eventually sold, there may be a difference between the reducing balance amount and the selling price of the asset. An appropriate adjustment must be made to ensure that the company receives allowances equal to the total allowance allowed (i.e. purchase price less final value).

Balancing allowances/charges

If a business buys a capital asset in one year and sells it several years later, the total tax relief it will receive is the tax on the cost of the asset less its eventual disposal value.

For example, if a business buys equipment for $100,000 in Year 0 and disposes of it in Year 5 for $20,000, it will receive tax relief on the net cost of $80,000. If the rate of corporation tax is 30%, the reduction in tax payments over the five years would be 30% × $80,000 = $24,000.

Balancing allowances are given as a final deduction to ensure the full fall in value has been allowed. Balancing charges occur where the total tax depreciation claimed exceeds the fall in value of the asset. The excess claimed is treated as a taxable amount in the year of disposal.

Timing of the tax savings associated with tax depreciation

It is likely that the corporation tax will be paid in four quarterly instalments. Hence, the benefit of tax saved because of tax depreciation is received when the corporation tax should have been paid. Thus, half the tax is saved in the current year, and half is saved in the year following.

> ### Example 4 – Balancing allowance
>
> An asset is purchased for $50,000. At the end of the fourth year it will be sold for $10,000. Tax depreciation is available at 25 per cent reducing balance and corporation tax is payable at 30 per cent per annum.
>
> Corporation tax is paid in two instalments, with half the tax payable in the year in which it arises, and the balance paid in the following year.
>
> **Required:**
>
> (a) Calculate the tax depreciation each year and the associated corporation tax saving.
>
> (b) Illustrate the timing of the tax savings calculated in part (a).

For tax purposes care must be taken to identify the exact time of asset purchase.

- Assets are assumed to be bought at T_0.

- It should be assumed that the asset is bought at the start of the accounting period and therefore the first tax depreciation is offset against the year 1 net cash flows.

5 Proforma layout for calculations

NPV with tax – Example pro forma

(assuming a two Year Project)

	Year 0	Year 1	Year 2	Year 3
	$	$	$	$
Cash inflows		X	X	
Cash outflows		(X)	(X)	
		—	—	
Net cash flow		X	X	
Tax on net cash flow		(X)	(X)	(X)
Investment	(X)			
Scrap value			X	
Tax depreciation savings (which would need a separate working)		X	X	X
Working capital	(X)		X	
Net cash flows	(X)	X	X	X
Discount factor	1.00	x	x	x
Present value	PV	PV	PV	PV

Example 5

Camp plc has produced and marketed sleeping bags for several years. The sleeping bags are much heavier than some of the modern sleeping bags being introduced to the market. The company is concerned about the effect this will have on its sales.

Camp plc are considering investing in new technology that would enable them to produce a much lighter and more compact sleeping bag. The new machine will cost $250,000 and is expected to have a life of four years with a scrap value of $10,000. In addition an investment of $35,000 in working capital will be required initially.

The following forecast annual trading account has been prepared for the project:

	$
Sales	200,000
Material	(40,000)
Labour	(30,000)
Variable overheads	(10,000)
Depreciation	(20,000)
Annual profit	**100,000**

The company's cost of capital is 10%. Corporation tax is charged at 30% and is paid in two instalments, with half the tax payable in the year in which it arises, and the balance paid in the following year. Tax depreciation of 25% on reducing balance is available on capital expenditure.

Required:

Calculate whether Camp plc should invest in the new technology.

6 Working capital

The next example has an investment of working capital included in it.

The treatment of working capital is as follows:

- It is treated as an investment at the start of the project, like any other investment. Any additional working capital requirements are invested when required. **Only *the change* in working capital is treated as a cash flow**.

- Working capital does not qualify for tax relief – so is ignored in the taxation and tax depreciation calculations.

- At the end of the project the working capital is 'released'. This is treated as a cash inflow at the end of the project, equal to the total investment in working capital (unless told otherwise).

In the examination, for a short life project, with cash flows inflating at different rates, it is best to set the NPV calculation out with the cash flows down the side and the time across the top.

7 The impact of inflation on cash flows

If an exam question involves inflation then we normally have to either:

- adjust the cash flows, or
- adjust the cost of capital.

Where cash flows have not been increased for expected inflation they are known as **current cash flows**, or **real cash flows**.

Where cash flows have been increased to take account of expected inflation they are known as **money cash flows**, or **nominal cash flows**. Remember, if they do take inflation into account, they represent expected flows of money, hence the term 'money cash flows'.

You can assume that cash flows you are given in the exam are the money cash flows unless told otherwise.

If the examiner specifies that the **cash flows are in current terms** you will generally need to put these in money terms before you can discount them. For example if the question tells you that sales for the next 3 years are $100 in current terms but are expected to inflate by 10%, then what he actually means is that the sales will be:

Year 1: $110
Year 2: $121   } i.e. these are the cash flows in money terms
Year 3: $133.10

Make sure you read the question carefully. Sometimes you will be given the **cash flows in Year 1 terms** with subsequent inflation.

- For example if the question says "Sales will be $100 in the first year, but are then going to inflate by 10% for the next two years", then the sales will be:

Year 1: $100
Year 2: $110 } compare these to the previous example – make sure
Year 3: $121   you understand why they are different!

8 Methods of dealing with inflation

The impact of inflation can be dealt with in two different ways – both methods give the same NPV.

```
┌─────────────────────────────┐
│ METHODS OF DEALING WITH     │
│         INFLATION           │
└─────────────────────────────┘
```

```
┌──────────────────┐                    ┌──────────────────┐
│   REAL METHOD    │                    │  MONEY/NOMINAL   │
│                  │                    │      METHOD      │
└──────────────────┘                    └──────────────────┘
```

┌──────────────────────────┐   ┌──────────────────────────┐
│ 1 Inflate each cash   │
│   flow by its spe-   │
│   cific inflation rate   │
│   ie convert it to a   │
│   **money flow.**   │
└──────────────────────────┘

┌──────────────────────────┐
│ 1 Do NOT inflate the cash │
│   flows – leave them in   │
│   real terms ie in today's│
│   (T_o) prices – **real flows.** │
└──────────────────────────┘

┌──────────────────────────┐   ┌──────────────────────────┐
│ 2 Discount using the   │   │ 2 Discount using the   │
│   real rate.   │   │   money rate.   │
└──────────────────────────┘   └──────────────────────────┘

Real/real   Money/money

Be consistent

The real rate of return

If money is invested in an account, it will earn interest. However, inflation will have the effect of reducing the value of the return. By deflating the future cash (money) we can find the real return from the investment, i.e. the return at today's prices.

Formula

To find the real rate of return we can use the following formula:

$$(1+r) = \frac{(1+m)}{(1+i)}$$

LEARN

This is where:

- **r** is the real rate of return
- **m** is the money cost of capital (this is the company's normal cost of capital)
- **i** is the rate of inflation

Illustration

$1,000 is invested in an account that pays 10% interest per annum. Inflation is currently 7% per annum.

Calculate the real return on the investment.

After 1 year $1,000 will have compounded up to $1,000 × 1.10 = $1,100.

Now deflate this figure to find the real return on the investment:

$$\$1,100 \div 1.07 = \$1,028$$

Therefore, the $1,000 has increased by 2.8% in real terms. This is the real rate.

It can be calculated using the formula as follows:

$$(1 + r) = \frac{(1 + m)}{(1 + i)}$$

$$(1 + r) = \frac{(1 + 0.10)}{(1 + 0.07)}$$

$$
\begin{aligned}
(1 + r) &= 1.028 \\
r &= 1.028 - 1 \\
r &= 0.028 = 2.8\%
\end{aligned}
$$

Using the real rate of return in questions

If there is one rate of inflation in the question both the real and money method will give the same answer. However it is easier to adjust one discount rate, rather than all the cash flows over a number of years. This is particularly true where the cash flows are annuities. The real method is the only possible method where they are perpetuities.

Although it is theoretically possible to use the real method in questions incorporating tax, it is extremely complex. It is therefore much safer (and easier) to use the money/nominal method in all questions where tax is taken into account.

Example 6 – NPV AND INFLATION

Storm Ltd is evaluating project X which requires an initial investment of $50,000. Expected net cash flows are $20,000 per annum for 4 years at today's prices. However these are expected to rise by 5.5% per annum because of inflation. The firm's cost of capital is 15%. Calculate the NPV by:

(a) discounting money cash flows

(b) discounting real cash flows.

9 Specific and general inflation rates

The examples given above had all cash flows inflating at the general rate of inflation. In practice, inflation does not affect all costs to the same extent. In some investment appraisal questions you may be given information on more than one inflation rate. In these situations you will have information on both specific inflation rates and general inflation rates.

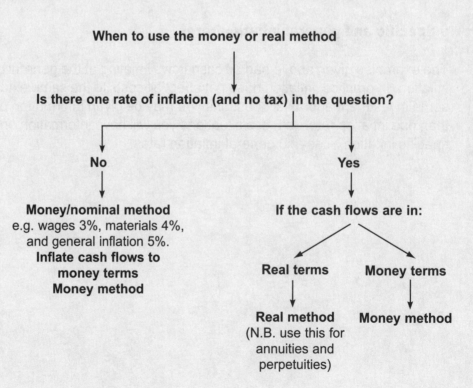

TWO TYPES OF INFLATION

SPECIFIC INFLATION RATE

Impacts all the individual cash flow items – each cash flow is affected by a specific rate.

GENERAL RATE OF INFLATION

Impacts the investors' overall required rate of return.

Investors in the project need compensation for their lost purchasing power, which relates to their ability to buy a basket of all goods, rather than any specific one.

Inflation can impact different types of products in different ways : prices don't rall rise at exactly the same rate. In situations where you are given a number of specific inflation rates, the real method outlined above cannot be used.

The following gives a useful summary of how to approach examination questions.

When to use the money or real method

↓

Is there one rate of inflation (and no tax) in the question?

No ← → **Yes**

No:
Money/nominal method
e.g. wages 3%, materials 4%, and general inflation 5%.
Inflate cash flows to money terms
Money method

Yes:
If the cash flows are in:

Real terms ← → **Money terms**

Real method
(N.B. use this for annuities and perpetuities)

Money method

If a question contains both tax and inflation, it is advisable to use the money method.

The money method

To use the real method when cash flows inflate at different rates (specific rates) is extremely complex and would involve a lot of calculations. It is therefore advisable to always use the money method in these situations. This involves:

- inflating the cash flows at their specific inflation rates

- discounting using the money rate

Very often the money rate will not be given in the question but will need to be calculated. This should be done using the real rate and the general inflation rate.

Example 7

Thunder plc has just developed a new product to be called the Lightening and is now considering whether to put it into production. The following information is available:

(i) Costs incurred to date in the development of Lightening amount to $480,000.

(ii) Production of Lightening will require the purchase of new machinery at a cost of $2,400,000 payable immediately. This machinery is specific to the production of Lightening and will be obsolete and valueless when production ceases. The machinery has a production life of four years and a production capacity of 30,000 units per annum.

(iii) Production costs of Lightening (at year 1 prices) are estimated as follows:

	$
Direct material	8.00
Direct labour	12.00
Variable overheads	12.00

In addition, fixed production costs (at year 1 prices), including straight-line depreciation on plant and machinery specific to this project, will amount to $800,000 per annum.

(iv) The selling price of Lightening will be $80.00 per unit (at year 1 prices). Demand is expected to be 25,000 units per annum for the next four years.

(v) The retail price index is expected to be at 5% per annum for the next four years and the selling price of Lightening is expected to increase at the same rate. Annual inflation rates for production costs are expected to be as follows:

	%
Direct material	4
Direct labour	10
Variable overheads	4
Fixed costs	5

(vi) The company's cost of capital in money terms is expected to be 15%.

You may ignore the effects of taxation.

Unless otherwise specified all costs and revenues should be assumed to arise at the end of each year.

Required:

Calculate whether Thunder plc should produce Lightening on the basis of the information above.

(15 marks)

Deflation

Many western economies have very low rates of inflation at present and some are even experiencing deflation. Deflation may also apply to certain hi-tech materials which get considerably cheaper when they go into mass production.

Deflation may affect business decision making in several ways:

• Investing in projects that have long payback periods may require some courage.

• Borrowing to finance the purchase of assets that are going to fall in value may also require some courage: money rates will be low, but real rates are higher.

• It may be difficult to reduce some costs – especially wages – in line with deflation.

- Consumers may defer purchasing decisions if they anticipate that prices will fall.

10 Dealing with questions with both tax and inflation

Combining tax and inflation in the same question does not make it any more difficult than keeping them separate.

Questions with both tax and inflation are best tackled using the money method.

- Inflate costs and revenues, where necessary, before determining their tax implications.

- Ensure that the cost and disposal values have been inflated (if necessary) before calculating tax depreciation.

- Always calculate working capital on these inflated figures, unless given.

- Use a post-tax money discount rate.

Example 8

Ackbono Co is considering a potential project with the following forecasts:

	Now	T_1	T_2	T_3
Initial investment ($million)	(1,000)			
Disposal proceeds ($million)				200
Demand (millions of units)		5	10	6

The initial investment will be made on the first day of the new accounting period.

The selling price per unit is expected to be $100 and the variable cost $30 per unit. Both of these figures are given in today's terms.

Tax depreciation is available at 25 per cent reducing balance and corporation tax is payable at 30 per cent per annum.

Corporation tax is paid in two instalments, with half the tax payable in the year in which it arises, and the balance paid in the following year.

The company has a real required rate of return of 6.8%.

General inflation is predicted to be 3% pa but the selling price is expected to inflate at 4% and variable costs by 5% pa

> **Calculate the NPV of the project.**
>
> **N.B.** work in $ millions.

11 Capital asset replacement decisions

As the title suggests, this section considers the need to replace old, worn out capital assets within a firm.

There are two distinct types of decisions to consider:

(1) Considering mutually-exclusive options with unequal lives.

(2) Calculating an optimum replacement cycle.

We shall consider each in turn.

Mutually-exclusive options with unequal lives

Companies considering the replacement of an asset may be faced with alternatives where the life spans of the various machines differ, but the asset is required for the foreseeable future. The options must be evaluated over a comparable number of years.

In order to compare like with like we will calculate an **equivalent annual cost**. This is similar to an average annual cash flow. Once both machines' costs have been annualised the cheapest machine can be chosen by comparing annual costs.

FORMULA

$$\text{Equivalent annual cost} = \frac{\text{PV of costs}}{\text{Annuity factor for year n}}$$

LEARN

where n is the machine life time.

This is best explained by working through an example (the solution at the end of the chapter includes an explanation of the technique):

Example 9 – REPLACEMENT DECISION

Donald Ltd is considering replacing an asset with one of two possible machines:

Machine X	Initial cost	$120,000
	Life	3 years
	Running costs	$20,000 p.a.
	Residual value	nil
Machine Y	Initial cost	$60,000
	Life	2 years
	Running costs	Year 1 : $40,000
		Year 2 : $35,000
	Residual value	nil

The machines will be required into the foreseeable future. The company's cost of capital is 10%.

Required:

Calculate which machine should be purchased.

Lowest common multiple method

There is an alternative method for comparing machines with different lives known as the lowest common multiple method.

This is where we find the smallest number, which we can divide into by each of a set of numbers and evaluate the NPV cost over this period.

Example

If we look again at the decision faced in Example 9 and apply the lowest common multiple method, we have two projects, one with a life of 2 years and one with a life of 3 years. The common multiple is 6 years. We then calculate the NPV of the two options over 6 years and compare the results as follows:

Machine X

Year	Description	Cash flow $	Discount rate 15%	Present value $
0	Outlay	120,000	1.000	120,000
1 – 3	Running cost	20,000	2.487	49,740
3	Replace	120,000	0.751	90,120
4 – 6	Running cost	20,000	1.868	37,360
			NPV =	**297,220**

Machine Y

Year	Description	Cash flow $	Discount rate 15%	Present value $
0	Outlay	60,000	1.000	60,000
1 – 2	Running cost	35,000	1.736	60,760
2	Replace	60,000	0.826	49,560
3 – 4	Running cost	35,000	1.434	50,190
4	Replace	60,000	0.683	40,980
5 – 6	Running cost	35,000	1.185	41,475
			NPV =	**302,965**

Machine X should be purchased as it has the least cost option (lowest NPV cost).

Optimum replacement cycles

Companies purchasing new plant and machinery must decide how often to replace them. Generally, as machinery ages its residual value decreases and the annual running costs increase. However, companies are unlikely to want to replace assets too frequently because of the capital outlay associated with the purchase.

In the next section we shall calculate the optimum replacement cycle in order to minimise long-term costs.

Factors in replacement decisions

The factors to be considered include the following:

- Capital cost of new equipment – the higher cost of equipment will have to be balanced against known or possible technical improvements.

- Operating costs – operating costs will be expected to increase as the machinery deteriorates over time. This may be the result of:
  - increased repair and maintenance costs
  - loss of production due to 'down-time' resulting from increased repair and maintenance time
  - lower quality and quantity of output.

- Resale value – the extent to which old equipment can be traded in for new.

- Taxation and investment incentives.

- Inflation – both the general price level change, and relative movements in the prices of inputs and outputs.

Example 10 – REPLACEMENT CYCLE

A supermarket is trying to determine the optimal replacement policy for its fleet of delivery vehicles. The total purchase price of the fleet is $220,000.

The running costs and scrap values of the fleet at the end of each year are:

	Year 1	Year 2	Year 3	Year 4	Year 5
Running costs	$110,000	$132,000	$154,000	$165,000	$176,000
Scrap value	$121,000	$88,000	$66,000	$55,000	$25,000

The supermarket's cost of capital is 12% per annum.

Ignore taxation and inflation.

Identify at the end of which year the supermarket should replace its fleet of delivery vehicles.

Method of solution

(1) Consider each possible replacement cycle in turn: 1 year, 2 year, 3 year etc.

(2) Calculate the PV of costs for each cycle.

(3) Divide this PV by the annuity factor to find the equivalent annual cost.

(4) Select the replacement cycle with the lowest equivalent annual cost.

Limitations of replacement analysis

The replacement analysis model assumes that the firm replaces like with like each time it needs to replace an existing asset.

However this assumption ignores

- changing technology – machines fast become obsolete and can only be replaced with a more up-to-date model which will be more efficient and perhaps perform different functions

- inflation – the increase in price over time increases the cost structure of the different assets, meaning that the optimal replacement cycle can vary over time

- change in production plans – firms cannot predict with accuracy the market environment they will be facing in the future and whether they will even need to make use of the asset at that time.

12 Capital rationing

If investment funds are unlimited then all projects with a positive NPV should be undertaken. Capital rationing occurs when insufficient funds are available to undertake all beneficial projects.

Hard and soft capital rationing

The term soft capital rationing is often used to refer to situations where for various reasons the firm internally imposes a budget ceiling on the amount of capital expenditure. If the capital is restricted because of external constraints such as the inability to obtain funds from the financial markets, the term hard capital rationing is used. The type of rationing imposed on a firm will not, however, affect our analysis.

The objective of all capital rationing exercises is the maximisation of the total NPV of the chosen projects' cash flows at the cost of capital. Thus it becomes necessary to rank projects to enable the optimum combination to be undertaken.

Underlying assumptions:

- Individual projects are divisible. The resulting NPV will be pro-rated. For example, if only 25% of the capital is available for a project only 25% of its NPV will be earned.
- Annual cash flows cannot be delayed or brought forward.
- Capital funds are restricted in just one period (year 0).

Technique

The decision aims to maximise NPV given a single limiting factor. As with other decisions with one scarce resource, the opportunities should be ranked according to NPV per $1 invested. This measure is called the profitability index (PI).

$$\text{Profitability index} = \frac{\text{NPV}}{\text{Initial Investment}}$$

LEARN

The optimal investment plan is determined by:

(1) calculating a PI for each project
(2) ranking the projects according to their PI
(3) allocating funds according to the projects' rankings until they are used up.

Example 11 – CAPITAL RATIONING

A company may undertake any of the following investment projects.

Project	Investment required	Net present value
	$000	$000
A	3,400	850
B	2,750	825
C	2,000	720
D	3,400	680
E	860	430
F	950	400
G	1,250	350

In the next budget period there is only $9 million available for capital expenditure projects. Each project is divisible.

Required:

(a) If the company ranks the projects according to highest NPVs, which projects will be undertaken? Calculate the total NPV.

(b) If the company selects projects according to their profitability index, calculate which projects will be undertaken. Calculate the total NPV now.

Dealing with indivisible projects

There may be scenarios where 'common sense' has to come into play and this general rule has to be ignored. Consider the following example:

Example

A company has an investment limit of $800,000 and has to choose between the following three projects:

Project	Investment	Inflow PV	NPV	PI	Rank
A	600,000	700,000	100,000	1.17	1
B	500,000	560,000	60,000	1.12	3
C	300,000	345,000	45,000	1.15	2

On the basis of the general rule, Project A only would be selected since it has the highest PI. But this precludes any other projects, generating an NPV of $800,000 and leaving $200,000 of the capital limit uncommitted. Consequently, NPV is maximised by adopting two projects (B and C) both of which have lower PIs than A. By adopting these two projects we raise total NPV to $105,000.

In these circumstances, the objective can only be achieved by selecting from amongst the available projects on a trial and error basis. Because of the problem of indivisibility this may leave some funds unutilised. Consider another example:

Example

PQ has $50,000 available to invest. Its cost of capital is 10%. The following indivisible projects are available:

Project	Initial outlay $	Return p.a. to perpetuity $
1	20,000	1,500
2	10,000	1,500
3	15,000	3,000
4	30,000	5,400
5	25,000	4,800

Solution

The first stage is to calculate the NPV of the projects.

Project	Initial outlay $	PV of cash flows $	NPV $
1	20,000	15,000	(5,000)
2	10,000	15,000	5,000
3	15,000	30,000	15,000
4	30,000	54,000	24,000
5	25,000	48,000	23,000

The approach is then one of considering all possible combinations of projects under the investment limit of $50,000.

The optimum selection of projects is as follows:

Project	Initial outlay $	NPV $
2	10,000	5,000
3	15,000	15,000
5	25,000	23,000
	50,000	43,000

Unused funds	Nil
Funds available	50,000

13 ABC in longer term decisions

The role of ABC

Activity-based costing (ABC) has been discussed in an earlier chapter. In this section we briefly discuss the role of ABC in longer-term decision making.

ABC systems are primarily designed to furnish management with cost information relating to an organisation's products. However, the production of this information is not an end in itself. Indeed it is the use to which such activity-based information is put that represents its real purpose and its value should be assessed against this end-result.

An ABC system produces historic information relating to its products or service provision which is of much assistance to management in analysing and explaining an organisation's profitability. However, many commentators including Robert Kaplan and Robin Cooper have viewed ABC as supporting major areas of strategic decision making with organisations, these being:

- decisions concerning product pricing strategy

- changes to the range and mix of products via the promotion and discontinuance of current lines, and

- new product development.

When ABC information is used in the above ways then it will underpin policy decisions of senior management and will therefore have a significant influence upon the longer-term prosperity of an organisation. Advocates of the use of ABC for strategic decision making maintain that its value lies in greater accuracy attaching to product costing which in turn increases the degree of reliability of cost information used for the above purposes. They further maintain that the use of ABC may give an indication of the long-term variable cost of products which arguably is the most relevant cost information for use in decisions of the above type. Given the inherent uncertainty involved in strategic decision making, management may use ABC information in decision-modelling and sensitivity analysis to assist in the making of such decisions.

The end product of an ABC system is an estimate of the historic cost of each of an organisation's products. However, strategic decision making involves future time periods and thus it is future outlay costs that need to be taken into consideration as opposed to historic costs. Therefore, it is arguable that the results obtained from an ABC system should only be used as a starting point in the determination of cost information that is aimed at assisting in the making of longer-term decisions. This is especially the case if ABC based product costs are viewed as estimates of longer term product costs as 'nothing is forever' and historic costs are susceptible to substantial change since all factors of production become variable in the longer term.

Any cost information which has been produced based on past activities must be used with caution with regard to longer-term decisions. Even so, ABC information may provide a sound starting point for the preparation of cost information to be used in strategic decision making. It has been argued that a significant advantage of ABC over conventional costing systems lies in its suitability for strategic decision making. Kaplan has argued that for decisions of a strategic nature a long-term perspective is usual and maintains that an ABC system gives product cost information which matches this requirement particularly well. This is evidenced by his assertion that 'conventional notions of fixed and variable costs are ignored because, for the purposes of product cost analysis, the time period is long enough to warrant treatment of virtually all costs as variable'.

14 Qualitative factors

The emphasis in this chapter has been on investment appraisal as a computational exercise: known numbers are inserted into formulae and a numerical result is produced. But, in reality, investment decisions are also influenced by many qualitative factors that must also be borne in mind in the investment appraisal exercise.

Qualitative factors

Consider the typical example of the proposed purchase of a new machine in a manufacturing plant. The machine offers both quantitative and qualitative costs and benefits, as below.

Quantitative costs include:

- the purchase price of the machine
- installation and training costs.

Quantitative benefits include:

- lower direct labour costs
- lower scrap costs and items requiring rework
- lower stock costs.

Qualitative costs include:

- increased noise level
- lower morale if existing staff have to be made redundant.

Qualitative benefits include:

- reduction in product development time
- improved product quality and service
- increase in manufacturing flexibility.

Because the qualitative factors are difficult to state in numerical terms, they are conventionally ignored in the investment appraisal exercise. However such an approach is flawed. If a question asks you to carry out a DCF analysis and then comment on what you have done, be certain to point out the qualitative factors that could additionally be brought into the decision.

15 Identifying real options in investment appraisal

Introduction

- Flexibility adds value to an investment.

- Financial options are an example where this flexibility can be valued.

- Real options theory attempts to classify and value flexibility in general by taking the ideas of financial options pricing and developing them.

- Conventional investment-appraisal techniques typically undervalue flexibility within projects with high uncertainty.

Illustration

- Flexibility adds value to an investment:
  - For example, if an investment can be staggered, then future costs can be avoided if the market turns out to be less attractive than originally expected.

  - The core to this value lies in reducing downside risk exposure but keeping upside potential open – i.e. in making probability distributions asymmetric.

- Financial options are an example where this flexibility can be valued.
  - A call option on a share allows an investor to 'wait and see' what happens to a share price before deciding whether to exercise the option and will thus benefit from favourable price movements without being affected by adverse movements.

- Real options theory attempts to classify and value flexibility in general by taking the ideas of financial options pricing and developing them:

  - A financial option gives the owner the right, but not the obligation, to buy or sell a security at a given price. Analogously, companies that make strategic investments have the right, but not the obligation, to exploit these opportunities in the future.

  - As with financial options most real options involve spending more up front (analogous to the option premium) to give additional flexibility later.

- Conventional investment-appraisal techniques typically undervalue flexibility within projects with high uncertainty.
  - High uncertainty within a NPV context will result in a higher discount rate and a lower NPV. However, with such uncertainty any embedded real options will become more valuable.

Different types of real option

There are many different classifications of real options. Most can be summarised under the following generic headings:

Options to delay/defer

The key here is to be able to delay investment without losing the opportunity, creating a call option on the future investment.

e.g

> **Illustration 2: Identifying real options in investment appraisal**
>
> For example, establishing a drugs patent allows the owner of the patent to wait and see how market conditions develop before producing the drug, without the potential downside of competitors entering the market.

(**Note:** Drugs patents was the subject of a past examination question on this area. However, there is some debate whether or not patents are real options. This debate is outside the scope of the syllabus.)

Options to switch/redeploy

It may be possible to switch the use of assets should market conditions change.

e.g

> **Illustration 3: Identifying real options in investment appraisal**
>
> For example, traditional production lines were set up to make one product. Modern flexible manufacturing systems (FMS) allow the product output to be changed to match customer requirements.

Similarly a new plant could be designed with resale and/or other uses in mind, using more general-purpose assets than dedicated to allow easier switching.

e.g

> **Illustration 4: Identifying real options in investment appraisal**
>
> For example, when designing a plant management can choose whether to have higher or lower operating gearing. By having mainly variable costs, it is financially more beneficial if the plant does not have to operate every month.

Options to expand/contract

It may be possible to adjust the scale of an investment depending on the market conditions.

Options to abandon

If a project has clearly identifiable stages such that investment can be staggered, then management have to decide whether to abandon or continue at the end of each stage.

Illustration 5: Identifying real options in investment appraisal

When looking to develop their stadiums, many football clubs face the decision whether to build a one- or a two-tier stand:

- A one-tier stand would be cheaper but would be inadequate if the club's attendance improved greatly.

- A two-tier stand would allow for much greater fan numbers but would be more expensive and would be seen as a waste of money should attendance not improve greatly.

Some clubs (e.g. West Bromwich Albion in the UK) have solved this problem by building a one-tier stand with stronger foundations and designed in such a way (e.g. positioning of exits, corporate boxes, etc.) that it would be relatively straightforward to add a second tier at a later stage without knocking down the first tier.

Such a stand is more expensive than a conventional one-tier stand but the premium paid makes it easier to expand at a later date when (if!) attendance grows.

Illustration 6: Identifying real options in investment appraisal

Amazon.com undertook a substantial investment to develop its customer base, brand name and information infrastructure for its core book business.

This in effect created a portfolio of real options to extend its operations into a variety of new businesses such as CDs, DVDs, etc.

16 Chapter summary

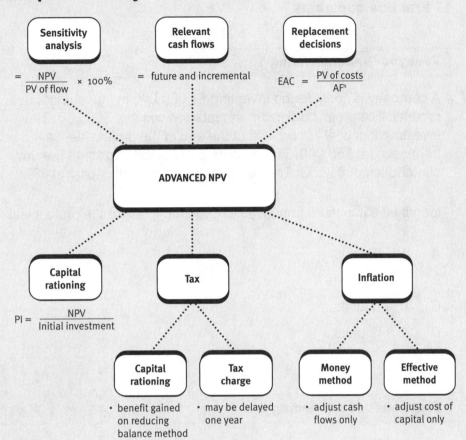

17 Practice questions

Test your understanding 1

A company is considering investing $1,000,000 in launching a new product. The project will incur annual fixed costs of $60,000. The investment capital will be sold at the end of the project life, seven years from now, for $50,000. The product is expected to generate a unit contribution of $12.50. The company has a cost of capital of 8%.

Identify the minimum annual sales required to make the project viable:

A   19,719 units

B   101,824 units

C   87,467 units

D   22,143 units

Test your understanding 2

Which of the following costs for a proposed project are relevant:

(i)   The salary to be paid to a market researcher who will oversee the development of a new product. This is a new post to be created specially for the new product but the $12,000 salary will be a fixed cost. Is this cost relevant to the decision to proceed with the development of the product?

(ii)   The $2,500 additional monthly running costs of a new machine to be purchased to manufacture an established product. Since the new machine will save on labour time, the fixed overhead to be absorbed by the product will reduce by $100 per month. Are these costs relevant to the decision to purchase the new machine?

(iii)   Office cleaning expenses of $125 for next month. The office is cleaned by contractors and the contract can be cancelled by giving 1 month's notice. Is this cost relevant to a decision to close the office?

(iv)   Expenses of $75 paid to the marketing manager. This was to reimburse the manager for the cost of travelling to meet a client with whom the company is currently negotiating a major contract. Is this cost relevant to the decision to continue negotiations?

(4 marks)

Test your understanding 3

ABC Ltd is deciding whether or not to proceed with a special order. Use the details below to determine the relevant cost of the order.

(a) Materials P and Q will be used for the contract. 100 tonnes of material P will be needed and sufficient material is in stock because the material is in common use in the company. The original cost of the material in stock is $1 per tonne but it would cost $1.20 per tonne to replace if it is used for this contract. The material Q required is in stock as a result of previous over-purchasing. This material originally cost $500 but it has no other use. The material is toxic and if it is not used on this contract, then ABC must pay $280 to have it disposed of.

(b) The contract requires 200 hours of labour at $5 per hour. Employees possessing the necessary skills are currently employed by the company but they are idle at present due to a lull in the company's normal business.

(c) Overhead will be absorbed by the contract at a rate of $10 per labour hour, which consists of $7 for fixed overhead and $3 for variable.

(d) The contract will require the use of a storage unit for 3 months. ABC is committed to rent the unit for 1 year at a rental of $50 per month. The unit is not in use at present. A neighbouring business has recently approached ABC offering to rent the unit from them for $70 per month.

(e) Total fixed overheads are not expected to increase as a result of the contract.

(10 marks)

Test your understanding 4

The management of a company are making a decision on whether or not to purchase a new piece of plant and machinery which costs $100,000. The new machine will generate a net cash flow of $30,000 each year for four years. At the end of the fourth year it will be sold for $20,000. The company's cost of capital is 5%. Tax depreciation is at 25% reducing balance and corporation tax is 30%. Corporation tax is payable in two instalments, with half paid in the current year and half paid in the following year.

Required:

Calculate the net present value of the project and advise management.

(5 marks)

Test your understanding 5

Dralin Co is considering an investment of $460,000 in a non-current asset expected to generate substantial cash inflows over the next five years. Unfortunately the annual cash flows from this investment are uncertain, but the following probability distribution has been established:

Annual cash flow ($)	Probability
50,000	0.3
100,000	0.5
150,000	0.2

At the end of its five-year life, the asset is expected to sell for $40,000. The cost of capital is 5%.

Calculate whether the investment should be undertaken.

(4 marks)

Test your understanding 6

Smith has decided to increase its productive capacity to meet an anticipated increase in demand for its products. The extent of this increase in capacity has still to be determined, and a management meeting has been called to decide which of the following two mutually exclusive proposals – A or B – should be undertaken.

The following information is available:

	Proposal A $	Proposal B $
Capital expenditure		
Buildings	50,000	100,000
Plant	200,000	300,000
Installation	100,000	15,000
Net Income		
Annual pre-depreciation profits (note (1))	70,000	95,000
Other relevant income and expenditure		
Sales promotion (note (2))	–	15,000
Plant scrap value	10,000	15,000
Buildings disposable value (note (3))	30,000	60,000
Working capital required over the project life	50,000	65,000

Notes:

(1) The investment life is ten years.

(2) An exceptional amount of expenditure on sales promotion of $15,000 will have to be spent in year 2 of proposal B. This has not been taken into account in calculating pre-depreciation profits.

(3) It is the intention to dispose of the buildings in ten years' time.

Using an 8% discount rate, calculate which of the two alternatives should be chosen.

(10 marks)

Test your understanding 7

A company has a money cost of capital of 21% per annum. The inflation rate is currently estimated at 9% per annum.

Identify the real cost of capital:

A   9%

B   11%

C   12%

D   14%

(2 marks)

Test your understanding 8

W is considering investing in a new machine which has a capital cost of $25,000. It has an estimated life of four years and a residual value of $5,000 at the end of four years. The machine qualifies for tax depreciation at the rate of 25% per year on a reducing balance basis.

An existing machine would be sold immediately for $8,000 if the new machine were to be bought. The existing machine has a tax written down value of $3,000.

The existing machine generates annual net contribution of $30,000. This is expected to increase by 40% if the new machine is purchased.

W pays corporation tax on its profits at the rate of 30%, with half of the tax being payable in the year that the profit is earned and half in the following year. The company's after tax cost of capital is 15% per year.

Calculate whether the investment is worthwhile.

(5 marks)

Test your understanding 9

A company is considering a cost-saving project. This involves purchasing a machine costing $7,000, which will result in annual savings (in real terms) on wage costs of $1,000 and on material costs of $400.

The following forecasts are made of the rates of inflation each year for the next five years:

Wage costs	10%
Material costs	5%
General prices	6%

The cost of capital of the company, in real terms, is 8.5%.

Calculate the NPV of the project, assuming that the machine has a life of five years and no scrap value.

(5 marks)

Test your understanding 10

Leo is contemplating spending $400,000 on new machinery. This will be used to produce a revolutionary type of lock, for which demand is expected to last three years. Equipment will be bought on 31 December 20X5 and revenue from the sale of locks will be receivable on the 31 December 20X6, 20X7 and 20X8. Labour costs for the three years, payable in arrears, are estimated at $500,000 per annum in current terms. These figures are expected to rise at the rate of 10% per annum.

Materials required for the three years are currently in stock. They originally cost $300,000; they would cost $500,000 at current prices although Leo had planned to sell them for $350,000. The sales revenue from locks in the first year is projected at $900,000. This figure will rise by 5% per annum over the product's life.

If Leo has a money cost of capital of 13%, identify the net present value of the project (to the nearest $000)

A ($130,000)

B ($23,000)

C $52,000

D $126,000

(4 marks)

Test your understanding 11

A contract is due to be commenced immediately. In one year's time it will require material XG. Price data relating to XG are as follows:

	$
Cost now	7,800
Cost in one year's time	8,800

The cost of storing XG for one year is $110, payable in one year's time.

If the cost of capital were 10% per annum, identify the present value of the cost of using material XG, assuming the contractor wished to maximise net present value:

A $7,800

B $7,900

C $7,910

D $8,000

(2 marks)

Test your understanding 12

November 2007

In early November 20X7, R Ltd considered manufacturing a new product called Sparkle. Up to that time $750,000 had been spent on researching the product. The company estimated that it would take two further years to develop Sparkle to the point of production and by that time it would probably have a lead of 18 months over its chief competitor. R Ltd expected to launch Sparkle on 1 November 20X9 and to produce and sell 100,000 units in the first year if $1.5 million was spent on pre-launch advertising. During the first year of production, R Ltd planned to spend $750,000 on advertising; this level of expenditure would be maintained each year.

From the second year onwards, the market was expected to increase to between 160,000 and 200,000 units. Once the competitor entered the market, it was thought that the competitor would win 50% market share very quickly because of its reputation.

The development and engineering costs of Sparkle were estimated to be $6 million, $2 million of which would be incurred in the first year of development, 20X7/X8. A special piece of equipment costing $500,000 would be required for production and this was to be installed in the month prior to the commencement of manufacture.

R Ltd planned to set a selling price of $249 a unit on the basis that variable manufacturing and distribution costs were expected to be $122 per unit. The company normally sets selling prices so that the contribution/sales ratio is 50% or slightly more. The fixed administrative and space costs that relate to the product, and which would be incurred from the commencement of production, were estimated to be $7.5 million per annum. It was also estimated that working capital of $2.5 million would be needed at the start of production in November 20X9.

The product was expected to have a life span of about five years, at which time the equipment would be scrapped as having no value. The company estimated its cost of capital to be 12% per annum.

November 20Y0

Development of Sparkle took six months longer than planned. This was largely because it proved necessary to employ two extra members of staff in the engineering department for the technical aspects of the product development.

The engineering department did not have a budget for this in year 1 (20X7/X8) and so employment was delayed until the start of the second year, November 20X8, when the budget for the extra funds had been approved. This caused the planned expenditure on development for year 2 to be spread over the 18 month period from the start of year 2 to the middle of year 3. The two new members of staff were employed at salaries of $45,000 each and employment costs were estimated to be 100% of the first year's salary. As a result, production started six months late in May 20Y0, the pre-launch costs were delayed accordingly and only 55,000 units were sold in the year November 20X9 to October 20Y0.

As expected, the competitor has decided to enter the market and is launching its rival product Glitter this month, November 20Y0.

R Ltd now predicts the market for 20Y0/Y1 to be 150,000 units and its share of this to be 50%. Thereafter the market size will be as forecast previously, i.e. between 160,000 and 200,000 units each year, and the product life cycle will stop at the same date as planned previously. The monetary value of all expenditures and revenues to date has been very close to the estimates and there is no reason to revise future forecasts in this respect.

Required:

Using the case of Sparkle in the scenario:

(a) Calculate the net present value of the project as perceived at the beginning of November 20X7, when R Ltd decided to manufacture Sparkle. State clearly any assumptions you make.

(11 marks)

(b) Calculate the revised net present value of the whole project as perceived at the beginning of November 20Y0.

(8 marks)

(c) Describe the position revealed by the figures you have calculated in (a) and (b) and on the events which have taken place. Identify what the company should do now?

(6 marks)

(Total: 25 marks)

Data Set Question: Bacher Co

Bacher Co is considering investing $500,000 in equipment to produce a new type of ball. Sales of the product are expected to continue for three years, at the end of which the equipment will have a scrap value of $80,000. Sales revenue of $600,000 pa will be generated at a variable cost of $350,000. Annual fixed costs will increase by $40,000.

(a) **Calculate whether, on the basis of the estimates given, the project should be undertaken, assuming that all cash flows occur at annual intervals and that Bacher Co has a cost of capital of 15%.**

(b) **Calculate the percentage changes required in the following estimates for the investment decision to change:**

I   initial investment

II   scrap value

III   selling price

IV   unit variable cost

V   annual fixed cost

VI   sales volume

VII   cost of capital.

Integration Style Question – Scotland Ski Runs

A landowner in Scotland proposes to develop a number of ski runs down the side of a mountain. The runs will be approximately 5 km long, dropping 1,000 metres from the mountain's summit to a car park.

You work as a strategy consultant and have been made aware that two alternative strategies (each giving the same capacity) are being considered for the development.

- *Low investment*, involving the construction of a series of tows to haul skiers from the car park to the summit: the initial cost of constructing the tows will be $250,000 and tow motors will have to be replaced after five years at a cost of $50,000; operating costs will be $90,000 per year (fixed) and $3.50 per skier (variable).

- *High investment*, involving the construction of a cable-car system giving a non-stop ride to the summit: the initial cost of constructing the lift will be $1,200,000; operating costs will be $30,000 per year (fixed) and $1 per skier (variable).

The Regional Tourist Board will subsidise the initial construction cost of the development (using either strategy) by providing a loan for half the value of the initial construction cost. The loan is at an interest rate of 4% repayable over six years on an annuity basis. The Tourist Board requires (as a condition of the loan) that a flat fee of $8 is charged for each skier towed/ lifted to the summit.

The number of skiers using the runs will be dependent on the quality of snow cover. The better the snow cover, then the more runs it will be possible to open and the longer the runs will be able to stay open. The landowner forecasts that in any 10-year period, and assuming an $8 fee, the seasons will be as follows:

Quality of snow cover	Number of seasons	Number of skiers
Good	3	60,000
Moderate	4	40,000
Poor	3	5,000

You have just received the following email from the landowner:

From: Mr L, landowner
To: AN Strategy Consultant
Date: 17 June 2014
Subject: Investment decision

Although the quality of snow cover is unpredictable for any one year, I am of the opinion that we can determine the expected outcome for an average year using probabilities and base our investment appraisal and business plan on that. I met with a business adviser yesterday who commented that the whole problem about winter sports in Scotland is the variability and unpredictability of snow cover. On average conditions are as good as any in Europe. However, he says, if our first three seasons are poor then this could have a devastating effect on project viability.

As you know, my cost of money is 12% per annum, and in appraising investments I consider cash flows over a 10-year period only. Could you help me identify which strategy I should adopt (low or high investment) on the basis of the expected value methodology I advocate, and assuming an $8 fee?

Regards
L

Test your understanding answers

Example 1 – SENSITIVITY ANALYSIS

(a)

Year		Cash flow $	15% discount rate	Present Value
0	Investment	(120,000)		(120,000)
1–15	Contribution	41,250	5.847	241,189
1–15	Fixed costs	(18,000)	5.847	(105,246)
15	Scrap value	25,000	0.123	3,075
				————
				19,018
				————

Net Present Value = $19,018

(b)

(i) If the capital outlay were to rise by more than $19,018 the project would cease to be viable. As a percentage increase this is:

$$\text{Sensitivity margin} = \frac{\$19,018}{\$120,000} \times 100\% = 15.85\%$$

(ii) If the PV of contribution were to fall by more than $19,018 the project would cease to be viable. As a percentage change this is:

$$\text{Sensitivity margin} = \frac{\$19,018}{\$241,189} \times 100\% = 7.89\%$$

(iii) If the PV of fixed costs were to rise by more than $19,018 the project would cease to be viable. As a percentage increase this is:

$$\text{Sensitivity margin} = \frac{\$19,018}{\$105,246} \times 100\% = 18.07\%$$

(c) The break-even point can be calculated as follows:

To remove the current NPV of $19,018, the PV of contribution would have to fall to $222,171 ($241,189 – $19,018). Calculating this as an annual amount can be done using the relevant annuity factor:

Annual cash amount	=	$222,171 ÷ 5.847 = $37,997
Let 'x' be minimum sales level		
Annual contribution	=	$2.75 × = $37,997
Therefore		× = 13,817 units

Example 2

The correct answer is **B**.

The initial $40,000 fee will be deemed to be a sunk cost – it has already been committed and won't be affected by any decision to proceed from this point.

The $20,000 is a future cost. Despite the fact that it is called a fixed cost it will only be incurred if the project proceeds. It is therefore and extra or incremental cost of the project and should be included in any future decision making.

Example 3

Activity 1

	$
Contribution per hour lost from normal working	3
Add back: labour cost per hour that is not saved	4
	7

The contract should be charged with 5,000 × $7 = $35,000

Activity 2

Nothing. The relevant cost is zero.

Example 4 – Balancing allowance

(a) Tax depreciation and the associated savings can be calculated as follows:

Year	$	Tax depreciation $	Tax saved at 30% $
0 – Investment	50,000		
1 – Tax depreciation (@25%)	12,500	12,500	3,750
	37,500		
2 – Tax depreciation (@25%)	9,375	9,375	2,813
	28,125		
3 – Tax depreciation (@25%)	7,031	7,031	2,109
	21,094		
4 – Disposal	10,000		
4 – Balancing allowance	11,094	11,094	3,328
Total tax depreciation/tax saved		40,000	12,000

The total tax depreciation will equal the difference between the initial cost ($50,000) and the residual value ($10,000). The total tax saving will be 30% of the tax depreciation (30% × $40,000).

(b)

Year	Cash benefit received	Total
1	$1,875	**$1,875**
2	$1,875 + $1,407	**$3,282**
3	$1,406 + $1,055	**$2,461**
4	$1,054 + $1,664	**$2,718**
5	$1,664	**$1,664**

Example 5

Corporation tax

Depreciation is not an allowable expense.

Therefore, taxable profit = $100,000 + $20,000 = $120,000 p.a.

Corporation tax at 30% = $36,000 p.a.

Half payable in current year, half payable in year following.

Tax depreciation

Capital cost:		$250,000
Scrap value:		$10,000
Total tax depreciation:		$240,000

Year	Reducing balance	Tax depreciation	Tax saved (30%)	Benefit received	Total cash benefit
1	$187,500	$62,500	$18,750	$9,375	**$9,375**
2	$140,625	$46,875	$14,063	$9,375 + $7,032	**$16,407**
3	$105,469	$35,156	$10,547	$7,031 + $5,274	**$12,305**
4	$10,000	$95,469	$28,641	$5,273 + $14,321	**$19,594**
5				$14,320	**$14,320**

Net present value

Year	0	1	2	3	4	5
	$	$	$	$	$	$
Net inflows		120,000	120,000	120,000	120,000	
Corporation tax		(18,000)	(36,000)	(36,000)	(36,000)	(18,000)
Tax depreciation		9,375	16,407	12,305	19,594	14,320
Investment	(250,000)				10,000	
Working capital	(35,000)				35,000	
Total net flows	(285,000)	111,375	100,407	96,305	148594	(3,680)
Discount factors	1.000	0.909	0.826	0.751	0.683	0.621
Present value	(285,000)	101,240	82,936	72,325	101,490	(2,285)

Net present value = $70,706

* working capital of $35,000 is injected in Year 0 and then released in Year 4.

Example 6 – NPV AND INFLATION

(a) **Discounting money cash flow at the money rate**

Year	Money cash flow $	Discount rate 15%	Present value $
0	(50,000)		(50,000)
1	21,100	0.870	18,357
2	22,261	0.756	16,829
3	23,485	0.658	15,453
4	24,776	0.572	14,172
		NPV =	14,811

(b) **Discounting the real cash flows at the real rate**

Calculate the real rate.

$$(1+r) = \frac{(1+m)}{(1+i)}$$

$$(1+r) = \frac{(1+0.15)}{(1+0.055)}$$

$$(1+r) = 1.0900$$

$$\therefore r = 0.09, \text{ i.e. } 9\%$$

Year	Real cash flow $	Discount rate 9%	Present value $
0	(50,000)		(50,000)
1–4	20,000 p.a.	3.240	64,800
		NPV =	14,800

Example 7

Notes:

$480,000 development cost is a sunk cost.

Depreciation is not a cash flow and should be excluded from the fixed costs.

Depreciation = $2,400,000/4 years = $600,000 p.a.

Therefore relevant fixed cost = $800,000 – $600,000 = $200,000.

Year 1 cash flows are:

		$000
Revenue	25,000 × $80	2,000 – rises at 5%
Direct material	25,000 × $8	200 – rises at 4%
Direct labour	25,000 × $12	300 – rises at 10%
Variable overheads	25,000 × $12	300 – rises at 4%
Fixed costs		200 – rises at 5%

Year	0	1	2	3	4
			$000		
Capital	(2,400)				
Revenue		2,000	2,100	2,205	2,315
Direct material		(200)	(208)	(216)	(225)
Direct labour		(300)	(330)	(363)	(399)
Variable OH		(300)	(312)	(324)	(337)
Fixed cost		(200)	(210)	(221)	(232)
Net cash flow	(2,400)	1,000	1,040	1,081	1,122
15% disc. factor		0.870	0.756	0.658	0.572
Present value	**(2,400)**	**870**	**786**	**711**	**642**

The net present value is $609,000.

Therefore the company should invest in the project.

Example 8

$ millions	T_0	T_1	T_2	T_3	T_4
Sales (W1)		520	1082	675	
Variable costs (W2)		(158)	(331)	(208)	
Net trading inflows		362	751	467	
Taxation (30%) – in year		(54)	(112)	(70)	
Taxation – in year (30%)			(55)	(113)	(70)
Initial investment	(1,000)				
Scrap proceeds				200	
Tax depreciation benefit (W3)		37	66	82	55
Net cash flows	(1,000)	345	650	566	(15)
DF @ 10% (W4)	1	0.909	0.826	0.751	0.683
PV	(1,000)	314	537	425	(10)
				NPV	266

(W1) Revenue

Revenue needs to be expressed in money terms.

Revenue at T_1 = 5m × $100 × (1.04) = $520m.

Revenue at T_2 = 10m × $100 × (1.04)^2 = $1,082m.

Revenue at T_3 = 6m × $100 × (1.04)^3 = $675m.

(W2) Costs

Costs need to be expressed in money terms.

Costs at T_1 = 5m × $30 × (1.05) = $158m.

Costs at T_2 = 10m × $30 × (1.05)^2 = $331m.

Costs at T_3 = 6m × $30 × (1.05)^3 = $208m.

(W3) Tax depreciation ($m)

Year	Bal b/f	Tax depr (25%)	Tax relief (30%)	Year relief received 1	2	3	4
1	1,000	250	75	37	38		
2	750	188	56		28	28	
3	562	362 *	109			54	55
				37	66	82	55

*Disposal = $200m when the TWDV was $562m. Therefore the balancing allowance = $362.

(W4) Discount rate

$(1+m) = (1+r) \times (1+i) = 1.068 \times 1.03 = 1.10$, giving a money rate (m) = 10%.

Example 9 – REPLACEMENT DECISION

Method and answer guide

Firstly calculate the NPV of costs:

		Machine X		Machine Y	
Year	Discount factor	Cash flow $000	Present value $000	Cash flow $000	Present value $000
0		120	120	60	60
1	0.909	20	18	40	36
2	0.826	20	17	35	29
3	0.751	20	15		
Net present value			170		125

It is not appropriate to compare these two NPVs. Machine X shows three years of costs whereas Machine Y only has two years worth of costs. Remember that the machines are needed into the foreseeable future, so do not pick the cheapest single purchase. The machine will be replaced many times over the next few years. Because of this we need to find a way of comparing the costs over an equal time period (not unequal years).

Machine X:

NPV of one life cycle = $170k

EAC = $170k ÷ 2.487

= $68k p.a.

Machine Y:

NPV of one life cycle = $125k

EAC = $125k ÷ 1.736

= $72k p.a.

Machine X is the cheapest.

Example 10 – REPLACEMENT CYCLE

		Replacement Cycle								
	Discount	1 year		2 year		3 year		4 year		5 year
Year	Factor	Cash	PV	Cash	PV	Cash	PV	Cash	PV	Cash	PV
0		(220)	(220)	(220)	(220)	(220)	(220)	(220)	(220)	(220)	(220)
1	0.893	11	9.8	(110)	(98.2)	(110)	(98.2)	(110)	(98.2)	(110)	(98.2)
2	0.797			(44)	(35.1)	(132)	(105.2)	(132)	(105.2)	(132)	(105.2)
3	0.712					(88)	(62.6)	(154)	(109.6)	(154)	(109.6)
4	0.636							(110)	(70.0)	(165)	(104.9)
5	0.567									(151)	(85.6)
Net present value			(210.2)		(353.3)		(486.0)		(603.0)		(723.5)
÷ Annuity factor		÷ 0.893		÷ 1.690		÷ 2.402		÷ 3.037		÷ 3.605	
		———		———		———		———		———	
Equivalent annual cost		(235.4)		(209.1)		(202.3)		(198.6)		(200.7)	
		———		———		———		———		———	

Notes:

- In year 0 the cost of the machine is shown

- In each year after that the cash column shows the running costs of the machine

- In the year of sale, net cash flow is scrap less running cost

- The PV (present value) column represents the cash column multiplied by the discount factor for that year

- The net present value is then the sum of the present values

- In order to compare net present values an equivalent annual cost is calculated by dividing the NPV by the annuity factor for the length of the investment. So, for example, the 4 year NPV of $603.0 is divided by the 4 year 12% annuity factor of 3.037 to give an annual equivalent cost of $198.6

- These equivalent annual costs are compared and the lowest one is the optimal replacement cycle.

Therefore, the most economical replacement cycle is four years.

Example 11 – CAPITAL RATIONING

Project	Investment Required $000	Net Present Value $000	NPV ranking	Profitability Index	Index ranking
A	3,400	850	1	0.25	6
B	2,750	825	2	0.30	4
C	2,000	720	3	0.36	3
D	3,400	680	4	0.20	7
E	860	430	5	0.50	1
F	950	400	6	0.42	2
G	1,250	350	7	0.28	5

(a)

Project	Investment $000	NPV $000
A	3,400	850
B	2,750	825
C	2,000	720
D	850	170 *
TOTAL	9,000	2,565

* NPV has been pro-rated: (850/3,400) × 680

(b)

Project	Investment $000	NPV $000
E	860	430
F	950	400
C	2,000	720
B	2,750	825
G	1,250	350
A	1,190	297.50*
TOTAL	9,000	3,022.50

* (1,190/3,400) × 850

Test your understanding 1

Year	Cash flow $000		Discount factor	Present Value $000
0	Initial cost	(1,000)		(1,000)
1–7	Fixed costs	(60)	5.206	(312.36)
7	Residual	50	0.583	29.15
				(1,283.21)

PV of annual contribution required:	$1,283,210
Annuity factor years 1 – 7	÷ 5.206
Annual contribution required	$246,486.75
Contribution per unit	÷ $12.50
Minimum number of units	19,719 units

Answer A

Test your understanding 2

(i)   The salary is a relevant cost of $12,000. Do not be fooled by the fact that it is a fixed cost. The cost may be fixed in total but it is definitely a cost that is relevant to the decision to proceed with the future development of the new product. This is an example of a directly attributable fixed cost. A directly attributable fixed cost may also be called product-specific fixed cost.

(ii) The $2,500 additional running costs are relevant to the decision to purchase the new machine. The saving in overhead absorption is not relevant since we are not told that the total overhead expenditure will be altered. The saving in labour cost would be relevant but we shall assume that this has been accounted for in determining the additional monthly running costs.

(iii) This is not a relevant cost for next month since it will be incurred even if the contract is cancelled today. If a decision is being made to close the office, this cost cannot be included as a saving to be made next month. However, it will be saved in the months after that so it will become a relevant cost saving from month 2 onwards.

(iv) This is not a relevant cost of the decision to continue with the contract. The $75 is sunk and cannot be recovered even if the company does not proceed with the negotiations.

Test your understanding 3

(a) The relevant cost of a material that is used regularly is its replacement cost. This will ensure that the business profits are unaffected by the use of the material for this contract. The relevant cost of material P is therefore $1.20 per tonne.

Material Q has a 'negative' cost if used for the contract. This is the saving that will be made through not having to pay the disposal cost of $280.

(b) The relevant cost of labour is zero. The labour cost is being paid anyway and no extra cost will be incurred as a result of this contract.

(c) The fixed overhead is not relevant because we are told that fixed overheads are not expected to increase. The relevant variable overhead cost is $3 per hour × 200 hours = $600.

Even if you are not specifically told that fixed overheads will remain unaltered, it is usual to assume that they will not increase, stating the assumption clearly.

(d) The rental cost $50 per month is not relevant because it will not be affected by the contract. The relevant cost of using the storage unit is the forgone rental income of $70 per month.

Summary of relevant costs

		$
(a)	Material P	120
	Material Q	(280)
(b)	Labour	–
(c)	Variable overhead	600
(d)	Rent foregone	210
(e)	Fixed overheads	–
		650

Test your understanding 4

Before you start a table of cash flows sort out corporation tax and tax depreciation benefits.

Corporation tax

30% of net cash flows (profits), i.e. 30% of $30,000 = $9,000.

Half is payable in the year of the profit, and half in the year following, i.e.:

Year	Corporation tax
1	$4,500
2	$9,000
3	$9,000
4	$9,000
5	$4,500

Tax depreciation

Capital cost: $100,000

Scrap value: $20,000

Total tax depreciation: $80,000

Year	Reducing balance	Tax depreciation	Tax saved (30%)	Benefit received	Total cash benefit
1	$75,000	$25,000	$7,500	$3,750	**$3,750**
2	$56,250	$18,750	$5,625	$3,750 + $2,813	**$6,563**
3	$42,188	$14,062	$4,219	$2,813 + $2,110	**$4,922**
4	$20,000	$22,188	$6,656	$2,110 + $3,328	**$5,437**
5				$3,328	**$3,328**

Now you can calculate the net cash flow each year, and discount:

Yr	Asset $	Profits $	Corporation tax $	Tax dep'n benefit $	Total net cash $	Discount factor	Present value $
0	(100,000)				(100,000)		(100,000)
1		30,000	(4,500)	3,750	29,250	0.952	27,846
2		30,000	(9,000)	6,563	27,563	0.907	25,000
3		30,000	(9,000)	4,922	25,922	0.864	22,397
4	20,000	30,000	(9,000)	5,437	46,437	0.823	38,218
5			(4,500)	3,328	(1,172)	0.784	(919)
						NPV =	12,542

Test your understanding 5

Expected annual cash flows are:

Annual cash flow (x)	Probability (p)	PV
50,000	0.3	15,000
100,000	0.5	50,000
150,000	0.2	30,000
		95,000

NPV calculation:

Time	Cash flow $	DF 5%	PV $
0	(460,000)	1.000	(460,000)
1–5	95,000	4.329	411,255
5	40,000	0.784	31,360
		NPV =	(17,385)

As the ENPV is negative, the project should not be undertaken.

An alternative approach would be to calculate three separate NPVs and then combine them, giving the following figures:

Annual cash flow	Probability	NPV
$		$
50,000	0.3	(212,190)
100,000	0.5	4,260
150,000	0.2	220,710

ENPV = 0.3 × (−212,190) + 0.5 × 4,260 + 0.2 × (220,710) =   (17,385)

Even though the ENPV is negative these figures show that there is a 70% chance of the project giving a positive NPV. Some investors may consider the project acceptable on this basis.

Test your understanding 6

Since the decision has been made to increase capacity (i.e. 'to do nothing' is not an alternative), the easiest approach is to discount the incremental cash flows.

The tabular approach of the previous chapter is still appropriate particularly as the project lasts for ten years (other forms of presentation will appear later).

Time		A	B	B – A	8%	PV
		$000	$000	$000	DF/AF	$000
0	Capital expenditure	(260)	(415)	(155)	1	(155)
0	Working capital	(50)	(65)	(15)	1	(15)
2	Promotion	–	(15)	(15)	0.857	(13)
1–10	Net income	70	95	25	6.710	168
10	Scrap proceeds	40	75	35	0.463	16
	Net present value					8

The present value of proposal B exceeds that of proposal A by $8,000 at 8% and therefore proposal B is preferred.

Assumptions

- The disposal value of buildings is realistic and all other figures have been realistically appraised.

- Expenditure on working capital is incurred at the beginning of the project life and recovered at the end.

- Adequate funds are available for either proposal.

- All cash flows occur annually in arrears.

Test your understanding 7

$1.21 \div 1.09 = 1.11$

Answer B

Test your understanding 8

(W1) The incremental increase in contribution earned as a result of using the new machine is $30,000 \times 40\% = $12,000 per year.

(W2) Tax due/paid on incremental contribution earned:

Year	Incr. Contribution	Tax due (30%)	1	2	3	4	5
1	12,000	3,600	1,800	1,800			
2	12,000	3,600		1,800	1,800		
3	12,000	3,600			1,800	1,800	
4	12,000	3,600				1,800	1,800
5	12,000	3,600					
			1,800	3,600	3,600	3,600	1,800

(W3) Tax depreciation/tax relief

Existing machine

The sale of the existing machine leads to a balancing charge of $8,000 – $3,000 = $5,000. Tax payable on this is $5,000 × 30% = $1,500. Assume this is paid half in year 0 and half in year 1.

New machine

Year	Bal b/f	Tax depr (25%)	Tax relief (30%)	Year relief received				
				1	2	3	4	5
1	25,000	6,250	1,875	937	938			
2	18,750	4,688	1,406		703	703		
3	14,063	3,515	1,055			528	527	
4	10,547	5,547*	1,664				832	832
				937	1,641	1,231	1,359	832

* Disposal = $5,000 when the TWDV was $10,547. Therefore the Balancing allowance = $5,547.

All figures $	Year 0	Year 1	Year 2	Year 3	Year 4	Year 5
Incremental contribution (W1)		12,000	12,000	12,000	12,000	
Capital	(25,000)				5,000	
Tax paid (W2)		(1,800)	(3,600)	(3,600)	(3,600)	(1,800)
Tax paid on existing machine (W3)	(750)	(750)				
Tax relief on new machine (W3)		937	1,641	1,231	1,359	832
Net cash flow	(25,750)	10,387	10,041	9,631	14,759	(968)
DCF @ 15%	1	0.870	0.756	0.658	0.572	0.497
Present values	(25,750)	9,037	7,591	6,337	8,442	(4.81)

Net present value = $5,176

The net present value is positive and therefore it is worthwhile purchasing the machine.

Test your understanding 9

Since the question contains both specific and general inflation rates, the money method should be used

Step 1

The money method needs to be calculated using the information provided on the real rate of return and the general rate of inflation

$(1 + i) = (1 + r)(1 + h)$

$(1 + i) = (1.085)(1.06)$

$i = 15\%$

Step 2

Inflate the cash flows using the specific inflation rates and discount using the money rate calculated above.

	T_0	T_1	T_2	T_3	T_4	T_5
	$	$	$	$	$	$
Investment	(7,000)					
Wages savings (inflating @ 10%)		1,100	1,210	1,331	1,464	1,610
Materials savings (inflating @ 5%)		420	441	463	486	510
Net cash flow	(7,000)	1,520	1,651	1,794	1,950	2,120
PV factor @ 15%		1.000	0.870	0.756	0.658	0.572	0.497
PV of cash flow	(7,000)	1,322	1,248	1,180	1,115	1,054

Therefore NPV = $(1,081) which suggests the project is not worthwhile.

Test your understanding 10

All cash flows shown are money cash ($000)

Year	Capital	Labour	Material	Revenue	Net cash	13% factors	Present value
0	(400)		(350)		(750)		(750)
1		(550)		900	350	0.885	310
2		(605)		945	340	0.783	266
3		(665.5)		992	326.5	0.693	226
							___
						NPV =	52
							___

Net Present Value = $52,000

Answer C

Test your understanding 11

If buy now PV of costs = $7,800 + $110 × 0.909 = $7,900

If buy in one year, PV of costs = $8,800 × 0.909 = $8,000

Therefore, buy XG now

Answer B

Test your understanding 12

(a) **Examination tip**: *Set up a table of cash flows. Keep all workings separate from this table.*

Year	Date	Advertising $000	Capital costs $000	Contribution $000	Working capital $000	Net cash flow $000	12% discount factor $000	Present value $000
0	1.11.07							
1	1.11.08		(2,000)			(2,000)	0.893	(1,786)
2	1.11.09	(1,500)	(4,500)		(2,500)	(8,500)	0.797	(6,775)
3	1.11.10	(750)		12,700		11,950	0.712	8,508
4	1.11.11	(750)		17,145		16,395	0.636	10,427
5	1.11.12	(750)		11,430		10,680	0.567	6,056
6	1.11.13	(750)		11,430		10,680	0.507	5,415
7	1.11.14	(750)		11,430	2,500	13,180	0.452	5,957
								27,803
				Less PV of fixed costs: 7,500 × (4.564 – 1.690)				(21,555)
								—
				Net present value				6,24
								—

Production:

Year

1	100,000 units
2	135,000 units*
3	90,000
4	90,000
5	90,000
*(160 + 200)/2	180
1st 6 months	90
2nd 6 months	45 (50% because of competitor)
Total for year	135

Contribution per unit: $249 – $122 = $127

Examination tip: *Stating assumptions is very important in this question.*

Assumptions:

- The amount already spent is not relevant – it is a sunk cost.
- The sales figures are the average of the range and the competitor takes 50% of market share after 18 months of sales.
- The equipment has no scrap value after five years.
- Working capital is released immediately production ceases.
- Inflation has been ignored.

Conclusion: the NPV is $6,248,000. Hence the project should be accepted.

(b)

Year	Date	Fixed cost $000	Advertising $000	Capital costs $000	Contribution $000	Working capital $000	Net cash flow $000	12% discount factor $000	Present value $000
0	1.11.07								
1	1.11.08			(2,000)			(2,000)	0.893	(1,786)
2	1.11.09			(2,847)		(2,500)	(2,847)	0.797	(2,269)
3	1.11.10	(3,750)	(1,875)	(1,923)	6,985		(3,063)	0.712	(2,181)
4	1.11.11	(7,500)	(750)		9,525		1,275	0.636	811
5	1.11.12	(7,500)	(750)		11,430		3,180	0.567	1,803
6	1.11.13	(7,500)	(750)		11,430		3,180	0.507	1,612
7	1.11.14	(7,500)	(750)		11,430	2,500	5,680	0.452	2,567
									——
					Net present value				558
									——

Development costs:

Year

1		= $2m
2	2/3 of $4m = $2.667m + $0.180	= $2.847m
3	1/3 of $4m = $1.333m + $0.090 + $0.5m	= $1.923m

Salary costs
in Year 2: $180,000

Salary costs
in Year 3: $90,000

Advertising
in Year 3: $1.5m + $0.375 (50% of $750,000) = $1.875m

Production:

Year

3	55,000 units @ $127	= $6.985m
4	150,000 × 50% @ $127	= $9.525m
5	90,000 units @ $127	= $11.430m

(c) The project is extremely sensitive to the sales in early years of the life cycle. These have been severely reduced due to the delay in the project (55,000 v 100,000 in Year 3) and the reduced total sales in Year 4 (down 30,000 units). This second reduction may also be attributable to the delay in product launch.

This large loss in profits is due to a budget constraint which involves a very small increase in the total development budget. The need for and the effects of not spending this small increase should have been made clear early on to avoid this ludicrous situation. If the sales figures in the remaining years are at the lower bound of the forecast, the project may well make a loss.

As the major cash outflows have already taken place (development, operating equipment and pre-launch marketing) the project should continue to reap the positive cash flows forecast for the next four years. The company can attempt to improve the size of the future positive cash flows by:

- finding ways to compete with its competitor that holds 50% of the market share

- further develop the product or market to extend the life cycle of the project

- an ongoing cost-reduction exercise.

Data Set Question: Bacher Co

Although part (a) could be completed most efficiently by finding the PV of net annual inflows ($600,000 − $350,000 − $40,000), i.e. of $210,000, part (b) would be most effectively negotiated if the separate PVs were found.

NPV calculation

Time		Cash flow	15% DF	PV
		$000		$000
0	Equipment	(500)	1.000	(500)
1–3	Revenue	600	2.283	1,370
1–3	Variable costs	(350)	2.283	(799)
1–3	Fixed costs	(40)	2.283	(91)
3	Scrap value	80	0.658	53
NPV ($000)				33

The project should, on the basis of these estimates, be accepted.

Sensitivity analysis

   (i) **Initial investment**

For the decision to change, the NPV must fall by $33,000. For this to occur, the cost of the equipment must rise by $33,000.

This is a rise of: $\dfrac{33}{500} \times 100 = 6.6\%$

   (ii) **Scrap value**

If the NPV is to fall by $33,000, the PV of scrap proceeds must fall by $33,000. The PV of scrap proceeds is currently $53,000. It must fall by: $33 \div 53 \times 100 = 62.26\%$, say 62.

(iii) **Selling price**

If sales price varies, sales revenue will vary (assuming no effect on demand). If the NPV of the project is to fall by $33,000, the selling price must fall by:

$$\frac{33}{1{,}370} \times 100 = 2.4\%$$

(iv) **Unit variable cost**

The project's NPV must fall by $33,000 therefore the PV of the variable costs must rise by $33,000. Since the PV of variable costs is $799,000, a rise of $33,000 is an increase of:

$$\frac{33}{799} \times 100 = 4.1\%$$

(v) **Annual fixed costs**

Since the PV of fixed costs is $91,000, a rise of $33,000 is an increase of:

$$\frac{33}{91} \times 100 = 36\%$$

(vi) **Sales volume**

If sales volume falls, revenue and variable costs fall (contribution falls). If the NPV is to fall by $33,000, volume must fall by:

$$\frac{33}{1{,}370 - 799} \times 100 = 5.8\%$$

(vii) **Cost of capital**

If NPV is to fall, cost of capital must rise. The figure which the cost of capital must rise to, that gives an NPV of zero, is the project's IRR.

NPV ($000) = − 500 + [210 × 2.210] + [80 × 0.624] = 14 The IRR is a little more than 17%, possibly 18%, but the formula can be used.

$$IRR \approx 15 + \frac{33}{33-14} \times (17-15)$$

≈ 18.47%, say 18.50%

To find the IRR, which is probably not much above 15%, the NPV at 17% can be found using the summarised cash flows.

The cost of capital would have to increase from 15% to 18½% before the investment decision changes

Integration Style Question – Scotland Ski Runs

Low investment

Year		Cash flow $000	12% discount factor	Present value $000
0	Initial cost	(250)	1.000	(250)
5	Replacement of motors	(50)	0.567	(28.35)
1–10	Fixed costs	(90)	5.650	(508.50)
1–10	Contribution (W1)	159.75	5.650	902.6
0	Loan	125	1.000	125.0
1–6	Loan repayment (W2)	(23.8)	4.111	(97.8)
				142.9

High investment

Year		Cash flow $000	12% discount factor	Present value $000
0	Initial cost	(1,200)	1.000	(1,200)
1–10	Fixed costs	(30)	5.650	(169.5)
1–10	Contribution (W1)	248.5	5.650	1,404.0
0	Loan	600	1.000	600
1–6	Loan repayment (W2)	(114.5)	4.111	(470.7)
				———
				163.8

Workings:

(W1) Expected values

Expected demand = 0.3 × 60 + 0.4 × 40 + 0.3 × 5 = 35,500 skiers

Low investment: Contribution per annum = ($8 − $3.50) × 35,500 = $159,750

High investment: Contribution per annum = ($8 − $1) × 35,500 = $248,500

(W2) Annuity

Initial loan = PV of repayments

PV of repayments = $x per annum × annuity factor

Low investment

$125,000 = $X × 5.242 (annuity factor, year 6, 4%)

∴ $X = $23,800

High investment

$600,000 = $X × 5.242

∴ $X = $114,500

Low investment: NPV = $142,900

High investment: NPV = $163,800

∴ Adopt high investment strategy.

The Pricing Decision

Chapter learning objectives

Syllabus Link

Lead C2: Discuss Pricing strategies and their consequences

Component C2a): Discuss pricing strategies and their consequences

- Pricing decisions for profit maximising in imperfect markets.

- Pricing strategies and the final consequences of market skimming, premium pricing, penetration pricing, loss leaders, product bundling/optional extras and product differentiation to appeal to different market segments.

1 Chapter summary

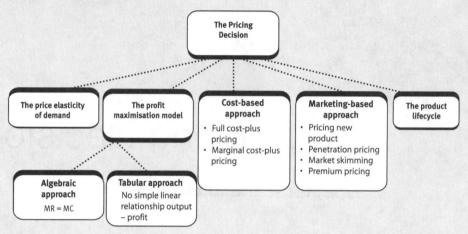

2 Introduction

In this chapter we will learn about the alternative strategies that an organisation may adopt in the pricing of its products or services.

The price to be charged to customers for the business's products or services is often one of the most important decisions to be made by managers. Not all businesses are free to determine their own selling prices: for example, some are unable to influence the external price and are obliged to accept the prevailing market price for their goods. For these businesses cost control is an important factor in maintaining profitability.

Other businesses are in a position to select their selling price. The objectives that they pursue in their pricing policy will affect the price to be charged for each product or service. For example, the business may be concerned with profit maximisation: in this chapter you will see how managers can use cost and demand analysis to determine the theoretical profit-maximising price.

Other objectives may also affect a company's pricing policy. For example, the company may be seeking to maximise revenue, to gain the largest share of the market, to utilise spare capacity or merely to survive. In this chapter, we will be looking at many of the different aspects which influence a company's pricing strategy, beginning with the price elasticity of demand.

3 Knowledge brought forward

There is no knowledge brought forward from Papers C01 and P1, but you may benefit from reading the Chapter on *Cost Behaviour and Pricing Decisions* from Certificate Level Paper C04.

4 Price elasticity of demand

Businesses make a profit by selling goods and services at a price that is higher than their cost. Profit is the result of the interaction between cost, volume and price:

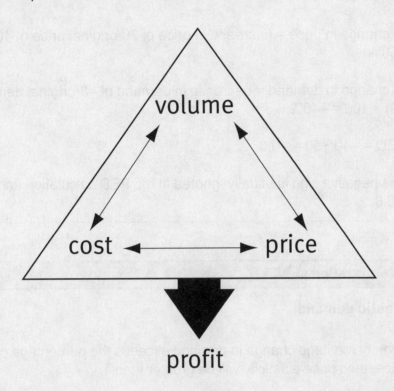

For instance, the volume of goods sold affects the cost per unit. If the volume increases, the fixed overheads are spread over more units, and so the cost per unit decreases. Lower costs give the seller the opportunity to reduce prices and so further increases volumes, or to increase profit margins. Cost is also influenced by price. This is discussed in target costing later in this text; the aim is to be able to produce at a target cost which is less than the target selling price. This chapter, however, concentrates on the link between *price* and *volume*, and its resulting effect on profit.

When a business proposes to change the price of a product or service, the key question is 'to what degree will demand be affected?'

The **price elasticity of demand** measures the change in demand as a result of a change in its price. It can be calculated as follows:

$$\text{Price elasticity of demand} = \frac{\text{Change in quantity demanded, as a percentage of demand}}{\text{Change in price, as a percentage of the price}}$$

The price elasticity of demand

Assume that the sales of a retailer fall from 20 per day to 12 per day when the price of a chocolate bar goes up from 40c to 60c. The price elasticity can be calculated as follows:

% change in price = (increase in price of 20/original price of 40) × 100 = +50%

% change in demand = decrease in demand of –8/original demand of 20) × 100 = –40%

PED = –40/+50 = –0.8

The negative sign is usually ignored in the PED calculation and the PED = 0.8.

Interpretation of PED

Elastic demand

If the percentage change in demand exceeds the percentage change in price, then price elasticity will be greater than 1.

Demand is 'elastic', i.e. very responsive to changes in price.

- Total revenue increases when price is reduced.
- Total revenue decreases when price is decreased.

Therefore, price increases are not recommended but price cuts are recommended.

Inelastic demand

If the percentage change in demand is less the percentage change in price, then price elasticity will be lower than 1.

Demand is 'inelastic', i.e. not very responsive to changes in price.

- Total revenue decreases when price is reduced.
- Total revenue increases when price is decreased.

Therefore, price increases are recommended but price cuts are not recommended.

More on price elasticity

Pricing decisions have a major effect on volume sold and, as a consequence, on profit generated. One of the major considerations of a pricing decision is therefore the effect of a change in price will have on volume sold. If price is reduced, by how much will demand increase?

If price is increased, will a small or large decrease in demand occur? A complete answer to these questions, if such an answer does indeed exist, will involve a number of different factors in the total marketing mix, but the basic microeconomic analysis of demand is the fundamental starting point. There are two extremes of the price/demand trade off, represented graphically here:

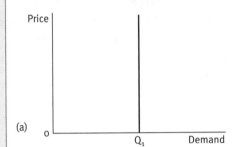

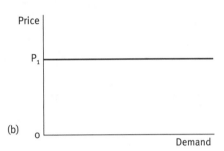

In (a), the same quantity, Q1, will be sold regardless of the selling price, as demand is completely unresponsive to changes in price. Demand is, therefore, completely inelastic, and the supplier would (theoretically) have unlimited scope, and considerable incentive, to increase price. In (b), demand is limitless at a particular price, P1, but it would vanish at prices above P1, that is demand is completely elastic. Under these circumstances there is obviously no point in reducing price below P1, as this will cause existing profits to fall. Needless to say, these two extremes are rarely seen in practice, and the more normal situation is represented by one of the following charts:

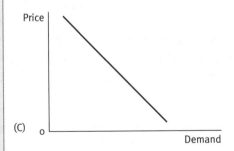

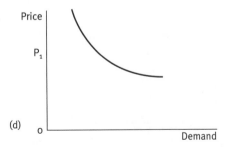

In both (c) and (d) the supplier is faced with a downward-sloping demand curve, in which reductions in price will result in increased demand and vice versa. This is a negative relationship, or negative correlation, as a decrease in price implies an increase in demand, and vice versa.

The slope of the line is the critical factor for a pricing decision, and is expressed by the following formula:

$$\textbf{Elasticity of demand} = \frac{\textbf{– \% change in quantity demanded}}{\textbf{\% change in price}}$$

The numerator and denominator are expressed in terms of percentage change rather than in any absolute amount, in order to avoid distortions caused by the use of different units of measurement. Given the slope of the curve, the negative sign in the numerator has the effect of making the outcome positive, which is generally considered a more convenient representation. If elasticity at a point on the curve is greater than 1, demand is considered elastic. This means that a fall in price increases demand considerably, so that total revenue increases, but an increase in price decreases demand substantially, so that total revenue falls. On the other hand, if point elasticity is less than 1 (i.e. it is inelastic) a fall in price will increase demand, but not by a sufficient amount to maintain the previous revenue level, yet a rise in price will increase total revenue:

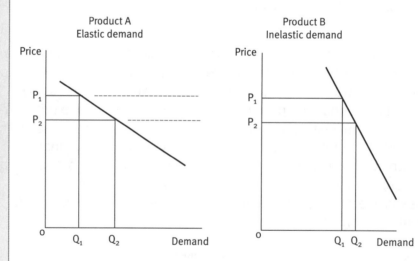

For product A, with elastic demand, a drop in price from P1 to P2 results in a relatively greater increase in sales volume. However, the same drop in price for product B, with inelastic demand, results in a far smaller change in volume.

Note that the formula measures movement between two discrete points on the curve, and that even though the slope itself is constant, elasticity will differ between different points on the curve:

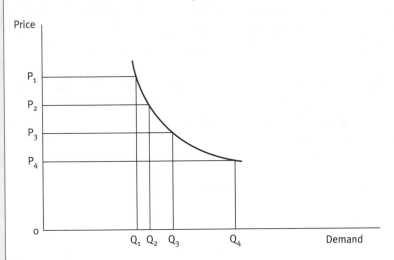

Note that although the price drops from P1–P2 to P3–P4 are equal, the impact on the quantity sold is greater with each fall in price.

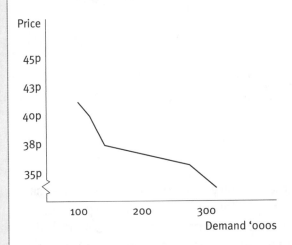

This is important information for an organisation. For example, when price elasticity is high (i.e. more than 1) the organisation will have difficulty in situations where cost inflation is higher than price inflation, because putting up prices in line with costs will cause a disproportionately large reduction in demand, and total revenues will decline. In times of inflation it is better to put up prices frequently by a small amount each time, as customers do not appear to notice the increases – or certainly do not react to them. If prices are held and then substantially increased in a single price rise, demand is likely to fall off sharply. In practice the prices of many products (e.g. consumer durable products) need to fall over time in order to increase demand. It is vital, therefore, to make costs fall by the same percentage if margins are to be maintained.

Different point elasticity can be seen in practice, as customers do not tend to react evenly to price increases. For example, $1 or $2 may be a psychological barrier and if price is increased over this level demand drops quite rapidly. If the product is sold in a supermarket the organisation needs to know how customers react to different prices in order to determine which price points are crucial. In the figure below, the rise between 38p and 40p triggers a large reduction in demand.

To complicate the issue an organisation does not decrease price with the aim of increasing volume in isolation. The effect on volume will depend on how competitors react to the price change, and on the price elasticity of the products.

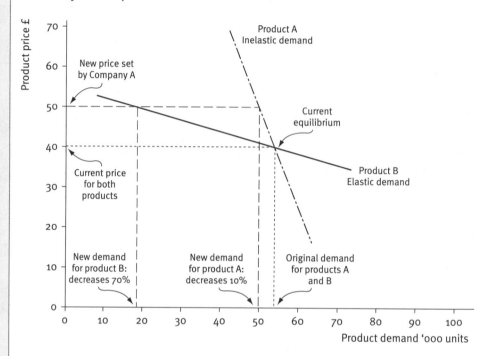

Different products in the same industry have different price elasticity because they are sold in slightly different markets due to product differentiation. This means that two or more products are sold that have different features, quality, sizes and so on. For example, a Volkswagen Golf GTI (the high-performance model) may enjoy lower price elasticity than the standard Golf 1.4E, so that the price of the former can be increased more safely than can that of the latter.

The figure above shows two companies. Company A's product A has a highly inelastic demand, while company B's product B has relatively elastic price elasticity:

In an industry in which costs of production are rising, the responsiveness of demand is an essential factor when deciding on price levels. In the above graph, the company producing product A could increase price by 25 per cent, from $40 to $50, with only a 10 per cent effect on volume (from about 54,000 down to 50,000 units). If the company that produces product B attempts to follow the price rise, its volume will fall from about 54,000 units to approximately 18,000 – the result of very elastic demand. In an industry where prices are falling, then the greater the price elasticity the greater the potential for increasing sales volume.

It is also important for an organisation to take account of expected competitors' reactions to any price increases the organisation makes.

One form of competitor reaction can be demonstrated with the kinked demand curve which shows 'price stickiness'. This occurs where competitors tend to follow price cuts with cuts of their own, but do not copy price rises. This is a pattern commonly found in the newspaper industry:

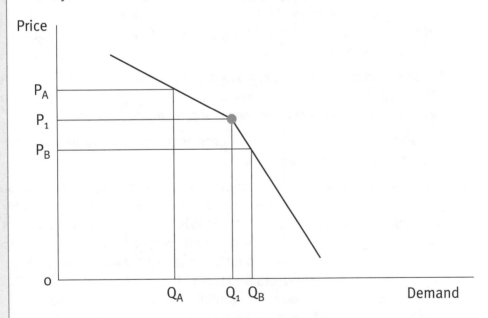

If the price is increased beyond the current price of P_1 to P_A, since competitors do not follow suit, demand will fall away sharply to Q_A (demand is elastic). If however, the price is dropped to P_B, competitors do follow, and little is gained in the way of extra sales (from Q_1 to Q_B) – demand is inelastic.

Where this occurs, firms may be reluctant to change their prices and the result is price stickiness.

5 Factors affecting price elasticity

When making decisions on products, markets and competitors, other factors, including the following, should be considered:

(1) **Scope of the market.** The larger the defined market, the more inelastic is the demand for the broader definition of product. For example, the total market for transport is relatively inelastic, whereas the market for 21-speed pedal cycles is comparatively elastic.

(2) **Information within the market**. Consumers may not know of the competing products in sufficient time to reassess their purchasing behaviour.

(3) **Availability of substitutes**. The less the differentiation between competing products, the greater the price elasticity of those products. Differentiated products benefit from customer awareness and preference, so their demand patterns tend to be more inelastic.

(4) **Complementary products**. The inter-dependency of products results in price inelasticity, because the volume sales of the dependent good rely on sales of the primary good. The consumer will make a purchase of the complementary product in order to achieve satisfaction from the primary good. For example, the purchase of a radio, remote control toy car or a torch, etc., all require the purchase of the complementary product – batteries.

(5) **Disposable income**. The relative wealth of the consumers over time affects the total demand in the economy. Luxury goods tend to have a high price elasticity, while necessities are usually inelastic.

(6) **Necessities**. Demand for basic items such as milk, bread, toilet rolls, etc., tend to be very price inelastic.

(7) **Habit**. Items consumers buy out of habit, such as cigarettes are usually price inelastic. In practice few organisations attempt to set prices by calculating demand and elasticity. This is probably because it is exceptionally hard to determine demand under different circumstances with any certainty. However, most organisations will have some idea of the elasticity of their products and this will have some bearing on the way prices are set. There are a number of different techniques for setting prices that depend on the type of market and product.

Different types of market structures

The price that a business can charge for its products or services will be determined by the market in which it operates.

In a **perfectly competitive** market, every buyer or seller is a 'price taker', and no participant influences the price of the product it buys or sells. Other characteristics of a perfectly competitive market include:

- **Zero entry/Exit barriers** – It is relatively easy to enter or exit as a business in a perfectly competitive market.
- **Perfect information** – Prices and quality of products are assumed to be known to all consumers and producers.
- **Companies aim to maximise profits** – Firms aim to sell where marginal costs meet marginal revenue, where they generate the most profit.
- **Homogeneous products** – The characteristics of any given market good or service do not vary across suppliers.

Imperfect competition refers to the market structure that does not meet the conditions of perfect competition. Its forms include:

(a) **Monopoly**, in which there is only one seller of a good. The seller dominates many buyers and can use its market power to set a profit-maximising price. Microsoft is usually considered a monopoly.

(b) **Oligopoly**, in which a few companies dominate the market and are inter-dependent : firms must take into account likely reactions of their rivals to any change in price, output or forms of non-price competition. For example, in the UK, four companies (Tesco, Asda, Sainsbury's and Morrisons) share 74.4% of the grocery market.

(c) **Monopolistic competition**, in which products are similar, but not identical. There are many producers ('price setters') and many consumers in a given market, but no business has total control over the market price.

For example, there are many different brands of soap on the market today. Each brand of soap is similar because it is designed to get the user clean; however, each soap product tries to differentiate itself from the competition to attract consumers. One soap might claim that it leaves you with soft skin, while another that it has a clean, fresh scent. Each participant in this market structure has some control over pricing, which means it can alter the selling price as long as consumers are still willing to buy its product at the new price.

If one product costs twice as much as similar products on the market, chances are most consumers will avoid buying the more expensive product and buy the competitors' products instead. Monopolistic products are typically found in retailing businesses. Some examples of monopolistic products and/or services are shampoo products, extermination services, oil changes, toothpaste, and fast-food restaurants.

6 The profit-maximisation model

A mathematical model can be used to determine an optimal selling price. The model is based on the economic theory that profit is maximised at the output level where **marginal cost is equal to marginal revenue**.

Full use of the model requires a knowledge of calculus, which is outside the scope of your syllabus. However, you are expected to understand the following basic principles:

It is worthwhile a firm producing and selling further units where the increase in revenue gained from the sale of the next unit exceeds the cost of making it (i.e. the marginal revenue exceeds the marginal cost). However, if the cost of the next unit outweighs the revenue that could be earned from it (i.e. the marginal cost exceeds the marginal revenue), production would not be worthwhile.

A firm should therefore produce units up to the point where the marginal revenue equals the marginal cost: **MR = MC**

The basic price equation is given as $p = a - bx$

where
p = price
x = quantity demanded
a and b are constants, where b is the slope of the curve and is calculated as (change in price/change in quantity)

For example, if you are told that demand falls by 25 units for every increase in price of $1, then b = (1/25) = 0.04

The **marginal revenue** equation can be found by doubling the value of b:
MR = a − 2bx

The marginal cost is the variable cost of production.

Illustration 1 – The MR = MC diagram

Marginal revenue is the additional revenue from selling one extra unit, for example:

Quantity	Price	Revenue	Marginal revenue
1	$70	$70	$70
2	$60	$120	$50
3	$50	$150	$30
4	$40	$160	$10
5	$30	$150	$(10)

Marginal cost is the cost from making one more unit. It is usually just the variable cost, e.g. MC = $30.

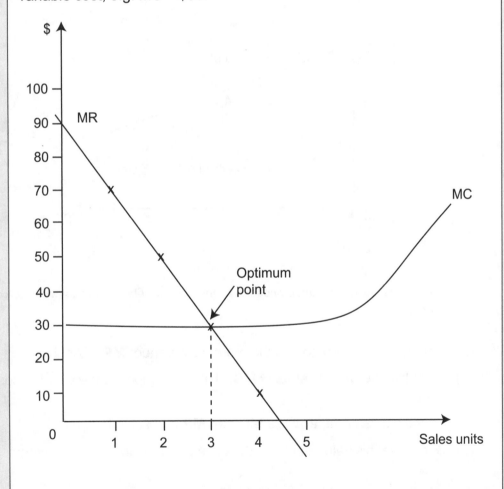

7 Procedure for establishing the optimum price of a product

This is a general set of rules that can be applied to most questions involving algebra and pricing.

(1) Establish the linear relationship between price (P) and quantity demanded (Q). The equation will take the form:

$$P = a + bQ$$

where 'a' is the intercept and 'b' is the gradient of the line. As the price of a product increases, the quantity demanded will decrease. The equation of a straight line P= a + bQ can be used to show the demand for a product at a given price:

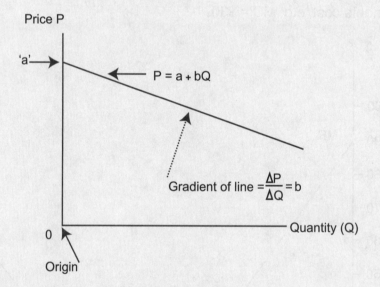

Note: 'b' is always negative because of the inverse relationship between price and quantity.

(2) Double the gradient to find the marginal revenue: **MR = a + 2bQ.**

(3) Establish the **marginal cost MC**. This will simply be the variable cost per unit.

(4) To maximise profit, **equate MC and MR** and solve to find Q.

(5) Substitute this value of Q into the price equation to find the optimum price.

(6) It may be necessary to calculate the maximum profit.

The algebraic approach

At a price of $200, a company will be able to sell 1,000 units of its product in a month. If the selling price is increased to $220, the demand will fall to 950 units. It is also known that the product has a variable cost of $140 per unit, and fixed costs will be $36,000 per month.

Required:

(a) Find an equation for the demand function (that is, price as a function of quantity demanded)

(b) Write down the marginal revenue function

(c) Write down the marginal cost

(d) Find the quantity that maximises profit

(e) Calculate the optimum price

(f) What is the maximum profit?

Example 1

Maximum demand for a company's product M is 100,000 units per annum. The demand will be reduced by 40 units for every increase of $1 in the selling price. The company has determined that profit is maximised at a sales volume of 42,000 units per annum.

What is the profit maximising selling price for product M?

Solution

In the demand equation, $p = a - bx$
where p = price
x = quantity demanded
a,b = constants

Maximum demand is achieved when the product is free, that is, when $p = 0$

When price = 0, demand, x = 100,000 $0 = a - 100,000b$ (i)
When price = 1, demand, x = 99,960 $1 = a - 99,960b$ (ii)
Subtract $1 = 40b$ so $b = 0.025$
Substitute in (i) $a = 100,000 \times 0.025$

so $a = 2,500$

427

The demand equation for product M is therefore p = 2,500 – 0.025b

When x = 42,000 units, p = 2,500 – (0.025 × 42,000)

so p= 1,450

Therefore, the profit-maximising selling price is $1,450 per unit.

Example 2

Another product, K, incurs a total cost of $10 per unit sold, as follows.

	$ per unit
Variable production cost	4
Variable selling cost	2
Fixed production cost	3
Fixed selling and administration cost	1
Total cost	**10**

The marginal revenue (MR) and demand functions for product K are:

MR = 200 – 0.4x
p = 200 – 0.2x

Where p – price, x = quantity demanded per period.

What is the profit-maximising selling price of product K, and what quantity will be sold per period at this price?

Solution

Marginal cost per unit of product K = variable cost per unit = $6

Profit is maximised when marginal cost marginal revenue
i.e. when 6 = 200 – 0.4x

x = 485

When x = 485, p = 200 – (0.2 × 485) = 103

Therefore the profit-maximising selling price is $103 per unit, at which price 485 units will be sold per period.

8 The tabular approach

When data in the exam is given in tabular form and there is no indication about the demand function, and/or when there is no simple linear relationship between output and profit – the tabular approach is likely to be the best to define optimum profit and the associated selling price.

Example 1 – Tabular approach

XYZ Ltd is introducing a new product. The company intends to hire machinery to manufacture the product at a cost of $200,000 per annum. However, this will only enable 60,000 units per annum to be produced, although additional machines can be hired at $80,000 per annum. Each machine hired enables capacity to be increased by 20,000 units per annum, but it is not possible to increase production beyond 90,000 units because of shortage of space.

The minimum rental period is for one year and the variable cost is estimated to be $6 per unit produced. There are no other fixed costs that can be specifically traced to the product. Marketing management has estimated the maximum selling prices for a range of output from 50,000 units to 90,000 units. The estimates are as follows:

Units sold	50,000	60,000	70,000	80,000	90,000	90,000*
Selling price ($)	22	20	19	18	17	15

* At $15 demand will be in excess of 90,000 units but production capacity will limit the sales.

Required:

Present relevant financial information to management for the pricing and output decision.

Answer guide

	$	$	$	$	$	$
Price per unit	22	20	19	18	17	15
Variable cost per unit						
Contribution per unit						
Number of units sold	50,000	60,000	70,000	80,000	90,000	90,000
Total contribution ($000)						
Less fixed costs ($000)						
Net profit ($000)						

9 Limitations of the profit-maximisation model

The profit-maximisation model does make some attempt to take account of the relationship between the price of a product and the resulting demand, but it is of limited practical use because of the following limitations:

(1) It is unlikely that organisations will be able to determine the demand function for their products or services with any degree of accuracy.

(2) The majority of organisations aim to achieve a target profit, rather than the theoretical maximum profit.

(3) Determining an accurate and reliable figure for marginal or variable cost poses difficulties for the management accountant.

(4) Unit marginal costs are likely to vary depending on the quantity sold. For example bulk discounts may reduce the unit materials cost for higher output volumes.

(5) Other factors, in addition to price, will affect the demand, for example, the level of advertising or changes in the income of customers.

10 Pricing strategies based on cost: Total cost-plus pricing

Cost-plus pricing involves adding a mark-up to the total cost of the product, in order to arrive at the selling price.

Unfortunately, since fixed costs are spread over the units of production, the full cost of a product will be a function of the number of units produced, which in turn will be a response to the number of units sold. Yet, sales quantity will depend on the price charged for the product, and so the argument is circular.

Where an order is placed with a jobbing company (a company that makes products to order) for a specific quantity of a product made to the customer's specification, cost-plus may be an acceptable pricing method. But for the majority of organisations this is not the case. Other factors will influence the pricing decision, such as competition and product differentiation. Nevertheless it is reassuring to have some knowledge of cost and price at particular volumes, even if the knowledge is not perfect.

If an organisation does use cost as the basis for pricing it has to decide whether to employ a standard mark-up or whether to vary the mark-up according to the market conditions, type of customer, etc. A standard mark-up is used by some organisations, such as government contractors and some job costing companies, but the majority of companies vary the percentage to reflect differing market conditions for their products. The example below demonstrates total cost pricing, using varying cost assumptions of total cost.

Total cost-plus pricing

A company is replacing product A with an updated version, B, and must calculate a base cost, to which will be added a mark-up in order to arrive at a selling price. The following variable costs have been established by reference to the company's experience with product A, although they may be subject to an error margin of + or − 10 % under production conditions for B:

	$
Direct material	4
Direct labour (1/4 hr @ $16/hr)	4
Variable manufacturing overheads (1/4 hr of machine time @ $8/hr)	2
Total variable cost per unit	**10**

As the machine time for each B would be the same as for A, the company estimates that it will be able to produce the same total quantity of B as its current production of A, which is 20,000 units. 50,000 machine hours may be regarded as the relevant capacity for the purposes of absorbing fixed manufacturing overheads. Current fixed costs are $240,000 for the production facilities, $200,000 for selling and distribution, and $180,000 for administration. For costing purposes, the 20,000 units of B can be assumed to consume 10 per cent of the total selling, distribution and administration costs.

Alternative 1, *using conventional absorption costing principles and building in the conservative error margin*

	$
Variable production costs (as above)	10
Add: allowance for underestimate 10%	1
Add: manufacturing cost 1/4 hour of machine time @ $4.80/hour ($240,000/50,000 hours)	1.2
Base cost	**12.2**

Alternative 2, *as 1 but including administrative costs*

	$
Base cost as under 1 above	12.2
Add: fixed administrative costs ($180,000 × 10% = $18,000/ 20,000 units)	0.9
Base cost	**13.1**

Alternative 3, *as 2 but including selling and distribution costs*

	$
Base cost as under 2 above	13.1
Add: fixed selling and distribution costs ($200,000 × 10% = $20,000/20,000 units)	1.0
Base cost	**14.1**

Depending on the analysis adopted, the base cost varies from $12.2 to $14.1. The base cost rises with each alternative, as an increasing proportion of the total costs is recovered. The profit mark-up built into the pricing formula is therefore likely to fall with each alternative from 1 to 3.

The profit mark-up needs to be based on some assumption. Normally it is fixed so that the company makes a specific return on capital based on a particular capacity utilisation.

A number of advantages are claimed for cost-plus pricing:

(i)   The required profit will be made if budgeted sales volumes are achieved.

(ii) It is a particularly useful method in contract costing industries such as building, where a few large individual contracts can consume the majority of the annual fixed costs and the fixed costs are low in relation to the variable costs.

(iii) Assuming the organisation knows its cost structures, cost-plus is quick and cheap to employ. Its routine nature lends itself to delegation, thus saving management time.

(iv) Cost-plus pricing can be useful in justifying selling prices to customers; if costs can be shown to have increased, this strengthens the case for an increase in the selling price.

However, there are a number of **problems** with cost-plus pricing:

(i)   There will always be problems associated with the selection of a 'suitable' basis on which to charge fixed costs to individual products or services. Selling prices can show great variation, depending on the apportionment basis chosen. This can lead to over-or under-pricing relative to competitors causing the firm to either lose business or make sales at an unintentional loss.

(ii) If prices are set on the basis of normal volume, and actual volume turns out to be considerably lower, overheads will not be fully recovered from sales and predicted profits may not be attainable.

(iii) Cost-plus pricing takes no account of factors such as competitor activity.

(iv) Cost-plus overlooks the need for flexibility in the different stages of a product's life cycle. It takes no account of the price customers are willing to pay and price elasticity of demand. The following example illustrates this point.

Illustration

The variable cost of product A is $10. Fixed manufacturing costs of $1m are spread over an estimated production and sales volume of 200,000 units, i.e. $5 per unit. This gives a total cost of $15 per unit. The cost-plus approach used by the manufacturer of A, based on a standard mark-up of 40 per cent on the product's total cost, dictates a selling price of $21. Assuming all costs were as anticipated, and the company managed to sell 200,000 units at the fixed price of $21, a gross profit of $1.2m ($6 × 200,000) would be earned. Suppose, however, that a market survey had indicated the price elasticity of demand for the product shown in the table below:

Price ($)	Demand (units)
19	250,000
20	240,000
21	200,000
22	190,000
23	160,000

A more correct analysis of the pricing problem would have concentrated on maximising total contribution, and therefore total profitability as shown in this table:

Price ($)	Variable cost	Contribution	Demand	Total contribution	Profit
19	10	9	250,000	2.25	1.25
20	10	10	240,000	2.40	1.40
21	10	11	200,000	2.20	1.20
22	10	12	190,000	2.28	1.28
23	10	13	160,000	2.08	1.08

The decision to use a full cost-plus price of $21 has an associated opportunity cost. In failing to take into consideration the market conditions the organisation has forgone an extra profit of $200,000 and its market share is lower than it could have been.

11 Marginal cost-plus pricing

To the accountant, marginal cost is the same as variable cost. Some of the reasons for using it in preference to total cost are as follows:

(1) It is just as accurate as total cost-plus pricing. A larger mark-up percentage is added because both fixed costs and profit must be covered, but the uncertainty over the fixed costs per unit remains in both pricing methods.

(2) Knowledge of marginal cost gives management the option of pricing below total cost when times are bad, in order to fill capacity.

(3) It is particularly useful in pricing specific one-off contracts because it recognises relevant costs and opportunity costs as well as sunk costs.

(4) It also recognises the existence of scarce or limiting resources. Where these are used by competing products and services it must be reflected in the selling price if profit is to be maximised. If there is a scarce or bottleneck resource the aim must be to maximise the total contribution from the limiting factor. The contribution that each alternative product or service makes from each unit of the scarce resource must be calculated and a suitable profit margin added.

Marginal cost-plus pricing

A company has been producing A successfully for a number of years, and demand appears to be static into the foreseeable future at a market price of $15 per unit. A market has just developed in product B, which the company could produce without additional investment in plant, and without increasing or retraining the existing labour force. Unfortunately, however, B uses the same basic direct material as product A, material C – which is in short supply. The company must determine a minimum selling price for B, below which it would not be worthwhile to divert resources from A.

Costs for the two products are given in the table below:

	A		B
Direct material: 6 units of C @ $0 .60	$3.60	5 units of C @ $0.60	$3.00
Direct labour: 1/2 hour @ $6.00	$3.00	1/2 hour @ $6.00	$3.00
Variable overhead	$2.40		$1.00
	$9.00		$7.00
Selling price	$15.00		
Contribution	$6.00		

Contribution per unit of material C = $6/6 units = $1

A produces a contribution of $6 using 6 units of C, that is, a contribution per unit of C, the limiting factor, of $1. B uses five units of C. The company must therefore seek a contribution of $5 (5 units of material C × $1). So the price must cover the cost of the unit and the lost contribution from C, i.e. be at least $7 + $5 = $12.

12 Criticism of marginal cost-plus pricing

Marginal costing as a basis for pricing has always had its sceptics. The main criticism is based on the following type of scenario:

There are two companies A and B competing with similar products in a market. The market is in recession and sales have decreased. Company A assesses its costs and lowers its price to below total cost, but well above marginal cost, in order to gain more market share. This tactic works; demand is elastic and so company A gains market share at the expense of company B. In order to get back its market share company B reduces its price below that of company A. Both companies now have their original market share but their margins are reduced. Company A then lowers the price again, etc. This continues, until one company is forced out of business. The remaining company now has to increase prices to the original level, which may well be difficult and can incur customer resistance.

13 Marketing-based pricing strategies

There are many different pricing strategies, and it may come as a surprise to would-be accountants that cost is only one of many methods and is certainly not universally used as the key method for pricing.

Premium pricing

Premium pricing is pricing above competition on a permanent basis. This can only be done if the product appears 'different' and superior to competition, which normally means establishing a brand name based on one of the following:

- Quality
- Image/style
- Reliability/robustness
- Durability
- After-sales service
- Extended warranties.

Brands and premium pricing

In order to establish a brand, heavy initial promotion is required and the name must be constantly advertised or promoted thereafter. Brand names, such as, Levi, Mars, Coca-Cola, etc., require many millions of pounds spent on them each year. The benefit is a higher selling price generating a larger profit per unit and customer loyalty, making the product relatively price inelastic. These benefits must, of course, outweigh the cost of keeping the brand name in front of the customers.

Market skimming

Skimming is a technique where a high price is set for the product initially, so that only those who are desperately keen on the product will buy it. Then the price is lowered, making the product more accessible. When the next group of customers have had a chance to buy at that price, the price is lowered again, and so on. The aim of this strategy is usually to **maximise revenue**. But, on occasions, it is also used to prolong the life of older products.

Market skimming and consumer durables

Consumer durable companies tend to skim the market. This is done, to a certain extent, to recover large research and development costs quite quickly. But the products also lend themselves to this treatment as trend-setters are willing to pay a high price to own the latest gismo, and the rest of the population follow their example in later years. Books are also sold this way, with new novels published in hardback at a high price. The hard cover costs little more than a soft cover. Avid readers of that author will buy the hardback book at the high price. A year or so later the book is reissued with a soft cover at a much cheaper price in order to reach a wider audience.

Price skimming was probably first employed at the end of the eighteenth century by Josiah Wedgwood, the famous ceramics manufacturer. He made classical-shaped vases decorated with sprigs of decoration, which he sold to the rich and well-to-do. Naturally he priced his products accordingly. As the designs became old and well known he reduced the price on those lines and introduced new designs at the high price. Thus, he created different tiers of markets for his products, and people who were not so well off could afford a piece which had been in production for some years. This marketing technique helps to prolong a product's life and extracts the maximum profit from it.

If demand for a new or innovative product is relatively inelastic, the supplier has the chance of adopting a market skimming price strategy. It is usually much easier to reduce prices than increase them, so it is better to begin with a high price, and lower it if demand appears more elastic than anticipated. If profitable skimming is to be sustained beyond the introductory phase, there must be significant barriers to entry to the market, in order to deter too many potential competitors entering attracted by the high prices and returns. In the case of books only one company own the rights to publish. Wedgwood had created an image/brand among the rich and famous which others could not copy, especially if they wished to undercut his prices. Consumer durable products have high manufacturing costs that deter too many companies entering the industry.

Penetration pricing

Penetration pricing occurs when a company sets a very low price for the new product initially. The price will usually be below total cost. The aim of the low price is to establish a large market share quickly by encouraging customers to try the product and then to repeat buy. This type of tactic is used, therefore, where barriers to entry are low. It is hoped to establish a dominant market position, which will prevent new entrants coming into the market because they could not establish a critical mass easily with prices so low.

Penetration pricing

In the past, companies used penetration pricing when they introduced a new product, such as a new spray polish, through supermarkets. The price would be, say, between 60 per cent and 80 per cent of the ultimate price. Customers would buy the new product largely because of its price and, it was hoped, repeat buy either because they did not notice the price increase or because they did not mind paying for a good product. If customers do notice the price increase they are likely to be put off further purchases if the increase is too large. If a company succeeds with this type of pricing it wins a large market share very quickly which competitors will find hard to break into.

[In the PEG September 2010, the Examiner highlights the necessity for candidates to be able to 'compare and contrast penetration and skimming pricing strategies'.]

Price differentiation

If the market can be split into different segments, each quite separate from the others and with its own individual demand function, it is possible to sell the same product to different customers at different prices. Marketing techniques can be employed to create market segmentation, if natural demarcation lines are not already in existence. Segmentation will usually be on the basis of one or more of the following:

- Time (e.g. rail travel is cheaper off-peak, hotel accommodation, telecommunications)

- Quantity (e.g. small orders at a premium, bulk orders at a discount)

- Type of customer (e.g. student and OAP rates)

- Outlet/function (e.g. different prices for wholesaler, retailer, end consumer)

- Geographical location (e.g. stalls and upper circle, urban and rural sites, wealthy and poor districts, different countries)

- Product content (e.g. sporty versions of a small car).

This type of pricing is of particular use where a service provider (theatre, leisure centre, train operator) has a high proportion of fixed costs. By attracting those willing and able to use the service at the less popular time/location will help to improve profitability.

Loss leader pricing

When a product range consists of one or more main products and a series of related optional 'extras', which the customer can 'add on' to the main product, the supplier can set a relatively low price for the main product and a high one for the 'extras'. Obviously, the aim is to stimulate sufficient demand for the former to ensure the target return from sales of the latter. The strategy has been used successfully by aircraft engine manufacturers, who win an order with a very competitively priced main product that can only be serviced by their own, highly priced spare parts.

Loss leader pricing – examples

Gillette did not invent the safety razor but the market strategy Gillette adopted helped to build market share. Gillette razors were sold at 1/5 of the cost to manufacture them but only Gillette blades fitted and these were sold at a price of 5 cents. The blades cost only 1 cent to manufacture and so Gillette made large profits once it had captured the customer. One of the best known uses of this technique in recent years has been the sale of printer ink for home printers.

Investigations by Which? and by Computeractive magazine showed that whilst the price of inkjet printers can be as little as $34, the cost of running the printer over an 18-month period could be up to $1,700. The top brand names for replacement ink cartridges cost more per millilitre than vintage champagne and even where the consumer only buys two replacement cartridges a year, the cost of the ink is likely to be significantly higher than the cost of the initial printer.

Discount pricing

Discount pricing is the long-term pricing strategy used by firms such as Ikea and Ryanair, based on low cost, high volume and low margins.

Products are priced lower than the market norm, but are put forward as being of comparable quality. The aim is that the product will procure a larger share of the market than it might otherwise do, thereby counteracting the reduction in selling price. However, care must be taken to ensure that potential customers' perceptions of the product are not prejudiced by the lower price. The consumer will often view with suspicion a branded product that is priced at even a small discount to the prevailing market rate.

Using discounts in pricing (short-term)

There are a number of reasons for using discounts to adjust prices:

(1) To get cash in quickly. This is a not always a financially sound strategy as the firm may lose more in sales revenues from the discount, than they would lose in interest from a bank loan for the same amount.

(2) To differentiate between different types of customer, wholesale, retail, etc.

(3) To increase sales volume during a poor sales period without dropping the price permanently.

(4) Some industries give discounts as normal practice, for example the antique trade, and some retail shops seem to have semi-permanent sales.

(5) Perishable goods are often discounted towards the end of their life or the end of the day, or seconds are often sold off cheaply. This may not be a good strategy as it does not improve the company image, and some customers may get wise and delay their purchase until the end of the day when prices are cheaper.

Controlled pricing

A significant proportion of the previously nationalised industries in the UK have been 'privatised' into the private sector, with a constraining influence usually called the industry 'regulator'. Examples of these regulating bodies are Oftel (telecommunications) and Ofwat (water).

Many of these companies are in a largely monopolistic situation and so regulation of these industries was perceived as desirable. Regulation largely takes the form of controlling price so that the monopolistic companies cannot exploit their unique position. The regulators use selling price as the means of controlling the volume of supply in the industry. They may also decide to specify the quality of the product or level of service that must be achieved or to prohibit the company operating in certain sectors.

When an industry is regulated on selling price, the elasticity is zero. No price change is allowed. Not only does this mean that 'small' customers pay less than they otherwise would, but large customers pay more than one might expect under more competitive positions. Over recent years all of the monopolistic industries have introduced some kind of discounted price for very large customers, which is beginning to allow genuine competition to enter the market. Gradually other billing companies have been allowed to enter the market and so price has become more flexible.

Product bundling

Bundling is putting a package of products together to make, for example, a complete kit for customers, which can then be sold at a temptingly low price. It is a way of creating value for customers and increasing company profits. It is a strategy that is often adopted in times of recession when organisations are particularly keen to maintain sales volume. One industry where this tactic started in the recession of the early 1990s is the computer industry. A manufacturer might decide to substantially reduce the profit margin on some hardware, such as printers. If, for example, only half its PC purchasers would also buy the company's model of printer, a bundled package which includes the PC and the printer for a lower combined price may well prove very successful. On the other hand, some customers will be put off by product bundling as they do not want the complete package; they will resent the increased price, however small it is.

Bundling

Bundling is profitable in situations in which some buyers value one of the items in a bundle relatively highly but the remainder slightly above or below cost price. Other buyers place a relatively high valuation on both or all of the items in the bundle. Four film exhibitors, A to D, are willing to pay the following prices for two films X and Y:

A values X at $16,000 and Y at $5,000
B values X at $14,000 and Y at $6,000
C values X at $11,000 and Y at $10,000
D values X at $10,000 and Y at $11,000

The distributor's marginal cost of supplying each film is $8,000.

The distributor offers X and Y separately at $14,000 and $8,000 respectively, or the pair as a package for $21,000. The result is that A, C and D hire the package and B hires film X only, as the cost of both the bundle and film Y exceed his particular valuations. The distributor's profit would be ($21,000 × 3) + ($14,000) − ($8,000 × 7) = $21,000.

However, A might also prefer to hire film X for $14,000, instead of taking the package, as the extra cost of the bundle exceeds his valuation of Y by $2,000. If A did choose this option, the distributor's profit would rise to $22,000, as he does not have to supply either A or B with film Y, which has a supply cost in excess of their valuations: ($21,000 × 2) × ($14,000 × 2) − ($8,000 × 6) = $22,000.

Bundling is a particularly efficient means of exploiting price differentiation. Buyers are offered a pricing structure in which they are charged higher prices for buying the items separately (X + Y = $22,000) than in a package (X + Y = $21,000). Bundling works as a discriminatory device by:

- Using the package to extract the most from those customers who value it most. (In our example C and D, who placed relatively high valuations on both films.)

- Charging a relatively high separate price for the item in the package that is valued very highly by some particular buyers. (In our example film X, which was valued very highly by both A and B.)

If the distributor did not bundle he would make a profit of $19,000, as A and B would purchase product X and C and D would purchase product Y.

Bundling: Amstrad

Bundling can be extremely successful, especially when tried on mature products for the first time. For instance, Amstrad had considerable success when it entered the hi-fi market and demystified the technology by being the first company to sell a complete package of amplifier, deck and speakers. This was more than just a pricing strategy: it was a complete marketing strategy. In recent years the telecommunications industry has successfully used this technique; first with TV channel packages, and then more recently extended to TV, broadband and phone bundles.

Whether a bundling strategy will succeed depends on the predicted increase in sales volume and the changes in margin. There are likely to be other cost changes such as savings in product handling, packaging and invoicing costs. Longer-term implications and competitors' reactions must not be ignored. For example, how will customers react when products are 'unbundled'? Will this result in a marked decline in sales? Will bundling be seen as an inferior product strategy which will have long-term implications for the brand's image? Will competitors retaliate by bundling their products? If they do this, will the strategy be successful?

Pricing with additional features

The decision to add extra features to a product is a similar decision to bundling products. Most people prefer to have extra features incorporated into the product but they may not be prepared to pay the extra price. Others do not require the extra features and view them as a definite disadvantage. This is likely to be the case with older customers and electrical or electronic equipment. Older people find mastering the equipment quite difficult and they do not want extra features that make operation even more difficult. The following exercise considers an extra feature, the resulting price and its effect on market share.

14 The product life cycle

Products and services, like human beings, have a life cycle. This is represented by the generic curve shown below:

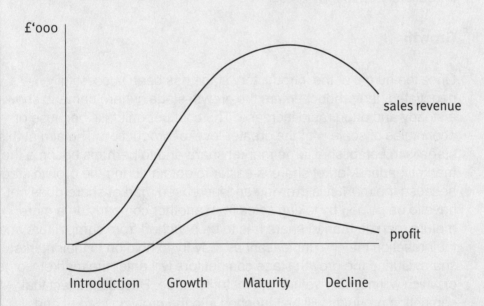

The length of the life cycle varies considerably from a year or so, for some children's toys, to hundreds of years, as in the case of binoculars, for example. The product life cycle is divided into four basic stages as shown in the figure above; each stage has different aims and expectations.

Price is a major variable over the product life cycle. Depending on market structure and demand, different pricing strategies will be appropriate for different stages in the cycle. The four stages in the life cycle and appropriate price strategies are described below:

(i) Introductory phase

Demand will be low when a product is first launched onto the market, and heavy advertising expenditure will usually be required to bring it to consumers' attention. The aim is to establish the product in the market, which means achieving a certain critical mass within a certain period of time. The critical mass is the sales volume that must be achieved in order to make the product viable in the medium term. Depending on the nature of the product, a price penetration (low entry price) policy may be adopted in order to reach the critical mass quickly. On the other hand the market may be skimmed (exploiting those purchasers keen to have the latest product such as plasma screen TVs) and so a high introductory price may be set.

(ii) Growth

Once the hurdle of the introductory stage has been successfully negotiated, the product enters the growth stage, where demand shows a steady and often rapid increase. The cost per unit falls because of economies of scale with the greater level of production. The aim at this stage is to establish a large market share and to perhaps become the market leader. Market share is easier to obtain during the growth stage because the market is growing and increased market share does not have to be gained by taking sales from another company. In a more mature market, market share has to be poached from competitors and their reaction may be unpleasant as they try to hold on to their market share. During the growth stage competitors will enter the market, some of which will not survive into the maturity stage. Despite the fact that competing products will be launched into the growing market and pricing is often keen in order to gain market share, it is usually the most profitable stage for the initial supplier.

(iii) Maturity

The increase in demand slows down in this stage, as the product reaches the mass market. The sales curve flattens out and eventually begins to fall. As market maturity is reached the organisation becomes more interested in minimising elasticity. Products have to be differentiated in order to maintain their position in the market and new users for mature products need to be found to keep demand high. Generally, profits will be lower than during the growth stage.

(iv) Decline

When the market reaches saturation point, the product's sales curve begins to decline. When the market declines price wars erupt as organisations with products which have elastic demand seek to maintain full utilisation of their production capacity.

Profits can still be made during the early part of this stage, and the products will be managed to generate cash for newer products. This will determine how prices are set. Eventually rapidly falling sales inevitably result in losses for all suppliers who stay in the market. This particular product has effectively come to the end of its life cycle, and alternative investment opportunities must be pursued.

Despite the recent general tendency to shorter life cycles, the length of any particular stage within the cycle and the total length of the life cycle itself will depend on the type of product or service being marketed. Although the curve will be characterised by a sustained rise, followed by levelling out and falling away, the precise shape of the curve can vary considerably. Life cycles are discussed further later in this text.

15 Other issues

The price/quality relationship

The price/quality relationship refers to the perception by most consumers that a relatively high price is a sign of good quality. The belief in this relationship is most important with complex products that are hard to test, and services, that cannot be tested until used. The greater the uncertainty surrounding a product, the more consumers depend on the price/quality hypothesis and the greater premium lights the importance of 'the relationship they are prepared to pay.

[In the PEG September 2010, the Examiner highlights the importance of 'the relationship between price and quality, and how this affects product decisions'.]

Income elasticity of demand

In economics, the income elasticity of demand measures the responsiveness of the demand for a good to a change in the income of the people demanding the good. For example, if, in response to a 10% increase in income, the demand for a good increased by 20%, the income elasticity of demand would be 20%/10% = 2.

A negative income elasticity of demand is associated with inferior goods; an increase in income will lead to a fall in the demand and may lead to changes to more luxurious substitutes.

445

A positive income elasticity of demand is associated with normal goods; an increase in income will lead to a rise in demand. If income elasticity of demand of a commodity is less than 1, it is a necessity good. If the elasticity of demand is greater than 1, it is a luxury good or a superior good.

A zero income elasticity (or inelastic) demand occurs when an increase in income is not associated with a change in the demand of a good. These would be sticky goods.

Ethical considerations

Whether or not to exploit short-term shortages through higher prices is an ethical decision faced, for example, by companies supplying essential commodities such as gas or fuel.

16 Practice questions

OT Question 1: Tabular Approach

ABC plc is about to launch a new product. Facilities will allow the company to produce up to 20 units per week. The marketing department has estimated that at a price of $8,000 no units will be sold, but for each $150 reduction in price one additional unit per week will be sold.

Fixed costs associated with manufacture are expected to be $12,000 per week.

Variable costs are expected to be $4,000 per unit for each of the first 10 units; thereafter each unit will cost $400 more than the preceding one. The most profitable level of output per week for the new product is:

A   10 units

B   11 units

C   13 units

D   14 units

E   20 units

OT Question 2: Optimum price

Market research by Company A has revealed that the maximum demand for product R is 50,000 units each year, and that demand will reduce by 50 units for every $1 that the selling price is increased. Based on this information, Company A has calculated that the profit-maximising level of sales for product R for the coming year is 35,000 units. The price at which these units will be sold is:

A $100

B $300

C $500

D $700

E $900

OT Question 3: Optimum price

Another product manufactured by company A is product M. At a price of $700 for product M there would be zero demand, and for every $40 reduction in the selling price the demand would increase by 100 units. The variable cost of producing a unit of product M is $60.

Company A knows that if the demand equation for product M is represented by $p = a - bx$, where p is the selling price and x is the quantity demanded at price p, then the marginal revenue (MR) for product M can be represented by $MR = a - 2bx$.

The profit-maximising output of product M is:

A   100 units

B   700 units

C   800 units

D   1,600 units

E   1,750 units

OT Question 4: Optimum price

A company is considering the pricing of one of its products. It has already carried out some market research with the following results:

The quantity demanded at a price of $100 will be 1,000 units.

The quantity demanded will increase/decrease by 100 units for every $50 decrease/increase in the selling price. The marginal cost of each unit is $35.

Calculate the selling price that maximises company profit.

OT Question 5: Optimum price

H is launching a new product which it expects to incur a variable cost of $14 per unit. The company has completed some market research to try to determine the optimum selling price with the following results.

If the price charged was to be $25 per unit, then the demand would be 1,000 units each period. For every $1 increase in the selling price, demand would reduce by 100 units each period. For every $1 reduction in the selling price, the demand would increase by 100 units each period.

Calculate the optimum selling price.

Data Set Question: AB Ltd

During the current year AB Ltd planned to produce 150,000 units of its main product, a cordless hand drill. Nearing the end of the current year, activity so far has corresponded to budget and it is anticipated that average costs for the whole year will be as shown below:

Average cost per unit (for 150,000 activity level)

	$
Direct material	18
Direct labour	10
Variable overhead	10
Fixed overhead	10
	48

The budget for next year is being developed and the following cost changes have been forecast:

Direct material: price increase of 33.3%

Director labour: rate increase of 10%

Variable overhead: increase of 5%

Fixed overhead: increase of 15%

The substantial price increase for materials is causing concern and alternative sources are being considered. One source quotes a material cost per unit of $20 but tests on samples show that the cheaper materials would increase labour costs by an additional 50c per unit and would lead to a reject rate of 5%. It would also be necessary to install a test and inspection department at the end of manufacturing to identify the faulty items. This would increase fixed costs by an additional $200,000 per year.

Selling prices are also considered when the budget is being developed. Normally, selling prices are determined on a cost-plus basis, the mark-up being 50% on unit cost, but there is concern that this is too inflexible as it would lead to a substantial price rise for next year. The sales director estimates that demand varies with price thus:

	$	$	$	$	$	$	$
Price/unit	64	68	72	76	80	84	88
Demand (000 units)	190	170	150	140	125	110	95

Calculate:

The **number of units** where the variable cost saving is equal to the incremental fixed costs:

The selling price that would maximise profit for next year $ [ ]

The maximum profit achievable $ [ ]

It has been realised that, through better organisation, it would be possible to reduce the extra fixed costs of $200,000 originally estimated in connection with the cheaper material.

Required:

The **increase** in fixed costs at which the company would be indifferent as to its choice of suppliers for materials. $ [ ]

PRE-SEEN MATERIAL

The Q Organisation is a large worldwide respected manufacturer of consumer electrical and electronic goods. Q constantly develops new products that are in high demand as they represent the latest technology and are 'must haves' for those consumers who want to own the latest consumer gadgets.

Recently Q has developed a new handheld digital DVD recorder and seeks your advice as to the price it should charge for such a technologically advanced product.

Market research has discovered that the price/demand relationship for the item during the initial launch phase will be as follows:

Price ($)	Demand (units)
100	10,000
80	20,000
69	30,000
62	40,000

Production of the DVD recorder would occur in batches of 10,000 units, and the production director believes that 50% of the variable manufacturing cost would be affected by a learning and experience curve. This would apply to each batch produced and continue at a constant rate of learning up to a production volume of 40,000 units when the learning would be complete.

Thereafter, the unit variable manufacturing cost of the product would be equal to the unit cost of the fourth batch. The production director estimates that the unit variable manufacturing cost of the first batch would be $60 ($30 of which is subject to the effect of the learning and experience curve, and $30 of which is unaffected), whereas the average unit variable manufacturing cost of all four batches would be $52.71.

There are no non-manufacturing variable costs associated with the DVD recorder.

You are Q's Senior Management Accountant and have recently received the following email:

From: Gianfranco Bolatelli
Sent: 03 June, 10.23 a.m.
To: Senior Management Accountant
Subject: Pricing

I am unclear about the best price to charge for our product. Would it have to change, now and then? Please draft me a report that, first of all, explains the relevance of the product life cycle to the consideration of alternative pricing policies that might be adopted by Q.

You have recently met the Production Director and looked at his figures: what rate of learning does he expect? What would the optimum price at which Q should sell the DVD recorder be, in order to maximise its profits during the initial launch phase of the product?

Personally, I expect that after the initial launch phase, the market price will be \$57 per unit. Estimated product specific fixed costs during this phase of the product's life are expected to be \$15,000 per month. During this phase of the product life cycle Q wishes to achieve a target monthly profit from the product of \$30,000.

How many units do we need to sell each month during this phase in order for Q to achieve our target monthly profit?

Test your understanding answers

The algebraic approach

(a) b = (220 – 200)/(950 – 1,000) = –0.4

200 = a –0.4 × 1,000

a = 200 + 400 = 600.

So the demand function is P = 600 – 0.4Q

(b) To find MR, just double the gradient so that MR = 600 – 0.8Q

MR = 600 – 0.8Q

(c) MC = 140

(d) The optimum quantity Q is achieved when the company produces units up to the point where marginal revenue equals marginal cost, i.e. when MR = MC

with MR = a + 2bQ

i.e. MR = $600 – 0.8Q

and MC = $140

so q is achieved when a + 2bQ = $140

i.e. when $600 – 0.8Q = $140

i.e. when Q = 575 units

(e) P= 600 – 0.4 × 575 = $370

(f) Revenue = Price × Quantity = $370 × 575 = $212,750

Cost = $36,000 + $140 × 575 = $116,500

Profit = $96,250

Example 1 – Tabular approach

	$	$	$	$	$	$
Price per unit	22	20	19	18	17	15
Variable cost per unit	(6)	(6)	(6)	(6)	(6)	(6)
Contribution per unit	16	14	13	12	11	9
Number of units sold	50,000	60,000	70,000	80,000	90,000	90,000
Total contribution ($000)	800	840	910	960	990	810
Less fixed costs ($000)	(200)	(200)	(280)	(280)	(360)	(360)
Net profit ($000)	600	640	630	680	630	450

To maximise profit, price should be $18, output 80,000 and 1 extra machine should be hired.

OT Question 1: Tabular Approach

The best approach is to calculate the profit for a range of outputs from 10 units upwards, then select the output with the highest profit.

The answer is B

Units	Total variable costs	Selling price per unit	Total select revenue	Total contribution
10	$40,000	$6,500	$65,000	$25,000
11	$44,400	$6,350	$69,850	$25,540
12	$49,200	$6,200	$74,400	$25,200
13	$54,400	$6,050	$78,650	$24,250

OT Question 2: Optimum price

Answer: B

In the demand equation p = a – bx
When price = 0, demand, x = 50,000 therefore 0 = a – 50,000b (i)
When price = 1, demand, x = 49,950 therefore 1 = a – 49,950b (ii)
Subtract   1 = 50b so b = 0.02

Substitute in (i)   a = (50,000 × 0.02) so a = 1,000

The demand equation for product R is p = 1,000 – 0.02x

When x = 35,000 units, p = 1,000 – (0.02 × 35,000) = 300

OT Question 3: Optimum price

Answer: C

In the demand equation p = a – bx

When price = $700, demand = 0 therefore a = 700

When price = $660, demand = 100 therefore 660 = a – 100b
Substitute for a 660 = 700 – 100b therefore b = 0 .4
The demand equation for product M is p = 700 – 0.4x
The marginal revenue equation is given by MR = 700 – 0.8x
Profit is maximised when marginal cost = marginal revenue, i.e. when 60 = 700 – 0.8x
i.e. **when x = 800.**

OT Question 4: Optimum price

Price at which demand equals zero = $100 + (1,000/100) × $50 = $600

P = $600 – 0.5x
MR = $600 – x
MC = $35
MC = MR
$35 = $600 2 x
x = $565
p = $600 – $(0.5 × 565)
p = $317.50

OT Question 5: Optimum price

Marginal cost (MC) = $14

Price (P) = $35 – 0.01q
Marginal revenue (MR) = $35 – 0.02q
So if MC = MR, then 14 = 35 – 0.02q

Q = 1,050
Price = $35 – (0.01 × 1,050) = $24.50

Data Set Question: AB Ltd

	Current material	Cheaper material
	$ per unit	$
Direct material	24.00	20.00
Direct labour	11.00	11.50
Variable overhead	10.50	10.50
Total variable cost	45.50	42.00

for 0.95 of a unit
$42

$$\therefore \text{ Cost per unit} = \frac{\$42}{0.95}$$

= $44.21 per unit

Fixed costs last year: $10 × 150,000 = $1,500,000
∴ Fixed cost in coming year: $1,500,000 × 1.15 = $1,725,000
If use cheaper material fixed costs increase
by $200,000: $1,925,000

When the company switches from the current material to the cheaper material, the cost per unit will decrease but the fixed cost will increase.

At low levels of activity the cheapest material would be the current one, taking advantage of the low fixed cost.

However, as production increases the cheaper material becomes more attractive, as one wishes to take advantage of the lower unit cost. At high levels of activity the cheaper material is preferable, the lower unit cost more than compensates for the higher fixed cost.

So, in conclusion, the material choice is dependent upon the activity level.

Ascertain the level of activity where the purchaser would be **indifferent** between the two materials.

When switch from regular to cheaper:

Saving in variable cost is $45.50 – $44.21 = $1.29 per unit.

Increase in fixed cost is $200,000.

Therefore, the number of units where the variable cost saving is equal to the incremental fixed cost is:

$200,000 ÷ 1.29 = 155,038.8 units

Conclusion

If production is expected to be **155,038** units or less, use the regular supplier. If production is expected to be **155,039** or more, use the cheaper material.

Price	Demand	Variable cost per unit	Contribution per unit	Total contribution	Fixed costs	Profit
$	000s	$	$	$000	$000	$000
64	190	(44.21)	19.79	3,760.1	(1,925)	1,835.1
68	170	(44.21)	23.79	4,044.3	(1,925)	2,119.3
72	150	(45.50)	26.50	3,975.0	(1,725)	2,250.0
76	140	(45.50)	30.50	4,270.0	(1,725)	2,545.0
80	125	(45.50)	34.50	4,312.5	(1,725)	2,587.5
84	110	(45.50)	38.50	4,235.0	(1,725)	2,510.0
88	95	(45.50)	42.50	4,037.5	(1,725)	2,312.5

From the table above, it can be seen that profit is maximised when 125,000 units are sold for $80 each.

The maximum profit is $2,587,500.

The regular supplier should be retained.

At 125,000 units the saving in variable costs if the firm switches to the cheaper supplier is

125,000 × $1.29 = $161,250

The company would be indifferent between the two suppliers if fixed costs increased by $161,250.

New fixed cost level = $1,725,000 + $161,250
= $1,886,250

Integration Style Question – Q Organisation

REPORT

From Senior Management Accountant to G. Balotelli

Re: Pricing

(a) The price of the product is likely to change over the four stages of the life cycle. We shall consider each stage in turn:

Introduction stage

When a new innovative product is launched to a market there are two commonly used pricing strategies used:

– *Market skimming*

This strategy involves selling the product at a very high price during the introduction stage. This policy is likely to be successful if the product is brand new and innovative. Also, if demand is inelastic, then the product will generate a much higher return at an initial high price. Market skimming will generate a high net cash in-flow initially, which hopefully will help recover the high development costs quickly.

Q may be able to take advantage of this pricing policy as its new DVD recorder incorporates the latest technology and Q is likely to be the first on the market with this cutting-edge item.

Selling at a very high price will attract strong competition to the product.

- *Price penetration*

    Q may choose to launch the product at a very low price or
    penetration price. Advantages of this approach include high
    growth is encouraged, competition is discouraged, and
    economies of scale may be taken advantage of. However, for
    this strategy to generate high profits, Q would need a high
    volume of sales, and be the dominant player in the market (high
    market share). Achieving high sales volume may be difficult with
    a brand new product.

- *Growth stage*

    During this stage of the products life cycle, the sales of the DVD
    player would be expected to grow rapidly. As the product starts
    to become accepted and established by the mass market,
    competition usually significantly increases. In order to maintain
    market share and dominance Q will find it necessary to lower
    the initial market skimming launch price.

- *Maturity stage*

    As product sales growth begins to slow down and level off, an
    established market price for the DVD recorder will become
    apparent. The price will often reach its lowest point during this
    stage. An average/going-rate price may be charged. However,
    Q has a good reputation and is respected worldwide, so it may
    be able to charge a premium price based on its reputation and
    a certain level of brand loyalty.

    Q may try to extend the maturity phase by launching upgrades
    or by trying to sell in new markets.

    The product must achieve its lowest unit cost during this stage.
    Profits are likely to be highest in the maturity stage.

- *Decline*

    The decline stage is the final stage of the product's life cycle.
    The initial new innovative technology has now been superseded
    by superior products.

    The DVD recorder may hold on to a small niche market. The
    group of loyal customers still purchasing the original DVD
    player may be willing to pay a price that is reasonable.
    Alternatively Q may use product bundling.

    At the final withdrawal of the product, prices may be slashed to
    sell off any surplus stock.

(b) (i)   Variable cost affected by the learning curve for the first batch

= \$60 – \$30 = \$30

Let 'r' be the learning curve rate.

Output in batches	Cumulative average cost per unit
x	y
1	30
2	30r
4	$30r^2 = 22.71$

If $30\,r^2$	= 22.71
r^2	= 0.757
r	= 0.87

The learning curve rate is 87%.

Note: This answer could be determined using the formula but this is a much more cumbersome method when doubling is possible. The approach using the formula would be:

$Y = ax^b$ so $22.71 = 30 \times 4^b$

$4^b = 22.71/30 = 0.757$

Taking logs b log 4 = log 0.757

b = log 0.757/log 4 = –0.2000

b = log learning rate/log 2

So   log learning rate = –0.200 × log2 = –0.06045

Learning rate = 0.87

(ii)

Price ($)	Demand (000s)	LC variable cost p.u. ($)	Non-LC variable cost p.u. ($)	Total V.C. p.u. ($)	Contribution per unit ($)	Total contribution ($000)
100	10	30.00	30.00	60.00	40.00	400.0
80	20	26.10	30.00	56.10	23.90	478.0
69	30	24.06	30.00	54.06	14.94	448.2
62	40	22.71	30.00	52.71	9.29	371.6

To maximise contribution the company should sell 20,000 units at $80 each.

Learning curve workings

Output in batches	Average cost per unit
x	y
1	30.00
2	26.10
3	24.06 **
4	22.71

$Y = ax^b$

$a = 30$

$b = \log 0.87 \div \log 2 = -0.2009$

$x = 3$ batches

$y = 30 \times 3^{-0.2009}$

$y = 24.06$

(iii)

$$\text{Target contribution} = \text{Fixed costs} + \text{Required profit}$$

$$= \$15{,}000 + \$30{,}000$$

$$= \$45{,}000 \text{ per month}$$

The initial launch phase represents the first 20,000 units (as per (b)(ii) above). However the learning effect continues until 40,000 units hence the unit cost decreases (and therefore unit contribution increases) until the 40,000 units have been completed.

The average unit cost of the batch of units from 20,001 – 30,000 is:

$$((30{,}000 \times \$54.06) - (20{,}000 \times \$56.10)) \div 10{,}000 = \$49.98$$

thus giving a unit contribution of $57.00 – $49.98 = $7.02 and a monthly sales target of:

$$\$45{,}000 \div \$7.02 = 6{,}411 \text{ units}$$

The average unit cost for 30,001 units and more is:

$$((40{,}000 \times \$52.71) - (30{,}000 \times \$54.06)) \div 10{,}000 = \$48.66$$

thus giving a unit contribution of $57 – $48.66 = $8.34

and thus the monthly sales target becomes:

$$\$45{,}000 \div \$8.34 = 5{,}396 \text{ units}$$

In the second month after the launch phase, the first 3,589 units (10,000 – 6,411) sold will generate a contribution of $7.02 per unit and the remaining units will generate a contribution of $8.34.

Target contribution	$45,000	
Contribution from first	3,589 × $7.02	($25,195)
Contribution still required	$19,805	

Number of units still to be sold $19,805 ÷ $8.34 = 2,375 units

Total unit sales in 2nd month = 3,589 + 2,375 = 5,964

The treatment of uncertainty and risk in decision making

Chapter learning objectives

Syllabus Link

Lead D1: Analyse information to assess its impact on long-term decisions

Component D1b): Analyse risk and uncertainty

- Quantification of risk.
- Probabilistic models and interpretation of distribution of project outcomes
- Decision Trees
- Bayes Theorem
- Decision making in conditions of uncertainty.

1 Chapter summary

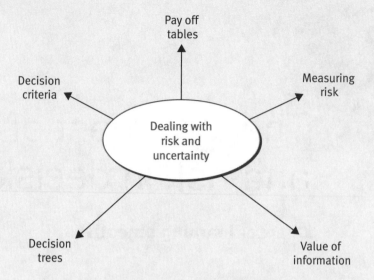

Topic overview

Over the next few chapters we explore some decision making problems such as whether to launch new products, whether to buy machines, choosing between products etc.

All of these decisions will involve an element of risk and uncertainty. This chapter looks at how risk and uncertainty can be built into the decision making process. This is often achieved by building in probabilities for expected outcomes and using expected values and decision trees to assess the problem.

Forecasting and decision making often include an element of risk or uncertainty. Because they look to the future they often involve estimates of future costs and benefits. In this chapter we look at how these risks and uncertainty can be built into the decision making process.

Decision making involves making decisions now about what will happen in the future. Events in the future can be predicted, but managers can rarely be 100% confident that these predicted future events will actually arise. As actual results emerge managers are likely to discover that they have achieved better or worse results than those predicted originally.

There are several ways of dealing with this variability of outcomes. In this session we will consider several different possible outcomes that may arise. It is common in practice to consider three possible outcomes; the most likely outcome, the pessimistic (worst possible) outcome and the optimistic (best possible) outcome. Analysts may consider more than these three possibilities, but more information will become more complicated and cumbersome to analyse and understand.

Examination questions will generally provide all the different possible outcomes that may arise, together with the associated chance (probability) of the outcome occurring. It is our task to analyse the information given, recommend an appropriate strategy for management to follow and finally to highlight the potential risk involved in the various choices.

2 Risk and uncertainty

The difference between risk and uncertainty

Investment appraisal faces the following problems:

- all decisions are based on forecasts
- all forecasts are subject to uncertainty
- this uncertainty needs to be reflected in the financial evaluation.

The decision maker must distinguish between:

- **risk** – quantifiable – possible outcomes have associated probabilities, thus allowing the use of mathematical techniques
- **uncertainty** – unquantifiable – outcomes cannot be mathematically modelled.

Illustration on risk and uncertainty

Risk: there are a number of possible outcomes and the probability of each outcome is known.

For example, based on past experience of digging for oil in a particular area, an oil company may estimate that they have a 60% chance of finding oil and a 40% chance of not finding oil.

Uncertainty: there are a number of possible outcomes but the probability of each outcome is not known.

For example, the same oil company may dig for oil in a previously unexplored area. The company knows that it is possible for them to either find or not find oil but it does not know the probabilities of each of these outcomes.

One possible approach to dealing with risk is to deploy sophisticated modelling techniques in an attempt to improve the reliability of business forecasts. The use of trend analysis, encountered earlier in this text, is one possibility. The key point is to develop a mathematical model to predict how future costs will behave having regard to labour becoming more adept at tasks (and hence unit resource requirements falling) the more times they are repeated.

3 Probabilities and expected values

An expected value summarises all the different possible outcomes by calculating a single weighted average. It is the long run average (mean).

The expected value is not the most likely result. It may not even be a possible result, but instead it finds the average outcome if the same event was to take place thousands of times.

Expected value formula

$$EV = \Sigma px$$ **LEARN**

where   x represents the future outcome

and   p represents the probability of the outcome occurring

Illustration 1

An organisation is considering launching a new product. It will do so if the expected value of the total revenue is in excess of $1,000. It is decided to set the selling price at $10. After some investigation a number of probabilities for different levels of sales revenue are predicted; these are shown in the following table:

Units sold	Revenue $	Probability	Pay-off $
80	800	0.15	120
100	1,000	0.50	500
120	1,200	0.35	420
		1.00	EV = 1,040

The expected sales revenue at a selling price of $10 per unit is $1,040, that is [800 × 0.15] + [1,000 × 0.50] + [1,200 × 0.35]. In preparing forecasts and making decisions management may proceed on the assumption that it can expect sales revenue of $1,040 if it sets a selling price of $10 per unit. The actual outcome of adopting this selling price may be sales revenue that is higher or lower than $1,040. And $1,040 is not even the most likely outcome; the most likely outcome is $1,000, since this has the highest probability.

Histograms

Probability data may be presented diagrammatically in the form of a histogram. The information given in the illustration immediately above might be presented as follows:

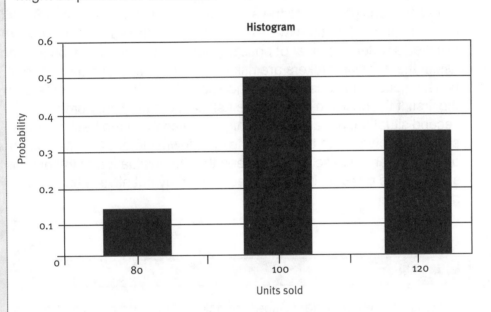

The single figure of the expected value of revenue can hide a wide range of possible actual results.

Furthermore, not all decision-makers will have the same attitude towards risk. There are three main types of decision-maker.

- **Risk neutral** decision-makers consider all possible outcomes and will select the strategy that maximises the expected value or benefit.

- **Risk seekers** are likely to select the strategy with the best possible outcomes, regardless of the likelihood that they will occur. They will apply the maximax criteria (covered later).

- **Risk averse** decision-makers try to avoid risk. They would rather select a lower, but certain, outcome than risk going for a higher pay-off which is less certain to occur. They will apply the maximin criterion or the minimax regret approach (both covered later).

Illustration 2

For instance, after investigation in the previous illustration the predicted revenues might have been different. They might have been as follows:

Units sold	Revenue $	Probability	Pay-off $
40	400	0.15	60.00
100	1,000	0.50	500.00
137	1,370	0.35	479.50
		1.00	EV = 1,039.50

Both situations give rise to the same expected sales revenue of $1,040 (to the nearest $), but the two situations are not the same. The second involves a wider dispersal of possible outcomes; hence it involves higher risk. If the decision-makers are risk averse they will judge the range of possible outcomes described in the second situation to be worse than the first. If the decision-makers are risk seekers they may prefer the second situation, because of the higher outcome in the best possible situation. However, in this case, the dire downside of $400 may put them off. Whatever the case it can be seen that the evaluation of the options solely on the basis of their expected value may not always be appropriate.

Utility theory

Utility is another important aspect of risk and uncertainty. The basis of the theory is that an individual's attitude to certain risk profiles will depend on the amount of money involved. For example, most people would accept a bet on the toss of a coin, if the outcome were that they would win $6 if it came down heads and if it came down tails they would pay $4. The average person would be happy to play secure in the knowledge that they would win if the game were repeated over a long enough period; if not it would still be a good bet. But if the stakes were raised so that the win was $6,000 on a single toss coming down heads and a loss of $4,000 if it came down tails, the average person might think twice and reject the bet as being too risky. Utility theory attaches weights to the sums of money involved; these are tailor-made to the individual's attitude towards winning and losing certain sums of money.

Therefore, considering a proposed option solely on the basis of its expected value ignores the range of possible outcomes.

Further expected value examples

Situation 1

A company buys in sub-assemblies in order to manufacture a product. It is reviewing its policy of putting each sub-assembly through a detailed inspection process on delivery, and is considering not inspecting at all. Experience has shown that the quality of the sub-assembly is of acceptable standard 90 per cent of the time. It costs $10 to inspect a sub-assembly and another $10 to put right any defect found at that stage. If the sub-assembly is not inspected and is then found to be faulty at the finished goods stage the cost of rework is $40.

Required:

Advise the company whether or not they should change their policy.

Solution

Four outcomes are possible:

(i) Inspect and find no problems – cost $10.

(ii) Inspect and find problems – cost $20.

(iii) Do not inspect and no problems exist – no cost.

(iv) Do not inspect and problems do exist – cost $40.

If sub-assemblies achieve the required standard 90 per cent of the time then there is a 10 per cent chance that they will be faulty.

The expected value of the cost of each policy is as follows:

Inspect $\qquad$ $[0.9 \times \$10] + [0.1 \times \$20] = \$11$
Do not inspect $\qquad$ $[0.9 \times \$0] + [0.1 \times \$40] = \$4$

Taken over a long enough period of time, a policy of not carrying out an inspection would lead to a saving in cost of $7 per sub-assembly. On a purely quantitative analysis, therefore, this is the correct policy to adopt.

However, in the real world such a high level of failures is incompatible with a requirement for a 'quality product', and the concept of continuous improvement. It would be more useful to ask the supplier some basic questions regarding his quality management, in order to bring about a fundamental shift towards outcome (iii), rather than simply implementing a policy on the basis of such an uncritical analysis of the situation.

Situation 2

An individual is considering backing the production of a new musical in the West End. It would cost $100,000 to stage for the first month. If it is well received by the critics, it will be kept open at the end of the first month for a further 6 months, during which time further net income of $350,000 would be earned. If the critics dislike it, it will close at the end of the first month. There is a 50:50 chance of a favourable review.

Required:

Should the individual invest in the musical?

Solution

The expected value of backing the musical is:

$[0.5 \times \$250,000] - [0.5 \times \$100,000] = \$75,000$

As this provides a positive return it would be accepted on the basis of expected values as the alternative yields zero. However, the expected value can be misleading here as it is a one-off situation and the expected profit of $75,000 is not a feasible outcome. The only feasible outcomes of this project are a profit of $250,000 or a loss of $100,000.

While almost everybody would welcome a profit of $250,000, not many individuals could afford to sustain a loss of $100,000 and they would place a high utility on such a loss. Many investors would be risk averse in such a situation because they would not consider that a 50 per cent chance of making $250,000 was worth an equal 50 per cent risk of losing $100,000; the loss might bankrupt them. On the other hand, if the individual were a multi-millionaire the return of 250 per cent would be very appealing and the loss of a mere $100,000 would have a low utility attached to it.

The two exercises have only had single-point outcomes, that is conformity or otherwise with a pre-set quality standard and a successful show or a flop. It is obvious that the two outcomes of the first exercise represent the only possible alternatives and so quantification of the related pay-offs along the lines of the example appears reasonable. It is also obvious that the profit of $250,000 predicted for a successful show in the case of the second exercise is far too precise a figure. It would be more realistic to assume a range of possible successful pay-offs, which will vary, according to the number of seats sold and the price of the seats. If probabilities are attached to each estimate, the expected value of a successful outcome will take account of the range of possible outcomes, by weighting each of them by its associated probability. The range of possible outcomes might be as follows:

Profit ($)	Probability	Expected value ($)
(100,000)	0.5000	(50,000)
200,000	0.1750	35,000
250,000	0.2000	50,000
300,000	0.0075	22,500
350,000	0.0500	17,500
	1.0000	75,000

The statement of a range of possible outcomes and their associated probabilities is known as a probability distribution. Presenting the distribution to management allows two further useful inferences to be drawn:

- *The most likely successful outcome.* That is the successful outcome with the highest probability (a profit of $250,000).

- *The probability of an outcome being above or below a particular figure.* The particular figure will either be the expected value or a figure of consequence, such as zero profit, where a lesser outcome might have dire consequences. By summing the probabilities for pay-offs of $200,000 and $250,000, it can be concluded that there is a 37.5 per cent probability that profits will be $250,000 or less if the musical is successful. By summing those for $300,000 and $350,000 it can be determined that the probability of a profit of $300,000 or more in the event of success is only 12.5 per cent.

Standard deviations

In order to measure the risk associated with a particular project, it is helpful to find out how wide ranging the possible outcomes are. The conventional measure is the standard deviation. The standard deviation compares all the actual outcomes with the expected value (or mean outcome). It then calculates how far on average the outcomes deviate from the mean. It is calculated using a formula.

The basic idea is that the standard deviation is a measure of volatility: the more that actual outcomes vary from the average outcome, the more volatile the returns and therefore the more risk involved in the investment/decision.

Further details on standard deviations

The standard deviation is calculated using the following formula:

$$\sigma = \sqrt{\frac{\Sigma (x - \bar{x})^2}{n}}$$

σ = standard deviation
Σ = sum of
x = each value in the data set
$\bar{x}$ = mean of all values in the data set
n = number of value in the data set

Let's examine how standard deviations are calculated and used by considering the following illustration.

Illustration

A company is considering whether to make product X or product Y. They cannot make both products. The estimated sales demand for each product is uncertain and the following probability distribution of the NPVs for each product has been identified.

Product X

NPV ($)	Probability	Expected value ($)
3,000	0.10	300
3,500	0.20	700
4,000	0.40	1,600
4,500	0.20	900
5,000	0.10	500
	1.00	4,000

Product Y

NPV ($)	Probability	Expected value ($)
2,000	0.05	100
3,000	0.10	300
4,000	0.40	1,600
5,000	0.25	1,250
6,000	0.20	1,200
	1.00	4,450

Using an expected value approach the company's decision would be to produce product Y. However, let's consider the standard deviation calculations for each product:

Product X

NPV Deviation from expected value	Squared deviation	Probability	Weighted amount ($)
3,000 – 4,000 = –1,000	1,000,000	0.10	100,000
3,500 – 4,000 = –500	250,000	0.20	50,000
4,000 – 4,000 = 0	0	0.40	0
4,500 – 4,000 = 500	250,000	0.20	50,000
5,000 – 4,000 = 1,000	1,000,000	0.10	100,000

Sum of weighted squared deviation	300,000
Standard deviation	547.72
Expected value	4,000

Product Y

NPV Deviation from expected value	Squared deviation	Probability	Weighted amount ($)
2,000 – 4,450 = –2,450	6,002,500	0.05	300,125
3,000 – 4,450 = –1,450	2,102,500	0.10	210,250
4,000 – 4,450 = –450	202,500	0.40	81,000
5,000 – 4,450 = 550	302,500	0.25	75,625
6,000 – 4,450 = 1,550	2,402,500	0.20	480,500

Sum of weighted squared deviation	1,147,500
Standard deviation	1,071.21
Expected value	4,450

The expected net present value for each product gives us an average value based upon the probability associated with each possible profit outcome. If net present value is used for decision-making, then on that basis Product Y would be produced as it yields the highest return.

However, the net present value for each product does not indicate the range of profits that may result. By calculating the standard deviation, this allows us to identify a range of values that could occur for the profit for each product. Product Y has a higher standard deviation than Product X and is therefore more risky. There is not a significant difference in net present value for each of the products. However, Product X is less risky than Product Y and therefore the final selection will depend on the risk attitude of the company.

The coefficient of variation

If we have two probability distributions with different expected values their standard deviations are not directly comparable. We can overcome this problem by using the coefficient of variation (the standard deviation divided by the expected value) which measures the relative size of the risk.

For example, the standard deviation of the numbers 2, 7 and 9 is 2.94. The mean is 6 {(2 + 7 + 9)/3}. The standard deviation is calculated by taking the squares of the three deviations from the mean (16 + 1 + 9 = 26) and then calculating the square root of their average ($\sqrt{(26/3)}$ = 2.94). In this case, equal weighting is given to the three figures. The coefficient of variation is the standard deviation of the series divided by its mean which is 0.49 in this case (2.94/6).

The standard deviation of a range of numbers gives a measure of the associated level of uncertainty. The measure is an absolute one and in order to allow comparison of two different series where the mean values of the two differ significantly, then the coefficient of variation is used.

Expected values, standard deviations or coefficient of variations are used to summarise the outcomes from alternative courses of action. However it must be remembered that they do not provide all the relevant information to the decision maker. The probability distribution will provide the decision maker with all of the information they require. It would be appropriate to use expected values, standard deviations or coefficient of variations for decision making when there are a large number of alternatives to consider i.e. where it is not practical to consider the probability distributions for each alternative.

Advantages and disadvantages of EVs

Advantages	Disadvantages
• takes account of risk • easy decision rule • simple	• subjective • not useful for one-offs • ignores attitudes to risk • answer may not be possible

Further explanation

Advantages:

- Takes risk into account by considering the probability of each possible outcome and using this information to calculate an expected value.

- The information is reduced to a single number resulting in easier decisions.

- Calculations are relatively simple.

Disadvantages:

- The probabilities used are usually very subjective.

- The EV is merely a weighted average and therefore has little meaning for a one-off project.

- The EV gives no indication of the dispersion of possible outcomes about the EV, i.e. the risk.

- The EV may not correspond to any of the actual possible outcomes.

4 Pay off tables and decision criteria

When evaluating alternative courses of action, management's decision will often depend upon their attitude towards the risk. To consider the risk borne by each alternative it is necessary to consider ALL the different possible profits/losses that may arise. A pay off table is simply a table that illustrates all possible profits/losses.

Two way data tables

Two way data tables are used to represent inter-related data in an easy to understand manner.

For example, consider a company who are unsure about both selling price and variable cost. They believe that selling price may be either $40 or $50 depending on differing market conditions, and that variable production cost will be either $20 or $30 depending on wage negotiations currently taking place. The company has therefore got a number of potential contributions per unit that could be represented in a two way table as follows:

	Selling price	
	$40	$50
Variable production cost		
$20	$20	$30
$30	$10	$20

A user can interpret the table quickly and easy. It can be seen, for example, that if selling price is $40 and variable production costs are $30, then the contribution per unit will be $10.

Two way data tables can be expanded to calculate expected contribution from different volume levels. This will be explored further in the following illustration.

Illustration 3

Geoffrey Ramsbottom runs a kitchen that provides food for various canteens throughout a large organisation. A particular salad is sold to the canteen for $10 and costs $8 to prepare. Therefore, the contribution per salad is $2.

Based upon past demands, it is expected that, during the 250-day working year, the canteens will require the following daily quantities:

On 25 days of the year	40 salads
On 50 days of the year	50 salads
On 100 days of the year	60 salads
On 75 days	70 salads

Total 250 days

The kitchen must prepare the salad in batches of 10 meals and it has to decide how many it will supply for each day of the forthcoming year.

Constructing a pay-off table:

- If 40 salads will be required on 25 days of a 250-day year, the probability that demand = 40 salads is:

P(Demand of 40) = 25 days ÷ 250 days

P(Demand 0f 40) = 0.1

- Likewise, P(Demand of 50) = 0 .20; P(Demand of 60 = 0.4) and P (Demand of 70 = 0.30).

- Now let's look at the different values of profit or losses depending on how many salads are supplied and sold. For example, if we supply 40 salads and all are sold, our profits amount to 40 × $2 = 80.

- If however we supply 50 salads but only 40 are sold, our profits will amount to 40 × $2 – (10 unsold salads × $8 unit cost) = 0.

- Note too that there is an upper limit to the potential profit in some instances. If, for example, we supply 60 salads then the maximum we can sell is 60 salads with a profit of $2 per unit (and $120 overall). If demand reaches 70 salads we can still only sell 60 salads and therefore the maximum profit we can make from supplying 60 salads is $120.

Solution

The pay off table would appear as follows:

		Probability	Daily supply			
			40 salads	50 salads	60 salads	70 salads
Daily demand	40 salads	0.10	$80	$0	($80)	($160)
	50 salads	0.20	$80	$100	$20	($60)
	60 salads	0.40	$80	$100	$120	$40
	70 salads	0.30	$80	$100	$120	$140

This could then be used to determine the expected value from each daily supply level:

EV (of supplying 40 salads) = 0.10(80) + 0.20(80) + 0.40(80) + 0.30 (80) = 80

EV (of supplying 50 salads) = 0.10(0) + 0.20(100) + 0.40(100) + 0.30 (100) = 90

EV (of supplying 60 salads) = 0.10(–80) + 0.20(20) + 0.40(120) + 0.30 (120) = 80

EV (of supplying 70 salads) = 0.10(–160) + 0.20(–60) + 0.40(40) + 0.30 (140) = 30

On the basis of expected values, the best strategy would be to supply 50 salads and gain an EV of 90.

5 Maximax, maximin and minimax regret

When probabilities are not available, there are still tools available for incorporating uncertainty into decision making.

Maximax

The maximax rule involves selecting the alternative that maximises the maximum pay-off achievable.

This approach would be suitable for an optimist who seeks to achieve the best results if the best happens.

e.g

Illustration 4 – The 'Maximax' rule

Let's apply the maximax rule to the previous illustration on Geoffrey Ramsbottom

Geoffrey Ramsbottom's table looks as follows:

		Probability	Daily Supply			
			40 salads	50 salads	60 salads	70 salads
Daily demand	40 salads	0.10	$80	$0	($80)	($160)
	50 salads	0.20	$80	$100	$20	($60)
	60 salads	0.40	$80	$100	$120	$40
	70 salads	0.30	$80	$100	$120	$140

The manager who employs the maximax criterion is assuming that whatever action is taken, the best will happen; he/she is a risk-taker.

Here, the highest maximum possible pay-off is $140. We should therefore decide to supply 70 salads a day.

Maximin

The maximin rule involves selecting the alternative that maximises the minimum pay-off achievable.

This approach would be appropriate for a pessimist who seeks to achieve the best results if the worst happens.

Illustration 5 – The 'Maximin' rule

Geoffrey Ramsbottom's table looks as follows:

		Probability	Daily Supply			
			40 salads	50 salads	60 salads	70 salads
Daily demand	40 salads	0.10	$80	$0	($80)	($160)
	50 salads	0.20	$80	$100	$20	($60)
	60 salads	0.40	$80	$100	$120	$40
	70 salads	0.30	$80	$100	$120	$140

If we decide to supply 40 salads, the minimum pay-off is $80.

If we decide to supply 50 salads, the minimum pay-off is $0.

If we decide to supply 60 salads, the minimum pay-off is ($80).

If we decide to supply 70 salads, the minimum pay-off is ($160).

The highest minimum payoff arises from supplying 40 salads.

The minimax regret rule

The minimax regret strategy is the one that minimises the maximum regret. It is useful when probabilities for outcomes are not available or where the investor is risk averse and wants to avoid making a bad decision. Essentially, this is the technique for a 'sore loser' who does not wish to make the wrong decision.

'Regret' in this context is defined as the opportunity loss through having made the wrong decision.

Illustration 6 – The 'Minimax Regret' rule

Following up from the pay-off table example, Geoffrey Ramsbottom's table looks as follows:

		Probability	Daily Supply			
			40 salads	50 salads	60 salads	70 salads
Daily demand	40 salads	0.10	$80	$0	($80)	($160)
	50 salads	0.20	$80	$100	$20	($60)
	60 salads	0.40	$80	$100	$120	$40
	70 salads	0.30	$80	$100	$120	$140

If the minimax regret rule is applied to decide how many salads should be made each day, we need to calculate the 'regrets'. This means we need to find the biggest pay-off for each demand row, then subtract all other numbers in this row from the largest number.

For example, if the demand is 40 salads, we will make a maximum profit of $80 if they all sell. If we had decided to supply 50 salads, we would achieve a nil profit. The difference, or 'regret' between that nil profit and the maximum of $80 achievable for that row is $80.

Regrets can be tabulated as follows:

		Daily Supply			
		40 salads	50 salads	60 salads	70 salads
Daily demand	40 salads	$0	$80	$160	$240
	50 salads	$20	$0	$80	$160
	60 salads	$40	$20	$0	$80
	70 salads	$60	$40	$20	$0

Conclusion

If we decide to supply 40 salads, the maximum regret is $60. If we decide to supply 50 salads, the maximum regret is $80. For 60 salads, the maximum regret is $160, and $240 for 70 salads. A manager employing the minimax regret criterion would want to minimise that maximum regret, and therefore supply 40 salads only.

Perfect and imperfect information

In many questions the decision makers receive a forecast of a future outcome (for example a market research group may predict the forthcoming demand for a product). This forecast may turn out to be correct or incorrect. The question often requires the candidate to calculate the value of the forecast.

Perfect information The forecast of the future outcome is always a correct prediction. If a firm can obtain a 100% accurate prediction they will always be able to undertake the most beneficial course of action for that prediction.

Imperfect information The forecast is usually correct, but can be incorrect. Imperfect information is not as valuable as perfect information. Imperfect information may be examined in conjunction with Decision Trees (see later in this chapter).

The value of information (either perfect or imperfect) may be calculated as follows:

Expected profit (outcome) WITH the information

minus

Expected profit (outcome) WITHOUT the information

Illustration 7 – The value of information

A new ordering system is being considered, whereby customers must order their salad online the day before. With this new system Mr Ramsbottom will know for certain the daily demand 24 hours in advance. He can adjust production levels on a daily basis. How much is this new system worth to Mr Ramsbottom?

Supply = demand	X Pay off	P Probability	px
40	$80	0.1	8
50	$100	0.2	20
60	$120	0.4	48
70	$140	0.3	42
			118

E.V. with perfect information = $118

E.V. without perfect information (from the original EV calculation) = $90

Value of perfect information $28 per day

6 Decision trees and multi-stage decision problems

A decision tree is a diagrammatic representation of a decision problem, where all possible courses of action are represented, and every possible outcome of each course of action is shown. Decision trees should be used where a problem involves a series of decisions being made and several outcomes arise during the decision-making process. In some instances it may involve the use of joint probabilities – where the outcome of one event depends of the outcome of a preceding event.

Joint probabilities

So far only a very small number of alternatives have been considered in the examples. In practice a greater number of alternative courses of action may exist, uncertainty may be associated with more than one variable and the values of variables may be interdependent, giving rise to many different outcomes.

The following exercise looks at the expected value of a manufacturing decision, where there are three alternative sales volumes, two alternative contributions, and three alternative levels of fixed cost. The number of possible outcomes will be 3 × 2 × 3 = 18.

Example

A company is assessing the desirability of producing a souvenir to celebrate a royal jubilee. The marketing life of the souvenir will be 6 months only. Uncertainty surrounds the likely sales volume and contribution, as well as the fixed costs of the venture. Estimated outcomes and probabilities are:

Units sold	Probability	Cont'n per unit $	Probability	Fixed cost $	Probability
100,000	0.3	7	0.5	400,000	0.2
80,000	0.6	5	0.5	450,000	0.5
60,000	0.1			500,000	0.3
	———		———		———
	1.0		1.0		1.0
	———		———		———

The next table shows the expected value of the net contribution to be $49,000. Totalling up the joint probabilities for each set of sales shows the project has a 56.5 per cent chance of making a net contribution, a 33 per cent chance of making a loss, and a 10.5 per cent chance of making neither a net contribution nor a loss. (For example, to calculate the probability of making a loss: we can see from the next table that a loss will arise in 7 situations. So if we add the overall probability of this happening we add up the joint probabilities associated with each of these outcomes – 0.150 + 0.090 + 0.025 + 0.015 + 0.010 + 0.025 + 0.015 = 0.33).

Units sold	Cont'n per unit $	Total Cont'n $ a	Fixed Cost $ b	Probability	Joint Prob. c	EV of net cont. $ (a-b) x c
100,000	7	700,000	400,000	0.3×0.5×0.2=	0.030	9,000
	7	700,000	450,000	0.3×0.5×0.5=	0.075	18,750
	7	700,000	500,000	0.3×0.5×0.3=	0.045	9,000
	5	500,000	400,000	0.3×0.5×0.2=	0.030	3,000
	5	500,000	450,000	0.3×0.5×0.5=	0.075	3,750
	5	500,000	500,000	0.3×0.5×0.3=	0.045	0
80,000	7	560,000	400,000	0.6×0.5×0.2=	0.060	9,600
	7	560,000	450,000	0.6×0.5×0.5=	0.150	16,500
	7	560,000	500,000	0.6×0.5×0.3=	0.090	5,400
	5	400,000	400,000	0.6×0.5×0.2=	0.060	0
	5	400,000	450,000	0.6×0.5×0.5=	0.150	−7,500
	5	400,000	500,000	0.6×0.5×0.3=	0.090	−9,000
60,000	7	420,000	400,000	0.1×0.5×0.2=	0.010	200
	7	420,000	450,000	0.1×0.5×0.5=	0.025	−750
	7	420,000	500,000	0.1×0.5×0.3=	0.015	−1,200
	5	300,000	400,000	0.1×0.5×0.2=	0.010	−1,000
	5	300,000	450,000	0.1×0.5×0.5=	0.025	−3,750
	5	300,000	500,000	0.1×0.5×0.3=	0.015	−3,000
			1.0		1.0	49,000

Decisions like this can be quite hard to visualise and it may be more useful to use a decision tree to express the situation.

Three-step method

Step 1: Draw the tree from left to right showing appropriate decisions and events/outcomes.

Symbols to use:

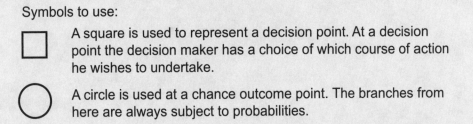

A square is used to represent a decision point. At a decision point the decision maker has a choice of which course of action he wishes to undertake.

A circle is used at a chance outcome point. The branches from here are always subject to probabilities.

Label the tree and relevant cash inflows/outflows (discounted to present values if necessary) and probabilities associated with outcomes.

Step 2: Evaluate the tree from right to left carrying out these two actions:

Calculate an EV at each outcome point.

Choose the best option at each decision point.

Step 3: Recommend a course of action to management.

Example on Decision Trees

An oil company has recently acquired rights in a certain area to conduct surveys and geological test drillings that may lead to extracting oil where it is found in commercially exploitable quantities.

The area is already considered to have good potential for finding oil in commercial quantities. At the outset the company has the choice to conduct further geological tests or to carry out a drilling programme immediately. On the known conditions, the company estimates that there is a 70% chance of further tests indicating that a significant amount of oil is present.

Whether the tests show the possibility of oil or not, or even if no tests are undertaken at all, the company could still pursue its drilling programme or alternatively consider selling its rights to drill in the area.

Thereafter, however, if it carries out the drilling programme, the likelihood of final success or failure in the search for oil is considered dependent on the foregoing stages. Thus:

(i) If the tests indicated that oil was present, the expectation of success in drilling is given as 80%.

(ii) If the tests indicated that there was insufficient oil present, then the expectation of success in drilling is given as 20%.

(iii) If no tests have been carried out at all, the expectation of finding commercially viable quantities of oil is given as 55%.

Costs and revenues have been estimated for all possible outcomes and the net present value of each is given below:

Outcome	Net present value
	$ millions
Geological testing	(10)
Drilling cost	(50)
Success in finding oil	150
Sale of exploitation rights:	
Tests indicate oil is present	65
Tests indicate 'no oil'	15
Without geological tests	40

Required:

(a) Prepare a decision tree diagram to represent the above information.

(8 marks)

(b) For the management of the company, calculate its best course of action.

(7 marks)

(c) Explain the value of decision trees in providing management with guidance for decision making. Illustrate examples of any situations where you consider their use would be of benefit.

(5 marks)

(Total: 20 marks)

More on decision trees

Decision trees force the decision maker to consider the logical sequence of events. A complex problem is broken down into smaller, easier-to-handle sections. The financial outcomes and probabilities are shown separately, and the decision tree is 'rolled back' by calculating expected values and making decisions. In the examination ensure that only relevant costs and revenues are considered, and that all cash is expressed in present value terms.

A number of other factors should be taken into account when considering decision tree-type problems:

- *Time value of money.* The time value of money should be incorporated in the calculations if the project is to last for more than one year. The time value of money is discussed in detail later in this text.

- *Assumes risk neutrality.* As mentioned under probability, some decision-makers do not choose options which give the greatest expected value, because they are either risk seekers or risk averse.

- *Sensitivity analysis.* The analysis depends very much on the values of the probabilities in the tree. The values are usually the subjective estimates of the decision-makers, and, no matter how experienced the people involved are, the values must be open to question. Sensitivity analysis can be used to consider 'break-even' positions for each variable – i.e. the value for a variable (such as probability) at which the decision would change. Sensitivity analysis is covered later in this chapter.

- *Oversimplification.* In order to make the tree manageable, the situation has often to be greatly simplified. This makes it appear far more discrete than it really is. In practice, it is much more likely that the outcomes would form a near continuous range of inflows and outflows. This cannot be shown on a decision tree, and so any decision tree usually represents a simplified situation.

e.g

Illustration 8

A manager is considering a make v buy decision based on the following estimates:

	If made in-house	If buy in and re-badge
	$	$
Variable production costs	10	2
External purchase costs	——	6
Ultimate selling price	15	14

Identify the sensitivity of the decision to the external purchase price.

Step 1: What is the original decision?

Comparing contribution figures, the product should be bought in and re-badged:

	If made in-house	If buy in and re-badge
	$	$
Contribution	5	6

Step 2: Calculate the sensitivity (to the external purchase price)

For indifference, the contribution from outsourcing needs to fall to $5 per unit. Thus the external purchase price only needs to increase by $1 per unit (or $1/$6 = 17%).

If the external purchase price rose by more than 17% the original decision would be reversed.

7 Conditional probabilities – the Bayes theorem

Introduction

Conditional probability is the probability of an event whose calculation is based on the knowledge that some other event has occurred.

The symbol P(A|B) is read as 'the probability of A occurring given that B has already occurred', and we can say that:

$$P (A \text{ and } B) = P (A|B) \times P (B)$$

This formula can be rewritten in a variety of ways, depending on what you are trying to find out.

$$P(A \text{ and } B) = P(B|A) \times P(A) \qquad P(A|B) \times P(B) = P(B|A) \times P(A)$$

$$P(A|B) = \frac{P(A \text{ and } B)}{P(B)}$$

$$P(B|A) = \frac{P(B \text{ and } A)}{P(A)}$$

However, this can get a bit mind-boggling. An easier way to deal with this sort of problem is to use what is known as a **contingency table.**

Contingency tables

Contingency tables are created by taking the given probabilities, multiplying by some convenient number, typically 100 or 1,000 (to make the numbers easy to work with), then drawing a table to show the various combinations of factors which may exist.

Contingency tables

40% of the output of a factory is produced in workshop A and 60% in workshop B.

Fourteen out of every 1,000 components from A are defective and six out of every 1,000 components from B are defective.

After the outputs from A and B have been thoroughly mixed, a component drawn at random is found to be defective. What is the probability that it came from workshop B?

Solution

The problem will be solved by drawing a contingency table, showing defective and non-defective components and output from workshops A and B.

Consider 10,000 components. We know that of these 4,000 (40%) will be from workshop A and 6,000 (60%) from workshop B.

	Workshop A	Workshop B	Total
Defective			
Non-defective			
Total	4,000	6,000	10,000

Of the 4,000 from workshop A, 14/1,000 – that is 56 – will be defective, and from workshop B 6/1,000 – that is 36 – will be defective. Hence, the table can be completed so far:

	Workshop A	Workshop B	Total
Defective	56	36	
Non-defective			
	———	———	———
Total	4,000	6,000	10,000
	———	———	———

All the remaining figures can be completed as balancing figures, and the final contingency table looks like this:

	Workshop A	Workshop B	Total
Defective	56	36	92
Non-defective	3,944	5,964	9,908
	———	———	———
Total	4,000	6,000	10,000
	———	———	———

The question was: what is the probability that a component came from workshop B, given that it is defective?

Given that it is defective, we know that we are dealing with one of the 92 components in the top row of the table. We can see that of these 92 components, 36 came from workshop B.

Hence

P(came from workshop B given that it is defective) = $\dfrac{36}{92}$

That is 0.39, or 39%.

There are other ways of solving such problems, but most students will find the contingency table method easier, and quicker.

Conditional probabilities

30% of the new cars of a particular model are supplied from a factory X, the other 70% from factory Y. 10% of factory X's production has a major fault, 12% of factory Y's production has such a fault.

A purchaser's new car has a major fault: what is the probability that it was made at factory Y?

8 Practice questions

Example 1 – Calculating an expected value

A company has identified four possible outcomes from a new marketing strategy as follows:

Outcome	Profit ($)	Probability
A	100,000	0.10
B	70,000	0.40
C	50,000	0.30
D	−20,000	0.20

Calculate the expected outcome of this strategy.

Example 2

- Hofgarten Newsagents stocks a weekly magazine which advertises local second-hand goods. Marie, the owner, can:
    - buy the magazines for 15c each
    - sell them at the retail price of 25c

- At the end of each week unsold magazines are obsolete and have no value.

- Marie estimates a probability distribution for weekly demand which looks like this:

Weekly demand in units	Probability
10	0.20
15	0.55
20	0.25
	————
	1.00
	————

Required:

(i) Calculate the expected value of demand?

(ii) If Marie is to order a fixed quantity of magazines per week, calculate how many should that be. Assume no seasonal variations in demand.

Example 3

A company is choosing which of three new products to make (A, B or C) and has calculated likely pay-offs under three possible scenarios (I, II or III), giving the following pay-off table.

Profit (loss)	Product chosen		
Scenario	A	B	C
I	20	80	10
II	40	70	100
III	50	(10)	40

Required:

Using maximax, which product would be chosen?

Example 3 continued

Required:

Using the information from Example 3, apply the minimax regret rule to decide which product should be made.

Example 3 continued

Required:

Using the information from Example 3, apply the maximin rule to decide which product should be made.

Example 3 continued

Following on from the data provided in Example 3, the company has made an estimate of the probability of each scenario occurring as follows:

Scenario	Probability
I	20%
II	50%
III	30%

However, an external consultant has some information about each likely scenario and can say with certainty which scenario will arise.

Calculate the value of the external consultants information.

Example 4 – Sensitivity analysis

A manager has identified the following two possible outcomes for a process

Outcome	Probability	Financial implications ($000s)
Poor	0.4	Loss of 20
Good	0.6	Profit of 40

The expected value has been calculated as EV = (0.4 × –20) + (0.6 × 40) = +16. This would suggest that the opportunity should be accepted.

Required:

(a) Suppose the likely loss if results are poor has been underestimated. What level of loss would change the decision? In effect we want a break-even estimate.

(b) Suppose the probability of a loss has been underestimated. What is the break-even probability?

Test your understanding 1

Identify the correct description of imperfect information:

A   costs more to collect than its value to the business

B   is available only after preliminary decisions on a business venture have been taken

C   does not take into account all factors affecting a business

D   may contain inaccurate predictions

(2 marks)

Test your understanding 2

A company is considering investing in one of the following projects.

Project	Expected value $000	Standard deviation $000
A	850	500
B	1,200	480
C	150	200
D	660	640

It wishes to select the project with the lowest risk factor (coefficient of variation). Identify which project should it select:

A   Project A

B   Project B

C   Project C

D   Project D

(2 marks)

Test your understanding 3

Three investors are considering the same investments. The net returns from the investments depend on the state of the economy and are illustrated as follows:

State of the economy	Returns from investment			Probability of economic state
	A $	B $	C $	
Good	6,000	14,000	3,000	0.1
Fair	5,000	3,000	5,000	0.4
Poor	4,000	500	8,000	0.5

Details on the attitudes to risk of the three investors is as follows:

- Micah is risk neutral

- Zhang is a risk seeker

- Jill is risk averse and typically follows a minimax regret strategy with her investments

Calculate which investment would be best suited to each investor's risk attitude.

(5 marks)

Test your understanding 4 – CHARITY ORGANISATION

For the past 20 years a charity organisation has held an annual dinner and dance with the primary intention of raising funds.

This year there is concern that an economic recession may adversely affect both the number of people attending the function and the advertising space that will be sold in the programme published for the occasion.

Based on past experience and current prices and quotations, it is expected that the following costs and revenues will apply for the function:

			$
Cost:	Dinner and dance:	Hire of premises	700
		Band and entertainers	2,800
		Raffle prizes	800
		Photographer	200
		Food at $12 per person (with a guarantee of 400 persons minimum)	
	Programme:	A fixed cost of $2,000 plus $5 per page	
Revenues:	Dinner and dance:	Price of tickets	$20 per person
		Average revenue from:	
		Raffle	$5 per person
		Photographs	$1 per person
	Programme:	Average revenue from advertising	$70 per page

A sub-committee, formed to examine more closely the likely outcome of the function, discovered the following from previous records and accounts:

Number of tickets sold	Number of past occasions
250 to 349	4
350 to 449	6
450 to 549	8
550 to 649	2

Number of programme pages sold	Number of past occasions
24	4
32	8
40	6
48	2

Required:

Calculate the expected value of the profit to be earned from the dinner and dance this year.

(10 marks)

Test your understanding 5 – RS GROUP

The RS Group owns a large store in Ludborough. The store is old-fashioned and profits are declining. Management is considering what to do – there appear to be three possibilities:

(1) Shut down and sell the site for $15m.

(2) Continue as before with profits declining.

(3) Upgrade the store.

The Group has had problems in the past and experience suggests that when stores are upgraded, 60% achieve good results and 40% poor results.

Because of the doubts, management is considering whether to contact a leading market research company to carry out consumer research in Ludborough for $1m. It has been fortunate in obtaining details of the track record of the research company, as follows:

		Actual outcome	
		Good	Poor
Attitude predicted by research	Positive	0.85 *	0.10
	Negative	0.15	0.90

* This means that when the actual results were good the research had predicted this 85% of the time.

If the research indicates a positive attitude, management will consider deluxe upgrading which will generate more profit but will cost $12m, as compared with standard upgrading costing $6m.

If the research indicates a negative attitude, then management will consider standard upgrading compared with shutting down and selling the site.

The time scale for the analysis is 10 years and the following estimates of returns have been made:

With Deluxe upgrading:	Good results	$40m total present value
	Poor results	$20m total present value
With Standard upgrading:	Good results	$25m total present value
	Poor results	$10m total present value

If operations continue as before, returns over the next 10 years will be $13.03m in present value terms.

Required:

(a) prepare a decision tree to represent the above information

(19 marks)

Note: No discounting is necessary for this question as the values are already expressed in present value terms.

(b) calculate what decisions should be taken

(3 marks)

(c) explain the basis of your analysis.

(3 marks)
(Total: 25 marks)

Test your understanding 6

A company can make either of two new products, X and Y, but not both. The profitability of each product depends on the state of the market, as follows:

Market state	Profit from product		Probability of market state
	X $	Y $	
Good	20,000	17,000	0.2
Fair	15,000	16,000	0.5
Poor	6,000	7,000	0.3

Calculate the expected value of perfect information as to the state of the market

A $0

B $600

C $800

D $1,000

(2 marks)

Test your understanding 7

The Venus Department Store operates a customer loan facility. If one of its new customers requests a loan then Venus either refuses it, gives a high loan limit, or gives a low loan limit. From a number of years past experience the probability that a new customer makes a full repayment of a loan is known to be 0.95, whilst the probability of non-repayment is 0.05 (these probabilities being independent of the size of loan limit). The average profit in $, per customer made by Venus is given by the following table.

	Loan limit	
	High	Low
Full-repayment	50	20
Non-repayment	−200	−30

Required:

(a) In the past the company has used a selection criterion that is totally arbitrary (i.e. it is not influenced by the customer's ability to repay).

Prepare a decision tree to represent the information. Calculate the expected value and explain what the management of Venus should do if a new customer requests a loan?

(6 marks)

(b) Venus can apply to an agency to evaluate the credit-rating of a customer. This agency would provide a rating for the customer as either a good risk or as a bad risk, this credit-rating being independent of the size of the loan being considered. Analysis of the last 1,000 customer ratings by this agency revealed the following information.

Agency	Type of customer		
Credit rating	**Full-repayment**	**Non-repayment**	**Total**
Good risk	790	10	800
Bad risk	160	40	200
Total	950	50	1,000

Determine the value of this credit rating to Venus

(9 marks)

(c) The Venus management believe that this first agency is not very good at selecting full-payers and non-payers. It considers contacting a second agency which guarantees perfect information concerning the credit rating of the customers.

Explain the meaning of the term 'perfect information' in the context of this question.

Calculate the value of this perfect information.

(5 marks)

(Total: 20 marks)

Data Set Question: Two-stage process

A product is manufactured in a two-stage process, the stages being designated A and B.

Each process has two machines, named A1 and A2 for process A, and B1 and B2 for process B.

Each unit of finished product must pass through either one of the two machines in process A, and then through either one of the two machines in process B. (50% go through A1 and 50% through A2. Similarly for B1 and B2.)

How many different ways may a product be manufactured?

The probabilities of a defective product from each machine are as follows: 2% for A1, 6% for A2, 4% for B1, 2% for B2. The defectives are thrown out as they occur.

What is the probability of a perfect item being produced?

The total production is 10,000 items started every year. The loss on each defective item is $10, and the profit on each item is $80.

The expected net profit is $

Integration style question – SITERAZE LTD

PRE-SEEN MATERIAL

Siteraze Ltd is a company which engages in site clearance and site preparation work. Information concerning its operations is as follows:

(a) It is company policy to hire all plant and machinery required for the implementation of all orders obtained, rather than to purchase its own plant and machinery.

(b) Siteraze Ltd will enter into an advance hire agreement contract for the coming year at one of three levels – high, medium or low, which correspond to the requirements of a high, medium or low level of orders obtained.

(c) The level of orders obtained will not be known when the advance hire agreement contract is entered into. A set of probabilities have been estimated by management as to the likelihood of the orders being at high, medium or low level.

(d) Where the advance hire agreement entered into is lower than that required for the level of orders actually obtained, a premium rate must be paid to obtain additional plant and machinery required.

(e) No refund is obtainable where the advance hire agreement for plant and machinery is at a level in excess of that required to satisfy the site clearance and preparation orders actually obtained.

A summary of the information relating to the above points is as follows:

			Plant and machinery hire costs	
Level of orders	Revenue $000	Probability	Advance hire $000	Conversion premium $000
High	15,000	0.25	2,300	
Medium	8,500	0.45	1,500	
Low	4,000	0.30	1,000	
Low to medium				850
Medium to high				1,300
Low to high				2,150
Variable cost (as a percentage of turnover)			70%	

You have just received the following email from the company's Finance Director:

From: Pedro Rodriguez
Sent: 03 June, 10.23 a.m.
To: Senior Management Accountant

Subject: Risk

How much money are we going to make this year? I would like you to prepare a summary which shows the forecast net margin earned by Siteraze Ltd for the coming year for each possible outcome _ I intend to present your numbers to the Board. On the basis of maximising expected value, could you tell me whether the advance contract for the hire of plant and machinery should be at the low, medium or high level?

Also, as you know, we have different risk profiles represented on the Board and I would appreciate it if you would explain how the risk preferences of the management members responsible for the choice of advance plant and machinery hire contract may alter the decision reached above.

After submitting your numbers, you then get a second email:

> **From:** Pedro Rodriguez
> **Sent:** 03 June, 10.23 a.m.
> **To:** Senior Management Accountant
>
> Subject: The value of perfect information
>
> Many thanks for all your work and figures. I am considering employing a market research consultant I have worked with in the past. He will be able to say with certainty in advance of the placing of the plant and machinery hire contract, which level of site clearance and preparation orders will be obtained. On the basis of expected value, what maximum sum should Siteraze Ltd be willing to pay the consultant for this information?

Task:

Reply to both emails from Pedro Rodriguez.

Test your understanding answers

Example on Decision Trees

(a) and (b)

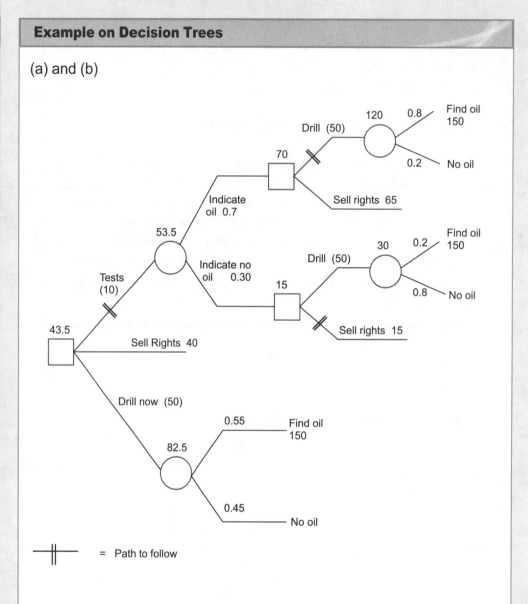

= Path to follow

Advice:

The company should undertake geological tests. If the tests indicate that oil is present then a drilling programme should be carried out. However, if the tests indicate that there is no oil then the company should sell the drilling rights.

This strategy will maximise expected returns at $43.5m.

(c) The main value of a decision tree is that it maps out clearly all the decisions and uncertain events and exactly how they are interrelated. They are especially beneficial where the outcome of one decision affects another decision. For example in the above, the probability of eventual success changes depending on the test outcomes. The analysis is made clearer by annotating the tree with probabilities, cash flows, and expected values so that the optimum decisions (based on expected values) can be clearly seen.

However, drawing a tree diagram is only one way of undertaking a decision. It is based on the concept of expected value and as such suffers from the limitations of this technique. For example, in this example, if the test drilling proves positive, the tree indicated the company should drill, as opposed to selling the rights. But if it does there is a 20% chance of it losing $50 million. A risk-averse company may well decide to accept the safer option and sell the rights and settle for $65 million.

Conditional probabilities

Using 1,000 as a suitable multiple, i.e. considering 1,000 cars are manufactured, the contingency table is:

| | *Made at factory.....:* | | |
	Factory X	Factory Y	Total
Has major fault	30	84	114
No major fault	270	616	886
Total	300	700	1,000

The question was : what is the probability that a car came from factory Y, given that it has a major fault?

Given that a major fault exists, we know that we are dealing with one of the 114 cars in the top row of the table. We can see that of these 114 cars, 84 came from Factory Y.

Hence P(made at factory Y|major fault exists) = 84/114

= 0.737

Example 1 – Calculating an expected value

Expected value calculation

Outcome	Profit ($)	Probability	Profit x Probability ($)
A	100,000	0.10	10,000
B	70,000	0.40	28,000
C	50,000	0.30	15,000
D	−20,000	0.20	−4,000
Expected value			49,000

Expected profit is $49,000.

Example 2

(i) EV of demand = $(10 × 0.20) + (15 × 0.55) + (20 × 0.25) = 15.25$ units per week.

(ii) The first step is to set up a decision matrix of possible strategies (numbers bought) and possible demand, as follows:

Outcome (number demanded)	Strategy (number bought)		
	10	15	20
10			
15			
20			

The 'pay-off' from each combination of action and outcome is then computed:

No sale: cost of 15c per magazine.

Sale: profit of 25c − 15c = 10c per magazine

Pay-offs are shown for each combination of strategy and outcome.

Probability	Outcome (number demanded)	Decision (number bought)		
		10	15	20
0.20	10	100	25	(50)
0.55	15	100	150	75
0.25	20	100	150	200
___	___	___	___	___
1.00	EV	100c	125c	81.25c
___	___	___	___	___

Conclusion: The strategy which gives the highest expected value is to stock 15 magazines each week.

Workings

(i) If 10 magazines are bought, then 10 are sold no matter how many are demanded and the payoff is always 10 × 10c = 100c.

(ii) If 15 magazines are bought and 10 are demanded, then 10 are sold at a profit of 10 × 10c = 100c, and 5 are scrapped at a loss of 5 × 15c = 75c, making a net profit of 25c.

(iii) The other contributions are similarly calculated.

Example 3

Using maximax, an optimist would consider the best possible outcome for each product and pick the product with the greatest potential.

Here C would be chosen with a maximum possible gain of 100.

Example 3 continued

In the pay-off matrix above, if the market state had been scenario I:

The correct decision would have been:	B (net income $80)
If A had been chosen instead:	The company would have been out of pocket by $60 (i.e. 80 – 20)
If C had been chosen:	It would have been out of pocket by $70 (i.e. 80 – 10)

- The opportunity loss associated with each product is: A = $60, B = $0, C = $70.

Scenario II and III can be considered in the same way and the results can be summarised in a regret table.

The completed opportunity loss ('regret') table is thus as follows.

		Decision		
State		**A**	**B**	**C**
I		60	0	70
II		60	30	0
III		0	60	10
Maximum regret		60	60	70

The maximum regret value for:

A = $60

B = $60

C = $70

The minimum value of these is $60, hence the minimax regret strategy would be either A or B.

B would probably be adopted because its second-highest regret outcome ($30) is lower than the second-highest for A ($60).

Example 3 continued

- Using maximin, a pessimist would consider the poorest possible outcome for each product and would ensure that the maximum pay-off is achieved if the worst result were to happen.

- Therefore, product A would be chosen resulting in a minimum pay-off of 20 compared to a minimum pay-off of (10) for product B and 10 for product C.

Example 3 continued

Firstly, we have to calculate the expected value without the information.

EV (A) = 0.2(20) + 0.5(40) + 0.3(50) = 39

EV (B) = 0.2(80) + 0.5(70) + 0.3(–10) = 48

EV (C) = 0.2(10) + 0.5(100) + 0.3(40) = 64

So the company would choose project C, with an expected pay-off of 64.

If the company had perfect information it would act as follows:

Scenario indicated by perfect information	Company's decision*	Pay-off
I	Invest in product B	80
II	Invest in product C	100
III	Invest in product A	50

* this will be based on the highest expected pay-off in that scenario. For example, if scenario I is predicted the company will face a pay-off of 20 from product A, 80 from product B, and 10 from product C. It will therefore decide to invest in product B.

The expected value from these decisions would be:

EV (C) = 0.2(80) + 0.5(100) + 0.3(50) = 81

This is 17 higher than the expected value (64) when the company had no information. Therefore the information has a value of 17.

Example 4 – Sensitivity analysis

(a) The EV would have to decrease by $16,000 before the original decision is reversed, i.e. this is the break-even point.

    – Let the loss be L

       Currently, EV = $(0.4 \times L) + (0.6 \times 40)$

       If EV falls to zero:

       EV of 0 = $(0.4 \times L) + (0.6 \times 40)$

       $0 = 0.4L + 24$

       $-24 = 0.4L$

       $-24 / 0.4 = L$

       $L = -60$

    – The loss would have to increase from $20,000 to $60,000 before the decision is reversed. This is a 200% increase in the loss.

(b) The EV would have to decrease by $16,000 before the original decision is reversed, i.e. this is the break-even point.

    – Let the probability of a loss be P and the probability of a profit be $1 - P$.

       Currently, EV = $(P \times -20) + [(1-p) \times 40)]$

       If EV falls to zero:

       EV of 0 = $(P \times -20) + [(1-p) \times 40)]$

       $0 = -20P + 40 - 40P$

       $60P = 40$

       $P = 40/60$

       $P = 0.67$

    – The probability of a loss would have to increase to 0.67 from 0.4 before the decision is reversed.

Test your understanding 1

D

Perfect information is certain to be right about the future. Imperfect information may predict wrongly.

Test your understanding 2

B

Project	Expected value $000	Standard deviation $000	Coefficient of variation
A	850	500	0.59
B	1,200	480	0.40
C	150	200	1.33
D	660	640	0.97

Test your understanding 3

Micah

As a risk neutral investor Micah will base his decision on the expected value of each investment. These are calculated as follows:

Investment A = ($6,000 × 0.1) + ($5,000 × 0.4) + ($4,000 × 0.5) = $4,600

Investment B = ($14,000 × 0.1) + ($3,000 × 0.4) + ($500 × 0.5) = $2,850

Investment C = ($3,000 × 0.1) + ($5,000 × 0.4) + ($8,000 × 0.5) = $6,300

Micah will therefore choose to invest in Investment C as it has the highest overall expected value.

Zhang

As a risk seeker Zhang will ignore the expected values and probabilities, and she will focus solely on the payouts. She will apply the maximax criteria and consider where the highest payout might arise. The highest possible return is the $14,000 that arises in a good market state for Investment B. Zhang will therefore choose to invest in Investment B.

Jill

To apply the minimax regret criteria Jill will have to create a regret table as follows:

State of the economy	Regret		
	A $	B $	C $
Good	8,000	0	11,000
Fair	0	2,000	0
Poor	4,000	7,500	0
Maximum regret	8,000	7,500	11,000

Jill will therefore choose to invest in Investment B as it has the lowest maximum regret ($7,500) of the three investments.

Test your understanding 4 – CHARITY ORGANISATION

Revenue per person = $20 + $5 + $1

Number of tickets	Probability	Revenue	Food cost	Net benefit	Prob. × benefit
		$	$	$	$
300	0.2	7,800	(4,800)	3,000	600
400	0.3	10,400	(4,800)	5,600	1,680
500	0.4	13,000	(6,000)	7,000	2,800
600	0.1	15,600	(7,200)	8,400	840
	1.0			**Expected value = 5,920**	

Number of pages	Probability	Contribution $65 per page	Prob. × contribution
		$	$
24	0.2	1,560	312
32	0.4	2,080	832
40	0.3	2,600	780
48	0.1	3,120	312
	1.0		Expected value = 2,236

Total contribution	$5,920 + $2,236	=	$8,156
Less fixed costs	$2,000 + $700 + $2,800 + $800 + $200	=	($6,500)
Expected profit			$1,656

Test your understanding 5 – RS GROUP

(a)

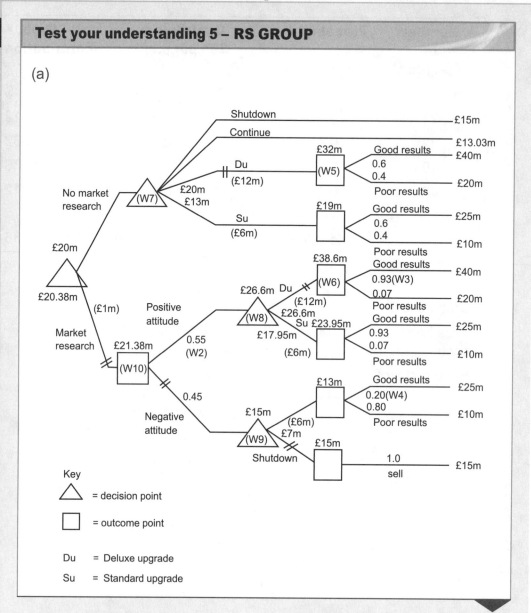

Key

△ = decision point

□ = outcome point

Du = Deluxe upgrade

Su = Standard upgrade

Workings 2, 3 and 4

A probability tree is the best way of understanding the dependent probabilities given in the question.

The probability of the prediction depends upon whether the results are good or poor.

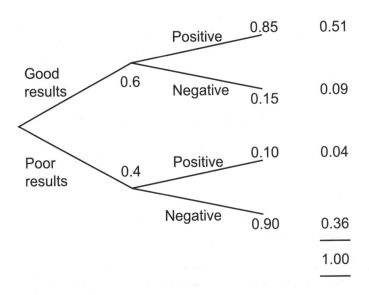

Joint probabilities

(W2)   p(positive attitude) = 0.51 + .04 = 0.55

(W3)   p(good results/positive attitude) =

$$\frac{p\ (good\ results\ and\ positive\ attitude)}{p\ (positive\ attitude)}$$

$$= \frac{0.51}{0.55} = 0.93$$

(W4)   p(good results/negative attitude) = $\frac{p\ (good\ results\ and\ negative\ attitude)}{p\ (negative\ attitude)}$

$$= \frac{0.09}{0.45} = 0.20$$

(W5)   Expected profit = $40m × 0.6 + $20m × 0.4 = $32m

(W6)   Expected profit = $40m × 0.93 + $20m × 0.07 = $38.6m

(W7) The deluxe upgrade provides an expected profit of ($32m – $12m) $20m

(W8) Deluxe upgrade profit = $38.6m – $12m = $26.6m

Standard upgrade profit = $23.95 – $6m = $17.95m

∴ Deluxe upgrade is recommended.

(W9) Standard upgrade profit = $7m

Shutdown and sell site = $15m

∴ Shutdown and sell is recommended

(W10) Expected profit = $26.6m × 0.55 + $15m × 0.45 = $21.38m

(b) In order to maximise expected profit:

Undertake the market research.

If the attitude is positive upgrade deluxe.

If the attitude is negative shutdown and sell the site.

(c) Comment
   (i)   This assumes that all estimates are correct; sensitivity analysis could be carried out on each estimate.

   (ii) It is assumed that the RS Group are risk neutral since expected values have been used – although the highest ENPV has a lower risk than the next highest.

   (iii) Ten years is a long time period over which to predict profits – a reasonable period for the life of the store but this makes estimation difficult.

   (iv) Comments on the courses of action open to the RS Group have been made in (a).

Test your understanding 6

B

Without information, the expected profits are:

Product X: $20,000 × 0.2 + $15,000 × 0.5 + $6,000 × 0.3   = $13,300
Product Y: $17,000 × 0.2 + $16,000 × 0.5 + $7,000 × 0.3   = $13,500

So without information, product Y would be selected.

With perfect information, product X would be selected if the market was good, and product Y in the other two cases. The expected value would then be:

$20,000 × 0.2 + $16,000 × 0.5 + $7,000 × 0.3   = $14,100

The expected value of perfect information is therefore
$14,100 – $13,500 = $600

Test your understanding 7

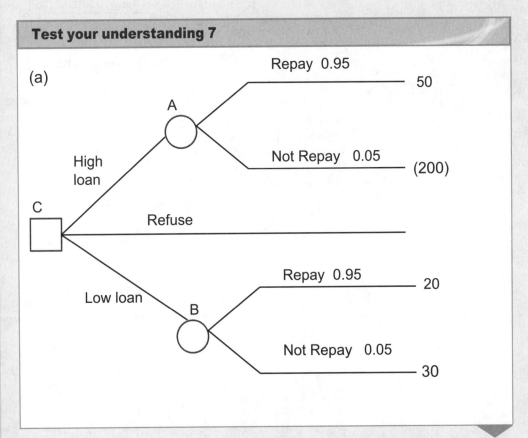

At points A and B calculate Expected Values

At A   EV = (0.95 × 50) + (0.05 × (200))   = **37.5**

At B   EV = (0.95 × 20) + (0.05 × (30))   = **17.5**

At C   compare the EVs of $37.5 and $17.5.

Recommendation; if a customer requests a loan give him/her a high loan limit.

(b)

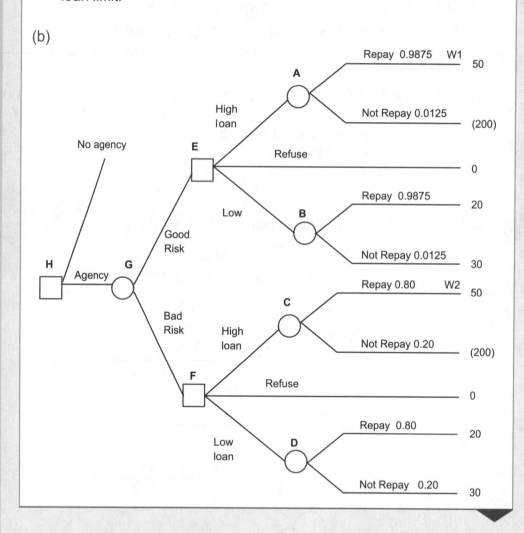

Workings

(W1) 800 customers have been assessed as being a good risk. Of these 790 did repay the loan. This represents 98.75% (790 ÷ 800) of the good risk customers.

Hence, the remaining 1.25% of the good risk customers did not repay the loan. (10 ÷ 800).

(W2) In a similar way to (W1), 160 out of the 200 bad risk customers did repay the loan, i.e. 80%.

40 out of the 200 bad risk customers did not repay the loan, i.e. 20%.

Expected values

At A	$(0.9875 \times 50) + (0.0125 \times (200))$	=	$46.875
At B	$(0.9875 \times 20) + (0.0125 \times (30))$	=	$19.375
At C	$(0.8 \times 50) + (0.2 \times (200))$	=	0
At D	$(0.8 \times 20) + (0.2 \times (30))$	=	$10.00

Decisions

At E compare A and B. Choose A, i.e. give customers a high loan

At F compare C and D. Choose D, i.e. give customers a low loan.

Expected values

At G $(0.8 \times 46.875) + (0.2 \times 10.00)$ = $39.5

Decision

At H compare "No agency" (return = $37.50) with the "agency" (return = $39.50)

The information from the agency is expected to increase profits by $2 per rating. This is the value of the information.

(c) Perfect information is a forecast that is 100% accurate. In the context of this problem it would be the credit rating agency providing an accurate forecast of the customer's ability to repay the loan.

If the new agency is approached

Forecast	Decision	Outcome	Profit	Probability	Expected value
Good risk	High loan	Repay	$50	0.95	47.50
Bad risk	Refuse loan	Nothing	$0	0.05	0
					$47.50

The expected return with perfect information   = $47.50

The expected return with no information   =   ($37.50)

_____

Therefore the value of the information is   = $10.00

Data Set Question: Two-stage process

The product can be manufactured in **four** mutually exclusive ways:

(i)   Through A1, then B1

(ii) Through A1, then B2

(iii) Through A2, then B1

(iv) Through A2, then B2

The probability of a perfect item being produced can be quickly solved with contingency tables. The first three columns are completed as illustrated previously, then the probabilities of producing a perfect item by each method are extracted and multiplied.

Contingency table   **Manufacturing method**

	A1	A2	Total	A1B1	A1B2	A2B1	A2B2
Defective (2%, 6%)	10	30	40				
Perfect	490	470	960	490/1,000	490/1,000	470/1,000	470/1,000
	500	500	1,000				

	B1	B2	Total				
Defective (2%, 6%)	20	10	30				
Perfect	480	490	970	480/1,000	490/1,000	480/1,000	490/1,000
	500	500	1,000				

				A1B1	A1B2	A2B1	A2B2
Probability of a perfect item				0.2352	0.2401	0.2256	0.2303

(e.g. 490/1,000 × 480/1,000)

Therefore, P (Perfect item) = P(A1B1 or A1B2 or A2B1 or A2B2)

= P(A1B1) + P(A1B2) + P(A2B1) + P(A2B2)

= 0.2352 + 0.2401 + 0.2256 + 0.2303

= 0.9312

Since the total production is 10,000 items pa, the expected number of perfect items is 0.9312 × 10,000 = 9,312.

The profit on each of these is £80, therefore the expected profit on the perfect items is 9,312 × $80 = $744,960.

P(perfect item) = 0.9312, and so P(defective item) = 1 – 0.9312 = 0.0688

Therefore, expected number of defects is 0.0688 × 10,000 = 688. The loss on each of these is $10, therefore the expected loss on the defective items is 688 × $10 = $6,880.

The expected net profit = $744,960 – $6,880 = **$738,080.**

This is the average profit that the company might expect to make per annum.

EMAIL

From: Senior Management Accountant

To: Pedro Rodriguez

Subject: The value of perfect information

Date: 06/05/2014

Hi Pedro,

Please find below some notes and calculations. I hope these will facilitate your decision about the maximum price to pay the consultant.

First, let's calculate the contribution for each turnover figure. There is a 30% C/S ratio :

Turnover $000	Contribution $000
15,000	4,500
8,500	2,550
4,000	1,200

Then, we calculate the net margin for each of the different possible outcomes:

Advance hire level	Demand level	Contribution $000	Advance hire costs $000	Extra hire costs $000	Net margin $000
High	High	4,500	2,300	–	2,200
	Medium	2,550	2,300	–	250
	Low	1,200	2,300	–	(1,100)
Medium	High	4,500	1,500	1,300	1,700
	Medium	2,550	1,500	–	1,050
	Low	1,200	1,500	–	(300)
Low	High	4,500	1,000	2,150	1,350
	Medium	2,550	1,000	850	700
	Low	1,200	1,000	–	200

We can then list the expected values at all different level. Starting with high hire level:

$$EV = (2,200 \times 0.25) + (250 \times 0.45) + (-1,100 \times 0.30) = \$332,500$$

At Medium hire level

$$EV = (1,700 \times 0.25) + (1,050 \times 0.45) + (-300 \times 0.30) = \$807,500$$

At Low hire level

$$EV = (1,350 \times 0.25) + (700 \times 0.45) + (200 \times 0.30) = \$712,500$$

We can see that the expected net gain is maximised at the medium hire level.

Managers could either seek risk or avoid it. While the calculations of expected values seem to indicate that the medium-usage advance hire contract was the best option, this is only the result when using the weighted average and probabilities. A risk-averse decision maker will examine the options to see which of the demand levels is providing the worst net gains. He will then select the best from these worst outcomes.

In the case of Siteraze, this would mean selecting the low hire level. With a low hire level a net gain of \$200,000 or higher is guaranteed. However, if the decision maker was a risk seeker, he would select the high hire level in the hope that demand would subsequently be high. This combination would yield a net gain of \$2,200,000.

Demand level	Hire decision	Net gain $000	Probability	px
High	High	2,200	0.25	550.00
Medium	Medium	1,050	0.45	472.50
Low	Low	200	0.30	60.00
				1,082.50

EV with perfect information   \$1,082,500

EV without perfect information   \$807,500

Value of the information   \$275,000

In conclusion, Siteraze should not pay more than \$275,000 to the consultant.

Risk Management

Chapter learning objectives

Syllabus Link

Lead D2: Discuss management's responsibilities with regard to risk

Component D2a): Discuss Risk Management

- Upside and downside risk.
- The TARA framework – transfer, avoid, reduce, accept.
- Business risks
- Ethical implications and the public interest.

1 Chapter summary

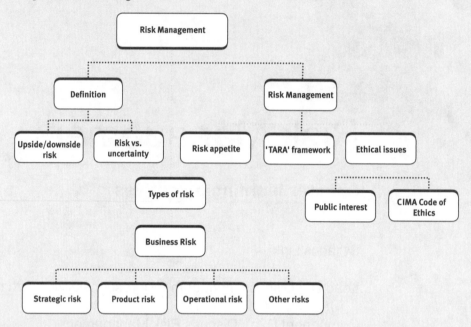

2 What is risk?

Risk in business is the chance that future events or results may not be as expected.

Risk is often thought of as purely bad (pure or **'downside'** risk), but it must be considered that risk can also be good – the results may be better than expected as well as worse (speculative or **'upside'** risk).

Downside risk examples

The term 'risk' is often associated with the chance of something 'bad' happening, and that a future outcome will be adverse. This type of risk is called '**downside' risk** or **pure risk**, which is a risk involving the possibility of loss, with no chance of gain.

Examples of pure risk are the risk of disruption to business from a severe power cut, or the risk of losses from theft or fraud, the risk of damage to assets from a fire or accident, and risks to the health and safety of employees at work.

Not all risks are pure risks or down-side risks. In many cases, risk is two-way, and actual outcomes might be either better or worse than expected. **Two-way risk** is sometimes called **speculative risk**. For many business decisions, there is an element of speculative risk and management are aware that actual results could be better or worse than forecast.

For example, a new product launch might be more or less successful than planned, and the savings from an investment in labour-saving equipment might be higher or lower than anticipated.

Risk and uncertainty

Risk is inherent in a situation whenever an outcome is not inevitable. **Uncertainty**, in contrast, arises from ignorance and a lack of information. By definition, the future cannot be predicted under conditions of uncertainty because there is insufficient information about what the future outcomes might be or their probabilities of occurrence.

In business, uncertainty might be an element in decision-making. For example, there might be uncertainty about how consumers might respond to a new product or a new technology, or how shareholders might react to a cut in the annual dividend. Uncertainty is reduced by obtaining as much information as possible before making any decision.

3 Why incur risk?

Businesses must be able to identify the principal sources of risk if they are to be able to assess and measure the risks that the organisation faces.

Risks facing an organisation are those that affect the achievement of its overall objectives, which should be reflected in its strategic aims. Risk should be managed and there should be strategies for dealing with risk.

4 Why incur risk?

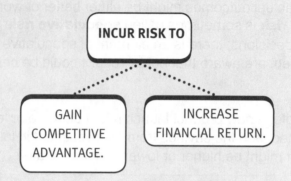

- To generate higher returns a business may have to take more risk in order to be competitive.

- Conversely, not accepting risk tends to make a business less dynamic, and implies a 'follow the leader' strategy.

- Incurring risk also implies that the returns from different activities will be higher – 'benefit' being the return for accepting risk.

- Benefits can be financial – decreased costs, or intangible – better quality information.

- In both cases, these will lead to the business being able to gain competitive advantage.

For some risks there is a market rate of return e.g. quoted equity – where a shareholder invests in a company with the expectation of a certain level of dividend and capital growth. However, for other risks there may not be a market rate of return e.g. technology risk – where a company invests in new software in the hope that it will make their invoice processing more efficient. The important distinction here is that the market compensates for the former type of risk, but might not for the latter.

5 CIMA's risk management cycle

Risk management should be a proactive process that is an integral part of strategic management.

This perspective is summarised in **CIMA's risk management cycle**, illustrated below:

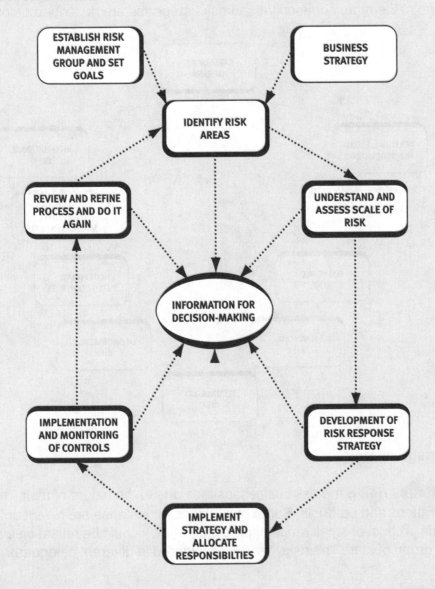

Source: Chartered Institute of Management Accountants (2002), Risk Management: A Guide to Good Practice, CIMA.

6 Identifying and categorising risks

Many organisations categorise risks into different types of risk. The use of risk categories can help with the process of risk identification and assessment.

There is no single system of risk categories. The risk categories used by companies and other organisations differ according to circumstances. Some of the more commonly-used risk categories are described below.

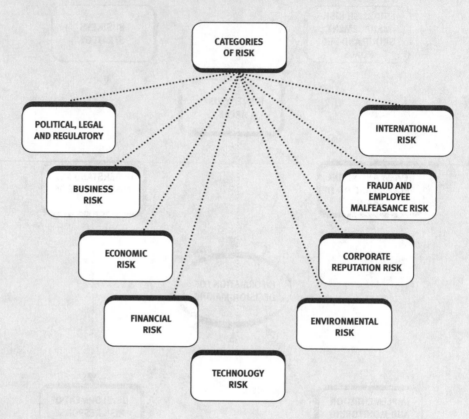

7 Business risk

Business risk is the risk businesses face due to the nature of their operations and products. Some businesses for instance are reliant on a single product or small range of products, or they could be reliant on a small key group of staff. The risks can be considered in different categories:

Strategic risk	Risk that business strategies (e.g. acquisitions/product launches) will fail.
Product risk	Risk of failure of new product launches/loss of interest in existing products.
Commodity price risk	Risk of a rise in commodity prices (e.g. oil).
Product reputation risk	Risk of change in product's reputation or image.
Operational risk	Risk that business operations may be inefficient or business processes may fail.
Contractual inadequacy risk	Risk that the terms of a contract do not fully cover a business against all potential outcomes.
Fraud and employee malfeasance	Considered separately later.

Business risks for a company are risks arising from the nature of its business and operations. Some businesses are inherently more risky than others.

Strategic risks are risks arising from the possible consequences of strategic decisions taken by the organisation. For example, one company might pursue a strategy of growth by acquisitions, whilst another might seek slower, organic growth. Growth by acquisition is likely to be much more high-risk than organic growth, although the potential returns might also be much higher. Strategic risks should be identified and assessed at senior management and board of director level.

Product risk is the risk that customers will not buy new products (or services) provided by the organisation, or that the sales demand for current products and services will decline unexpectedly. A new product launched on to the market might fail to achieve the expected volume of sales, or the take-up will be much slower than expected. For example, the demand for 'third generation' (3G) mobile communications services has been much slower to build up than expected by the mobile telephone service providers, due partly to the slower-than-expected development of suitable mobile phone handsets.

Commodity price risk. Businesses might be exposed to risks from unexpected increases (or falls) in the price of a key commodity. Businesses providing commodities, such as oil companies and commodity farmers, are directly affected by price changes. Equally, companies that rely on the use of commodities could be exposed to risks from price changes. For example, airlines are exposed to the risk of increases in fuel prices, particularly when market demand for flights is weak, and so increases in ticket prices for flights are not possible.

Product reputation risk. Some companies rely heavily on brand image and product reputation, and an adverse event could put its reputation (and so future sales) at risk. Risk to a product's reputation could arise from adverse public attitudes to a product or from adverse publicity: this has been evident in Europe with widespread hostility to genetically-modified (GM) foods. There could also be a risk from changes in customer perceptions about the quality of a product. For example, if a car manufacturer announces that it is recalling all new models of a car to rectify a design defect, the reputation of the product and future sales could be affected.

Operational risk refers to potential losses that might arise in business operations. It has been defined broadly as 'the risk of losses resulting from inadequate or failed internal processes, people and systems, or external events' (Basel Committee on Banking Supervision). Operational risks include risks of fraud or employee malfeasance, which are explained in more detail later. Organisations have internal control systems to manage operational risks.

Contractual inadequacy risk may arise where a business has negotiated contracts and other business transactions without adequate consideration of what may happen if things don't go according to plan. For example, a builder may have a fixed completion date to complete the construction of a house. If he does not complete on time, he may have to pay compensation to the house purchaser. Similarly, there is also a risk that the purchaser does not have the funds when payment is due. This risk may be mitigated by having terms in the contract as to what rights he will have in such circumstances. Clearly, if the builder does not consider either or both of these possibilities when agreeing to build the house, then there is an unidentified and unquantified risk of loss.

 8 Risk management

Risk management is defined as **'the process of understanding and managing the risks that the organisation is inevitably subject to in attempting to achieve its corporate objectives'**

CIMA Official Terminology

The traditional view of risk management has been one of protecting the organisation from loss through conformance procedures and hedging techniques – this is about avoiding the **downside** risk.

The new approach to risk management is about taking advantage of the opportunities to increase overall returns within a business – benefiting from the **upside** risk.

The following diagram shows how risk management can reconcile the two perspectives of conformance and performance:

Source: IFAC (1999) Enhancing Shareholder Wealth By Better Managing Risk

534

Risk management and shareholder value

Ernst and Young (2001) have developed a model of shareholder value in which

Shareholder value = Static NPV of existing business model + Value of future growth options

which more simply put is 'the sum of the value of what a company does now and the value of what they could possibly do in the future'.

Good risk management allows businesses to exploit opportunities for future growth while protecting the value already created. By aligning risk management activity to what the shareholders consider vital to the success of the business, the shareholders are assured that what they value is protected.

Ernst and Young identify four stages:

(a) Establish what shareholders value about the company – through talking with the investment community and linking value creation processes to key performance indicators.

(b) Identify the risks around the key shareholder value drivers – the investment community can identify those factors that will influence their valuation of the company. All other risks will also be considered, even if not known by investors.

(c) Determine the preferred treatment for the risks – the investment community can give their views on what actions they would like management to take in relation to the risks. The risk/reward trade-off can be quantified by estimating the change in a company's market valuation if a particular risk treatment was implemented.

(d) Communicate risk treatments to shareholders – shareholders need to be well informed, as a shared vision is important in relation to the inter-related concepts of risk management and shareholder value.

9 Risk management strategy

For many businesses the specific formulation of a risk strategy has been a recent development.

In the past a formal strategy for managing risks would not be made but rather it would be left to individual managers to make assessments of the risks the business faced and exercise judgement on what was a reasonable level of risk.

This has now changed: failure to properly identify and control risks has been identified as a major cause of business failure (take Barings Bank as an example).

A framework for board consideration of risk is shown below:

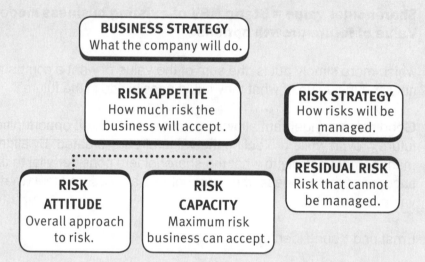

 Risk appetite can be defined as the amount of risk an organisation is willing to accept in pursuit of value. This may be explicit in strategies, policies and procedures, or it may be implicit. It is determined by:

- **risk capacity** – the amount of risk that the organisation can bear, and
- **risk attitude** – the overall approach to risk, in terms of the board being risk averse or risk seeking.

The way that the organisation documents and determines the specific parts of its risk strategy will have to link to the business strategy and objectives.

Overall the risk management strategy is concerned with trying to achieve the required business objectives with the lowest possible chance of failure. The tougher the business objectives, however, the more risks will have to be taken to achieve them.

Residual risk is the risk a business faces after its controls have been considered.

10 Risk management – The TARA framework

An alternative way of remembering risk management methods is via the mnemonic '**TARA**':

Transference. In some circumstances, risk can be transferred wholly or in part to a third party, so that if an adverse event occurs, the third party suffers all or most of the loss. A common example of risk transfer is insurance. Businesses arrange a wide range of insurance policies for protection against possible losses. This strategy is also sometimes referred to as **sharing**.

Avoidance. An organisation might choose to avoid a risk altogether. However, since risks are unavoidable in business ventures, they can be avoided only by not investing (or withdrawing from the business area completely). The same applies to not-for-profit organisations: risk is unavoidable in the activities they undertake.

Reduction/mitigation. A third strategy is to reduce the risk, either by limiting exposure in a particular area or attempting to decrease the adverse effects should that risk actually crystallise.

Acceptance. The final strategy is to simply accept that the risk may occur and decide to deal with the consequences in that particular situation. The strategy is appropriate normally where the adverse effect is minimal. For example, there is nearly always a risk of rain; unless the business activity cannot take place when it rains then the risk of rain occurring is not normally insured against.

Risk mapping

A common qualitative way of assessing the significance of risk is to produce a '**risk map**'.

- The map identifies whether a risk will have a significant impact on the organisation and links that into the likelihood of the risk occurring.

- The approach can provide a framework for prioritising risks in the business.

- Risks with a significant impact and a high likelihood of occurrence need more urgent attention than risks with a low impact and low likelihood of occurrence.

- Risks can be plotted on a diagram or map, as shown below; the map can provide a useful framework to determine an appropriate risk response:

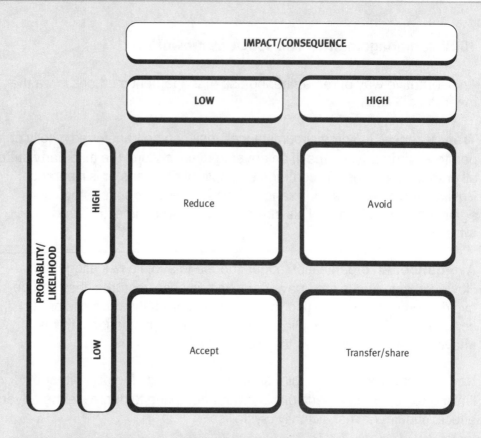

More on risk mapping

The potential loss from an adverse outcome is a function of:

- the probability or likelihood that the adverse outcome will occur, and
- the impact of the outcome if it does occur.

When an initial review is carried out to identify and assess risks, the assessment of both probabilities and impact might be based on judgement and experience rather than on a detailed statistical and numerical analysis.

- In an initial analysis, it might be sufficient to categorise the probability of an adverse outcome as 'high', 'medium' or 'low', or even more simply as 'high' or 'low'.
- Similarly, it might be sufficient for the purpose of an initial analysis to assess the consequences or impact of an adverse outcome as 'severe' or 'not severe'.

Each risk can then be plotted on a risk map. A risk map is simply a 2 × 2 table or chart, showing the probabilities for each risk and their potential impact.

Example

The following simple risk map might be prepared for a firm of auditors:

	Impact/consequences	
	Low	**High**
High	New audit regulations for the profession	Loss of non-audit work from existing clients
Low	Increases in salaries above the general rate of inflation	Loss of audit clients within the next two years.

Probability/likelihood

Using a risk map

A risk map immediately indicates which risks should be given the highest priority.

- High-probability, high-impact risks should be given the highest priority for management, whether by monitoring or by taking steps to mitigate the risk.

- Low-probability, low-impact risks can probably be accepted by the organisation as within the limits of acceptability.

- High-probability, low-impact risks and low-probability, high-impact risks might be analysed further with a view to deciding the most appropriate strategy for their management.

For each high-probability, high-impact risk, further analysis should be carried out, with a view to:

- estimating the probability of an adverse (or favourable) outcome more accurately, and

- assessing the impact on the organisation of an adverse outcome. This is an area in which the management accountant should be able to contribute by providing suitable and relevant financial information.

11 Ethical issues as sources of risk

A conceptual framework that requires a management accountant to identify, evaluate and address threats to compliance with the fundamental principles, rather than merely comply with a set of specific rules which may be arbitrary is in the **public interest.**

CIMA's Code of Ethics has a 'threats and safeguards' approach. If identified threats are other than clearly significant, a management accountant should apply safeguards to eliminate the threats or reduce them to an acceptable level such that compliance with the fundamental principles is not compromised.

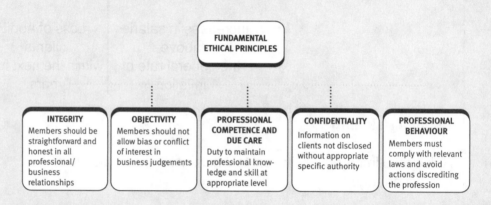

FUNDAMENTAL ETHICAL PRINCIPLES				
INTEGRITY Members should be straightforward and honest in all professional/ business relationships	**OBJECTIVITY** Members should not allow bias or conflict of interest in business judgements	**PROFESSIONAL COMPETENCE AND DUE CARE** Duty to maintain professional knowledge and skill at appropriate level	**CONFIDENTIALITY** Information on clients not disclosed without appropriate specific authority	**PROFESSIONAL BEHAVIOUR** Members must comply with relevant laws and avoid actions discrediting the profession

The CIMA Code of Ethics

As Chartered Management Accountants, students throughout the world have a duty to observe the highest standards of conduct and integrity, and to uphold the good standing and reputation of the profession. They must also refrain from any conduct which might discredit the profession. Members and registered students must have regard to these guidelines irrespective of their field of activity, of their contract of employment or of any other professional memberships they may hold.

The Institute promotes the highest ethical and business standards, and encourages its members to be good and responsible professionals. Good ethical behaviour may be above that required by the law. In a highly competitive, complex business world, it is essential that CIMA members sustain their integrity and remember the trust and confidence which is placed on them by whoever relies on their objectivity and professionalism. Members must avoid actions or situations which are inconsistent with their professional obligations. They should also be guided not merely by the terms but by the spirit of this Code.

CIMA members should conduct themselves with courtesy and consideration towards all with whom they have professional dealings and should not behave in a manner which could be considered offensive or discriminatory.

CIMA has adopted a code of ethics based on the IFAC (International Federation of Accountants) code of ethics which was developed with input from CIMA and the global accountancy profession.

The CIMA Code of Ethics is freely available on CIMA's website – cimaglobal.com > Standards and ethics > Code of ethics.

If a member cannot resolve an ethical issue by following this code or by consulting the ethics support information on CIMA's website, he or she should seek legal advice as to both legal rights and any obligations (s)he may have.

The code of ethics is in three parts:

- Part A establishes the fundamental principles of professional ethics and provides a conceptual framework for applying those principles.

- Parts B and C illustrate how the conceptual framework is to be applied in specific situations:
    - Part B applies to professional accountants in business.
    - Part C applies to professional accountants in public practice.

12 Example threats and safeguards

Ethical threat	Safeguard
Conflict between requirements of the employer and the fundamental principles For example, acting contrary to laws or regulations or against professional or technical standards. (Intimidation threat)	• Obtaining advice from the employer, professional organisation or professional advisor. • The employer providing a formal dispute resolution process. • Legal advice.
Preparation and reporting on information Accountants need to prepare/report on information fairly, objectively and honestly. However, the accountant may be pressurised to provide misleading information. (Intimidation threat)	• Consultation with superiors in the employing company. • Consultation with those charged with governance. • Consultation with the relevant professional body.

Having sufficient expertise Accountants need to be honest in stating their level of expertise – and not mislead employers by implying they have more expertise than they actually possess. Threats that may result in a lack of expertise include time pressure to carry out a duty, being provided with inadequate information or having insufficient experience.	• Obtaining additional advice/ training. • Negotiating more time for duties. • Obtaining assistance from someone with relevant expertise.
Financial interests Situations where an accountant or close family member has financial interests in the employing company. Examples include the accountant being paid a bonus based on the financial statement results which he is preparing, or holding share options in the company. (Self-interest threat)	• Remuneration being determined by other members of management. • Disclosure of relevant interests to those charged with governance. • Consultation with superiors or relevant professional body.
Inducements – receiving offers Refers to incentives being offered to encourage unethical behaviour. Inducements may include gifts, hospitality, preferential treatment or inappropriate appeals to loyalty. Objectivity and/or confidentiality may be threatened by such inducements. (Self-interest threat)	• Do not accept the inducement! • Inform relevant third party such as a senior manager.

Inducements – giving offers	• Do not offer the inducement!
Refers to accountants being pressurised to provide inducements to junior members of staff to influence a decision or obtain confidential information. (Intimidation threat)	
Confidential information Accountants should keep information about their employing organisation confidential unless there is a right or obligation to disclose, or they have received authorisation from their client. However, the accountant may be under pressure to disclose this information as a result of legal processes such as anti-money laundering/terrorism – in this situation there is a conflict between confidentiality and the need for disclosure.	• Disclose information in compliance with the relevant statutory requirements, e.g. money laundering regulations
Whistleblowing Situations where the accountant needs to consider disclosing information, where ethical rules have been broken.	• Follow the disclosure requirements of the employer, e.g. report to those responsible for governance. Otherwise disclosure should be based on the assessment of: legal obligations, whether members of the public will be adversely affected, gravity of the matter, likelihood of repetition, reliability of the information and reasons why employer does not want to disclose.

13 The public interest

The distinguishing mark of a profession is the acceptance of a responsibility to the public. The accountancy profession's public includes:

- Clients
- Credit providers
- Governments
- Employees
- Employers
- Investors.

The public interest can be defined as that which supports the good of society as a whole, as opposed to what serves the interests of individual members of society, or of specific sectional interest groups.

For an accountant, acting in the public interest is acting for the collective well-being of the community of people and institution that it serves.

The concept of public interest may affect the working of an organisation in a number of ways. The actions of the organisation itself may be harmful to society, for example from excessive pollution or poor treatment of the labour force. The government may then decide, in the public interest, to limit the actions of that organisation for the greater good of society as a whole.

14 Organisations as 'shapers of society'

Businesses can manage their reputational risk either by applying their own positional power, or in more specific terms by changing society for the better in terms of the 'public interest.'

For example, organisations can amend or shape society by the products that are made available. It can be argued that McDonald's has assisted poor eating habits in society overall, by making available cheap 'fast food'.

To be a shaper of society in the public interest, organisations must 'improve' society, however that term is defined. For example, it can be argued that Toyota's research into solar powered cars is seen as an obligation to society of providing pollution free transport rather than continuing to manufacture petrol-burning cars. The act of investment in solar power not only shows the company's commitment to this area, but shapes society by raising the issue of environmental concern.

15 Practice questions

Objective Test Question 1: TARA framework

Chen Products produces four manufactured products: Products 1, 2, 3 and 4. The company's risk committee recently met to discuss how the company might respond to a number of problems that have arisen with Product 2.

After a number of incidents in which Product 2 had failed whilst being used by customers, Chen Products had been presented with compensation claims from customers injured and inconvenienced by the product failure. It was decided that the risk committee should meet to discuss the options.

When the discussion of Product 2 began, committee chairman Anne Ricardo reminded her colleagues that, apart from the compensation claims, Product 2 was a highly profitable product.

Chen's risk management committee comprised four non-executive directors who each had different backgrounds and areas of expertise. None of them had direct experience of Chen's industry or products. It was noted that it was common for them to disagree among themselves as to how risks should be managed and that in some situations, each member proposed a quite different strategy to manage a given risk. This was the case when they discussed which risk management strategy to adopt with regard to Product 2.

Using the TARA framework, place each of the following strategies in a grey cell, against the 'TARA' element to which it is most likely to relate:

Transfer	
Avoid	
Reduce	
Accept	

Strategy 1: this would involve discontinuing the activity that is exposing the company to risk. In the case of Chen, this would involve ceasing production of Product 2. This would be pursued if the impact (hazard) and probability of incurring an acceptable level of liability were both considered to be unacceptably high and there were no options for transference or reduction.	Strategy 2: this would involve the company accepting only a portion of the risk. Although an unlikely possibility given the state of existing claims, insurance against future claims would serve to limit Chen's potential losses and place a limit on its losses. Outsourcing manufacture may be a way of transferring risk if the outsourcee can be persuaded to accept some of the product liability.
Strategy 3: This would involve seeking to retain a component of the risk (in order to enjoy the return assumed to be associated with that risk) but to reduce it and thereby limit its ability to create liability. Chen produces four products and it could reconfigure its production capacity to produce proportionately more of Products 1, 3 and 4 and proportionately less of Product 2. This would reduce Product 2 in the overall portfolio and therefore Chen's exposure to its risks. This would need to be associated with instructions to other departments (e.g. sales and marketing) to similarly reconfigure activities to sell more of the other products and less of Product 2.	Strategy 4: This would involve taking limited or no action to reduce the exposure to risk and would be taken if the returns expected from bearing the risk were expected to be greater than the potential liabilities. The case mentions that Product 2 is highly profitable and it may be that the returns attainable by maintaining and even increasing Product 2's sales are worth the liabilities incurred by compensation claims.

Objective Test Question 2: Risk appetite

Use the words and phrases in the table provided below to complete the following paragraphs:

high risk	reduction	risky
avoidance	low risk	TARA
transference	more	appetite

An organisation is likely to have a portfolio of projects, some incurring more risk than others, so that the overall risk _____ is met from that portfolio.

A _____ appetite will indicate that the organisation will normally seek a higher number of higher-risk/return activities as the organisation is willing to accept _____risk and its risk capacity has not been reached. However, a _____ appetite indicates that a higher number of low-risk/lower-return activities will be preferred.

The way that an organisation manages risk will also affect its risk strategy. Using _____ as an example of risk management, the overall risk strategy of an organisation can be explained as follows:

- A strategy of primarily self-insurance may limit the organisation's strategy regarding undertaking _____projects. Self-insurance implies risk minimisation as an overall strategy.

- A risk strategy of risk _____ may imply an overall strategy that incorporates a higher level of risk. However, risk will then be limited by the amount of insurance premiums. Where premiums become too high, the risk strategy determines that, overall, the organisation will seek less risky projects.

- A strategy of _____ implies that the organisation wants to limit the total amount of risk.

- Finally, a strategy of risk _____ may imply that the risk capacity of the firm is being reached and while additional risk can be accepted, the amount of risk that can be taken on is limited.

Risk capacity is also important when determining the desired method of expansion within an organisation. Where the organisation has a high risk capacity the overall risk strategy is likely to be directed to taking on higher risk projects. However, where the organisation's total risk capacity is being reached, then projects with a lower amount of risk will be expected.

Case Style Question: The ZXC Company

The ZXC company manufactures aircraft. The company is based in Europe and currently produces a range of four different aircraft. ZXC's aircraft are reliable with low maintenance costs, giving ZXC a good reputation, both to airlines who purchase from ZXC and to airlines' customers who fly in the aircraft.

ZXC is currently developing the 'next generation' of passenger aircraft, with the selling name of the ZXLiner. New developments in ZXLiner include the following.

- Two decks along the entire aircraft (not just part as in the Boeing 747 series) enabling faster loading and unloading of passengers from both decks at the same time. However, this will mean that airport gates must be improved to facilitate dual loading at considerable expense.

- 20% decrease in fuel requirements and falls in noise and pollution levels.

- Use of new alloys to decrease maintenance costs, increase safety and specifically the use of Zitnim (a new lightweight conducting alloy) rather than standard wiring to enable the 'fly-by-wire' features of the aircraft. Zitnim only has one supplier worldwide.

Many component suppliers are based in Europe although ZXC does obtain about 25% of the sub-contracted components from companies in the USA. ZXC also maintains a significant R&D department working on the ZXLiner and other new products such as alternative environmentally friendly fuel for aircraft.

Although the ZXLiner is yet to fly or be granted airworthiness certificates, ZXC does have orders for 25 aircraft from the HTS company. However, on current testing schedules the ZXLiner will be delivered late.

ZXC currently has about €4 billion of loans from various banks and last year made a loss of €2.3 billion. ZXC's chief executive has also just resigned taking a leaving bonus of around two years salary.

You have received the following email from the newly appointed Acting Chief Executive:

From: Jack Van Gus, Acting Chief Executive
To: A.N Accountant
Date: 15 June 2014

Subject: Risks

Hi A.N.
Unlike my predecessor, I am keen to proactively manage risks in this business—please could you Identify and explain the sources of business risk that could affect ZXC? I intend to use your report as a basis for a presentation to the Board

Many thanks in advance
Jack

Test your understanding answers

Objective Test Question 1: TARA framework

Transfer	Strategy 2
Avoid	Strategy 1
Reduce	Strategy 3
Accept	Strategy 4

Objective Test Question 2: Risk appetite

An organisation is likely to have a portfolio of projects, some incurring more risk than others, so that the overall risk **appetite** is met from that portfolio.

A **high-risk** appetite will indicate that the organisation will normally seek a higher number of higher-risk/return activities as the organisation is willing to accept **more** risk and its risk capacity has not been reached. However, a **low-risk** appetite indicates that a higher number of low-risk/lower-return activities will be preferred.

The way that an organisation manages risk will also affect its risk strategy. Using **TARA** as an example of risk management, the overall risk strategy of an organisation can be explained as follows:

- A strategy of primarily self-insurance may limit the organisation's strategy regarding undertaking **risky** projects. Self-insurance implies risk minimisation as an overall strategy.

- A risk strategy of risk **transference** may imply an overall strategy that incorporates a higher level of risk. However, risk will then be limited by the amount of insurance premiums. Where premiums become too high, the risk strategy determines that, overall, the organisation will seek less risky projects.

- A strategy of **avoidance** implies that the organisation wants to limit the total amount of risk.

- Finally, a strategy of risk **reduction** may imply that the risk capacity of the firm is being reached and while additional risk can be accepted, the amount of risk that can be taken on is limited.

Risk capacity is also important when determining the desired method of expansion within an organisation. Where the organisation has a high risk capacity the overall risk strategy is likely to be directed to taking on higher risk projects. However, where the organisation's total risk capacity is being reached, then projects with a lower amount of risk will be expected.

Case Style Question: The ZXC Company

EMAIL

TO: Jack Van Gus

FROM: AN Accountant

SUBJECT: ZXC – Sources of business risk

DATE: 19 June 2014

Hi Jack,

In response to your email, please find below some notes about the potential sources of risks that may affect our business in the coming months.

Product/market risk

This is the risk that customers will not buy our new products (or services), or that the sales demand for current products and services will decline unexpectedly. For ZXC, there is the risk that demand for the new aircraft will be less than expected, either due to customers purchasing the rival airplane or because airports will not be adapted to take the new ZXLiner.

Commodity price risk

Businesses might be exposed to risks from unexpected increases (or falls) in the price of a key commodity.

Part of the control systems of the ZXLiner rely on the availability of the new lightweight conducting alloy Zitnim. As there is only one supplier of this alloy, then there is the danger of the monopolist increasing the price or even denying supply. Increase in price would increase the overall cost of the (already expensive) ZXLiner, while denial of supply would further delay delivery of the aircraft. ZXC needs to maintain good relations with their key suppliers to mitigate this risk.

Product reputation risk

Some companies rely heavily on brand image and product reputation, and an adverse event could put its reputation (and so future sales) at risk. While the reputation of ZXC appears good at present, reputation will suffer if the ZXLiner is delayed significantly or it does not perform well in test flights (which have still to be arranged). Airline customers, and also their customers (travellers) are unlikely to feel comfortable flying in an aircraft that is inherently unstable. ZXC must continue to invest in R&D and good quality control systems to mitigate the effects of this risk.

Credit risk

Credit risk is the possibility of losses due to non-payment by debtors or the company not being able to pay its creditors, which will adversely affect the company's credit rating.

Given that the ZXLiner has not been sold at present, there are no debtors. However, ZXC is heavily dependent on bank finance – any denial of funds will adversely affect ZXC's ability to continue to trade. Credit risk is therefore significant at present.

Currency risk

Currency risk, or foreign exchange risk, arises from the possibility of movements in foreign exchange rates, and the value of one currency in relation to another. ZXC is currently based in Europe although it obtains a significant number of parts from the USA. If the €/$ exchange rate became worse, then the cost of imported goods for ZXC (and all other companies) would increase. At present, the relatively weak US$ is in ZXC's favour and so this risk is currently negligible.

Interest rate risk

Interest rate risk is the risk of unexpected gains or losses arising as a consequence of a rise or fall in interest rates. Exposures to interest rate risk arise from borrowing and investing. As ZXC do have significant bank loans, then the company is very exposed to this risk. As interest rates are expected to rise in the future then ZXC would be advised to consider methods of hedging against this risk.

Gearing risk

Gearing risk for non-bank companies is the risk arising from exposures to high financial gearing and large amounts of borrowing. Again, ZXC has significant amounts of bank loans. This increases the amount of interest that must be repaid each year. In the short term ZXC cannot affect this risk as the bank loans are a necessary part of its operations.

Legal risk or litigation risk

The risk arises from the possibility of legal action being taken against an organisation. At present this risk does not appear to be a threat for ZXC. However, if the ZXLiner is delayed any further there is a risk for breach of contract for late delivery to the HTS company. There is little ZXC can do to guard against this risk, apart from keep HTS appraised of the delays involved with the ZXLiner.

Regulatory risk

This is the possibility that regulations will affect the way an organisation has to operate. In terms of aircraft, regulation generally affects noise and pollution levels. As the ZXLiner is designed to have lower noise and pollution levels than existing aircraft then this risk does not appear to be a threat to ZXC.

Technology risk

Technology risk arises from the possibility that technological change will occur or that new technology will not work. Given that ZXC is effectively producing a new product (the ZXLiner) that has not actually been tested yet, there is some technology risk. At worse, the ZXLiner may not fly at all or not obtain the necessary flying certificates. ZXC appear to be guarding against this risk by not decreasing its investment in product development.

Economic risk

This risk refers to the risks facing organisations from changes in economic conditions, such as economic growth or recession, government spending policy and taxation policy, unemployment levels and international trading conditions.

Demand for air travel is forecast to increase for the foreseeable future, so in that sense there is a demand for aircraft which ZXC will benefit from. The risk of product failure is more significant than economic risk.

Environmental risk

This risk arises from changes to the environment over which an organisation has no direct control, such as global warming, to those for which the organisation might be responsible, such as oil spillages and other pollution.

ZXC is subject to this risk – and there is significant debate concerning the impact of air travel on global warming. At the extreme, there is a threat that air travel could be banned, or made very expensive by international taxation agreements, although this appears unlikely at present. ZXC need to continue to monitor this risk, and continue research into alternative fuels etc. in an attempt to mitigate the risk.

Business probity

This is the risk that a company does not follow rules of good corporate governance or show appropriate ethical awareness.

In ZXC, the departure of the chief executive with a bonus of more than two years salary appears to act against business probity – why should the chief executive obtain a bonus when ZXC is making a loss and workers may be made redundant? However, the impact of this risk on ZXC is unclear. It is unlikely to affect sales as customers are more interested in the ZXLiner than the departure of the chief executive. There is more of an association risk in terms of business probity not being followed in other areas such as perceived cost cutting in research and development affecting the quality of the product. Again, ZXC are guarding against this risk.

However, the board of ZXC should ensure that the remuneration committee review directors' service contracts to ensure risk in this area does not occur in the future.

With regards

AN Accountant

Collecting and using information

Chapter learning objectives

Syllabus Link

Lead D2: Discuss management's responsibilities with regard to risk

Component D2b): Discuss the risk associated with the collection and use of information

- Costs and benefits associated with investing in information systems
- Big Data

1 Chapter summary

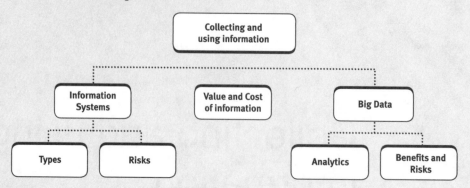

2 Information systems to support management

To meet their information needs, managers use information systems, of which there are a number of different types. The different types of system meet the different information needs of the different managers.

The main systems can be summarised in the following diagram:

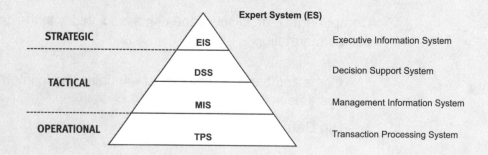

As a basic idea the systems towards the top of the tree will support the strategic decisions and they will use the data from systems in the levels below.

3 Benefits of an information strategy

The **benefits** of an information strategy include:

*   Achievement of **goal congruence** between the information system's objectives and the corporate objectives. Failure of computer systems to work can result in the failure of some organisations to function at all. This, for example, would be the case for Amazon and eBay.

*   The organisation is more likely to be able to create and sustain **competitive advantage**. The company's computer system will likely impact on the customer these days, if they order over the internet or rely on order information for a delivery date.

*   The high levels of expenditure on information systems will be more focused on supporting key aspects of the business.

- Developments in IT can be exploited at the most appropriate time – which is not always when they are first available.

- Computers are often of strategic importance in a company. Having an information strategy is a costly business and unmanaged development can lead to costly mistakes.

- IT affects all levels of employees and management. Having a plan that can be communicated to these employees should ensure that they 'buy in' to the ideas within it and efficiency will be increased more quickly.

Research continues to show that over 70 percent of Information Systems and Technology (IS/IT) investments fail to deliver the expected business benefits. In any case, evaluating the benefits of investing in information systems is complex. Information on these benefits is not always available, or easy to obtain, and benefits are both tangible and intangible benefits.

Tangible benefits are straightforward to identify: they can be quantified and assigned a monetary value. However, intangible benefits, such as more efficient customer service or enhanced decision making, cannot easily be quantified..

Information system types

System	Purpose	Features	Example(s)
Transaction processing system.	Captures and stores transaction data.	Batch, on-line or real time processing.	• Sales order processing. • Accounting system.
Management information system.	Integrated system for supporting operations and decision making.	Data gathered from TPS. Pre-determined output format.	• Databases. • Reporting systems.
Enterprise resource planning system.	Integration of information across the company.	Commercial software package installed on a Database Management System.	• Customer relationship management (CRM). • Balanced scorecard performance reporting.

Decision support system.	Manipulation of information to support decision making.	User-friendly style and assists with unstructured problems.	• Budgeting on a spreadsheet.
Executive information system.	Present selected/ focused information for senior executives.	Highly visual and incorporates internal and external data.	• Executive performance 'dashboard'.
Expert system.	Present decision options to 'non-expert' users.	Modify its knowledge database in accordance with its own results.	• Tax advice. • Legal advice. • Selection of training methods.
Strategic enterprise management system.	Assists with strategic decision making.	Incorporates tools such as ABM.	• Significant investment decisions. • Acquisition decisions.

4 Risks

Computer systems have unique risk and control issues that need to be addressed by the business. As with any risk factor the company needs to make an assessment of the risks and decide on the appropriate level of control to reduce the risks to an acceptable level.

A risk to a computer system could be anything that prevents the managers getting the information they need from the system at the time that they need it.

Risks to information processing facilities may arise from:

- Dissatisfied employees might deliberately modify or destroy information in the system.

- A hacker or industrial spy might break into the system.

- Viruses or malicious software could be introduced.

- Accidental mistakes could be made on input to the system.

- Inadequate security of the hardware or data.

- Faults in the hardware system.

Such risks result in the loss of information (or the loss of its integrity or confidentiality), business disruption and a loss of time and money. Costs may be incurred.

Further detail on risks

Risks to information security can be categorised as follows:

Risks	Description
Risk of hardware theft	This risk might seem fairly obvious, but the theft of computer hardware is common.
Physical damage to hardware and computer media (disks, etc)	Physical damage can be caused by: • malicious damage • poor operating conditions causing damage to equipment and magnetic files • natural disasters, such as fire and flooding.
Damage to data	Data can be damaged by hackers into the system, viruses, program faults in the software and faults in the hardware or data storage media. Software, particularly purpose-written software, can become corrupted. Programs might be altered by a hacker or computer fraudster. Alternatively, a new version of a program might be written and introduced, but contain a serious error that results in the corruption or loss of data on file.
Operational mistakes	Unintentional mistakes can cause damage to data or loss of data; for example, using the wrong version of computer program, or the wrong version of a data file, or deleting data that is still of value.
Fraud and industrial espionage	This can lead to the loss of confidentiality of sensitive information, or the criminal creation of false data and false transactions, or the manipulation of data for personal gain.

Data protection legislation

Some countries give individuals the right to seek compensation against an organisation that holds personal data about them, if they suffer loss through the improper use of that data. In the UK, for example, rights are given to 'data subjects' by the Data Protection Act. There could be a risk that an organisation will improperly use or communicate personal data about individuals, in breach of the legislation.

Erroneous input

Many information systems, especially those based on transaction processing systems and with large volumes of input transactions, are vulnerable to mistakes in the input data.

- Some input items might be overlooked and omitted. Other transactions might be entered twice.

- There might be errors in the input data, particularly where the data is input by humans rather than by electronic data transfer. For example, in a system relying on input via keyboard and mouse, data accuracy depends on the ability of the operator to input the data without making a mistake.

Where input errors are high, the integrity of the data and information becomes doubtful.

Hacking

Hacking is the gaining of unauthorised access to a computer system. It might be a deliberate attempt to gain access to an organisation's systems and files, to obtain information or to alter data (perhaps fraudulently).

Once hackers have gained access to the system, there are several damaging options available to them. For example, they may:

- gain access to the file that holds all the user ID codes, passwords and authorisations

- discover the method used for generating/authorising passwords

- interfere with the access control system, to provide the hacker with open access to the system

- obtain information which is of potential use to a competitor organisation

- obtain, enter or alter data for a fraudulent purpose

- cause data corruption by the introduction of unauthorised computer programs and processing on to the system (computer viruses)

- alter or delete files.

Viruses

A virus is a piece of software that seeks to infest a computer system, hiding and automatically spreading to other systems if given the opportunity. Most computer viruses have three functions – avoiding detection, reproducing themselves and causing damage. Viruses might be introduced into a computer system directly, or by disk or e-mail attachment.

Viruses include:

- trojans – whilst carrying on one program, secretly carry on another

- worms – these replicate themselves within the systems

- trap doors – undocumented entry points to systems allowing normal controls to be by-passed

- logic bombs – triggered on the occurrence of a certain event

- time bombs – which are triggered on a certain date.

Risks and benefits of internet and intranet use

Many organisations have intranet systems or use the Internet directly. Using an intranet or the Internet has obvious advantages, but also creates substantial risks.

The advantages of intranets and the Internet

- Employees have ready access to vast sources of external data that would not otherwise be available. Using external information can help to improve the quality of decision making.

- Organisations can advertise their goods and services on a website, and provide other information that helps to promote their image.

- Organisations can use the Internet to purchase goods or supplies, saving time and money. For example, the Internet is used regularly by businesses to purchase standard items such as stationery, and to reserve hotel rooms and purchase travel tickets.

- The Internet/intranet provides a means of operating an e-mail system. Communication by e-mail is fast and should remove the requirement for excessive quantities of paper. Using e-mails might also reduce the non-productive time spent by employees on the telephone.

- Intranets create the opportunity for more flexible organisation of work. For example, employees who are away from the office can access the organisation's IT systems and files through the Internet. Similarly, employees can work from their home but have full access to the organisation's systems.

The disadvantages of intranets and the internet

There are disadvantages with using intranets and the Internet.

- E-mail systems can become inefficient if too many messages are sent and users have to look through large amounts of 'junk mail' to find messages of value.

- E-mails can be disruptive, especially if a prompt appears on an individual's computer screen whenever a new message is received.

- Senders of e-mails often expect an immediate reply to their messages, and a delay in responding can create bad feelings and ill-will.

- Employees might waste too much time looking for information on the Internet, when the value of the information is not worth the time spent looking for it.

- Without suitable controls, employees might spend large amounts of time on the Internet or exchanging e-mails for their personal benefit, rather than in carrying out their work responsibilities.

The greatest problem with using intranets and the Internet, however, is the vulnerability of the organisation's IT systems to:

- unauthorised access by hackers, including industrial spies

- the import of viruses in attachments to e-mail messages and other malicious software.

 5 Value and cost of information

Cost-benefit analysis (CBA) can be used to assess the expected costs and benefits of the system design to be recommended. It is often called a method for 'system justification' – if the system is justified, then it will be recommended.

(This section does not relate solely to IT projects but to all projects a business could undertake – be prepared in the exam to discuss a cost-benefit analysis from more than an IT viewpoint.)

The **net value of information** in decision-making situations could be calculated as:

- the difference in the values of outcomes in a decision with and without the information, minus
- the cost of obtaining the information.

In other words a manager will make a decision based upon the information currently known. If additional information is available, which makes the manager take a different decision, then the value of that information is:

- the savings or profits made as a result of taking the different decision
- adjusted for the cost of obtaining the information, which may be:
  - a cost arising from preparing the information internally
  - the cost of purchasing the information from external sources
  - the cost of the delay to the decision whilst the information is prepared.

Cost of information

The cost of information could be classified under three general headings:

(a) The cost of **designing and setting** up the system that produces the information including:
  - systems design
  - systems testing
  - capital costs of equipment (e.g. IT equipment)
  - installation
  - training.

(b) The **day-to-day running** costs of the system providing the information, including:
  - staff salaries
  - supplies (paper, disks, etc)
  - other running expenses such as premises costs and security costs.

(c) **Storage** costs including:
  - hardware costs
  - retrieval costs
  - security costs.

Assessing the value and cost of information

In order to assess the value of information, the following questions can be asked:

- What information is provided?
- What is it used for?
- Who uses it?
- How often is it used?
- What benefit is achieved by using it?
- Is it used as often as it is provided?
- What other relevant information is available that could be used instead?

Unfortunately, the value of information is not always easy to quantify in terms of benefits obtained. An alternative approach might therefore be to assess the consequences of not having the information, taking into account the quantity of the information and its availability (e.g. on-line), accuracy, level of detail and other information qualities.

Budgeting and IS/IT costs

The description of cost-benefit analysis above assumes that there are identifiable IT projects whose costs and benefits can be estimated and evaluated. In practice, although some new projects can be evaluated in this way, much spending on IT does not take the form of spending on identifiable new projects. A considerable amount of spending is incurred on maintaining, expanding and upgrading existing systems.

This type of spending, particularly IT running costs but also some capital expenditure (e.g. on new PCs and printers) is included within the normal budgeting process. Where an organisation uses an incremental approach to budgeting, annual IT spending could be agreed simply by taking spending for the previous year and adding a percentage for anticipated growth and cost inflation.

There is clearly a risk that when IT costs are budgeted in this way, they could easily grow more quickly than necessary and get out of control. For example:

- New PCs, laptops or other equipment might be purchased without due consideration to the benefits as well as the cost.

- Systems upgrades might be purchased in the same way, when an upgrade is not necessary.

- Spending on system maintenance, such as providing protection against software viruses, or 'cleaning up' systems affected by viruses, might escalate without the costs being adequately monitored and controlled.

Budgeting for IT costs might benefit from:

- a zero-based budgeting approach, although this will depend on whether the organisation uses ZBB for all its budgeting

- an activity-based budgeting approach, where the costs of IT activities (and cost drivers for those activities) are identified and used as the basis for budgeting.

The use of IT systems and services might also be controlled through a system of charging for the use of central IT systems.

6 Big Data

What is Big Data?

There are several definitions of Big Data, the most commonly used referring to large volumes of data beyond the normal processing, storage and analysis capacity of typical database application tools.

Although Big Data does not refer to any specific quantity, the term is often used when speaking about petabytes and exabytes of data.

The definition can be extended to incorporate the types of data involved. Big Data will often include much more than simply financial information and can involve other organisational data which is operational in nature along with other internal and external data which is often unstructured in form.

One of the key challenges of dealing with Big Data is to identify repeatable business patterns in this unstructured data, significant quantities of which is in text format. Managing such data can lead to significant business benefits such as greater competitive advantage, improved productivity and increasing levels of innovation.

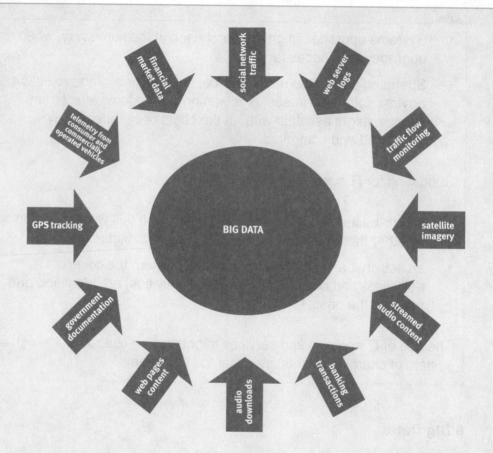

7 The three V's

The three V's represent the defining characteristics of Big Data:

Velocity

Data is now streaming from sources such as social media sites at a virtually constant rate and current processing servers are unable to cope with this flow and generate meaningful real-time analysis.

Volume

More sources of data and an increase in data generation in the digital age combine to increase the volume of data to a potentially unmanageable level.

Variety

Traditionally data was structured and in similar and consistent formats such as Excel spreadsheets and standard databases. Data can now be generated and collected in a huge range of formats including rich text, audio and GPS data amongst others.

(Also **Veracity** – because of so many different sources there is an increased risk of inaccuracies)

8 Big Data Management and analytics

Big Data management is the storage, administration and control of vast quantities of both structured and unstructured data.

The main aim of Big Data management is to ensure the data stored is high quality and accessible. Effective Big Data management can leverage large sets of data from a variety of relatively new sources such as social media sites.

New technologies combine traditional data warehouses with Big Data systems in a logical data warehousing architecture.

Big Data analytics is the process of scrutinising Big Data to identify patterns, correlations, relationships and other insights. This information can have a wide reaching effect on the organisation's competitive strategy and marketing campaigns and can therefore have a direct impact on future profitability.

Big Data sources may not fit into currently available data warehouses and Big Data analytics may require more advanced software tools than those commonly used in traditional data mining. Open source technologies such as Hadoop are increasingly utilised to manage the constantly evolving data processing requirements of Big Data.

Hadoop is an open source programming framework which enables the processing of large data sets by utilising multiple servers simultaneously.

9 Big Data: Benefits and risks

Why is Big Data so important?

Several major business benefits arise from the ability to manage Big Data successfully:

(1) Driving innovation by reducing time taken to answer key business questions and therefore make decisions

(2) Gaining competitive advantage

(3) Improving productivity

There are risks associated with Big Data:

(1) **Availability of skills** to use Big Data systems, which is compounded by the fact that many of the systems are rapidly developing and support is not always easily and readily available. There is also an increasing need to combine data analysis skills with deep understanding of industry being analysed and this need is not always recognised.

(2) **Security of data** is a major concern in the majority of organisations and if the organisation lacks the resource to manage data then there is likely to be a greater risk of leaks and losses.

(3) **Data Protection issues** as organisations collect a greater range of data from increasingly personal sources (e.g. Facebook).

It is important to recognise that just because something CAN be measured, this does not necessarily mean it should be. There is a risk that valuable time is spent measuring relationships that have no organisational value.

If organisations are to effectively utilise Big Data, this will require a change in perspective to ensure sense can be made of the information.

How do we use it? Examples of data which may input into Big Data systems include:

* social network traffic
* web server logs
* traffic flow monitoring
* satellite imagery
* streamed audio content
* banking transactions
* audio downloads
* web pages content
* government documentation
* GPS tracking
* telemetry from consumer and commercially operated vehicles
* financial market data

How is Big Data is used? Examples

Consumer facing organisations monitor social media activity to gain insight into customer behaviour and preferences. This source can also be used to identify and engage brand advocates and detractors and assess responsiveness to advertising campaigns and promotions.

Sports teams can use data of past fixtures to tracking tactics, player formations, injuries and results to inform future team strategies.

Manufacturing companies can monitor data from their equipment to determine usage and wear. This allows them to predict the optimal replacement cycle.

Financial Services organisations can use data on customer activity to carefully segment their customer base and therefore accurately target individuals with relevant offers.

Health organisations can monitor patient records and admissions to identify risk of recurring problems and intervene to avoid further hospital involvement.

10 Practice questions

Objective Test Question 1: benefit of an information system

Access to a larger market, targeted marketing, reduced costs and the elimination of intermediaries are just some of the benefits that could result from the implementation of:

A   knowledge management systems

B   e-commerce

C   web 2.0 tools

D   enterprise-wide systems

Objective Test Question 2: Intangible Costs of an Information

Which of the following is NOT an intangible cost of a new information system?

A   The opportunity cost of other projects foregone

B   Day to day running costs such as heating and insurance

C   Staff disruption during the implementation phase

D   The cost of dysfunctional behaviour due to resistance to change

Case Style Question: ZZ

ZZ is a music streaming company specialising in classical tracks and opera. It has a growing loyal customer base, which has largely been created through word of mouth and magazine adverts and editorials.

You have received the following email from the new Chief Executive:

From: Donald Picton
To: A.N. Accountant
Date: 25.06.2014
Subject: Big Data

Good morning to you!

As you know, ZZ does not use social media as I believe our customer base is largely comprised of an age bracket that wouldn't be likely to engage in such channels. However, I have just discovered that recently, a Twitter account has been created by an enthusiastic customer entitled @iloveZZ. It has several thousand followers already!

This is all about 'Big Data', isn't it. Can you prepare me a report about it? I would like to understand the risks and benefits of Big Data to ZZ.

With many thanks and regards,
D

Test your understanding answers

Objective Test Question 1: benefit of an information system

Answer B

E-commerce refers to the conducting of business electronically via some sort of communications link and may result in access to larger markets, targeted marketing, reduced costs and elimination of intermediaries.

Objective Test Question 2: Intangible Costs of an Information

Answer B

Day to day running costs, such as heating and insurance, should be tangible costs. Answers A, C and D all describe intangible costs.

Case Style Question: ZZ

EMAIL

TO: D. Picton

FROM: AN Accountant

SUBJECT: Big Data

DATE: 19 June 2014

Good Morning Donald,

In response to your email, please find some notes about Big Data.

Big Data management involves using sophisticated systems to gather, store and analyse large volumes of data in a variety of structured and unstructured formats. Companies are collecting increasing volumes of data through everyday transactions and marketing activity. If managed effectively, this can lead to many business benefits, although there are risks involved.

Benefits

As ZZ is a web-based business it is likely that all of its sales transactions take place over the internet. This is likely to result in a greater volume of data being collected for each transaction, which ZZ can use to better understand its customer preferences and buying patterns. This can help to ensure that the right type of track is available to customers and can also drive more targeted and effective marketing campaigns.

One ever-growing source of largely unstructured data is the wide range of social media channels now available. ZZ have chosen not to develop social media networks in the belief that customers will not want to engage in this way. The @iloveZZ Twitter feed, along with its followers, suggests that this may no longer be the case and so ZZ have an opportunity to gather data from this source in order to obtain a greater insight into customer interests.

As ZZ has a loyal customer base, they can also harness the data collected through transactions and social media networks to maximise this loyalty. Certain customers may be defined as key advocates of the company's product and this can be used effectively in marketing campaigns to show the positive customer feedback ZZ receives.

Risks

ZZ is currently not using social media and therefore not collecting data in this way. There is a risk that the company falls behind its competitors who may well be harnessing the powerful data available from this source. Although ZZ currently has a loyal customer base, these customers may be tempted to switch to other streaming services if they are engaged through Twitter and Facebook based marketing.

Even if ZZ decides that they should develop a social media strategy there is a danger that significant volumes of data are collected and stored but not used properly. Not only will this be a waste of potentially useful information, but it will also cost money and use up storage space on the company's systems.

Index

Index

Index

Index